MW00344524

A PRIVATE IN THE TEXAS RANGERS

NUMBER THREE

Canseco-Keck History Series

Jerry Thompson, General Editor

A PRIVATE IN THE TEXAS RANGERS

A. T. Miller of Company B, Frontier Battalion

JOHN MILLER MORRIS

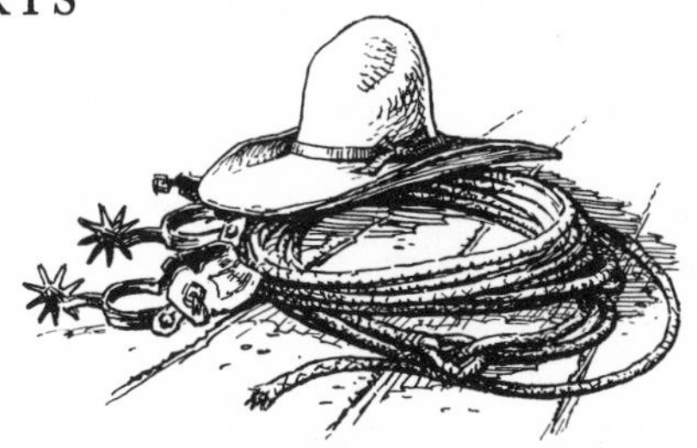

Texas A&M University Press, College Station

First edition

Frontispiece: Abner Theophilus Miller, 1858–1931
(circa 1887 Daniel P. Sink Photograph, Vernon, Texas).
Courtesy Naomi Morris Green, Clarendon, Texas

The paper used in this book meets the minimum requirements
of the American National Standard for Permanence
of Paper for Printed Library Materials, Z39.48-1984.
Binding materials have been chosen for durability.

♾

LIBRARY OF CONGRESS CATALOGING-IN-PUBLICATION DATA

Morris, John Miller.
A private in the Texas Rangers : A. T. Miller of Company B, Frontier Battalion / John Miller Morris.— 1st ed.
p. cm. — (Canseco-Keck history series ; no. 3)
Contains excerpted and annotated material from three diaries written by Miller.
Includes bibliographical references and index.
ISBN 0-89096-964-7 (alk. paper)
1. Miller, A. T. (Abner Theophilus), 1858–1931—Diaries. 2. Texas Rangers—Biography. 3. Soldiers—Texas—Diaries. 4. Frontier and pioneer life—Texas. 5. Texas—History—1846–1950. I. Miller, A. T. (Abner Theophilus), 1858–1931. II. Title. III. Series.
F391.M637 M67 2001
976.4′06′092—dc21

00-011316

DEDICATED TO THREE WISE WOMEN

Lena Mae Morris,

Patsy Blair Heflin,

and Erin Claire Morris

I came to see how ancestors could appear less fallen than their descendants and thereby serve, when revered, as doorways to transcendence. I saw how virgin nature—especially in its grand phenomena: sun, wind, moon, thunder, lightning, and the sky and earth that are their containers—could be venerated as the most transparent symbols of the divine.

—Huston Smith
Beyond the Post-Modern Mind

CONTENTS

ILLUSTRATIONS

MAPS

ACKNOWLEDGMENTS

Writing a book about the dead is a surefire way to run up literary debts with the living. A lot of good folks assisted during the five-year co-evolution of this work. I must single out some special folk in particular: Carl Bernard Morris, Jr., and Joan Morris of Horseshoe Bay, Texas; Naomi Morris Green and the late Horace A. Green of Clarendon, Texas; and historian Frank Heflin of Amarillo, Texas. These very special people told me family stories, gave me access to the key documents, provided copies and photographs, answered questions, and furthered my understanding of the distant diarist Abner Theophilus Miller in a thousand and one ways. This book is your book.

Many others gave freely of their time. Mae M. Naylor of Vernon, a granddaughter of A. T. Miller, was a keen supporter. Her encouragement is much appreciated. Paul Francis Schmidt, an inspiring mentor, unfortunately died during the completion of this work. Nevertheless, his values, scholarship, and literary advice influenced every page. The eminent historian T. Lindsay Baker read the manuscript closely and made a number of very helpful suggestions and corrections. Dr. Baker's detailed comments and advice amounted to a quantum improvement in the manuscript. E. P. Taylor of Amarillo and Lewis Buttery of Lampasas provided bibliographic and cartographic assistance respectively. Ty Cashion and Mike Cox suffered my questions, gave good advice, and lent me their encouragement and scholarship. The maps are by the incomparable historian-illustrator Jack Jackson of Austin. Jack's cartographic expertise also forced me to rethink some old assumptions, and thus led to new insights into the travels of the Company B rangers.

The editors at Texas A&M University Press shaped this work in profound ways. They greatly improved my "grammer," thereby transmuting a raw manuscript into a well-done book. I must especially thank both my copy editor, Stephanie Radway Lane, and the managing editor. Trust me, their professionalism and long hours of work transformed the manuscript. I am equally grateful to the staff, faculty, and students of the University of Texas at San Antonio. Marian L. Martinello was especially supportive and encouraging of this project, while Dean Dwight Henderson kindly arranged a course release. Thanks also to my patient colleagues in Social and Policy Sciences and Education at UTSA.

Some of the most pleasant hours spent on this work occurred at libraries and institutions open to the public. As every researcher knows, Texas is blessed to have superb human resources working at its public research facilities. The state librarians, archivists, and research assistants really do deserve a raise from the taxpayers. This work particularly benefited from the professional resources and staff at the Texas State Library in Austin, the Amarillo Public Library in Amarillo, the Western History Collections at the University of Oklahoma in Tulsa, and the Texas Ranger Hall of Fame and Museum in Waco. I would also single out the wonderful staff at the Research Center, Panhandle-Plains Historical Museum in Canyon, and the Center for American History in Austin. At the Texas Ranger Hall of Fame and Museum in Waco, Dan Agler and Christina Stopka arranged for the reproduction of photographs from the Moody Texas Ranger Memorial Library. Insights into the Miller family ancestry primarily came from Naomi M. Green, Patricia Friesen, Joan and Carl B. Morris, Jr., and the Carolina Room of the Public Library of Charlotte and Mecklenburg County, North Carolina.

I must also thank my mentors and scholar-heroes, Robin Doughty, William H. Goetzmann, Richard Jones, and Ron Tyler for their advice and counsel while I was completing this manuscript. Other support—including nutritious food—was provided by David Pittard, Carol Dawson, Bill and Jean Norton, David Reynolds and Ann Martin, David Rice, Kelly Ignatov, Julie Blair, and Randall, Belinda, and Sean Durrett, among a number of supportive friends.

Few people have seen this project unfold from beginning to end. One person who has done so—and to whom I am eternally in debt—is Patricia A. McGee. Dr. McGee has been indispensable in the completion of this work. Thank you.

Above all I am indebted to Lena Mae Morris and Patsy Blair Heflin, gifted, kind, and generous Texas women who taught their children to value education.

A PRIVATE IN THE TEXAS RANGERS

PROLOGUE

The west is best.

—*Jim Morrison*

There has been a lot of ink spilled in describing the trails, usually bloody trails, of the famed Texas Rangers. The present spillage flows from a premise that differs considerably from any late twentieth-century mythologizing. I do not seek to present glorious heroes or transcendent lawmen in the pursuit of justice. Instead the inquiry turns on the reality of ranger life in the 1880s, and in particular, the ordinary life and social geography of just one company of Texas Rangers—Company B, Frontier Battalion. Readers will ride with "the boys" over the course of a tumultuous year and a half on the fading frontier of Texas and Oklahoma. There are exciting exploits and chases, arrests and escapes, stabbings and shootings. Unlike the movies though the tales are told in laconic style with few references to gore. There may not be enough gratuitous violence for some mass consumer taste. But this lacking is good, for the reality of a closing frontier life—its land and water, its law and order, as named on the specific days and places herein—is a complex, fascinating, and adventurous story. These rangers are seeing the last of the Old West in Texas.

Company B

There is some gunplay and violence to be sure, but Company B is no Wild Bunch. They like the semantic distinctions of "peace officers" and "peacemakers." Their job is to discourage and suppress violence, not feed it or exploit it. One of the first myths to fall must be the relentlessly violent image of the last frontier. Twentieth-century American media presents the West by "telescoping," stringing together one sensational event after another. Such programming hardly sensitizes us to the long periods of effort and fruitless activity that may precede the capture of a wanted man, much less the rarity of a killing. Myth-mongering images of the Texas Rangers may have to give way to a more complicated and ambiguous perspective on the lawmen of the passing West.

However terse or low-key it may appear, the gritty, day-to-day story of a private in Company B deconstructs some myths and reconstructs many realities for the Texas Rangers. We can expect insights into the kind of personalities that are really behind the six-guns and Winchesters. The narrative is also very useful in understanding the social and geographic changes sweeping this last realm of frontier. Ranger techniques of scouting were ideally suited to exploration. Rangers examined nature and studied the vast territories around and beyond them. They travelled widely in all kinds of weather, met a variety of folk, and soon learned the lay of the land and its society. Charles Goodnight first heard of Palo Duro Canyon while rangering toward the Llano Estacado during the Civil War. George Washington "Cap" Arrington set up Camp Roberts in Blanco Canyon in the fall of 1879 as a ranger base. From a pretty bluff above the Rio Blanco, his Company C, Frontier Battalion, explored the conquered plains and "lost lakes" of the Panhandle and South Plains. In the process of scouting, the Texas Ranger—like the Turnerian scientific explorer before him—discovered bygone settlements, old camps, wonders of nature, and interesting inhabitants.

Company B's privates called themselves "boys" although they were all grown men. Some had long years of state service. This story of their lives and friendships aspires to be more than the usual selected recollections, filtered hearsay, or testimonial account of great exploits. Indeed ranger social geography proved more complex and subtle than I at first thought possible. The story of a private in Company B is also a personal window into crime and punishment on the passing Texas frontier. As such it opens our minds to the truer measure of justice and the more lasting experience of a western lawman.

At the heart of this work are three diaries preserved by A. T. Miller's descendants and now annotated by the author, a great-grandson. These diaries record the recruitment of Private Abner Theophilus Miller into Company B of the famed Frontier Battalion in early 1887, and his subsequent experiences on the ranchlands and farms of North Texas and Southwest Oklahoma. Company B was newly stationed in the Hardeman County area, a vast frontier embracing the modern Texas counties of Foard and Hardeman, and closely tied to the "Texas Alsace" of Greer County or "Old Greer"—now three and a half counties in Southwest Oklahoma. Throughout 1887 and over half of 1888 A. T. Miller wrote

Figure 1. The Boys of Company B (circa 1887 Fletcher Photograph, Quanah, Texas). Back Row: "(1) John Platt, (2) A. T. Miller, (3) J. F. Green"; Middle Row: "(4) D. A. Peal[e], (5) J. M. Bradbury, (6) Sterling Price"; Front Row: "(7) E. E. Furman, (8) Tom Platt." Courtesy Texas Ranger Hall of Fame and Museum, Waco

daily entries, unique jottings that now provide an insider's view on life in a Texas Ranger company.

Through the candid observations of the newest company recruit it is possible to re-experience ranger life against the twilight of the American frontier. We can saddle up for the wild trails of Old Greer County, or ride the new iron rails crossing the Great Panhandle Route from Fort Worth to Denver. We can watch meteor showers at night, flirt with the misses, listen to a boy preacher try to save our soul, pose for a photographer, and explore a thousand other verities of the time and place. Often it is not the spectacular that is lost to time, but rather the ordinary and tangible meanings of life.

Above all we can learn from the boys—the highly-skilled team of fellow Texas Rangers around the diarist. Rangers in the late 1880s still collectively addressed themselves as boys, a noticeable colloquialism dating back to 1870 or earlier.[1] They lived together in the old ranger camp ways, and they irritated each other often enough. Sergeant W. J. L. Sullivan once stepped between two enraged Company B privates, both men ready to gun each other down over a trivial breakfast incident. Each man has flaws. Nevertheless officers and men alike are linked by the strongest of bonds—loyalty and danger. They have sworn an oath. The job requires them to work together and to trust each other with their life as possible forfeit. This part of the ranger legend is true. The boys in the Miller diaries include the legendary likes of Sam McMurry, Bill Jess McDonald, Jim Green, Tom and John Platt, Grude Britton, and John McNelly. These professional lawmen contributed personally to the enduring image of late nineteenth-century Texas Rangers. It is remarkable to have such a candid, sincere, and honest account of their comings and goings now available.

Journals and similar documentary sources for the Texas Rangers in the nineteenth century are hardly known. One work, A *Texas Ranger's Diary & Scrapbook* contains only the limited writings, transcriptions, and jottings of a Texas Ranger, Alonzo Van Oden, in the 1890s Trans-Pecos and South Texas. Van Oden's work is quite significant, but it is essentially a scrapbook or miscellany and not a true journal.[2] A very important published work on the Northwest Texas rangers is W. John L. Sullivan's *Twelve Years in the Saddle for Law and Order on the Frontiers of Texas*. The 1909 edition and 1966 reprint are difficult to find, but a new reprint will be available May, 2001.[3] The colorful Sergeant Sullivan served with Company B at Amarillo in the 1890s. Despite the disjointed nature of his book's narrative, it does offer considerable insight into Company B's activities toward the end of the century. Ranger Sullivan, wrote bibliographer John H. Jenkins, "served under Bill McDonald and others between 1888 and 1900, a period for which there are few surviving ranger recollections."[4] With the Miller diaries, of course, we have more than "recollections." We have in our hands daily windows into the West.

"So Good Night Diary"

Two years after the Miller diaries end the United States Census of 1890 gathered the damning evidence that the American frontier had closed in all but name. After looking at the data, historian Frederick Jackson

Turner announced in 1893 the academic termination of the American frontier. By the 1890s the rest of the West was all "in-filling" so to speak. If the reality was gone, the spirit nevertheless remained. The frontier lived on in American culture, where it lodged deeply and mutated creatively in twentieth-century media and literature. The Miller diaries suggest though that the frontier was a considerably different place than we now commonly imagine.

His diaries largely conjure a lost world: a geography of bypassed pioneer towns, dispersed and displaced people of all sorts, old stage trails and fresh steel rails, hopeful "razzoopers" or town boomers, and the old, labor-intensive economies of farmstead and ranch. The entries also shed considerable light on "the ending" of the frontier, a daily window into a profound economic and social transformation that *was* refashioning the 1880s landscape.

The young lawman's dispassionate observations on court trials, crime, gun control, drug abuse, sexual misconduct, and other social ills are inevitably subject, *mutatis mutandis,* to contrast with the same social issues of today. How do present American communities compare with those of the "wild, wild" 1880s? Do we project our current violence onto the past? Consider a vision of Texas where prostitutes are tolerated in town—but guns are not—and where death by suicide is more likely than death by gunfight.

Abner Theophilus Miller publicly preferred his spoken initials—"A. T."—to his given names. "Theophilus" had been a better idea in the Greek Revival 1850s than in the Industrial 1880s. It was common for aquaintances and friends to hail him on the streets as "A. T." He often signed documents as A. T. Miller. Within the family he was often addressed familiarly as "Abner." The Miller name stuck around, passing on as a middle name to a second grandson, my father, and he passed it straight along to me.

A. T.'s dairies contain entries from January 1, 1887, to July 23, 1888. They record a wealth of experiential information on the settlement of the frontier. Abner Miller's writing style reveals a world of familiar, even contemporary semantics: "Have a nice day" and "Go see whats going on" are common expressions. There are also pleasant subtleties of archaisms and pre-modern speech patterns. His word choices are keyed to the Upper Southern dialect of his youth with strong admixtures of western slang and criminal justice jargon. Although some entries are sparse or abbreviated, taken together the diaries portray a twenty-nine-year-old newcomer sensitive to the nature, climate, and people of the "beautifull" new land. They record an Easterner falling in love with the Western "Prarie" environment. Miller's preoccupation with sunrises, weather, and rainfall was constant. Interspersed with his romancing the landscape, there is the further maturation of a young man in the company of real men.

We find the diarist of Company B writing typically at dawn and at night, but he writes at other intervals as well. Often he tells us where he is writing—in saloons, courthouse yards, mercantile stores, around campfires, or sprawling on the new spring grasses of the plains. A happy feature is the *dailiness* of these introspective entries on ranger life. Seasons come and go, and we watch them unfold and pass. (But perhaps "seasons" is too mild a term for the winds and blizzards of '87 and '88.) Within a few months of daily writing the journal becomes a trusted companion. After noting a hard day's ride and the day's news, A. T. sometimes closed with the affectionate phrase, "So good night diary." He kept his current journal close to him, often taking it out while on lonely herd duty, or unpacking it from his saddlebags while traveling around the Texas Panhandle.

A. T. Miller's three diaries were preserved by his descendants, Morris family members whose assistance and information has been invaluable in this inquiry. The diaries are somewhat frail from their passage through time. The first one contains entries from January 1, 1887, to July 23, 1887. It is a soft, red-leather bound, plain ledger book containing some 100 gilt-edged pages with a page size of 4 by 6⅝ inches. At the end are a few random notes, meticulous accounts of various debts owed, settled, and paid, and a few "discripsion"s of wanted men, stolen horses, owner brands, and the like. The second and smallest volume is a soft, black-leather bound ledger volume of 108 pages, dated from July 24, 1887, to March 25, 1888. Two pages were cut out. On the 3½ by 5¾ inch gilt-edged pages, Miller penned some of the most poignant vignettes of Texas Ranger life on the Rolling Plains frontier, in particular the gloomy holiday season of 1887–88. His description of Christmas Day, 1887, is a never-to-be-forgotten glimpse into the loneliness, frustration, and pathos of lawmen on the closing frontier. The final 4 by 6¾ inch, red-leather volume runs from March 26, 1888, to July 23, 1888. The entries cease on page 42 of the 116 hand-numbered pages. Scattered throughout many of the remaining pages are various accountings and enumerations. Taxes paid, notes, debts, boarding house meal tallies, and the like provide a glimpse into Miller's private affairs and life. A few of the later extraneous entries are dated as late as the 1930s, mainly concerning Miller's tax obligation on a family farm property in Jones County, North Carolina.

Writing in a small, bold, Victorian style, the pencilled script is very difficult to interpret. Especially difficult are the phonetic renderings of the ethnic names of people. Miller's orthography is ceaselessly erratic in any case. Although clearly a literate young man, sometimes the abundant and variant misspellings suggest a touch of dyslexia. Probably the orthography is characteristic of the Texas time and plains place. Indeed, Miller's spelling is often so bad as to have become "good," a unique mode of expression to be preserved in its naivete.

In editing the diaries, however, a decision had to be reached as to Miller's missing capitalization and punctuation. Both elements were routinely deficient or erratic. Commas and apostrophes were usually lacking or rare. Capitalization was simply a matter of whim. Considering that these diaries would have been touched up—if any thought of bringing them before the public was in mind—the editor has engaged in a mild effort to remedy some of Miller's deficient capitalization and punctuation. Purists may wince, but many sentences will start with an initial capital letter and will end with a period not always present in the original holograph entry. This editing helped remove annoying difficulties for the modern reader (as otherwise separate sentences and thoughts tended to glide together chaotically). In rare instances I have added clarifying articles and pronouns, or sought other minor grammatical remedies where the meaning might be obscured. Miller's shorthand penchant for ampersands has been converted to "and." Otherwise, I rejected unwarranted and excessive improvement. It was important to preserve the original voice, spelling, and thought of the diarist.

While transcribing and researching the diaries I often found myself entering into a dialogue with my great-grandfather, both privy to his secret thoughts and willing to share my own reflections on the events of his day. The result of these trans-ancestral lucubrations was a series of editorial comments that began to pepper the raw transcription of the entries. After fighting the urge to comment and clarify—and losing—and after trying to put my comments into footnotes—where they withered—I finally abandoned all pretense and embraced the concept of accompanying annotations. Many diary entries are therefore followed by an editorial intrusion. These italicized expressions are simply a personal statement on the context, one editor's exegesis. In practice there are many interpretations of the literary text. Purists can certainly ignore the accompanying annotations, but some readers may benefit from the contextual and historical-geographical notations.

"The Boys"

As a junior Texas Ranger, A. T. Miller met and rode with some of the finest peace officers of the plains: William Jesse "Bill" McDonald, George Washington Arrington, Sheriff J. A. Williamson, Sheriff James Allee, Sheriff W. N. Barker, Sheriff Al Gentry, Deputy John T. Williams, Deputy John Hammond, and ex-ranger Sam Platt. He served in Company B of the Frontier Battalion under the doughty Captain Samuel A. "Soft Voice" McMurry. He was acquainted with Charles Goodnight, J. G. Witherspoon, Doss Swearingen, Pat Wolforth, Sam White, and other famed ranchers and trail bosses of the West.

Despite the dominant legends of sensational frontier violence and lawlessness, the Miller diary entries portray a considerably more polite and socialized state of affairs. Much of an ordinary Texas Ranger's time was spent in routine duties: serving warrants, paperwork, saloon walk-throughs, chasing outlaws, guarding a few hapless prisoners from time to time, looking after the ranger remuda of horses (the dreaded and lonely "Hurd day"), transporting water, wood, and supplies, and going into town to poke around—to see and be seen.

Only rarely does a sense of direct or personal danger intrude. The laconic style of the diarist often lightens the true element of danger. Terse expressions such as "No harm done" may be applied to near-miss shootings and potentially fatal fights. Indeed, the *apparent* lack of sensational violence or ever present danger may disappoint the contemporary mind. Much of Texas Ranger work was routine and even dull. The diarist faithfully records the routine, the everyday, and the mundane. This approach is different from the memoirist or biographer, who strings together one exciting incident or embellished anecdote after another. Instead these raw entries usefully remind us of other realities of late nineteenth-century Texas Ranger duty: parties, saloons, chasing outlaws who often get away, going fishing, looking after the drunks, fighting depression, keeping an eye peeled, settling lots of trouble in town by their mere presence, and loafing and visiting with the locals.

The rangers of Company B move widely around the Rolling Plains and Panhandle. Despite the legend that only one ranger is needed to quell one riotous mob of men—a legend encouraged by the grandiloquent Bill Jess McDonald of Quanah, Texas—A. T. Miller's entries often refer to the deeply *companionate* nature of 1880s ranger life. Captain McMurry dispatches small teams frequently, for there is safety and power in numbers. Only if a job seems perfectly ordinary will he send a lone ranger instead. The men spend a lot of time together. Many become boon companions. The veteran captain is brave and true—although he likes a little off-duty poker from time to time. The company sergeant, John McNelly, is a crude and weathered veteran, but he had ridden in the 1870s with the wildest of his famous uncle's bandit-busting company—Leander H. McNelly's Special Force of Texas Rangers.

And then there are the boys, the enlisted men of Company B: brothers John and Tom Platt, Sterling Price, Ed Furman, Dennis Peal, Jim Green, J. M. Bradbury, Grude Britton, John Hammond, George Adamson, Tom O'Hare, Jim Bishop, A. T. Miller, and company teamsters like Mike Cahill and Tom Mulhall. They were decent men, but not without flaws. They shared common masculine values, but often went different ways in their private life. Sharing risk, duty, and hardship led to loyalty, trust, and affection. Ranger camaraderie linked these different men together.

The entries cover a considerable amount of Texas-Oklahoma frontier geography. From Gainesville to Fort Worth, then up the Red River frontier, through the Texas Panhandle, into Southwest Oklahoma, and eventually as far afield as Denver, Colorado, the Miller diaries give us firsthand impressions of a new land and its most recent settlers. Company B of the Frontier Battalion also spent regular time in their humble canvas tent and dugout quarters outside the new railroad town of Quanah, Texas. There camp life was a ceaseless cycle of chores, rumors, chases, and gossip. It was also a training program, a school in the ways of frontier criminal justice.

Radiating outward from their Quanah camp the boys ranged across the last frontier. They rode the historic roads to Vernon, Quanah, Margaret, Benjamin, Clarendon, Childress City, Kirkland, Panhandle City, Tascosa, Mobeetie, Fort Elliott, Amarillo, and especially to Mangum. At that time Mangum and the million and a half acres of "Old Greer County" were claimed fiercely—and probably rightly—by Texas officials. Sam Houston signed the legislation in 1860 authorizing Greer County of Texas. The United States government thought otherwise. A slow, protracted, border dispute was underway for decades between officials in Washington, D.C., and Austin, Texas. The Quanah Texas Rangers were part of this process, special state lawmen used to assert Texas law into land then known for terrorism and lawlessness. Old Greer, a "beautifull land" in the words of the diarist, was plucked from Texas in 1896 by the United States Supreme Court and given to the Oklahoma Territory. The loss of Greer was a serious territorial contraction for the expansive Anglo-Texas Homeland.

Of special importance the diarist also witnessed the construction of the mighty Fort Worth & Denver City Railroad across the Texas Panhandle. This railroad ushered in an industrial economy that transformed North Texas. Company B's assignment included dampening the lawlessness and settling labor unrest that threatened the building of the FW&DC railroad. The salaried presence of rangers was very much a state benefit promoting a corporate interest. But the larger interest promoted was the settlement process. And such settlement! The railroad vastly stimulated the economy of each county it crossed. The old landscape of big ranches and distant headquarters gave way to new towns and mechanized farms. Merchants, laborers, farmers, teachers, fugitives, and rangers alike arrived in the new train stations. The frontier was in transition.

These slender, sincere, Victorian-era journals provide a unique one-and-a-half-year window into the day-to-day life of a 1880s Texas Ranger recruit on the fading frontier. They also record the story of a young man who falls in love with a new region: a geographic relationship that deepens until Miller eventually takes up residence as a farmer near Thalia—not far from the Old Margaret settlement on Mule Creek. But this anticipates the story, which begins so casually with a winter day resolution and the purchase of a blank diary in Gainesville, Texas.

CHAPTER 1

"What Now Shal Be My Fate?"

WINTER OF 1887

When reading Ranger scout reports, reviewing the monthly returns, or examining laconic telegrams, it is easy to believe the Rangers were the stuff of legend and myth rather than very real men who possessed the foibles and faults of all men. Rangers had to eat and sleep, liked to have a drink and chased women on occasion, and a few were thrown out of the force for excessive fondness for some or all of these habits. Very little of the reality of daily Ranger life is revealed in official records. . . .

—*Frederick Wilkins,* The Law Comes to Texas

The Great Plains frontier was a national frontier, nationally advertised. What happened there was magnified in the press and exaggerated in the imagination, and nothing was more magnified than its unconventionality, its romantic aspects, and its lawlessness.

—*Walter Prescott Webb,* The Great Plains

Abner Theophilus Miller was twenty-nine years old when he set out to change his circumstances and to charge his life with new purpose. He would leave the embraces of his siblings, ride to the frontier of Texas, and there make a singular life for himself. The first line of his diary, "New Year's Day Saturday in Gainesville 1887," tells us he is in a resolving mood. We sense a desire to better one's fortune in the year ahead. This introspective impulse can be given discipline by the purchase of a diary, a solemn record of a pilgrim's progress on a new road. Miller's initial entries are tentative, sparse, and incidental, as if he was only gradually adjusting to daily acts of self-reflection. Once on the frontier though he begins to open up, to confide to a silent friend, to confess his thoughts, and to record a wealth of gossip and insight about his new companions in Company B, Frontier Battalion.

A. T. Miller was the fourth of six children born to John Alexander and Margaret Steele Miller of historic Jones County, North Carolina. Jones County was a fertile, forested lowland along the Trent River of North Carolina. The Atlantic Ocean was not far away. As early as 1710 various refugees arrived in the area from war-torn Europe. From 1734 to 1752 a particular migrational stream poured into Jones County from the German Palatinate and Switzerland. The newcomers joined the scattered Scotch-Irish and English settlers in taming the land.[1] *These Protestant Germans were meticulous farmers, otherwise weary of the religious feuding in the Old World. They epitomized German traditions of hard work, communal life and church, and progressive agriculture. Together the emigrants carved out farms and mercantile settlements like Trenton and New Bern.*

Among these early families were Muellers or Müllers, soon corrupted into the Anglicized surname Miller.[2] *The region was a battleground during the Revolutionary War, when Tobias Miller's sons and relatives fought for American independence. Jones County, formerly upper Craven County, was organized in 1779 when there were a fair number of Miller families present and participating. It is possible that John A. Miller, born on August 8, 1828, was a descendant of these early North Carolina Millers.*

John Alexander Miller married Margaret Lenora Steele on April 25, 1849. He was twenty-one and the bride was twenty-four. A daughter, Agnes Silome, blessed the marriage in 1851 and a first son, Thomas Aushine, in 1856. Their second son and our diarist, Abner Theophilus, was born on August 2, 1858, in Mooresville, Iredell County, some twenty-five miles north of Charlotte, North Carolina.[3] *Abner was six when his father died in January of 1864 during the Civil War. Subsequently he grew up close to his mother's family; later in life he kept in touch with the Steeles and other maternal relatives by correspondence.*

Abner Miller learned farming as a youth in the fields along the streams of the Trent River. While in his early twenties a sister and then his mother died. Bereft of parents, Abner Miller, his older sister, Adda, and three other brothers—Thomas Aushine Miller, R. L. "Lucius" Miller, and John Victor "Johnnie" or "Johnie" Miller—left a Reconstruction-battered North Carolina shortly after their mother's death on September 30, 1879. According to a grand-

daughter, A. T. Miller left North Carolina on November 25, 1879, and arrived in McKinney, Texas, in Collin County on November 29, 1879.[4] *The Millers were part of a wave of southern refugees seeking a better life in Texas, a state relatively untouched by the battles and destruction of the Civil War. After a spell in Collin County, Thomas Miller at least, and perhaps other family members, resettled in the nearby Red River settlement of Gainesville, Texas, around or before 1883.*[5] *Joining his older brother there, Abner Theophilus Miller further acclimated to Texas and her ways.*

The journey farther west begins with the tenth entry of Abner Miller's diaries—January 10, 1887. The three Miller brothers and their sister Adda commemorate the fateful occasion with a last group photograph—a relict object to capture time, to preserve their momentary togetherness forever. Will they ever be together again? Sadly within a year half their number will be dead. They leave by train for Fort Worth on the evening of January 10 for separate journeys ahead. Thomas and Adda are traveling to Southern California. For A. T. and Johnnie the destination is a distant urban mirage—the frontier "city" of Margaret, Texas.

Margaret was a promising hamlet founded in 1884 on a beautiful Pease River plain, just west of Mule Creek. It was the first county seat of the enormous Hardeman County frontier in Northwest Texas. The warm community spirit Miller found there is personified in the frequent diary appearance of "Mr. and Mrs. Wesley." John and Mary Wesley were indeed the guiding spirits of this pioneer settlement near the junction of Mule Creek and the Pease River. John Wesley founded the town and renamed his youthful community of "Pease" to "Margaret" to celebrate a new daughter's birth. The child, Margaret Wesley, the baby "Virginia Dare" of her day, was said to be the "first white child" born in Hardeman County, out of which Foard County was carved in 1891.

Clearly the Western Hotel is the place to be seen in 1887 in Margaret, Texas. Local teenagers like "Miss Kittie" gather there, and notables like Charles Goodnight turn up during travels to and fro. Abner Miller chronicles parties, singings, conversions, and socials in Margaret that winter. This winter socializing wove the community together in a spirit of fun and fellowship, necessarily offsetting the depressing burials, the darkness, and the bitter cold winds of the '87 northers.

After a spell of equipping, familiarizing, and partying, A. T. Miller formally enlists in the Texas Rangers under Captain Samuel A. McMurry on February 12, 1887. "I will try to do the best I can," he writes earnestly. The new job requires an immediate relocation to the rough, raw, and half-constructed terminus town of Quanah, Texas. Miller arrives to the canvas tent and dugout camp for Texas Ranger Company B of the Frontier Battalion, quartered a short ride away from the boom town. Ranger camps were a feature of many new frontier communities. This typical camp was located near the Quanah town water tank. With its first lot sale in December of 1886, Quanah was barely two months old. Alcohol and drunkenness—the drug abuse problem for the 1880s Texas lawmen—was noticeably prevalent. "An awful site of drunk men to night," Miller noted, "lying in a sallon near the P.O."

The underlying tension and violence breaks out on February 24, 1887, with an understated "shooting scrape" in Dutch Henry's Saloon. In this incident the legendary Pat Wolforth coolly fires a pistol shot of discouragement toward John Davidson and then toward Comanche Bill. Texas Rangers arrive, arrest Wolforth for his own safety, and defuse the potentially lethal situation.

Shortly thereafter A. T. Miller sets off for the first of many trips into the gang-infested wilderness of "Old Greer," an immense region of prairies, cedar brakes, sand hills, gypsum bluffs, meandering creeks, braided rivers, and numerous hideouts. Both the State of Texas and the United States government formally claimed this giant county between the forks of the Red River and east of the 100th meridian. Neither claimant had been able to impose firm law and order. But with numbers of Anglo-Texan settlers moving into Greer County after 1886, state officials assigned the Texas Rangers the job of upholding the law from their new headquarters at Quanah.

Through Abner Miller's morning weather reports, we also see the gradual changing of the seasons. His interest in the climate of the land is keen. He reads the sky like a text, always looking for signs of nature's intent. Rains, fog, mists, and drizzles finally appear, heralds of an advancing seasonal warmth that signals a happy end to the crippling '86 drought and the '87 blizzards. Having "a nice day" becomes almost a mantra in March. Miller's diary travels with him, because we even find him sitting on the prairie, writing in it while herding the ranger remuda and enjoying "these beautiful prairies."

But by mid-March the forces of delinquency, theft, and murder are active as well. The rangers will have to start a spring roundup—of men not cattle. The last winter entry grimly notes, "Bill Turner near Seymour was shot and killed on the night of the 14th. Was shot five times."

The story begins with a sudden and violent shift in the wind on New Year's Eve, the last day of 1886. An arctic front is pouring down the Great Plains, plunging temperatures, killing stock, and threatening unprotected citizens. Abner Theophilus Miller begins his diary the next morning in Gainesville. For a young man soon far from family and distant from old friends, that blizzard marks a cold but adventurous trail ahead.

Winter of 1887
New Year Day

JAN. 1, 1887 SATURDAY. IN GAINSVILLE.

Clear and cold. Street car tore up by a flat car. I bought my Author book. Gone and returned them and I will get another book.

[The first blizzard of '87 seizes Gainesville in an icy grip. Located on the edge of the Western Cross Timbers, Gainesville was the county seat of Cooke County in the Red River Valley.]

JAN 2ND, 1887 SUNDAY.

Little cloudy apart of the day. And a few drops of Snow. Went to ME [Methodist Episcopal] church. Sermon by Worley. In evening a very cold beautiful night.

JAN 3RD, 1887 FIRST MONDAY IN GAINSVILLE.

Cold, nice and clear. I met Miss Nannie Wallis. Had some fine music from her. Went to the theater that night. [A show] by Patti Rosa. It is a little cloudy and moderating. Had som Photoes taken.

[The "First Monday" of each month was a popular day for shopping, entertainment, and socializing in town. Victorians often took photographs before separations or long travels.]

JAN 4TH, 1887 (GAINESVILLE)

This morning is cloudy and raw. Cloudy most all day. I met Bob Right this evening at the train. To night I am up in Town. Nice and clear overhead and thin clouds all around.

JAN 5TH, 1887 (GAINESVILLE)

Thin mist of clouds and cold. The air is damp and smokey. I went down to R. R. building, cotton platform, swich, &C [etc.]. It is a nice day. I met Ben Burnsides to day. He's working in The Nation on the railroad. Miss Nannie Wallis is at Dr. Landis to night. It is a cloudy night and warm.

[Abner Miller may be checking schedules and purchasing railroad tickets at the Gainesville depot of the Missouri, Kansas, and Texas Railroad. "The Nation" refers to the nearby Indian Nation—the 1880s "Indian Territory" of present Oklahoma. Dr. Landis is an old friend of the Miller family.]

JAN 6, 1887 WEDNESDAY IN GAINSVILLE

I rose with the fire alarm this morning. The house was burned up. I met Mrs Edwards. Noon is nice but cloudy and cold. In the evening I went to see the Water Works Fire Engine & Machinery &C. The evening is cold and cloudy. Had an oyster supper. Big Ball in Town to night.

JAN 7, 1887 FRIDAY MORNING IN GAINESVILLE

It is beautiful and clear and cold. By 10 oclock it became cloudy and cold, an indication of a Norther. I met Will Talkington in Town. After dinner it is clear with thin clouds. I went out with Dr. Landis to John O'Brians and met with old Mrs. Jeff Robinson of Collin Co., about 8 miles N.W. Town. The evening is cold and windy.

[Another cold front is pouring into Texas. Miller and Dr. Landis have a cold ride back to town.]

JAN 8, 1887 SATURDAY MORNING IN GAINSVILLE.

The ground is about covered with snow and still snowing hard. Snow all day. I went to see Henry Graham this evening for Dick Cofee. No good. Then I went to the 10 ct Store. Got our photoes.

JAN 9, 1887 SUNDAY MORNING IN GAINESVILLE.

Thin mist of clouds around. It is very cold at 10 oclock. Nice day. Dr Landis and family have gone to Sunday School and church. The Sun is shining warm and nice. The Evening is beautiful and a little cold. Sang some good pieces of music this evening at Dr. Landises.

[Dr. Landis kept in touch with the Millers. After Thomas and Adda Miller traveled to California, Dr. Landis also ventured west to look over "The Golden State," even staying with Thomas and Adda Miller.

JAN 10, 1887 MONDAY MORNING IN GAINESVILLE.

Nice and clear, it looks to be a fine day. We all went up and had our Photos taken in a group. Thomas and Adda, Johnnie and myself. Still is a fine day. I met old Mr. Nicolas in Town today. I left one of Ma's Photos to have a large one taken. We will start to Ft. Worth this evening.

Now I am on the Gulf Coast & Santa Fe Railroad traveling from Gainesville to Ft. Worth. Valley view of a little place. Nice country around. Next [station] is Nolan. Nice county. No Town. Next station is "Krum," a small town near Denton. There is nothing but a depot, near Bob Rights. We got to Ft Worth about 8 oclock. Stayed at the Mansion. Had a nice Trip.

[The four Miller children are now setting out on their western odyssey. One last group photo is taken in Gainesville to commemorate the occasion. They board their train and roll southward over the Grand Prairie. New and hopeful little towns appear like Krum, Texas, near Bob Wright's place. Krum started as a tiny 1886 railroad townsite eight miles northwest of Denton, named after the engineer of the first train to arrive. After struggling and dying for decades, Krum now prospers on the suburban frontier of the Dal-worth megalopolis.[6] *Arriving in Fort Worth the Millers check into the prestigious "Mansion," a popular 1880s hotel for travelers.]*

JAN 11, 1887 TUESDAY MORNING

Leaving Ft. Worth on the train. It is nice and clear. We are on our way to Decatur to William Lawrence's. Got to Decatur about ½ past 11 oclock. I find Decatur to be a real nice Town. We went around town with coz [cousin] William. I met several men and we went on top of the court house and had a beautifull view. A Prairie lies on the East and South, and Timber is on the North and West. I came up on the train with a Mr. Holman, who has a large pastur in Knox Co., near Benjamin.

[The Miller siblings split up at this point. Thomas and Adda leave Fort Worth on a different train to an unfortunate destiny. A. T. and Johnnie Miller catch a Fort Worth & Denver City train northwest to Decatur in Wise County. They pause in Decatur to visit with their cousin and his family. The center of town and chief tourist attraction was of course the courthouse. The Fort Worth & Denver City Railroad was the main artery of a new civilization overtaking the Old West. In its passenger cars you could meet a paragon of progress like Mr. Holman. Only the year before Knox County voters had chosen Benjamin as the first county seat.]

JAN 12, 1887 DECATUR WEDNESDAY MORNING.

Starting to Vernon. A fine day, clear as can be. We bid coz Cordie and William our farewells. We've had a nice Trip up to Alvord which is in the Cross Timber. It is a small and finely built Town. Stopped at Bowie for dinner. We got to Vernon about 5 oclock. It is a nice evening, a little cloudy. I went around tonight and bought me a matress for $5.00.

[The two brothers catch an outward bound train at Decatur. Alvord (Wise County) and Bowie (Montague County) were 1882 railroad townsites along Grenville M. Dodge's Fort Worth & Denver City Railroad. Both towns grew rapidly in the mid-1880s. The Miller brothers get off at Vernon in Wilbarger

County, an even more recent terminus and boomtown. From here on they must ride.]

JAN 13, 1887 THURSDAY MORNING IN VERNON

I am lodged at George McTaylors. It is cloudy and cold. We will start for Margaret, Texas this morning now, in just a few minits. Arrived at Margaret about 12 oclock. It was a very pleasant ride. Found all was well.

[A. T. and Johnnie Miller checked out of McTaylor's Boarding House in Vernon, probably caught the stageline, and therefore followed the rutted road that ran west-southwest upstream the Pease River. Their destination was the small town of Margaret, Texas. Margaret was unprepossessing, but it was the most important town established in Hardeman County before 1887 (see Map 1). Hardeman County was legislated into being on February 21, 1858, and named for two brothers from Tennessee, Bailey and Thomas Jones Hardeman, both of whom came to Texas in 1835.[7] The 1880 census showed about fifty people in all of Hardeman County, with one hundred citizens estimated for 1884. Voters were scarce, but by the end of the year just enough emerged to organize the county officially on December 31, 1884. At the same time forty voters, a majority, chose John Wesley's Mule Creek hamlet of Margaret for the first county seat.

Margaret was less than three years old when Abner Miller arrived in town, but it was still the official seat of a land empire with impacts in five modern counties in two states.]

JAN 14, 1887 MARGARET. FRIDAY MORNING

Nice clear morning. To day is warm and nice. I got a letter from S. S. Steele at Mooresville, N.C., saying he would send us some money.

[The Miller siblings had moved away from North Carolina for good, but they still owned a little land near Raleigh, a sentimental legacy from their mother. They leased this land to Mr. Steele, a maternal relative, who forwarded small payments to be divided pro rata. Abner Miller maintained correspondence habits with family and tax officials in North Carolina. Another North Carolina young man who started fresh on the northeast frontier of Texas was Leigh ("Lee") Hall. Captain Hall achieved fame as a Texas Ranger in the 1870s, tracking down the likes of Sam Bass and John Wesley Hardin.]

JAN 15, 1887 SATURDAY MORNING. MARGARET

It is beautiful and clear this morning. Well I must go to breakfast. This has been a nice day. Very warm. Sales no good to day. I wrote S. S. Steele and T. N. Steele and C. H. Hathcox on business.

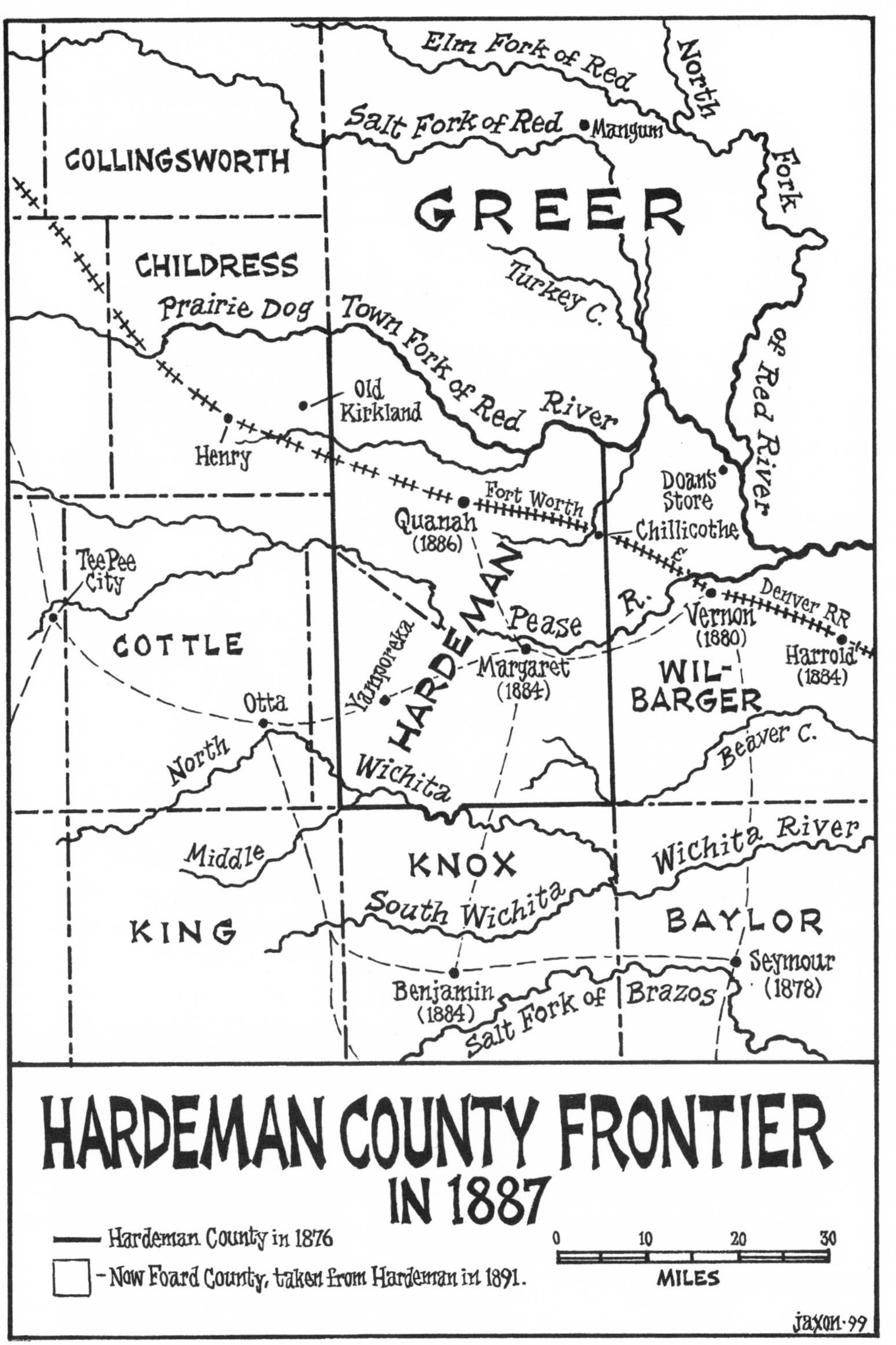

Map 1. Hardeman County Frontier in 1887. Map by Jack Jackson

JAN 16, 1887 MARGARET. SUNDAY MORNING.

Down at the Graveyard. We are comencing to Dig a Grave for a son of Mr. Gobles. The crew is composed of W. R. Wheat, Joe Brown, George Burk, Bart Abbott, A. T. & J. W. Miller. We have just taken George Burk to dinner. This has been the windiest day I ever saw. The dust is terrible. I went in to see John Bland. He is sick. We are having a lively time at the Western Hotel to night. Miss Kittie Morrow is in Town to night.

[Within a few days of their arrival in Margaret, the Miller brothers are treated as instant members of the fledgling community. A. T. and Johnnie make themselves useful by digging a grave and attending a bleak Sunday funeral service to comfort a distraught family. The wind is howling again. One imagines the mother's grief and father's anguish over a lost child, the grit of this winter dust storm, and the sense of death in the community. The romantic image of the frontier fades when we recall that the lack of pediatric care contributed to high infant mortality.

Most of the personages mentioned were significant pioneers of northwest Texas. George L. Burke, for example, left his endless winter home in Michigan in 1882 and settled into a rustic dugout on the Pease River near Mule Creek. Burke's interest in local political affairs was keen and practical. He worked with John Wesley and other entrepreneurs to organize Hardeman County in 1884. He also lobbied for Margaret as the county seat. Later George Burke became county judge of Foard County.[8]

George Burke and Abner Miller, both bachelors, struck up a friendship in the small town that year. A. T., like George, often boarded and socialized with the Wesleys. George Burke taught school for a living, but he soon gave up his single life to marry Miss Lula Prewitt on August 22, 1888. About three years later, George Burke's sister, Naomi Burke Nixon, moved to Margaret and joined her brother. A native Michigander, young widow, and new schoolteacher, Mrs. Nixon was introduced to A. T., still a bachelor. They courted, fell in love, married, and George Burke became A. T.'s brother-in-law.[9]*]*

JAN 17, 1887 MARGARET. MONDAY MORNING.

This is a beautifull morning, clear and cool. Wind is blowing a little. This evening is beautiful clear and still. I gave Miss Kittie Morrow a drink of Whisky for a joak. We will have a surprise partie at Mr. Wesleys to night. I anticipate a nice time. We had a real nice time tonight.

[Miss Helen Catherine "Kittie" Morrow, age fourteen and a minor, is clearly a more demure and respectable young lady than Amanda Blake's "Miss Kittie" in the classic (but warped) 1960s television series "Gunsmoke." Before

radio and television packaged amusement and beamed it into the hinterland, practical jokes, surprise parties, and the much-relished badger pull were staples of small community life. In the badger pull, townspeople convinced a newcomer or greenhorn that a mysterious container held a fierce, wild badger. They watched with glee as the innocent man pulled the "badger's" leash—out came a chamberpot!]

JAN 18, 1887 TUESDAY MORNING MARGARET

Nice and clear this morning by 10 oclock. This morning the wind is very high and dusty and increasing all the time. Up until now is 11 ½ very dusty. Mail is not here yet. This Evening has been very windy. To night the wind is still high. A little cloudy this evening. Not much to night. Cool. Charley Loskwoods wife came up today to see the town. I made her acquaintance while she was here. (Notice in the paper today that Miss A. L. Reynner and Preston Culp was married on the 12th instance).

[High winds envelope the days—and nights. Everyone depended on the mail to keep in touch and chase away the loneliness. When the mail was late a certain impatience crept over the community.]

JAN 19, 1887 WEDNESDAY MORNING IN MARGARET

Terrible windy and dusty. A little cloudy soon this morning. And to night it is as dusty as ever. Oh but how I do long to see the wind cease once more. I have wrote a letter to day to Lucius and one to Lonie.

[The wind has been blowing hard for days now. The terrible dust, scoured from drought-stricken and overgrazed plains, seeped through doors and windows.]

JAN 20, 1887 THURSDAY MORNING. MARGARET

Nice and still this morning. Cloudy and thretning rain. A long train of wagons passed through to the Matador Ranch. Now at dinner at 4 oclock. Mr and Mrs [Marshall M.] Hankins is with us. A stranger came through Town last night on his way to Quanah. He's from Colorado—he sais.

[The Matador Ranch, some 94,000 cattle on 300,000 acres spread over four counties, lay southwest of Margaret. It was purchased in 1882 by the Matador Land and Cattle Company, Ltd., of Dundee, Scotland. Scottish investors financed a number of improvements and bought ranch supplies in bulk. The Matador was one of the largest and best managed of the new syndicate ranches.[10]]

JAN 21, 1887 FRIDAY MORNING IN MARGARET

Another nice, still morning. A little cloudy and warm. By 10 oclock the wind is beginning to blow. And by 12 oclock its up prettie high and the dust is right bad now. Severel boys are in Town today. Cloudy all evening and to night. We had a nice Social at Mr. Hankins and enjoyed ourselves well. Had some nice music on the Guitter by Robert Henry.

[The prominent host Marshall M. Hankins came from Missouri to Texas. Like A. T. Miller he left Gainesville, Texas, for the northwest frontier of Hardeman County. Hankins had arrived two years earlier, opened a law office, and was appointed county attorney in 1885.[11] *Bob Henry ran a small retail store in Margaret. The wind returns, enveloping Margaret in dusty gales.]*

JAN 22, 1887 SATURDAY MORNING IN MARGARET

Nice still morning and will be a nice day if the wind dont rise. A little cloudy by Noon. Norther and a little cloudy. There is a new driver to day on the hack. To night it is cold and the wind is high. We spent an hour or so over at the Western Hotel playing checkers, and Robert Henry, W. B. Abbott, A. T. and J. W. Miller were the boys. The Two Miss Rambos and Miss Kittie Morrow were the ladies. We had some nice music. I now have my bed made and think I had better retire.

JAN 23, 1887 MARGARET. SUNDAY MORNING

This is a beautifull morning, clear and cool and Plesant. Mr and Mrs Wesley's gone to Yamporeka to day. I went to church to hear Mr Crutcher. His subject was "Husbands love your wives." I stayed at the Wesley House with the children to night.

[The single boys and single ladies gather at the Western Hotel on Saturday night for board games, music, and socializing. Then it is off to church on Sunday morning to hear Mr. Crutcher deliver a sermon on marital consequences and proper relations—truly an age of innocence.

Yampareka, Texas, was a small dugout community at the B. Frank Sheffield place, westward on the forlorn trail to the town of Otta in Cottle County. Miss Ashsa Sheffield ran a post office there from March, 1886, to 1890, when "Yampareka, Texas" became just another ghost town. The name refers to a northern Comanche tribe, the Yampahreekuh or "Eaters of Yap Root."[12] *Frank Sheffield's town died, but not his grip on the land. Frank continued to work his place well into the next century and became a well-known old-settler.]*

JAN 24, 1887 MARGARET MONDAY MORNING

The wind is rising this morning. At noon the wind is as high as ever it gets and dusty. (I sent the Tax money to C. Askin at Trenton, Jones Co., North Carolina, amount $1.70) This evening late it is nice and calm, some streaks of clouds. To night it is getting cold and the wind is rising right fast. I sat a few minits at the Western Hotel. Goodnight, Latimore of the Matador is in Town. Logan came down today from Austin.

[When Miller writes with foreboding, "The wind is rising," he is chronicling the gritty and blusterous unpleasantries of the disastrous 1886–87 weather. Wailing wind and swirling dust have been lashing the eroded Plains for several weeks. Complaints about "the wind" are commonplace. On January 19 Miller had lamented, "Oh but how I do long to see the wind cease once more."

A young girl in Sweetwater, Texas, about 120 miles to the southwest in Nolan County, found the '87 wind more than just an irritation—Miss Dorothy found it a force against the mind. Her father, John Bledsoe Scarborough, moved his law practice to Sweetwater in 1882 to dry out his wife's tubercular lungs. But after the '86 drought and the dusty '87 winter, the family rather happily moved east to the college town of Waco. Their daughter, Dorothy Scarborough, grew up there, graduated from Baylor University, became a folklorist, and went on to a distinguished academic and literary career in New York City.

She never forgot her childhood in windy West Texas though. In New York City in the mid-1920s, Dorothy Scarborough shared a taxi ride one day with Edna Ferber. The subject of high wind and human nerves came up. Scarborough told Ferber "of our Texas winds and sands, and how hard they are on women. I told her of the story I meant to write, of the effect of wind and sand and drought on a nervous, sensitive woman not used to the environment. I quoted our Texas saying, 'Never mind the weather so the wind don't blow.'" Edna Ferber thought the story idea was marvelous, and she encouraged her companion.[13]

Remembering again the wailing, whistling, dust-laden wind of her Sweetwater youth, and recalling tales of her mother's coping with the drought, dust storms, and blizzards of '86–'87, Dorothy Scarborough wrote a stunning 1925 novel entitled The Wind. *Published anonymously in its first edition (as a ploy), the book wove a stark portrait of a young woman moving to the Sweetwater area. Letty is soon driven murderously mad by the West Texas wind, "a demon lover." Some prominent West Texans were offended and angered at the unflattering regional portrayal of their environment. After Miss Scarborough emerged as the author, some of the furor died down. The author had lived in Texas after all, and she claimed the narrative sprang from the weather troubles of the late 1880s. At a national level* The Wind *was a significant commercial success. In one of the last great silent films, Lilian Gish starred as Letty, the tragic heroine driven to madness by West Texas. This 1928 Metro-Goldwyn-Mayer film adaptation of the work came complete with a new "happy" ending. When the balmy 1920s gave way to the Dust Bowl of the 1930s, even West Texans could see their land sometimes had a dark climatic side.*

Charles Goodnight and other notables stopped over in Margaret while going to and from their ranches farther in the interior. Goodnight and John Adair were still partners in the 1.2 million acre JA Ranch, but in June they would go their separate ways. Goodnight was enjoying a spell of notoriety at this time. In a bitter dispute with state authorities, he had refused to pay a state lease on school grassland. The populist press had excoriated him as the symbol of greedy cattle barons.[14]*]*

JAN 25, 1887 MARGARET TUESDAY MORNING

The sun rose clear and nice, but not long until the wind begins to rise. At noon the Wind is as high as it ever gets and the dust awful bad. So all evening until late which is quiet. Old man J. H. Taylor will stay in the yard to night and J. L. Austin. Also Frank Sheffield came in Town [from Yampareka]. Kirk McGee will bunk with me to night. He is just back from Denton.

JAN 26, 1887 WEDNESDAY MORNING. MARGARET

This is as prettie a morning as I ever saw, beautifull and clear, perfectly still. Oh, how lovely cool and nice by 11 oclock. Still nice and cool, a little tinge of clouds. The boys are making up a crowd to day for a partie out at John Kleppers tomorrow night. I see the wagons coming with the Relief Supplies and will have to help to unload. It has been a very nice evening and tonight is still and nice. I have severel men in with me to night. Frank Sheffield, Frank Sherman, Mr King, and Hardisty all will sleep in here.

[The reference to relief supplies is an important reminder that the crippling West Texas drouth of 1885–86 was not yet considered over. Moisture had fallen off rapidly in June of 1885. The subsequent winter moisture and spring rains failed as well for most of West Texas. The Rolling Plains dried up and began to blow away. In 1886 John Campbell left Dallas County with his family, heading for Hardeman County. On the way he saw sere plains, ghostly dead-tree landscapes, and dying cattle "in all directions."[15] *By the summer of 1886 frontier settlements were seriously distressed. Ranchers who could not afford to relocate or ship their herds to better pastures watched in horror as faithful water-*

holes dried up and herds died off. Other desperate cattlemen launched their crazed herds down the gyppy waterholes of the rivers, losing control, and sending a tidal wave of maddened animals southeastward into suffering farm communities. The failure of two crops in a row was the end of the line anyway for many small-time, low-credit farmers on the Rolling Plains. A wave of farmers abandoned their fields, some in near panic. Wagons ladened with household goods rolled eastward—long lines of environmental refugees fleeing the aridity.[16]

News of the "Texas Drouth" aroused all Texans and eventually the nation. The Texas press quickly seized upon the issue, publishing appeals and pathetic descriptions of conditions: "The very air is now quivering and throbbing with the cries of the poor and needy," wrote the Dallas Morning News *on September 4, 1886, "for bread to eat and food to sustain life."*[17] *The Reverend John Brown, sent east to appeal for aid and to fight cattleman counter-propaganda, claimed at a meeting in Buffalo, New York, that 100,000 families or about 500,000 Texans were in dire want.*[18]

Clara Barton of the Red Cross rushed supplies and came to Texas herself to assess the claims and counterclaims. She found a complex situation. A class war between cattlemen and nesters was raging, with drought aggravating the trouble. The farmers wanted the newly opened school lands in the region. For years their wagons had pushed deeper into West Texas. But the big ranchers now saw the aridity side of the environment, and they warned—in their own interest, of course—that West Texas was simply not good farming country. They were often happy to see the farmers going back east, leaving the best grasslands for them to exploit when the rains returned. A second factor was the shameless railroad promotions for the new lands. Clara Barton noted that boomers provided "glowing descriptions, both false and dangerous, to encourage immigration," with no provisions for the unexpected.[19] *Indeed, land agents, boomers, and others frankly argued against appeals for aid outside of Texas. In a more practical vein, some railroad officials shipped in supplies of seed wheat for new plantings along their lines.*

Hardeman County pioneers like Frank Sheffield and John W. Klepper were determined to outlast the drought. Some were worried that inflamed reports of conditions would stop immigration, discourage investment, and lead to catastrophic economic decline. In any event only a trickle of state and private aid, mainly in the form of seed wheat and oats, reached Hardeman County. Most of the pioneers survived with each other's help. They also adapted, learning from the plainsmen how to place macerated cactus into the gyppy water available to treat it for drinking. Although they told tall tales of nesters booting up potatoes from their fields already baked and ready to eat, they were anxious for rain. It is difficult for modern urbanites to relate to climatological preoccupation, but A. T. Miller was ceaselessly watching the weather, looking for signs of moisture. Would 1887 be another drought year?]

JAN 27, 1887 THURSDAY MORNING MARGARET

Cloudy and looks very much like rain. There is a big cloud in the N.W. Ples Sanders started to Gainesville this Morning. He came over last night with Jim Allee. Now it is 3 ½ oclock and looks very much like rain. We will have a party at John Kleppers on Saturday night. It is cloudy to night and the wind has begun to blow. I must go to bed. Now 11 oclock.

[John W. Klepper and James Milton Allee epitomized the best of the early settlers in the upper Pease River Valley. Like many other Margaret pioneers, the Allees and Kleppers had moved westward to Margaret from Collin County, just north of Dallas County. In 1885 the Allees, Kleppers, and Beverlys led a migration of Collin County families to a new settlement at the confluence of Mule Creek with the Pease River. As a form of chain migration it was extremely effective, providing an instant sense of community, shared values, and sociable traditions. Other Collin County families followed over the years, like Sarah Fergeson and nine of her fourteen children in 1886, each filing on a section of school land. By 1890 the Plano Enquirer *of Collin County maintained a special local correspondent to report stories on the Margaret colony. This daughter colony migration also brought a number of women into the closing frontier, where their values and morality made a lasting impact.*

Like other arrivals, James Milton or "Jim" Allee had traveled to the Pease Valley alone at first, to check out the country before sending for his family. He liked the land, bought a town lot in Margaret in 1885 from John Wesley, and built a one-room shack with a lean-to for his family's arrival.[20] *Despite the 1886 drouth he elected to stay and opened a small freight line between Vernon and Margaret. He bought a section east of Margaret known as the "Belle Allee Place," and he was elected sheriff of Hardeman County in 1886. He was honest, well-intentioned, and severely understaffed for the demanding job.*

After checking out the land with Jim Allee, John W. Klepper also brought a new wife, Lucinda Klepper, westward to join him. The popular young couple were from Plano in Collin County. Mr. Klepper also freighted for a living at first, and later settled down in Foard County to farm.[21]

A. T. Miller meets Ples Sanders this Thursday, a genial soul killed a year later. Down in Sweetwater, Texas, Miss Dorothy Scarborough celebrates her ninth birthday on this day. That night, as Abner Miller informs us, the West Texas wind begins "to blow."]

JAN 28, 1887 FRIDAY MORNING MARGARET

Cloudy this morning and the wind blowing from the North and tolerably cold. Frank Spoon and [Tom] Latham came to Town this morning. This has been a nice day and I hope we will have a nice time at the party to night at Mr Wesleys at [Bob] Henrys Birthday Party. I will take Miss Ellen Coltharp to night. Well we had a real nice time to night. Babe Deberry stayed with me to night.

JAN 29, 1887 SATURDAY MORNING IN MARGARET

This is a fine morning. Clear and cool and bids fare well for a nice day. And so it has been. One of the nicest days we have had in some time. [Charles] Goodnight in Town to day. Billie Burus came back this evening from Thackerville, I. T. To night is a beautiful night, clear and cool.

[Charles Goodnight had many memories of the Pease River Valley. Comanche raids into Palo Pinto County in the fall of 1860 caused a young Goodnight to forsake his Keechi Valley ranch for the life of a ranger and scout. He explored beyond the Western Cross Timbers, across the fantastic Rolling Plains of the Brazos, Pease, and Red Rivers. He endured the torturing gyp water country to reach the freshwater springs and creeks draining from the great Llano Estacado mesaland. While serving as a scout for Cureton's troopers in December of 1860, he rode again up the Pease River Valley. On December 19, 1860, Charles Goodnight rode into the thick of the legendary Pease River Battle between Captain Sul Ross's Texas Rangers and Nocona's band of Comanches—mostly women, children, and servants, as Nocona and many other warriors were away.

The battle—or slaughter—took place within sight of 1887 Margaret. Twenty-seven years before, Goodnight had deduced that a Comanche band was camped along Mule Creek, and was leading Cureton's strung-out troopers in this direction from the east, when he rode into sight of Sul Ross's rangers shooting down the startled Comanches. As Goodnight told J. Evetts Haley:

> *From the creek [Mule Creek] to the foot of the first hills to the west was about a mile and a half of perfectly level ground, as smooth and naked as a floor, as the buffaloes had eaten off the grass. The Indians apparently lost their heads when they saw Ross' command so close. Instead of going into the [Pease*

River] sand hills, they crossed the creek twice, where it made some short bends, then struck a bee-line for the foothills with Ross and his men after them. The rangers passed through the squaws and shot the bucks as they came to them. The Sergeant and his men fell in behind on the squaws, whose horses were loaded so heavily with buffalo meat, tent poles, and camp equipage that they could not run, and killed every one of them, almost in a pile.[22]

Mr. and Mrs. M. F. Thacker piled their belongings in a wagon and moved to Margaret in 1885 from Thackerville, Indian Territory. The Thackers settled in Margaret and opened a mercantile store. Later they moved to Crowell and opened the first store there too.]

JAN 30. 1887 SUNDAY MORNING IN MARGARET

This is a clear, cool morning. Looks like it will be a nice day. I was late to breakfast this morning. I came half past nine and all was right, no Grumbling at all. I had a good breakfast, and then I sat down and played marbels with little George. Now I comence to read my Book. Its now 4 oclock and I have just finished it. *Married in Haste & Fair but False!* It is good. I hope it will do me some good. This has been a real nice day. Cool all day and now a few tinges of clouds in the North but no signs of rain. We had a nice little Social at Nelsons to night. We sang a few pieces and played Snap. I saw Babe Deberry go to see his Girle to night.

[A. T. Miller is eating and relaxing in the John Wesley home. The Wesleys were the founders and best promoters of the Margaret townsite. The first known settlers in Hardeman County were the Snyder clan, who rode into the Pease Valley wilderness in December of 1878. The next year three more adventurers—John Wesley, Fred Ditman, and Benjamin F. Lower—rode north from the raw town of Seymour, Texas. They used a compass to guide their party to the Pease River. They struck the Worsham Camp on the Pease River near Vernon, but Wesley claimed the area was "too crowded," so they wandered upstream and poked around for weeks.

Wesley was a Union veteran accustomed to taking risks, including the authorship of original poetry. He was farming in the Weatherford area of Parker County when he decided to explore the last frontier in Texas.[23] *His partner, B. F. Lower, was a talented engineer, surveyor, and an architect if needed. He was also a fast-talking, slightly delusional visionary. Frederick Ditman was a German emigrant hoping to get in with the others on the establishment of a prominent new town site. The three dreamers wandered through the Pease*

River Valley in the summer of 1879, hunting, gathering wild plums and grapes, and searching for that perfect spot. They finally decided upon the general locale where the freshwater Mule Creek drains into the Pease River. There were springs, good soils, other townsites in the nearby uplands, and fair timber along the regional drainages. Good country.

Wesley, Ditman, and Lower returned a year later in 1880 with their wives and families. They would stake claims and organize not just a town, but a metropolis. B. F. Lower and Fred Ditman dreamed of greatness with their new "Pease City" townsite, about five miles north of present-day Crowell, Texas, in Foard County. The trio sweet-talked Mary Wesley into serving as postmistress, built a large stone outpost and store, and started booming.[24] *Lower and Ditman worked themselves into a frenzy of environmental deception as they put together promotional tracts and grandiose town plans.*

Pease City was to become "The Metropolis of the West," a city destined to the greatness of a St. Louis or Fort Worth. Lower drew up elaborate plans for a sprawling city. Pease City would even have wharves teaming with workers offloading merchandise from steamboats plying the Pease River. In their eyes prospective visitors would travel on these steamboats upstream through fertile country, past vast citrus orchards, until they reached the docks, jumped ashore, and began wandering through the maze of streets. It was such a good fantasy that Lower and Ditman took it on the road. After the carpetbaggers of Reconstruction, the South returned the favor with its 1880s land boomers sent to the North and abroad.

More specifically, the pair of promoters set out on a determined tour of northern and East Coast towns. John Wesley stayed behind to run local affairs. Cattle fever had already swept many Yankee communities; it was said fabulous fortunes were being made in the closing West. In many towns and cities the Ditman slick materials and the Lower fancy plans combined nicely with their smooth-talking ways. They sold hundreds of well-situated town lots on various and sundry respectable streets—all in a city that existed only on paper. How could their victims know the Pease River could barely float a canoe much less a steamboat? Eventually, the two confidence men earned so much money that they rather lost interest in actually building the great metropolis. After working so hard to sell the dream, they preferred to retire.

John Wesley made the best of a bad situation. Pease City was abandoned as a hopeless swindle, even though Mary continued to handle some mail. John Wesley moved over to Mule Creek and renamed Pease City to "Margaret" to commemorate the birth of his daughter, Margaret or "Maggie" Wesley. Margaret Wesley, aged "1 mo." was one of fifty residents enumerated for the county in the 1880 census.[25] *Despite their keen attention to affairs and a big welcome to newcomers, the Wesleys struggled to build Margaret. Although an 1884 dugout election gave the community the precious county seat location, by 1887 the railroad was building into Quanah, well to the north.*

Little George Wesley was about three years old when A. T. was playing marbles with him. With the great drouth still around, signs of rain were eagerly sought.]

JAN 31, 1887 MONDAY MORNING MARGARET

I rose with the sun this morning and a fine morning it is, clear and cool. Will Richards was in Town this morning. He came down last night. Yesterday I got an invitation to the wedding of Tom Latham and Miss Minnie O'Neal for next Wednesday evening. We have a Norther blowing tonight. It has been cold all evening. Dance at Kirkmans to night. I did not go. (Chanolt came over this evening with a palitive but I think no good.)

[The word palitive was probably a reference to a palliative or a pain-killing agent, that is, a nostrum or medicinal aid for the relief of pain and/or bodily discomfort.]

FEB 1, 1887 TUESDAY MORNING MARGARET

Cloudy and looks as if it might rain. Still as cold as Blazes. Down to about 20°. Williams and Latham came in Town this morning and went on to Vernon. They will be back to morrow and Tom Latham will marry, if Mrs. O'Neal is able to. Johnnie [Miller] has started to Cottle and Motley to assess those two counties for tax [revenues]. This evening is still cold as whis. Mr. Latimer and F. A. Lewinthall of the Matador Ranch came in Town to night. And Mr. [J. L.] Austin from Cottle Co. is in Town to night. I got a letter today from Lonie and CK and have opened one for Johnnie [Miller] from Miss Joe Goodlet in Gay Hill.

FEB 2, 1887 WEDNESDAY MORNING MARGARET

Cloudy and threatning rain very much. The wind is from the East and cold. The mercury stands at 30° in the house. Now 8 oclock. I must go to breakfast. This is 6 in the evening now. It looks very much like rain and still cold as whis. Good big crowd here for the [Latham-O'Neal] wedding to night at 7 ½ oclock. We have had a real nice time at the wedding and dance. They were married by Mr. Hayne at 8 oclock. Then we had a nice supper and came on over to the Western Hotel and danced 10 sets.

Everything went off nice. Tonight is very cold and cloudy and the wind is blowing right hard.

Good night diary.

[The diary now holds affectionate qualities. We sense the sentimental link that Miller has established between himself and his daily entries. "Good Night Diary" appears for the first time as a testament to the relationship between the author and his work. Weddings, couples, and honeymoons against a backdrop of howling bitter wind—does A. T. want a relationship as well? Note the diarist's habit of an entry in the early morning—usually date, place, weather, and plans—followed immediately by a further entry made near the end of the day, one that relates daily events, current weather, and his mood.]

FEB 3, 1887 THURSDAY MORNING MARGARET

This morning is cold and cloudy. The mercury was down to 15° by hanging on about 15 minits on the North side. We will go out to the ULA Ranch to day, I suppose. To night is the supper of Mr and Mrs Lathams. We got to the ranch in good time, about 6 oclock. We had a nice supper and danced until 1 oclock. I danced with Miss Vina, and Miss Kittie Morrow, and Miss Ethel Hardisty, and Miss Emma Rambo. Frank Spoon and W. T. McConel got drunk as H— [Hell]. We had a real nice dance.

[The pioneer ranch supper is a staple of western lore. Folks gathered from miles around for the food, festivity, fiddling, and dancing. The ULA was a famous early ranch owned by the Witherspoons. Harriet C. Witherspoon was the proud hostess of this wedding supper for newlyweds Tom and Minnie Latham. A kind and generous person, she earned the enduring affection of locals and ULA cowboys. Like several other early women, she was also a postmistress, running the "Ula, Texas" post office out of her ranch home. Her husband, J. G. Witherspoon, was a wily but otherwise honorable rancher who led the 1890 movement to detach the southern portion of Hardeman County. Combining the Hardeman land south of the Pease River with some other county scraps, he carved out the proposed new county of Beaver in a deal cut with the Quanah power interests.[26]

Even loyal local historians note the political cynicism behind the eventual county name. Witherspoon's bill was held up in the state legislature until a key committeeman, Senator Wells Townsend, agreed to carry it forward, provided the proposed new county of "Beaver" would bear instead the name of Townsend's close friend and law partner, Major Robert Foard. Witherspoon agreed and the bill was carried to the House and Senate in 1891. In the capitol it did not hurt that "Foard" sounded identical to "Ford." Enough legislative members thought the proposed new county was named in honor of John S. "RIP" Ford, the famous explorer, Texas Ranger, and Confederate colonel, that the bill actually passed into law. Thus Foard County came into being in 1891, an obscure law partner from Columbus, Texas, got more than his due, and the famous John Ford went without honor in the county pantheon of names. The townspeople of Margaret hoped to dominate this new county as they once had the old.[27]]

FEB 4, 1887 FRIDAY MORNING ULA RANCH

The ground was covered with snow. And cold, oh hush as whis. We started back for Margaret about 10 oclock. Had a right cold ride. We got here about 12 ½ oclock. This has been a cold day. The mercury stood at 18° this morning. Down at Mr Wesleys in the House this evening it is not so cold as this morning. George Ranes has his Team in the yard to night and will sleep with me.

[The ULA partygoers ride back through freezing weather to Margaret. A. T. shares his boarder's bed. On this day Congress enacted the Interstate Commerce Act. The legislation was designed to curb the excesses of powerful railroads, but the scope of the act soon expanded.]

FEB 5, 1887 SATURDAY MORNING. MARGARET

Snow still on the ground. The mercury is at 25° after hanging it out 10 or 15 minutes on the North side of the House. I received a letter to day from Bunion Goodlet in Sanbarnadina [San Bernadino] California and one for Johnie from Lonie. Got word from Capt Mack Murrey [McMurry] to day to report at once to Quanah. W. B. Houston came up to day to attend court. This has been a gloomy day all day. It has been raining this evening and is still drizzling as it falls.

[These were the blizzard snows and icy rains that gradually eased the grip of the drought. Captain Samuel A. McMurry commanded Company B, Frontier Battalion, of the Texas Rangers. The Texas Rangers had only recently advanced from the railheads of Vernon and Harrold to the new boomtown of Quanah, Texas. The railroad was just laying track into the new town.]

FEB 6, 1887 SUNDAY MORNING MARGARET

Terrible misty and dark. Not very cold. Noon is still misty. There is no church today. To bad. Sampson came in and he and George Burk will fix up and change their rent contract from Sampson to George. Mr Hoby and Bob Murray came in Town this evening from Quanah. Hoby lost $40 Dollars and thinks Murray got it. The snow all left to day and the ground is wet. The ground was covered this morning but it is all gone.

FEB 7, 1887 MONDAY MORNING MARGARET

This morning is still cloudy but the mist is gone. Right smart like rain. Yet, I will go to Quanah to day as Capt Mackmuray has wrote me to report at once. Well I came over with Mr Hollie in the buggy and led my horse. I found Quanah to be growing conciderably. There is a big dance in Town to night, but did not take it in. Some nice looking young ladies at the dance. The train will be in Quanah in three or four days. I met Dr Sumpter and his wife this evening. I met Mr Berry of Lakes Hardware in Ft Worth.

[The course of the mighty Fort Worth & Denver City Railroad would determine future settlement patterns far more than the Collin County pioneer families and their agrarian traditions. The townfounders of Margaret rightfully feared the economic and political consequences caused when the railroad resumed building west of its terminus at Harrold, Texas. The Fort Worth & Denver City tracks completely missed Margaret, skirting instead a crude dugout hamlet now called Quanah. After the company released its railroad survey in 1886, some boomers rushed onto the Quanah site in anticipation of the railroad, arriving in good time. The first organized town lot sale took place in December of 1886, a few months before A. T. Miller rode into town.

The raw, new town was named after Quanah Parker, the famous son of Peta Nokona and Cynthia Ann Parker. Ironically, Margaret had a much stronger geographic claim to the name than the railroad survey dugout site. Margaret was virtually on the Mule Creek site where Captain Sul Ross rode upon a Comanche encampment, his men massacring as many natives as possible. Ross incidentally spared the life of a runaway squaw, a woman he recognized as a white captive from her intensely blue eyes. It was thus near Margaret that Quanah escaped to become a famous chief and his mother was forced to return to her biological kinship. The name "Quanah" was given by Cynthia Ann Parker to her son shortly after his springtime birth. It was the Comanche expression for the smell of the spring prairies in bloom, when the air is fresh and scented with a thousand fragrances from the earth.]

FEB 8, 1887 QUANAH TX. TUESDAY MORNING 1887

The wind has changed last night in the North. This morning its a little cool but Plesunt enough. I will start to Margaret this morning to return

Friday. Well on my way to day I saw four nice Deer. I went up the Pease River to hunt a horse for Mr Wesley that his little boy has. It was given to him by J. A. Williamson. I got to Margaret between one and two oclock. Sam Britt of Vernon came in Town to night. A Gentleman from Bell Co[unty] came up with him. Tom Latham beat his case to day. Good for him. I had the Pleasure of meeting Miss Eva Grim this evening for the first time in several months. Our Photographs came in to day from Gainesville. Good night Diary.

[The newlywed Tom Latham "beat his case," as A. T. noted approvingly. This case may refer to Tom Latham's gunfight in front of Fred Rip's saddle shop in Quanah; his opponent, Doc Shaw, died from his wounds. Latham was lucky to be both a newlywed and a man acquitted of murder. By the turn of the century Tom Latham was a champion roper at cowboy reunions around the country.[28]*]*

FEB 9, 1887 WEDNESDAY MORNING MARGARET

It is a little cloudy this morning but pleasant. Well, I will work the Road to day. Not but four hands on the Road to day. Well, I will hunt a horse this evening. I went to Mr Keens house and to Mr Frys and to Mr Bamtries and Gobles and on back to Town. No horse to day. Well, Mrs [Frank] Sheffield is at Mr Wesleys to night. She is on her way to Dallas. I sold Johnie's Scrip to Mr Hollie to day for 90 ct [percent]. Sold him $64.00 and got in cash $57.60. Well, about enough for to day. So Good night Diary.

[Captain Sam McMurry has given Miller a few days back in Margaret to straighten his affairs, pack, and obtain a horse and saddle. Miller visits various residents near Margaret in search of a good horse to buy.]

FEB 10, 1887 THURSDAY MORNING MARGARET

Cloudy this morning and warm. I think it will rain. I have been in the courthouse listening at a trial between Chipman & Cartwright. Jim D[Illegible]'s case came up. They found him gilty, fined $1.00 and costs. This evening is very warm. It looks as if it may rain to night.

[Sitting in on trials was not only amusing, it was recommended as an education on the process of law. As the county seat, Margaret attracted both lawyers and lawsuits. Conveniently, the new courthouse and jail were located right next to one another. Because so many families were related or close friends, justice to locals (like newlywed Tom Latham) might be fairer than the swift justice meted out to ugly strangers.]

FEB 11, 1887 MARGARET. FRIDAY MORNING.

Norther came up fast last night. Cold as whis this morning. And I must go to Quanah to day for sure. I have bought a horse from W. R. Wheat. A black horse, about 14 ½ hands high, with one white hind foot left and saddle marks, black face, at $75.00 for Horse and saddle. And I put in a watch at $20.00. The watch I got of barder. Well, I got to Quanah about 2 oclock. Had a cold trip here. He took Mr Kelly back with him.

[After several days of looking, A. T. buys a fine horse from local rancher Riley Wheat, and reports for duty at the new Quanah ranger camp.]

FEB 12, 1887 QUANAH. SATURDAY MORNING.

Cool and cloudy. First morning in Ranger Camp. I met Sterling Buster in Town this Morning. He was on his way to the Mill Iron Ranch. Capt McMurray and Tom Plat will go to Margaret to day. (Well I enlisted in Ranger force this morning and what now Shal be my fate.) I will try and do the best I can. Capt and Plat came home about 6 oclock. Ulysses Grant was drunk as a fool to night. Ples Sanders closed his Saloon to night and will go in with Hoby.

[On this day Abner Miller subscribed to the oath and enlisted as a private in Company B of the famous Frontier Battalion of the Texas Rangers.[29] *Miller had obviously been in prior contact and correspondence with Captain McMurry over the enlistment. A ranger captain interviewed a candidate closely, because a life might depend on the new man's abilities and character. Miller's purchase of a good horse from rancher Riley Wheat was simply part of the equipment that every ranger had to furnish for himself. The state government was notoriously stingy in supplying and equipping its state police force.*

Company B was commanded by veteran Texas Ranger Captain Samuel Alexander McMurry. Sam McMurry came to Texas from Tennessee after the Civil War. He cowboyed for a spell, made good friends in Colorado County, then turned to criminal justice as another paying business that rounded up strays. Sam "Soft Voice" McMurry earned his ranger badge the hard way—as a young 1877 private serving under the legendary Captain Lee Hall.[30] *Captain Hall and his young ranger privates saw plenty of action. They continued the virtual guerrilla war against bandits, feuds, and thefts begun by McNelly's rangers in South Texas. McMurry rode after outlaws in Live Oak, McMullen, San Patricio, Nueces, Jim Wells, La Salle, and other lawless counties. In 1879 McMurry reenlisted under Captain Hall as part of the "Special Force for the Suppression of Crime and Lawlessness."*[31]

Sam McMurry and Lee Hall also became good friends. McMurry was

Figure 2. Captain "Soft Voice" Sam McMurry. Courtesy Texas Ranger Hall of Fame and Museum, Waco

dedicated, professional, intelligent, and highly disciplined. He advanced rapidly in the ranks. He made sergeant under Captain Hall, then lieutenant under Captain Thomas L. Oglesby. (Oglesby replaced Lee Hall when the latter fell in love and resigned to marry a twenty-one-year-old belle.) Lieutenant McMurry was noted for his reticence and calm as an officer; some folks even called him "Say Nothing" McMurry. He was a lieutenant in Company F in the summer of 1881 when the new adjutant general, W. H. King, turned to him to solve a serious problem. Captain Bryan Marsh's Company B was in a serious mess from its stint in Colorado City.

The best man, Sergeant Dick Ware, had resigned after winning the first election for sheriff of Mitchell County. A little later Jeff Milton and two other Company B rangers had shot Ware's opponent, W. P. Patterson, during one of Patterson's drunken altercations. Allegations of ranger brutality were ballyhooed, and the three rangers suddenly found themselves indicted for murder!

Captain Marsh was said, according to complaints and a quartermaster inquiry, to be drinking more often than normal. Stress was a factor. Company B moved westward to Hackberry Springs, and then on to the raw whistlestop at Big Spring, but the unit's morale and discipline were at a low ebb. Adjutant General W. H. King filed the paperwork and officially disbanded the entire company.[32]

King then reorganized the unit, giving Sam A. McMurry the captaincy of a new Company B, Frontier Battalion. The adjutant general gave Captain McMurry authority both to reenlist the best men and to hire new ones. Officially McMurry's duties began on September 1, 1881, but already "Soft Voice" had caught a train to join Company B near the Pecos City "tent town." McMurry assembled not only a new company, but also a new image for Company B. Disliking a press or public image of rangers as motley brutal shootists, McMurry encouraged a new vision: well-dressed, professional, and respected lawmen. Following the Texas & Pacific Railroad west across the Staked Plain, Captain McMurry invigorated the company with his leadership, quiet orders, and detached professionalism. He was beginning a remarkable—if undersung—career as one of the greatest ranger captains in an era of distinguished lawmen. Company B was certainly his creation for almost all of the 1880s.

McMurry sometimes visited his old mentor Lee Hall, who managed the Dull Ranch in La Salle County. Hall had signed on some of his former rangers as cowboys. Shortly after making captain, S. A. McMurry met a droll young man named William Sydney Porter at the Dull Ranch. Willie Porter was an iconoclastic North Carolina teenager who spent two years at the ranch to shake the tuberculosis that had killed his mother.[33] *Later known as "O. Henry," Willie Porter grew his hair out long at the Dull Ranch, strummed a guitar, and drew witty caricatures. He relished the reunions of McMurry and Hall where anecdotes and stories abounded.*

Sam McMurry commanded Company B for almost a decade, seeing a lot of action in the western half of the state.[34] *Company B fought fence cutters, tracked down rustlers, and supervised courts, elections, and trials. McMurry's men worked well as a crime suppression force around the "whiskey men" at Big Spring, Pecos City, and Toyah during the building of the Texas & Pacific to its junction with the Southern Pacific Railroad in West Texas.*[35] *After 1883–85 stints back at Colorado City and Big Spring, Company B was transferred in 1885 to Wichita Falls. McMurry's skill in taming railroad towns got his company assigned to accompany the Fort Worth & Denver City Railroad.*[36]

Company B's mission was to tame the Northwest and Panhandle frontier, to suppress all the crime and lawlessness they could find. Company B had closely followed the construction of the FW&DC Railroad westward: from Wichita Falls in 1885 to Harrold in early 1886, then from Harrold to Vernon that same year. As the fall of 1886 approached, Captain S. A. McMurry turned his attention to Hardeman County more and more. On September 1, 1886, the captain wrote the Frontier Battalion quartermaster that he was starting to Hardeman County "to-day with four men."[37]

McMurry traveled widely and arrested scores of men. His job was a dangerous one. A month and a half earlier, on December 26, 1886, former ranger captain and La Salle County Sheriff Charles B. McKinney was assassinated near Cotulla while investigating an apparent report of child molestation.]

FEB 13, 1887 SUNDAY MORNING QUANAH

Cloudy and misting rain. The wind is from the Southeast. It is my day for Herding Horses. Well this has been a drizzly day all day. I got along fine. Kept all the Horses together. I bought a winchester to day. Paid $15.00 for it off Capt McMurray.

[Miller likely purchased one of the Model 1873 Winchesters popular with the rangers. Ever since Captain Richard King introduced them to McNelly's men in South Texas, the Texas Rangers preferred this efficient and lethal weapon over the state-supplied .50 Sharps carbines.]

FEB 14, 1887 QUANAH MONDAY MORNING

This is a fine clear morning. Very different to yesterday. Well this has been a nice day. Captain and Plat went over to Margaret to day and back. Johnie [Miller] and Will Rambo came over to day. Porter Drace went to Margaret. Plat made an arrest to night with a man for breaking out a window at Mrs Dixon. And we had a dance to night. I took it in. Had a good time.

[Captain McMurry and Tom Platt were old friends with common memories of Columbus, Texas. It was natural for them to ride together. Their families had known each other since the days when Sam McMurry and the Platts lived in Colorado County, Texas. Like the Collin County clans of Margaret, McMurry and the Platt brothers shared a former county identity. (Captain Lee Hall, in turn, had recruited heavily from his friends and connections in Washington County.)

Tom Platt was one of eight brothers and a daughter in the Platt family. The father was a tough-talking sergeant who served in the Mexican-American War under the incomparable John S. "RIP" Ford. His martial spirit was imparted to five sons who grew up to become Texas Rangers and to bear arms pro-

fessionally—Sam M., John, Tom, Jake, and Radd. The Platt brothers saw much service in the Frontier Battalion.[38]*]*

FEB 15, 1887 QUANAH TUESDAY MORNING

Misty this morning. Johnie [Miller] came down to the camp this morning on his way to Margaret. I went to see Mrs Burnsides this morning. She told me of all her troubles. I hope she will do better in the future than in the past. The Day train came in to day about 4 oclock. For the first time a passenger ever has come out this far west. This has been a fine day all day. I met Fred M. Campbell to day for the first time in a long time. And he is on a drunk today.

FEB 16, 1887 QUANAH WEDNESDAY MORNING

This is a nice morning and I think we will have a nice day. Well, I have made me a bedsted to day and think it a right good ruff sted. Fred Campbell is still drunk in town yet. Plat and Gray are playing dominoes. An awful site of drunk men to night lying in a sallon near the P.O. One was Big Bill Williams. Most of them are Irish. Working on the R.R. Poor old fellows.

[Big Bill Williams was a Quanah butcher with a big drinking problem. He was widely rumored not to care particularly where his beeves came from, lending credence to stories of connections with local rustlers. Later on, Texas Ranger Bill McDonald insisted that he be shown the hides of butchered animals to ensure that stolen livestock was not being sold on the streets of Quanah. Stories of the hard-drinking Irish railroad workers were routine. Fred Campbell owned a town lot in Margaret, but like others he rode to Quanah for a drink or two, or too many.]

FEB 17, 1887 QUANAH THURSDAY MORNING

This is an awful windy day. As bad as I have ever saw, I think. I got a letter to day from W. M. Kerr. He gave me a good deal of news. Johnie sent it to me and a paper from North Carolina. He wrote me that our money from S. S. Steele had come by PO Order on Vernon. He had sent it down to have it cashed. I sent him a note by Bob Murray to pay W. R. Wheat $40 and take a receipt. Sterling Price came over from Margaret to night. His trial will come off the 2nd. Tom Plat and Green went out this evening and arrested Wesley Ashburn. They brought him to Camp and we have him to gard to night. Dennis Peal and I stand from ½ after 11 to 3 oclock. This day was the windiest day I ever saw in my life. The house belonging

Figure 3. Captain Bill McDonald. Courtesy Texas Ranger Hall of Fame and Museum, Waco

to Cahn blew all to pieces and som Tents were all a total reck. Oh, its a pictur to see the like.

[From out of a fierce duststorm, we begin to see the new ranger's Company B companions now: the brothers John and Tom Platt, Jim Green, Sterling Price, J. M. Bradbury, and Dennis Peal. Many of these privates have been with the Frontier Battalion for years. With a little money from the family property in North Carolina, A. T. pays off the debt on his horse. Despite the supposed frontier ethic of a "man's word is his bond" and deals done with a handshake, Miller always got a receipt. The relentless West Texas wind blows down the flimsiest parts of the new town.]

FEB 18, 1887 FRIDAY MORNING IN QUANAH

Beautiful morning, clear and nice. We will have to go to Mangum to take a Prisner, Wesley Ashburn. [Private J. M.] Bradberry and I will go. Well we now are at Mangum. Got here about Sundown. We have had a hard days ride. We have passed over some of as prettie a land to day as I ever saw. And some awful ruff places and mountains. Still you cant rest. We went through a valley about six or eight miles across about eight miles South of Mangum. Some deliteful land and valleys. On Turkey Creek there is right smart timber. Salt Fork valley is emence and fine. Mangum is situated on a rise North and East of the Salt Fork about a mile.

[Mangum was the lonely county seat, indeed the only seat of any consequence for the Greer County frontier. In 1883 Henry Sweet surveyed a veteran's state land grant for Colonel John Swisher in the area. Sweet returned the next year and started a small community soon called "Tin City" after the town's abundant use of flattened tin cans to seal drafty houses and buildings. Tin City became "Sweet's Camp," and finally took the Mangum name to honor the original landowner, A. S. Mangum. The Texas legislature created Greer County in early 1860; Governor Sam Houston signed it into law on February 8, 1860. The county was an enormous stretch of promised land between the North Fork and Prairie Dog Town Fork of the Red River west to the 100th meridian. Little was done about law and order until a few more settlers and major cattle interests entered these grasslands in force in 1885.

Texas officials belatedly started to administer the claimed and leased land, often tapping the scanty resources of adjacent Hardeman and Wheeler County. Only seven months earlier in July of 1886, all the Greer settlers who could do so rode west from their dugouts and half-dugouts to Mobeetie for the official election to organize the county. Not all the new county residents were upstanding citizens. In the secluded brakes, sand hills, and watered valleys between the forks of the Red River, various and often indeterminate combinations of hired cowhands, outlaws, and settlers sheltered herds of stock. Some of these animals had been stolen from elsewhere, but legitimate stock was also subject to theft and removal from Greer.

Despite the supererogatory assumptions of Texas officials, the million and a half acres of Greer were equally claimed by the United States government as federal territory. The entire county was therefore "disputed territory" between state and federal officials. Two questions of geography were key to the dispute. The first question concerned the 100th meridian. Texans noted that the 1819 Melish Map that accompanied the Adams-Oñis Treaty—a map famed for its inaccuracies—located the 100th meridian about a hundred miles east of its actual location, a favorable situation for Texas legal claims. The United States insisted that the boundary should reflect improved and modern surveying on the ground.

A second question was which branch *of the upper Red River was intended upon annexation as the boundary between Texas and U.S. territory? According to the 1819 treaty and map the boundary was to have been the principal (and only marked) branch of the Red River. Texas claimed with good cause that this principal branch was the North Fork. Had not the government's own explorer, Captain Randolph Marcy, chosen to follow the North Fork branch during his 1852 investigation of the mysterious sources of the Red River? U.S. attorneys insisted that the principal branch was the Prairie Dog Town Fork. They even obtained later testimony from Marcy that the Prairie Dog Town Fork had had the greater flow, and he had regarded and published it as the "main branch." If Texas won on either question then Greer County belonged to the people of Texas.[39] Even the good guys were locked in a power struggle for Greer County in 1887.]*

FEB 19, 1887 MANGUM SATURDAY MORNING

Cloudy and looks very much like rain. We have another big days ride before us. We have to go to Quanah. Well we got here about 7 oclock. Got caught in a rain. We have come over some more beautiful land on a line from here back to Mangum, Greer Co. We left poor Wesley Ashburn to wait his trial in Mangum. I do [not] know how he may come out. About 2 inches of snow in Greer Co. to night.

[Poor "Wes" Ashburn was arrested by Captain McMurry in Hardeman County on February 17 for stealing horses in Greer County. Miller and Bradbury delivered the prisoner to the authorities at Mangum. Miller obviously felt sympathetic to the man.[40]]

FEB 20, 1887 SUNDAY MORNING QUANAH

It rained last night and is still cloudy this morning. I must go up town. Well I met Capt. [McMurry] and we must go right back to Mangum. Eight of us will have to go. Well we got to Mangum in good time.

[The trail from Quanah to Mangum was about forty-five miles long. It crossed the Prairie Dog Town Fork almost nine miles north of Quanah, then advanced north-northeast in Greer County across Boggy Creek and Turkey Creek. Crossing a low divide the trail descended to the Salt Fork of the Red River, crossed a ford, and a mile away reached the raw town of Mangum—supposedly in Texas.

Figure 4. 1887 Greer County Half-Dug-Out (Kubala Family near Willow). Courtesy Old Greer County Museum and Hall of Fame, Mangum, Oklahoma

Figure 5. 1896 Mangum Street Scene. Courtesy Old Greer County Museum and Hall of Fame, Mangum, Oklahoma

McMurry's "Record of Scouts" noted for February 20, "Sergeant McNelly and four men went to Greer Co. in pursuit of Horse thieves."[41]*]*

FEB 21, 1887 MONDAY MORNING ON OUR (WAY) TO MANGUM.

I think we will have a nice day as its clear and nice. We got to Mangum about 2 oclock and have come 15 miles N. E. over the mountains. We have had a nice camp to day. The mountains are nice, and good water in Mangum and around. We arrested J. A. Williamson this evening at old man Hickmans.

[Greer County had two settlers named Williamson. The more prominent Mr. Williamson was the sheriff of Greer County based at Mangum. After a pause at the county seat for information and a short rest, the rangers ride out northeast for Lee Hickman's place. Their travels take them through the scenic Quartz and Granite Mountains, more than a thousand feet of granite mountains rising from the grassy plains. The Texas Rangers locate "Jenks" Williamson at Old Man Hickman's place. They arrest Jenks for "theft of horses."[42] *Lee Hickman is later accused of horse theft as well, possibly a reflection of the poor company he kept.]*

FEB 22, 1887 TUESDAY MORNING GREER CO. AT MR HICKMAN

Near the North Fork of the Red River. This is a nice morning and I think we will have a nice day. Well we are all on Turkey Creek, Greer Co., to night. We have a good place to camp to night. We have had a good days ride to day. Have come several miles to day.

[The rangers wake up at Lee Hickman's place near the North Fork edge of Greer County. The Comanche, Kiowa, and Apache reservation is just across the river to their east. Newcomers from Texas, like the storied Marlow brothers, were settling into these lands as well in 1887. The ranger detachment starts back to Quanah with their alleged horsethief. The men make about half the distance and stop for the night along the better (non-gyppy) waters of Turkey Creek.]

FEB 23, 1887 TURKEY CREEK, GREER CO.

WEDNESDAY MORNING AT CAMP

Cool and a little cloudy this morning. I am afraid we will have a cold ride to day. Well, we got to Quanah about 2 oclock this evening. Had a very nice days ride. The wind blew right hard. We ate our dinners and Mr Moore took the prisner and started to Margaret with him. He was arrested for Stealing Horses. Well I must go up Town. Bob Murray was arrested this evening and brought to camp for being drunk.

[Turkey Creek is a northern tributary of the Prairie Dog Town Fork of the Red River near Duke, Oklahoma. It lies about halfway between Mangum and Quanah. It is not a hard ride from a morning camp at Turkey Creek back to Quanah, but a cold wind adds to discomfort.]

FEB 24, 1887 QUANAH THURSDAY MORNING

This is a nice morning and I think we will have a nice day. Well we've had a nice day. Had Shooting Scrape in Town this evening. (Pat Woolford Shot two shots at John Davidson and Comanchie Bill in Dutch Henrys Saloon. But done no harm. One ball went through the crack of the dore.) Capt. and the boys came over from Margaret to day on the trial of Sterling Price. His case was put off.

[The context for this shooting was the bad blood between Pat Wolforth and tough locals like John Davidson and "Comanche Bill" (the drunken butcher we met earlier as Big Bill Williams). Davidson and Williams were rumored to have gang connections. The brilliant, upright, and honest Pat Wolforth was seen as a challenging new force, one of legitimacy and Victorian morality. He was also talking too much, turning unwanted attention to the questionable activities of some neighbors. John Davidson was a colorful man from Wilbarger County, just to the east of Hardeman. He was a loud, proud, and clannish individual, often boisterous and sociable, sometimes quick-tempered, and invariably well armed. He also carried the public confidence of having killed several men. Already Davidson had clashed with a friend of Wolforth's, the blue-gray-eyed, new deputy sheriff of Quanah—Bill McDonald. To Davidson's utter surprise, McDonald consistently managed to disarm him when he came to Quanah.

William Jesse and Rhoda Isabel McDonald arrived in Hardeman County in 1885. Bill McDonald had sold out his lumberyard interest in Harrold, and the McDonalds bought good ranch land near Wanderer's Creek and stocked the range.[43] *McDonald had grown up in Alabama, but after the death of his father in the Civil War the family moved to Henderson, Texas, in 1866. As a young man in Rusk County he worked for a time in law enforcement, getting a routine background, but then he turned to business affairs and moved westward.*

The loose ways and blatant theft of the "free" enterprise Hardeman County frontier deeply offended Bill McDonald's sense of moral order. McDonald's thirty-three years of maturity and his bold demeanor crystallized into a new persona—the avenging angel of the Hardeman frontier. Needing all the help he could get, Sheriff Jim Allee quickly agreed to appoint McDonald as a deputy. The new deputy gradually lost interest in his ranch, and he left his wife Rhoda to cope with long absences. But Deputy McDonald used his humble office to launch an anti-crime crusade that eventually made him the most feared lawman in a 3,500 square mile region.

McDonald employed a suddenness and stealth in disarming men that was considered amazing. It was done gracefully and quickly, with an expert's touch. After first doing so to John Davidson, McDonald marched him to the office, where Davidson paid a fine for flourishing his firearm on the streets of Quanah. A little later Davidson, like the Earps and others, inveigled himself into a more respectable position. He became the new deputy sheriff in Wilbarger County, the adjacent jurisdiction. Once again he appeared on the streets of Quanah, boasting that as a deputy himself, McDonald now had no right to take his gun away. Nevertheless McDonald did so, apparently saying, "Your Commission won't do you much good up here. If Sheriff [W. N.] Barker wants to appoint a man that throws in with thieves, all right. But in Hardeman County we don't have to recognize him."

In 1909 Albert Bigelow Paine wrote a celebrated biography of Bill McDonald that included a more detailed account of this famous incident involving Pat Wolforth, John Davidson, and Comanche Bill. Contrary to the popular mythology, gun control was often applied to Texas frontier towns and settlements, and it was often strict. There were accidents in applying gun control. Not long before, the sheriff of Tascosa had called to an exuberant newcomer to turn over his gun for safe-keeping while in the town. Feeling challenged, unsure of city ways, the youth hesitated, then made for a fast draw. The sheriff automatically shot the adolescent boy off his saddle. It was a sickening experience.

Pat Wolforth was aligned with the new deputy sheriff and was an outspoken leader of the other do-gooder newcomers. Toward him Davidson and "Comanche Bill" Williams decided to vent their feelings at being usurped. Albert Bigelow Paine provides no date but describes the action of February 24 thusly:

> *There was never such a stubborn man, Davidson decided, as that fool deputy, Bill McDonald. He decided to wait until McDonald should be absent, and then have it out with Wolforth. When the time came, Davidson brought a gang along with him and they followed Wolforth about with pestering remarks, until their victim suddenly grew tired of the annoyance, and opened fire. This was unexpected and the gang retired for reorganization. Then some rangers, quartered at Quanah, appeared on the scene, and Wolforth was put under arrest.*
>
> *He was taken before a justice, who fixed his bond at a thousand dollars,*

which he was unable to raise, because of the dread in which Davidson and his crowd were held. It was just about this moment that Deputy McDonald returned, and the Rangers delivered Wolforth into his hands.

"What's the matter, Pat?" McDonald asked.

His co-worker explained how he had fired on the Davidson gang, though without damage to anybody.

And they put you under a thousand dollar bond for it?" commented Deputy Bill.

"Yes."

"Well, they ought to have made it a good deal heavier for your not being a better shot. Never mind, I'll fill your bond all right," and this McDonald did, immediately.[44]]

FEB 25, 1887 QUANAH FRIDAY MORNING

Cool and a little cloudy. There is a right good cloud in the East. The wind is in the East. My day on hurd. Expect I will have a cold day.

FEB 26, 1887 SATURDAY MORNING QUANAH

Nice morning, cool, but think we will have a nice day. Plat and Price and I have to go right back to Mangum, Greer Co. to day. Well to night we will camp in the brakes near Mangum. After a hard days ride we got here about 7 oclock.

[Is it possible that Jenks Williamson has been talking about his associates in horse stealing? Suddenly the rangers are going back to Hickman's place in Greer County to round up more suspected rustlers.]

FEB 27, 1887 SUNDAY MORNING

IN CAMP NEAR MANGUM, GREER CO.

This is a beautifull morning. We will go and get the Sheriff, Mr. Williamson, and go for Wooten and Hickman 15 miles N.E. of Mangum. Well we got both of the boys we went after, but had a race after Wooten. Price and Sheriff Williamson followed him and out run him. So we are back in Mangum to night again. We got in about 8 oclock. We got a good dinner in the gap of the mountain today.

[For ten years Texas Rangers rounded up outlaws in an area of Oklahoma bigger than Delaware. Greer County Sheriff Williamson used the rangers as an auxiliary force in his manhunts. They were state lawmen assigned to aid local officials. Thus, they chased, caught, guarded, and transferred prisoners like the rustlers Tom Hickman and William Wooten. The rustlers apparently made

a business of stealing and selling back and forth between Hardeman and Greer Counties.]

FEB 28, 1887 MANGUM MONDAY MORNING

Last day of February and a nice morning. I think we will have a good day to go to Quanah with our Prisner. Gray Will of Wood & Dixon is in Town and will go over with us. Well, we have had a hard days ride to day. Three of our horses very near give out. Got in Town about 9 ½ oclock. All safe and sound with our men.

[Hard riding was routine by now for the boys. Camping together in the open under the sky also forged strong bonds and built company camaraderie. Campfire stories, ranger history and personalities, and the humor and profundity of the outdoors worked to lessen the hardships of long hours in the saddle. John W. Bracken wrote in a short 1929 reminiscence: "I have made some hard old rides with Tom and John Platt on the plains and if you want to find out what a man is, the place to do so is in the Ranger service or in a cow camp. You will learn more about a man in a week in camp than you can anywhere else in years."[45]]

MARCH 1, 1887 TUESDAY MORNING QUANAH TEX

This is a nice clear morning. I hope we have a nice month, but may we have more rain in this month than we had in the last. Enoch Boren and family came over to Town this evening. I met John Coltharp to day, also Mr [William] Reed and Billie Powers. I forwarded to Johnnie [Miller] to day some letters that came in return to me, which I had sent to him at Teepee.

["Teepee" or Tee Pee City began as a wild 1875 trading post along Tee Pee Creek near the Middle Pease River in eastern Motley County. Once the semi-violent, demimonde hangout of buffalo hunters, skinners, pimps, and common renegades, Tee Pee City was considerably more sedate when Johnnie Miller arrived to do tax assessments. When the Quanah, Acme, & Pacific RR skipped the town a decade later, the settlement died quickly. The last resident abandoned the community at the turn of the century. Only the legend of Tee Pee City lingers.[46]]

MAR 2, 1887 QUANAH WEDNESDAY MORNING

This is a nice morning and looks as we will have a nice day today. Well I will go with the Teamster to day after a load of wood. John Bland and Porter Drace came over to day. Robinson Bros. opened their house today.

[John Bland was an early attorney in Hardeman County, a resident of Margaret, and a familiar face at the courthouse. The growth of Quanah can be measured in the openings and "firsts" chronicled by the diary, a consequence of the economic boom brought about by the advancing industrial culture.]

MAR 3, 1887 QUANAH THURSDAY MORNING

This is a nice cool morning. A right good Norther came up last night. Well I wrote Uncle Silas and Thomas to day. I want to write Lonie to night. Old man Hawkins was in Town to day. Sheriff [Tom] Williamson of Greer Co. came over to day with Mrs Wooten as a witness.

[William Wooten had given the rangers a "race" before his arrest on February 27. Perhaps Mrs. Wooten had some words of explanation in general on her husband's behalf.]

MAR 4, 1887 QUANAH FRIDAY MORNING

Cloudy and cool. It looks very much like it will rain. A very raw morning. And it is my Hurd day. Still looks as if it would rain to night. I had my Horse Shewed to day and it cost me $1.50 at Rabbs.

[The weather always seems lousy when it is A. T.'s turn on herd day. Keeping track of the remuda and the pack animals was evidently a boring, lonely, and day-long chore. Watching animals graze contrasted sharply with manhunting. It was also much more fun to go into a booming new town and see and be seen—even if prices were getting high.]

MAR 5, 1887 QUANAH SATURDAY MORNING

Cool and cloudy. Sprinkling rain a little. I hope it will come a good rain. McNelly left this morning for Ft Worth. Well everything has went on quiet to day. But the boys are keeping their eyes open this evening. Expecting a row. McDonnell came in this Evening. I mailed a letter this evening to Ed Correll at Dallas.

["McDonnell" is Abner Miller's initial spelling for William Jesse McDonald. Note the profusion of Scotch-Irish names joining and running the Texas Rangers. There were rumors of Scotch-Irish and Irish power struggles within the ranger force and some allegations of ethnic discrimination. Within two decades William Jesse "Bill" McDonald would become the most famous Texas Ranger of his day. He was an old friend of progressive Texas Governor James Hogg, and after the turn of the century he hobnobbed with the powerful. Teddy Roosevelt and Woodrow Wilson were eventual fans. The A. T. Miller entries document McDonald's presence on the Hardeman County frontier at a time

when he was just getting established as a career law enforcement officer. They provide important contemporaneous commentary.[47]

McDonald's literary fame is due in large measure to the earnest attentions of an old friend, Colonel Edward M. House. Rich and powerful, the confidant of Woodrow Wilson and state leaders, Colonel E. M. House greatly admired the frontier spirit of the "Old Texans," a genius he saw reflected in Alabama's Bill McDonald. In 1908 Colonel House conceived the idea of a promotional biography for his friend. He asked William Sydney Porter (O. Henry) to do the honor to a fellow Texan, but House's letter was delayed by a mother-in-law, and the job went instead to Albert Bigelow Paine.[48] *Bill McDonald came to New York at Colonel House's invitation, where Paine interviewed him for days at the fancy Player's Club. Needless to say, Paine's dates and time frames are inexact, and the reader gets McDonald's cock-of-the-walk version of events. Few other law officers receive credit where due.*

Albert Bigelow Paine claimed in his biography that after McDonald returned to Quanah, he and Bill Williams had it out in front of a Quanah saloon. McDonald was not intimidated by the size of "Big Bill"—the town butcher—or the fierceness of his moniker, "Comanche Bill." After the usual verbal provocations, and with the apparent threat of a butcher knife stuck in his body, Bill McDonald picked up a loose piece of stout lumber and hit Williams so hard in the head that he almost killed him. Unquestionably effective but not recommended for the modern peace officer.]

MAR 6, 1887 QUANAH SUNDAY MORNING

Tis a beautiful morning. Plesant as can be and not much sign of rain soon. This is Prices Hurd day. Well this has been a nice day and everything has gone off quiet.

MAR 7, 1887 QUANAH MONDAY MORNING

Capt McMurray left this morning for Ft Worth. Well this has been a nice day. Bart Abbott and Robert Henry came over to day. Allen Snyder. Also George Ranes and Dr Anderson of the copper mines. And old man J. Y. Henderson and son. I was glad to see him.

[Boom towns were very sociable places. In contrast to the loneliness of ranch country, on the new streets of Quanah one encountered old friends and met interesting strangers. J. Y. Henderson had a new farm not far from Quanah. His cows and chickens supplied milk and eggs for the ranger camp. Margaret's guitar-playing merchant Bob Henry and early settler Bart Abbott were recent friendships of Miller. Consider also the mention of Allen Snyder, formerly of

Iowa. As a twenty-one-year-old, Allen joined his parents, William and Ann Snyder, in one last family migration.

The Snyders settled in Hardeman County in 1878, said to be the first permanent Anglo settlers in the region. Allen Snyder witnessed the passing of the frontier in about a decade, a shock wave of economic settlement and environmental transformation. An early traveler happened upon the Snyders when he rode up to investigate a strange column of smoke pouring from the ground. The Snyder home was a Mule Creek dugout so snug as to be part of the landscape; only the trailing column of smoke from their wood stove signaled a human presence.

Dr. Anderson "of the copper mines" refers to a bizarre 1880s business scheme by Abraham Lincoln's former presidential opponent, General George B. McClellan. As a young officer Lieutenant McClellan had joined Marcy's 1852 expedition to determine the source of the Red River. The ambitious lieutenant had taken careful note when the expedition found copper ores in the Pease River country. Wealthy and famed after the Civil War—for somewhat inexplicable reasons given his shortcomings—McClellan recalled the copper ore deposits of Texas. He hired former ranger captain L. Seiker as a guide and returned to Hardeman County in 1877, determined to locate ores sufficient for production. His journey to the copper beds of Southwest Hardeman (today Foard) County defined decadence for the time: a freight wagon of expensive champagne and wines, luxurious tents and carpets, a number of servants, and a huge metal bathtub laboriously hauled through the brakes even when water could seldom be found to fill its bulk. After shipping good ore eastward to assayers, McClellan lost interest when elected governor of New Jersey.

By 1883 McClellan renewed his interest. Using his prestige he sweet-talked a number of investors into sinking some $12 million into "The Grand Belt Copper Company." The promotions were glorious and the profits assured. In 1884 and 1885 crews of men and giant machines arrived in Southwest Hardeman County to establish the mines. With no railroad nearby—a huge oversight—supply and transport costs were high. A further constraint was the lack of water. A newly fashioned diamond-tipped drill probed a thousand feet into the geology in the search for pure water. About 150 people worked the mines at their height. A small company town sprang up with a "Notch House" nearby. Improbably, McClellan wanted to smelt the ore on the site, so fuel coke was hauled all the way from Pittsburgh, Pennsylvania, to the Fort Worth & Denver terminus, then freighted overland to company headquarters. Production began in 1885 but major problems quickly developed.

McClellan escaped the worst of it by dying that same year, but it took until

1887 for other investors to face the ruin before them. The local clays refused to smelt, instead baking around the low-grade copper ore. Operators attempted sluicing the ore with precious water, then shipping the poorly refined result back east for regular smelting, but here too problems ensued. Dr. Anderson could do little to salvage the situation during its last gasp in 1887. The problems of transport and costs proved insurmountable, and the entire enterprise was abandoned.[49]

Captain McMurry left for Fort Worth to attend the Northwest Texas Cattle Raisers Association meeting there.[50] *Organized in 1877 at Graham, Texas, the association represented the interests of large cattle barons. At first the big ranchers were less concerned with rustlers—according to J. Evetts Haley because "Much theft was by big men"*[51]*—but by 1887 they were strongly interested in lawmen suppressing the predation on their established herds. The Northwest Texas Cattle Raisers Association later became the Texas and Southwestern Cattle Raisers Association.]*

MAR 8, 1887 TUESDAY MORNING QUANAH

Foggy and damp this morning. We had a heavy dew last night. Breakfast is ready and the Train is leaving. This has been a nice day, but looks very much like it would rain to night. Heavy cloud in the west. As a Norther has come up to night I fear it will blow the rain away. A little cloud in the N.E. and lightening once in a while. But there is not much sign of rain now.

MAR 9, 1887 WEDNESDAY MORNING QUANAH

Cool and clear this morning. The Norther blew all the rain away last night. Harry Husher and Bob Erwin had a fight last night and will have a trial this morning at 10 oclock. Well its my Hurd day and I must go and round up the horses.

MAR 10, 1887 THURSDAY MORNING QUANAH

Another nice morning and no hopes of rain yet. It is now evening at 6 oclock. And this has been a nice day. A Special coach came up this evening. I went looking for Capt. [McMurry] but he did not come. A good crowd came in this evening. A letter from Ed Conell this evening. Said he was well. Still at the St George.

[Miller consistently maintains a correspondence with Ed Conell. This individual is probably not Edward F. "Big Ed" Connell, who joins Company B in 1892 in Amarillo and works as a protection man for the XIT Ranch.]

MAR 11, 1887 FRIDAY MORNING QUANAH

Another nice morning and not any hopes rain yet. John Deberry came over last night. Well this has been another nice day and everything has gone in line. Pat Woolford . . .

[The diary page is torn and stained and the rest of the comment lost. We must wonder.]

MAR 12, 1887 SATURDAY MORNING QUANAH

Another nice morning. It looks as if spring has come one time more. The grass has begin to show and look towards the sun. Well I must go up Town and see whats going on up there. Well everything has went on all right and I must go to camp and go to bed. W. F. Reed of Mexico, Mo. [Missouri] came in town this evening from Margaret with his Lawyer. And James A. Reed, his brother.

MAR 13, 1887 SUNDAY MORNING QUANAH

Another nice clear cool morning. Only a little tinge of cloud to be seen. Well its now nearly bed time again and everything has gone on all right to day. Capt McMurray came up to day from Ft Worth.

[The captain of Company B naturally lived a different and more interesting lifestyle than the new recruits and privates. Sam McMurry was often absent on official business, but the monthly records suggest he still managed to arrest plenty of men.]

MAR 14, 1887 MONDAY MORNING QUANAH

Another nice cool morning. A thin tinge of cloud all about. The air is cool and chillie. I am now on hurd. Sitting down on the Prarie writing up my diary. I am in a beautiful valley up above the R. R. tank. There is a nice scene of cattle and horses grazing over the Prarie around me. I can look and see the tents and houses in Town. Oh what a nice cenery out on these beautiful prairies. L. M. Logan was in Town this evening but did not get to see him.

[The diarist now takes a moment to jot some impressions of the landscape while on herd duty. Everything is peaceful and orderly with the herd, so he slips off his horse, stretches out, and commences to writing an entry. The land is starting to appeal to him. After northers and dust storms, the "beautiful valley" before him is cheered by the presence of grazing cattle and horse herds. A welcome hint of sociability rises from the town in the distance.]

MAR 15, 1887 TUESDAY MORNING QUANAH

This morning looks a little something like it may rain. Smoky all around. A little thin clouds almost all around. This is pay day on the R. R. and we will have a lively crowd in Town to night. Goodmany drunk this evening. Saw two Horses running away with the front wheels of a wagon. Did no harm. J. Y. Henderson was in Town this evening. J. N. Cobb, N.J. Ayers, Bob H[Illegible] were in Town to day. . . . got a . . . . [letter] this evening with. . . . Photograft in it.

[The seasonality of frontier community life is often missing in television, where the streets are always crowded with sober Western extras. Payday in Quanah really meant a crowd in the town, with the saloons, gambling dens, and brothels at their busiest as well. A lot of men came, drank hard, and enjoyed their inebriation. As a touch of surrealism, a wild team races through town dragging the broken front end of a wagon, eliciting the laconic "Done no harm." Miller enjoyed photographs. Like his diary, photographs were important documents of bourgeois realism.]

MAR 16, 1887 WEDNESDAY MORNING QUANAH

The Sun rose this morning in a cloud. It was very red almost hidden. Paul Hoffle, Sterling Buster, and John Hammond stayed at camp last night with us. Well its now most bed time, about 10 ½ oclock. I have just come from Town. Everything Quiet. I met Billie Trumble and Dud Melton in Town to night and George Brandt this morning. A little Norther blew up this evening and it is right cool to night. Well I will close for this time, so good night diary.

[Neither William "Billie" Trumble nor Dud Melton were strangers to the law. Trumble had legal troubles from gunning down a man in Otta, Cottle County, Texas, in 1886, and Melton was a suspected rustler. Both men will be arrested by the Texas Rangers in the future.]

MAR 17, 1887 THURSDAY MORNING QUANAH

Another nice morning but looks as it might rain. Well I will go up to Town this morning awhile. P[orter] P. Drace left this morning for Red River to run a Saloon. Well I will go to Margaret to night if nothing happens. Well I went to church to night and heard the Boy Preacher. He preached a good surmon. I saw on my way over here this evening that the grass was starting to grow. It is as fine as could be for not to be any rain lately.

[A boy preacher was a good draw for a traveling revival. Featuring a religious prodigy, a young boy preached, shouted, and exhorted the audience with old-time religion. Revivals were an important part of community life. Many of these meetings provided spiritual comfort and a form of entertainment in remote areas. Boy preachers were often highly skilled in verse, oratory, and delivery, although one is suspicious of an exploitative edge to the profession.]

MAR 18, 1887 MARGARET FRIDAY MORNING

Cloudy all around and hope it will rain soon. I am at Mr Wesleys now and must go up Town soon and attend to my business so I can go to Quanah as soon as I can. Well J. and L. Kahn came over together. We had a plesant trip. We got to Quanah about Sundown. This has been a terrible warm day.

MAR 19, 1887 SATURDAY MORNING QUANAH

Cloudy and cool and looks very much like it will rain soon. As there are a little more appearanc every day I am in good hopes of its raining soon. J. Y. Henderson came and got the May Saddle this evening. Well it's turned right cold to night. And I expect I'll have a cold day tomorrow to Hurd. I wrote a letter to Lucius and one to Thomas to night. Everything is quiet this evening and night. Well its now 10 minits after 11 oclock and I must go to bed. So goodnight diary.

MAR 20, 1887 SUNDAY MORNING QUANAH

Clear and cool. No hopes of rain this morning. My Hurd day. I must see about the Horses. Well I went to the singing to night at Misses McC[Illegible]. A nice little crowd out. Well as its bedtime I will go down to camp and go to bed.

MAR 21, 1887 MONDAY MORNING QUANAH

Another cool and cloudy day. Mr. Hankins and Ferguson came over to day. This has been a cold day all day and this evening looks very much like rain. Hick Garrisons brother is in Town to night. Look out for He— [Hell] popping between him and Jno. Davidsons. Well everything went off all OK.

[Marshall M. Hankins and Sterling Price Ferguson were first cousins and pioneer law partners at Margaret. They actively participated in organizing Hardeman County. Hankins was elected as the first county attorney in 1886,

and he became the Hardeman County judge in 1890. Deputy John Davidson and his rowdy friends had more enemies than just Deputy McDonald or Superintendent Pat Wolforth. Davidson wronged Garrison and was called into Quanah for a trial. After weeks of socializing in the streets and saloons, the rangers of Company B had a penchant now for spotting trouble and heading it off. Their appearance and watchful eyes provided significant deterrence.]

MAR 22, 1887 TUESDAY MORNING QUANAH

Another cold day. It has been cold all day and cloudy a good part of the day. John Davidsons trial came off to day. The jury hung. Four for clearing and two for conviction. Old Fant was arrested to day for getting d____ and holering up the streets. Everything has went off all OK to day. Well as I have a bad cold I will go to bed as it is time anyway 10 ½ oclock.

Bill Turner near Seymour was shot and killed on the night of the 14th. He was shot five times.

[At the end of a one-day trial, Deputy John Davidson, "The Terror of Wilbarger County," walked out a free man after the six-man jury failed to reach a decision. Bill Turner was not so lucky. Some claimed William Turner's bad luck started during an unfortunate spell in earlier days, when he rode with two wild and crazy brothers—Bill and Bood Brooken. The Brookens started as opportunistic cattle thieves, then graduated into serious rustling, train-robbing, and murder apparently. They used the secluded cedar brakes along the Wichita River for hideouts and liberated livestock. John Davidson was also said to have had dealings with the delinquent brothers. Turner soon left the gang, according to Paine's biography of McDonald, and walked the straight and narrow path thereafter. But the Brookens brooded over his intimate knowledge of the gang. At some point perhaps they felt he had talked too freely and decided to lay an ambuscade. This version at least is the account told by McDonald to Albert Bigelow Paine.[52]

A gang of men rushed Turner at a lonely spot on the Western Trail near the nine-year-old town of Seymour in Baylor County, about forty miles southeast of Margaret. William Turner and Samuel Lazarus, the intriguing Jewish cattleman and owner of the Diamond-Tails, were traveling together in a carriage when the Brooken gang rushed them from behind. Sam Lazarus leaped over the front end and clung to the cross-bar, but a fusillade of shots killed Bill Turner quickly. Lazarus clung to the carriage cross-bar as the frightened horses raced all the way back to the town of Seymour.]

CHAPTER 2

Quanah Crime and Punishment

SPRING OF 1887

Meantime, the railroad had reached Hardeman and the town of Quanah . . . had sprung up. It was the typical tough place and certain bad men still at large came there to proclaim vengeance and to 'lay' for the men who were making them trouble.

—*Albert Bigelow Paine,* Captain Bill McDonald, Texas Ranger

The town of Quanah appeared like a mushroom. The coming of the railroad was responsible for the new settlement and it had the hard character of such towns the West over. The railroad construction gangs were attended by the usual procession of gamblers, red light women, parasites and killers of various calibers.

—*Eugene Cunningham,* Triggernometry

The first day of spring in 1887 finds Private Miller contemplating the fresh prairie grasses and enjoying the more temperate weather. The rangers are still living in their dugout and tent quarters near the water tank, not too far from the bustling railroad town of Quanah. Daily life in the ranger camp has enough drudgery that Miller always seems glad to go "up Town and see whats going on." Quanah's social life is vibrant and energetic. Miller is always bumping into old friends and making new acquaintances. News circulates in the stores and saloons.

In the boisterous streets of Quanah, this raw ranger recruit begins to learn the strange ways of justice. Quanah is an introduction to crime and punishment, a training school for Texas Ranger life. This spring A. T. Miller further interacts with a remarkable group of lawmen and associates. There is the intelligent and ethical Pat Wolforth, already mentioned for coolly firing warning shots when pressed too close by aggressive local thugs. Wolforth bosses Diamond Tail herds as the superintendent, effectively running the ranch and trailing herds to distant markets. Rounded out by these experiences, Pat Wolforth becomes one of the greatest range detectives of Texas, a Sherlock Holmes of the plains. There is also Hardeman County Sheriff Jim Allee, honest but understaffed for the extent of both petty and serious crime. Paine claims the good sheriff was handicapped after the Turner murder, when the dastardly Brookens stole his horse. And there is the incomparable Bill McDonald, fast-moving, tough, even obsessive in his pursuit of malefactors. The late John Jenkins called McDonald "the most famous Texas Ranger of the time." He glides through Miller's diaries like a legendary avenging angel, a relentless spirit tracking evildoers.

Captain McMurry appointed Bill McDonald as a "Special Texas Ranger" in the summer of 1887 to help with the organized state effort to clean out Hardeman and Greer Counties. McDonald was a gifted marksman, a local rancher, and a superb choice of personal intimidation to do the job. In the process of taming Hardeman County he did not mind making a name for himself. Eventually his career as a lawman led to lasting fame and the celebrated ranger biography, Captain Bill McDonald Texas Ranger, A Story of Frontier Reform. *This commissioned 1909 biography written by Albert Bigelow Paine popularized McDonald's life. Later writings like Madeline Mason's* Riding for Texas: The True Adventures of Captain Bill McDonald of the Texas Rangers *continued the adulation after his death.*[1] *A. T. would have enjoyed the hyperbolic bravado of the book, but his own style lay with laconic understatement.*

The Miller diaries shed light as well on the toughs and villains of the day. There is Old Bill Williams, a reputed butcher of stolen beef. He was a big man with an equally big drinking problem. Then as now one wonders about drugs and crime. Apparently, he links up with Quanah's more disreputable set. And there is roguish John Davidson, the "Terror of Wilbarger County," an engaging and tough man who seemed to work on both sides of the law. Reputed to have been—and possibly still be—a gang member, Davidson was also the deputy sheriff of Wilbarger County. It was Davidson who stalked Pat Wolforth, drawing the latter's fire on February 14, and precipitating a later and legendary Davidson-McDonald saloon showdown.

A. T. Miller also joins his Company B companions in combing the notorious Greer County. This huge and disputed land between the North Fork of the Red River and the Prairie Dog Town Fork of the Red River lay only eight miles north of Quanah. It was full of new settlers and old outlaws. The rangers also rode for the desperadoes of the Brooken gang, considered the worst gang of the place and time. The Brooken gang preferred to hide in the rough brakes along the Wichita River. A. T. Miller never seems to thirst for blood or violence, but the diarist never betrays the slightest fear either. Only on "Hurd day" do we detect a sense of loneliness and boredom—the Lonesome Ranger.

Like their hard-riding forebears, these Texas Rangers are also going to range, to travel at will over the new land of settlements, farms, and ranches. On April 28, 1887, Company B loads its wagons, leaves Quanah, and sets out on an old-fashioned ranger tour. Their extended swing through the big Texas Panhandle will occupy them until May 21. Among other things their tour is meant to reinforce the rule of law over a wide area. Fortunately Private Miller recorded detailed observations of Company B in the field. Miller's remarks on old Clarendon, Tascosa, and Mobeetie were made just as the oncoming Fort Worth & Denver Railroad was redirecting Panhandle urbanization into new sites and settlements.

Indeed, the boys are making the last ranger company tour of the fading Panhandle frontier. By 1887 there were hardly any frontiers left at all for the increasingly misnomered "Frontier" Battalion. Historian Frederick Wilkins writes convincingly that the frontier was vanishing for the Texas Rangers as early as 1881–82.[2] *Cutbacks and transportation improvements were at the heart of the change. Low appropriations from the legislature in the 1880s forced strict economies on the Frontier Battalion. Reduced travel allocations from the quartermaster and the growing convenience and speed of railroads combined to outdate the old ranger tour.*

But Company B rides as a company one last time this spring of 1887. The rangers are riding trails and streets that will be largely deserted in only a few more years. It is sad that so many pre-industrial features of that cultural landscape, the ranch towns, stage roads, and ghostly settlements beyond the advancing railroad, must disappear. Yet all are swallowed by relocation, atrophy, or abandonment. There are times when Company B rides along next to the advancing railroad, even stopping to dine at the boarding car, and two diametric lifeways stand contrasted. A year later the Panhandle Rangers will be riding the railroad instead of riding by it. The railroad will draw a spatial noose around the criminals of yore, hastening a cycle of constriction that inevitably transforms pioneer criminality.

As before, the entries also provide a lot of quotidian reality, environmental observations, and plenty of small-town gossip. The days grow warmer, then turn hot. There are suspicious strangers, religious conversions, subpoenas to deliver to friends, letters from family, rumors the Brooken gang was in town last night, and important ranger fishing expeditions. It was an engaging life, and a suitable introduction to crime and punishment on the closing frontier.

Spring of 1887

MAR 23, 1887 WEDNESDAY MORNING QUANAH

Another cool and clear morning. It looks as if it would be a nice day. These cold days are liable to put the grass back some. It will be too bad as it's looking well. Well this has been a quiet and nice day. Johnie [Miller], Bart, and Guss Abbott came over to day. And John Bland.

[More and more people coming to Quanah is not a good augury for the boosters of Margaret. Especially because the named individuals are mostly from Margaret.]

MAR 24, 1887 THURSDAY MORNING QUANAH

Another cool and nice morning and it looks as we will have another nice day. Johnie [Miller] and Bart [Abbott] left this morning about 10 oclock. Guss [Abbott] will stay over here. I'm now waiting to see the train come in. It's a little late. George Hansard will start his Butcher shop this evening. He goes in with Tom Gipson. Four men arrested this evening on suspician and locked up in a box car to night for safe keeping.

MAR 25, 1887 FRIDAY MORNING QUANAH

Another clear and cool morning. There are not much hopes of any rain yet. I met J. N. Coleman in Town last night. He told me he had a steer stole off him that was branded **H** on left side. Still holding those men. They are in the caliboos to night and are the first it has had. The brands of the horses and names of the men are

O. M. Carpenter—black bay pony about 14 hands high, on left sho[ulder], X on left hip, **H** on left thigh, and scar on left rump.

W. B. Winkler—one bay Horse about 14 hands high, on left sho[ulder], on left hip IS, on left thigh, and a scar on right hip.

J. E. Jernigan—one dark 15 hands h[igh] Iron Gray, on left sho[ulder,] on left side of neck, on left gam.

Name Will Beanbine—one white or gray Stalione, about six or seven years old, about 15 hands high, no brands on him at al.

[These entries add interesting details on the detention and description of suspects. McDonald was later accused of cruelty because of his use of railroad boxcars, posts, and leg chains, and other convenient forms and instruments of incarceration. He admitted the practice later in a crucial interview with Governor Hogg, but placed it in the context of Mineola, Texas, a tough East Texas town where Hogg and McDonald both worked as young men to uphold the law: "That's so, Jim, I do put 'em in box-cars when there ain't a jail; the way I used to back in Mineola—you recollect, when the jail was full . . ."[3] *Nevertheless, the diary makes it clear that the rangers and deputies used a boxcar only until they had a public jail of sorts thrown together.*

Texas Ranger treatment of arrested men tended to reflect the times, racism, and state of law. In the 1870s McNelly's rangers in the Las Cuevas War had brutally tortured suspected "spies," then hanged them, sometimes in wholesale lots. Or rather than turn the worst criminals over to local juries of sympathetic friends and relatives, there were disturbing reports that rangers sometimes shot a man "trying to escape"—the so-called ley de fuga.[4] *Among other outrages McNelly's men had invaded Mexico in conducting their authorized guerrilla war against bandits. But after the chaos of Reconstruction the 1880s saw the increasing acceptance of the rule of law in Texas.*[5]

For the Texas Rangers this meant a shift from bloody guerrilla warfare to supporting more mundane police work in the newly opened western lands. It also meant more lawful restraints on their own actions and activities. "The quieter Texas became," writes historian Frederick Wilkins, "the more the Rangers came under scrutiny. People wanted them posted on every street corner, but they also expected more and more in the way of deportment."[6]

Note how an 1880s suspect is described by reference to his horse. Automobiles now command the kind of attention lawmen once paid to horses.]

MAR 26, 1887 SATURDAY MORNING QUANAH

Cool and cloudy this morning. The sun rose behind a cloud at 7 oclock. It looks very much as if it might rain. Well I went over to Margaret to day, for to see if the county attorney would allow the carpenters to work tomorrow on a special job to accomodate the people coming to the converrsion on next Tuesday. And he could not deside the matter. They were digging a grave for old man Hammer in Margaret. I also served my first sapoenia [subpoena]. They were on John Wesley and John Bland and Babe Deberry and J. W. Murray. Two of our prisners was turned out to night. Osker Carpenter and J. E. Jernigan. Pat Woolforth is in Town to night.

MAR 27, 1887 SUNDAY MORNING QUANAH

Another cold and cloudy day it is going to be. And it is my day off. Well I am now on the Prarie over towards Wanders Creek. I have had a time to day with an old M mule. She ran away from me this morning and I ran her about 10 or 15 miles before I got back to the hurd. This has been a cold day all day. I went to the Singing to night but did not enjoy it one bit and don't know as I will go any more.

[We like to think of dashing Texas Rangers chasing killer outlaws over the prairie, but sometimes the reality of a hot pursuit is a private chasing a runaway mule. One ranger is dispatched for one riot, and sometimes one ranger rides for one ornery mule.]

MAR 28, 1887 MONDAY MORNING QUANAH

Another cool clear morning. D. A. Peal is on hurd to day. Well this has been a real nice day. Mr and Mrs [J. G.] Witherspoon came over to day for the conversion tomorrow. A good crowd of boys in town to night but everything went off quiet.

MAR 29, 1887 TUESDAY MORNING QUANAH

Another cool, nice, and clear morning and I think we will have a nice day for the conversion. Well I will go up Town this morning and see whats going on up there.

[It is likely this "conversion" refers to one of several great revivals held in 1887. The arrival of the Witherspoons, owners of the ULA Ranch, added the approval of important community leaders. Prominent citizens, cowboys, and a few hard-scrabble farmers alike rode into town to participate in revivals and conversions. Back in 1880 when the county had only a couple dozen settlers and a score or so of cowboys on the R2 ranch, there was little thought of an organized church. An occasional religious service was held in a dugout with a sky pilot like Methodist circuit-rider the Reverend James Hosmer. After the new jail and schoolhouse were built in Margaret, more regular services were possible. The two-year spurt of colonists from 1885 to 1887 now made it practical to organize official churches.

There was little doubt that the first churches would be Methodist. This creed was particularly strong in the area due to the arrival of hard-core Collin County Methodists. Indeed, Margaret was known as the "Mother of Methodism" for the strong influence of this denomination over local residents. The

Reverend Sam Hardy was the newly appointed pastor at Margaret in 1887. A young attorney who gave up the bar for the Bible, Hardy decided to hold a brush arbor revival in the summer of 1887. There were fears that ULA cowboys would cause trouble, but Hardy ensured that the Witherspoons and other prominent residents would attend the service. In the presence of their employer, the rough-and-tumble cowboys became meek, worshipful lambs. They met at John Bannister's brush arbor to sing hymns and pray fervently. At the conclusion of the meeting they agreed to establish a new Methodist church, with John Bannister donating land for a building and cemetery.[7]*]*

MAR 30, 1887 WEDNESDAY MORNING QUANAH

Clear and cool and looks as if it will be a nice day. Well I shall go up Town and see what is going on. Well everythings went on all right to day. I met Bill Tilson in Town to day for the first time in two years. He is still on the Mill Iron Ranch. Well I will go to bed now as its eleven oclock. Everything has went off quiet to day and night.

[Located northeast of Quanah, the Mill Iron Ranch eventually embraced over 200,000 acres in Hall and Collingsworth Counties from 1886–89. The capitalist successor to the Millet Ranch of Baylor and Throckmorton Counties and the famed Hashknife Ranch (Couts and Simpson partnership) near Seymour, the Mill Iron Ranch was part of the holdings of the Continental Land and Cattle Company, a powerful and well-funded corporation under the direction of financier Colonel A. C. Hughes and pioneer cattleman John S. Simpson. The Mill Iron Ranch was typical of the 1880s corporate investment and development interests that dominated the closing of the grassland frontier.[8]*]*

MAR 31, 1887 THURSDAY MORNING QUANAH

Another nice cold morning but thin clouds all around. Well I must go to bed now. Everything has went off all OK today and it has been a real nice day and this is a cool night. Jim Green and John Platt put old Bill Williams in the caliboos this evening.

[It seems clearer that many frontier terrors like Comanche Bill were serious alcoholics. These anti-heroes appear in contemporary Westerns as rather sober villains of great ability, but the reality is a substratum of pathetic drunks and gamblers with medical problems and criminal histories.

Not long after this incident the lawman Jim Gober encountered Comanche Bill in Rag Town. Bill had punched his red-haired, freckled girlfriend for flirting—and been clubbed by a cowboy with a .45-caliber Colt. Gober washed off the blood from Comanche Bill, "got some sugar and turpentine, mixed the two, then bandaged his head with his jane's panty leg. She was kissing him and calling him 'Honey,' seemingly forgetting that her eye was swollen and black from the blow Comanche had given her a few minutes before."[9]]

APR 1, 1887 FRIDAY MORNING QUANAH

Another nice cool morning with a thin tinge of clouds all around. Well I have been down at camp all day and now as its most train time I will go up Town and see what is going on. The boys say there was some excitement on the streets to day over a man having a winchester on the street.

[Some Texans just do not like having their guns taken away in town. Yet the extension and enforcement of reasonable gun-control laws was considered logical in the 1880s. Many citizens saw gun-control as the insertion of communitarian values into the otherwise individualistic, anti-statist Texas frontier. Gun-control social issues still stir the towns and cities of modern Texas. Current fringe "militias" and some National Rifle Association officials argue that "jackbooted government thugs" are trying to strip people of their constitutional right to bear arms. The Miller diaries and ranger records suggest in fact that this stripping is hardly a new or unknown process. One of the commonest charges recorded in Captain McMurry's monthly arrest records was the offense "Carrying Pistol." The Quanah rangers also wore boots, carried firepower, worked for the government, and sometimes shot people of guilt—or even innocence. Most of them assuredly had less training and restraints than the modern law officer. They probably made up for this deficit by taking more risks.

The rangers and sheriffs did establish an effective form of urban gun control, despite the occasional First or Second Amendment appeal to cowboy free expression in firing off shots. Sheriff Cape Willingham typically greeted arrivals in 1880s Tascosa with the pronouncement: "Hand over your guns or ride out of town." Enforcing gun control in frontier communities had its own dangers, as there were accidents and incidents of course. Fred Leigh, a hungover LS boss in a bad mood, entered Tascosa one morning with his cowhands. Leigh was still offended that Sheriff Willingham had relieved him of his gun the previous night. Passing a peaceable woman feeding a backyard flock of ducks, Fred Leigh was tempted by the devil. He pulled his pistol and shot into the ducks for a scare, whereupon there was a dead duck. Frightened by the shot the lady passed out in a faint. Responding to the sound of the shot, Sheriff Willingham came running up and saw an apparently "dead" and dear woman sprawled on the earth. Catching up with the laughing shootist, the sheriff instantly demanded Leigh's gun. The LS boss was not thinking clearly—he made for a quick draw. Cape Willingham shot the poor jester off his saddle.[10]

Nevertheless, practical experience suggested that crowds of people and the agitated flourishing of firearms led to too much trouble. More—not less—gun control was considered the obvious advancement of 1880s civilization. Therefore, when a lawman demanded your weapons, the safe response was to give them up with a friendly smile and polite demeanor. Only a few souls tried any exceptions. John Wesley Hardin perfected one: he would calmly offer both his guns up, then dexterously reverse them in mid-air to get a sudden drop on the demander. Certainly for most people it was not worth a coroner prying your cold, dead, stiff fingers off the trigger when a Texas Ranger asked you to stop scaring the ladies or threatening an associate with your gun while in town.

Moreover, the adage that "Guns don't kill people, people kill people" was not true on the frontier either. Defective guns blew up. Firearms also discharged accidentally with depressing regularity, often wounding and maiming the public, and sometimes killing someone completely innocent like a child. Improved design and safety releases eventually slowed down the accidental discharge carnage in towns, trains, and hunting camps. Nevertheless the Miller diary reinforces the notion that an increased level of gun control was an important component of law enforcement on the Texas town frontier of the 1880s.[11]

Ironically, the Texas legislature voted in 1995 to allow eligible and licensed Texans to carry concealed handguns in public space again. There are important restrictions to observe involving schools, churches, bars, and the like. The bill passed as a reaction to perceived wide-spread lawlessness on modern streets and within urban communities. After a short training course, an eligible citizen is permitted to carry a hidden firearm to defend herself or himself in public space from desperadoes, the contemporary Comanche Bills. A subliminal part of the campaign was an appeal to the Texas "frontier spirit" of bearing arms. "We're in the days of the Old Wild Wild West right now," Texas Governor George W. Bush said in 1995. "Hopefully, this [concealed-handgun] bill will take us out of the Wild Wild West."[12]

The Miller diary and contemporary ranger records suggest, paradoxically, that more *gun control was thought logical for the violence threatening Victorian frontier communities. The Second Amendment right to bear arms seemed equally subject to being well regulated, as with state militias. The Texas Constitution also gave the right to bear arms but further reserved the power to regulate the activity. The application and extent of these regulations has never been anything but a cultural choice. In the 1880s this choice undoubtedly reflected the opinions of women. The pioneer women of Hardeman County were familiar with guns; many used them skillfully to terminate rattlesnakes, pests, and vermin. But when all those "good" farm and ranch guns moved into a tumultuous public space, the women felt threatened. They wanted the public situation "well-regulated." Accidents, arguments, random discharges, and wild shootings after all might claim one of their innocent family members.*

Thus, the "pioneer spirit" of the 1880s was a predilection for more, not less gun control in public space. Over a century ago Texans looked to a progressive future and took guns away from public space; in the 1990s Texans harked to a mythic past to justify their reappearance and concealment in public space.]

APR 2, 1887 SATURDAY MORNING QUANAH

Another nice clear and cool morning. I must go after a load of wood to day over on Groesbeck Creek. Well we got wood and water by 12 oclock and I must take a sleep. No mail to day except two papers for Capt. Noticed in the *Dallas News* that Capt Scott and one of his men was badly wounded and one killed down near Hemphill SE Texas.

[Abner Miller read the news accounts in McMurry's newspapers with great interest. Captain Scott's bloody fight in the Big Thicket with the backwoods Conner clan soon became a legend around ranger campfires.

Captain William Scott first set out for the Conners in July of 1886 from the Wilbarger County town of Vernon, the former Fort Worth & Denver terminus below Quanah and above Harrold. In a July 3, 1886, letter to Quartermaster Sieker, Captain Scott noted breezily that as soon as their informant, Mr. Weathered, ascertained that the Conners are back in East Texas, "I will start for that section and make a descent on the Sabine County Desperados."[13] *A followup letter on July 31 from Hemphill in East Texas soberly noted the complete failure of their first scout: "I have just gone through fifteen days of the 'toughest Ranging' that you ever saw. I had rather be a pack mule out west than a million heir [*sic*] in this brush. We have been going out every day and each man brings back Ticks, enough to keep him scratching and 'Kussing' all night. Yes it is sure rough country on man and beast . . . I have made quite a failure on this scout but can stand it if I can only get back to the Prairie alive. I will return to Vernon on or about August 6th."*[14]

Nine months later Captain William Scott, five other good rangers of Company F, and the informer rode once more into the deep forests of Sabine County. They were determined to get Old Man Conner and his sons this time. Conner was a cagey, tough, and desperate criminal, one unusually skilled in and at home in the Big Thicket forests on the Texas-Louisiana border. He shifted his camp frequently that March. Prudently, Conner had taken the bell off his regular pack animal. The consequent silence confused the informer trying to locate his camp. In effect Company F walked into a deadly East Texas backwoods ambush at dawn on April 1, 1887.

The rangers were hit hard. They completely underestimated the guile and woodcraft of the pursued foe. The Texas Ranger habit of dawn arrests made the outlaw family exceedingly wary. Alerted to the rangers' stealthy approach, the Conners prepared an ambush. They suddenly turned a pack of vicious hunting dogs on the rangers and at the same time opened up with accurate rifle and shotgun fire from behind big longleaf pine trees. Almost immediately four of the six rangers were hit: Captain Scott shot through the lungs, Sergeant Brooks shot in both hands (with several fingers blown away on the left one), John Rogers wounded twice, and the unfortunate Jim Moore killed with a shot in the heart. As a student of ranger lore, William Warren Sterling described the Conner fight as intense: "Bright blazes from the black powder cartridges lit up the battlefield, where the range was never more than twenty or thirty feet."[15]

Texas Ranger Jim Carmichael probably saved all their lives. His determined return fire and resolute stand discouraged the Conners from rushing up and killing off the survivors and wounded. Eventually, the man-killing dogs were shot or driven off and further ranger gunplay killed one Conner and wounded another, who was captured. The wounded were taken to Hemphill.[16] *The Conner fight was a devastating lesson on the danger of attacking well-armed and desperate men in an unfamiliar environment.]*

APR 3, 1887 SUNDAY MORNING QUANAH

A little cloudy this morning and looks as if we might have some rain. Well I have got breakfast and must go see about the Horses as its my Hurd day. McNally started to Capt Scotts company to day to see what is needed I suppose. Well I have been after the horses. They are all ok to day. A large circle around the sun to day and I think we will have rain soon. A big wind and dust from the East.

[The "McNally" mentioned is Sergeant John McNelly, the five-foot-nine-inch, blue-eyed nephew of the great Texas Ranger Captain Leander H. McNelly.[17] *Like Sam Platt and G. W. Arrington, John McNelly served as a private in his uncle's famous "Special Force State Troops" company in South Texas during the 1870s Sutton-Taylor feud and Las Cuevas border troubles. This native West Virginian also enlisted in Captain Lee Hall's successor company, where he got to know rising leaders like Sam McMurry. From March to August in 1881 McNelly joined Company F in protecting the Texas & Pacific Railroad during its construction across the plains.*

On February 15, 1882, Captain McMurry enlisted John McNelly into the reorganized Company B, a reflection of McMurry's resolve to stiffen the new company with a well-tested ranger veteran. A year later McMurry appointed

McNelly as first sergeant for the company. He loyally served Company B in this capacity for over four years.[18] *Adjutant General King dispatched the tough and experienced Sergeant McNelly to Hemphill, Texas, to assist in the resolution of the Conner fight.]*

APR 4, 1887 MONDAY MORNING QUANAH

A cold Norther blew up last night and is right cold to day. I think the Norther has blown the rain away. Well I believe I'll stay at camp to day and not go up Town before Noon. Two Negros and three white boys arrested to night. One Negro for shooting and the other for dastarbing the peace. The White boys arrested for opening a cealed car and going in.

[Invariably in his entries A. T. Miller refers to African Americans as Negroes. His word choice suggests a politeness level far above low southern racism. With racial epithets then prevalent in Texas society, the diarist's language and lack of derogation suggest an uncommon fairness and toleration of diversity. Not all Texas Rangers were bigots.

Many were. The Texas Rangers gained a serious reputation for racism during the 1870s border and bandit troubles in South Texas. Much of that ugly reputation survived well into the twentieth century. Tejanos dreaded the arrival of rangers, feared their tactics, and coined ugly phrases to express their disgust: "Rinche, pinche, cara de chinche—*Ranger bastard, scum, face of a bedbug!*"

Once the frontier was over though, the Texas Rangers found their most persistent and deadly foes were armed white men.]

APR 5, 1887 TUESDAY MORNING QUANAH

Another nice morning. Oh, how I wish it would rain but not much hopes of it. Well Sheriff Alley and Mr [County Attorney Marshall M.] Hankins came over to day. Also Mr [Tom] Williamson, the Sheriff of Greer Co. came in on the train this evening. Look out for some riding to do.

APR 6, 1887 WEDNESDAY MORNING QUANAH

Well a little cloudy this morning and we have to start to Greer Co. on a big ride after Bill Brookin and a couple more bad men. $2,000. Dollars reward for the men. Sterling Price, [Jim] Green, [J. M.] Bradbury, John Plat, and myself has to go. Well we have had a nice days ride and we are camped near Mangum to night. Look out for a ride tomorrow. Lots of young calves on the road to day.

[Five rangers load up and ride north-northeast into Greer County, a county as big as all of Delaware and half of Rhode Island. The scouts cross Boggy and

Turkey Creek, stopping for the night not far from Mangum. McMurry's monthly "Record of Scouts" noted that on April 6 Private Bradbury and three men "went to Greer Co. in persuit of horse thieves."[19] *But these thieves were no ordinary stock bandits, rustlers to be picked up casually or chased down at Old Man Hickman's place outside Mangum.*

The Brooken Brothers were the consanguine regional version of Butch Cassidy and the Sundance Kid for the closing frontier. By 1887 they were the most notorious outlaws of the North Rolling Plains. Bill and Bood Brooken knew the country from the Wichita cedar brakes to Greer County intimately. They moved stolen livestock back and forth and they were always armed. Only a few weeks earlier they had apparently assassinated William Turner near Seymour. With Captain Scott's unfortunate recent experience with the Conners in mind, the rangers were undoubtedly alert.]

APR 7, 1887 THURSDAY MORNING-GREER CO. CAMP.

A fine morning and think we will have a nice day to ride. Well we will go over to Town and see what we will do. Well we have had a ride sure enough today and will have another tonight. I have been on the top of the Wichita Mountains to day and one of the prettiest ceneries I ever looked at in my life of the kind. I could see all over the Nation for miles and miles. I had a glass but not a good one. Oh, what a terrible ruff place we came through to day. We had to lead our horses over the mountains. Sheriff Williamson of Greer Co. and Sheriff [W. N.] Barker of Wilbarger Co. and his deputies, [Pink] Coldwell and John Hammond, was with us to day. They met us in Margaret this morning. Oh, what a nice dinner and supper we have had to day by Mr. Elliot. Well we must go for a ride to night. And if we do meet the parties the little thing will pop sure beyond a doubt.

[After breakfast the five Company B rangers ride on, cross the Salt Fork River, and reach Mangum just beyond. There they join forces with four other lawmen, two Texas sheriffs and two deputies, for the Brooken manhunt. This combination of Wilbarger and Greer County lawmen together with the large party of Texas Rangers indicates a very serious purpose. Someone could get killed.

Northeast of Mangum, Texas, just across the Elm Fork, the lawmen encounter the remarkable granite outliers of the Wichita Mountains. Small chains of granite mountains, the last gasp of the great Appalachians, lie nestled between the Elm Fork and North Fork of the Red River. The lawmen ride to vantage points in the Quartz Mountains and the Granite Mountains beyond Mangum, and then use field glasses to sweep large stretches of the country. To the east, beyond the North Fork of the Red River, Private Miller espies the farther mountains and prairies of the Indian Territory. After a day of scenery, spying, and rough riding in the outliers of the Wichita Mountains the lawmen prepare for a moonlight night ride and surprise visitation.

As professionals, Texas Rangers often liked to take wanted men at night or early dawn when consciousness was dim and outlaw reflexes slow and uncertain. Sometimes they surrounded a house unawares, then shouted and hallooed for the residents to make a light and come on out. Because the occasional dirty assassin used the same technique, some residents were understandably nervous in responding. An important variation therefore involved surreptitiously surrounding a house, then tiptoeing indoors, often at first light, to poke a loaded Winchester into a sleeping man.[20]*]*

APR 8, 1887 FRIDAY MORNING MANGUM TX

Another fine morning. Well we had a big ride last night for nothing. We did not see anything of our men. We rode until about 2 oclock before we got to Town. And what a beautifull night it was. So we will start for Quanah this morning. A 45 mile ride. Well we got in Quanah about Sundown or a little before. Tired and hungry. As we have rode all day without any thing since morning. The water on the road was gippy and salty and we did not get a good drink since we left the good water at Mangum. The finest water in the mountains was at Mr Elliots where we drank. Well now after reading a good letter from Miss Joe Goodlet I will go to bed. So goodnight diary. Maby the boys will bring you some news to night.

[Thursday night in the Wichita Mountain country was indeed "a beautiful night"—a big full moon rose in the east as the sun set in the west.[21] *The nine-man force rides for the Brookens by the bright moonlight, but to no avail, so around midnight they turn their tired mounts back to Mangum. With no signs of the Brooken gang, the rangers turn southward on Friday for a long day's ride back to their camp. The brine springs and gypsum cliffs of Greer taint many of the waters along the trail. Rufus Elliot was an early pioneer of the Greer County granite country.]*

APR 9, 1887 SATURDAY MORNING QUANAH

Well, well. It did rain. A nice little shower last night. Still cloudy this morning and sprinkling a once and a while. Capt [McMurry] and Tom Platt, Dennis Peal and Tom Mulhall has gone up the R.R. to day for some one. [Jim] Green and I hauled some corne and water this morning. Whole company of U.S. Soldiers are camped on the other side of the RR.

[McMurry's detachment rode northwest into Childress County to quell a disturbance there over the railroad right-of-way. As usual their mere presence was enough to quiet things down.[22]]

APR 10, 1887 SUNDAY MORNING QUANAH

Still its cloudy and looks as if it would rain. I thought sure it would rain last night from the looks of the cloud. I met Mr. Hester last night from near Boggy [Creek], I. T. He brung to me news from Thomas. I met him in the Carter Hotel. He said Thomas had bought out a store and was selling goods on his own hook. Well to day has been cloudy and windy all day and it looks very much like rain. Jim Ellison of Greer Co., Deputy Sheriff, came in this evening. I have learned the Lieutenant in charge of the U.S. Souldiers that have camped here is waiting on recrutes, and a good many came in to day.

[The soldiers were headed north for Fort Elliott, a pretty U.S. Army post established in 1876 on Sweetwater Creek. Named for Major Elliott, the unfortunate commander left by Custer to a gruesome fate at the Battle of the Washita, the fort was home to some four hundred officers, soldiers, Kiowa and Tonkawa scouts, and sutlers. Many companies of Buffalo Soldiers served a monotonous stint at Fort Elliott. In 1890 the army abandoned the fort; the nearby town of Mobeetie survived a spell then relocated.]

APR 11, 1887 MONDAY MORNING QUANAH

Still its cloudy and the air is damp and the wind is high. I am afraid it will blow the rain all away. Well its my Hurd day and I must go, so after the horses. Its now 10 oclock, and the boys in the other mess has not got up yet, except [Jim] Green and he has gone after wood. Well I had no trouble with the Horses to day. Price swaped for a new horse to Sterling Buster. A very good one. Well I must go up Town now as all the boys has gone to see whats going on.

APR 12, 1887 TUESDAY MORNING QUANAH

Cloudy and drizzling rain a little and looks as if it may come down right smart before it clears up. I hauld a barrel of water this morning. It's thundering around right smart. Well I met Bill Richards up Town and eat dinner with him. Got a letter from T. B. Hoskins and a card from Thomas [Miller]. I did not go up Town to night, but read a lecture of Talmage, and a letter concerning the life of old Sam Houston of early Texas. Well its raining nice and slow now and it looks as if it will rain all night.

[A. T.'s reading reflects his middle-class ways. Thomas De Witt Talmage was an American divine whose moralistic lectures and histrionic sermons proved popular in the 1870s and 1880s. The letter on the life of "old Sam Houston" shows the enduring appeal of Texana.]

APR 13, 1887 WEDNESDAY MORNING QUANAH

Still cloudy and looks as if it is not done raining. It rained all night slow and steady. So the ground is right muddy this morning. Well I must shave and parch coffee and wash up the dishes before I go up Town. Tom [Platt] has gone up now for some corne and grub. Well Tom has came back with corne and flour and onions, potatoes, pickles, soap etc. So we will have dinner before we go up Town. Well dinner is over and we eat with the other men. The boys had a time of running McNellys Horse to catch him for McDonnald to ride up to Kirkland. Dennis [Peale] is going with him. Well they got the man they went for. His name is Blankenship. He is wanted in Coriel [Corryel] Co. for stealing horses. I learned to night where Wiley Bill is. He is at Billie B— to night. Shock came in Town this evening. He's a St. Louis Drummer for Barnard & Co.

[Sometimes there is just no substitute for a great dinner with good companions, followed by a successful manhunt. McDonald and Peale catch their man, R. R. Blankenship, just ahead of the railroad building into Childress County. Coffee was "parched" in the morning, meaning the green coffee beans were roasted before grinding and brewing a fresh cup.]

APR 14, 1887 THURSDAY MORNING QUANAH

Another nice clear and a Plesant morning. And the grass looks beautiful and every thing looks living around. Well I must go up Town and see what I can see going on. Well this has been a beautifull day and everything has went on all OK. I met Mr Hosmer this evening. Well the Programe is changed at camp this morning. For the one to herd tomorrow will stay at camp to night and so from now own.

[The Reverend James T. Hosmer was the assigned Methodist leader for the Vernon District, a thirty-four-county area that included the Hardeman Mission. The Reverend Hosmer preached the first sermon in Vernon in 1880. He was active throughout the 1880s in furthering the cause of Methodism on the frontier, including Greer County.[23] Known for his tact and spirituality, the Reverend Hosmer was one of the last frontier sky pilots, the old-fashioned, circuit-riding preachers.]

APR 15, 1887 FRIDAY MORNING QUANAH

A little cloudy this morning and cool. This is Prices herd day and he has not come to camp yet. Well I will go up Town and see whats going on up there. Oh my, if there isnt Dewberries or Blackberries, one or the other, this soon in the seson. The first I have heard of. Well I'll stay at camp to night with Brad[bury] as I have such a cold and not go to Town. It looks very much like it will rain anyway. Dr. Sumpter was put in the caliboos last night for disturbing the Peace.

[Even the town's more plausibly respectable citizens, like Dr. Sumpter, can drink too much and find themselves with the law on their tail. "Disturbing the peace" was a new and more fashionably phrased charge to replace the older and vulgar "Drunk and Disorderly." Around 1887–88 the new legal phrase took hold in the Panhandle.[24] *It covered the arrest of the obnoxiously drunk.]*

APR 16, 1887 SATURDAY MORNING QUANAH

Cloudy and raining a little. I do hope it will rain good before it stops. Well its now nearly 11 oclock and the boys have all gone to Town. All but [Sterling] Price and he has gone after a load of wood. So I will go and see what is going on. Well I have orders to stay down at camp to night to gard the horses and not go to sleep. Mr [Ed] Furman will stay to night as he came home this evening. The Brookin Boys and gang were supposed to have been in Town last night and the boys will see about it to night.

APR 17, 1887 SUNDAY MORNING QUANAH

Well we had another fine rain last night again. [Private] Furman and I was called near the tank last night to take care of some drunk men that had killed one of there horses with a club. McDonald and Green was there when we got there. Still looks as if it will rain more before it stops. Well it's now about 12 oclock and I must go up Town. I met Porter Drace in Town this evening and brought him down to sleep with me. I saw John Deberry down at Mart Cunninghams. He has been there now for two nights and Blowing in his money.

[Bill McDonald is still a deputy sheriff, but he is starting to hang out with the boys, and he shows up with a ranger or two wherever there is trouble. Mart Cunningham, a natural boomer, runs a popular Quanah dance hall, where one could "blow in his money" with drink and women—for days apparently. Porter Drace and John DeBerry are Margaret residents who increasingly turn up in Quanah for business, followed by a little liquid refreshment and intemperate fun.]

APR 18, 1887 MONDAY MORNING QUANAH

Cloudy and still looks as it will rain some more before it closes down. Well this has been another Plesant day. Cool and cloudy all day. Peter Ferguson came over this evening. Pat Wolforth is in Town again. This is my night to gard as I will have to hurd tomarrow. Tis a nice night. Tom Platt and Dennis Peal went out to Henry this evening.

[Pat Wolforth was a busy cattleman in the spring of 1887. A no-nonsense, strong-willed, and active man, he was the superintendent of Bill Curtis's famed Diamond Tail Ranch for a decade. He knew the land around Quanah well. Curtis's Diamond Tails had grazed along Groesbeck Creek in 1878 before settling into Childress and Collingsworth Counties. The FW&DC Railroad was building across the lower end of the ranch that spring, adding to Wolforth's interest and concerns.

Tom and Dennis catch a train to Henry. They arrive to find a nothing, a surveyed but otherwise almost empty townsite on the railroad right-of-way in Childress County. Henry was not a community. It was a machination of R. E. Montgomery, masterful town agent for the FW&DC and Grenville Dodge's son-in-law. The trouble with Henry was that most locals hated it. An intense power struggle between pioneers and railroad officials was underway. Childress County was being organized in April of 1887. Bob Montgomery demanded Henry as the new county seat. He offered to build a depot—and a free courthouse.

A week before Miller's Monday entry, the available and angered voters gathered four miles west of Henry. A rival and bright-prospected townsite had sprung up along the line—Childress City. It was a bustling place of good people, and not half-owned by the greedy railroad interests. The voters organized Childress County on April 11 and voted heavily for Childress City—not Henry—as the county seat. Happy county officials ordered a new courthouse built there at once. Montgomery was perturbed at their disrespect, but not at all intimidated.

Round one went to the pioneers and old-settlers of Childress County.]

APR 19, 1887 TUESDAY MORNING QUANAH

Another damp, cloudy, gloomy morning and I have to herd to day. I hope I will have a good day for it. Well I killed a nice Kerlloo [curlew] to day and had a nice mess. Well the boys, some of them, are on a drunk to night. [Private] Green and I was Sopeonead [subpoenaed] to appear at court at the Town of Margaret the 1st monday in May.

Figure 6. Scene on Groesbeck Creek, in the Panhandle. From Texas Live Stock Journal *(Oct., 1887).*

APR 20, 1887 WEDNESDAY MORNING QUANAH

Another nice morning and the grass looks well and every thing lovely. Tom Mulhall went up Town before Breakfast and got drunk as hell. So Price, John Platt, Mr Kahn and I will go over to Groesbeck Creek after a load of wood and fish while we are over there. Well we got no fish. Came home and found Tom M[ulhall] still drunk. Well we have word this evening that four men were killed by the Indians yesterday evening over in the Nation near Harrold. A little excitement this evening by old Uncle Pood shooting a blank cartridge at a fellow for throwing water on him.

[Uncle Pood has an interesting approach to incivility. One imagines the intimidation and bullying, followed by the final insult as the stranger splashes the old man with water. Uncle Pood returns with a gun and shoots the taunter at point-blank range. It probably takes awhile before the dead man realizes he is alive—the victim of a cruel hoax. Was it a cure? Will he insult a stranger so casually again? Colonel E. M. House claimed that Southerners were praised for their "courteous demeanor," and that they learned such demeanor to avoid being shot for saying a cross word to a quick-tempered stranger.[25]

Most rangers spent a fair amount of time in saloons because their presence there discouraged excessive rowdiness. Saloon walk-throughs were also a routine in law enforcement. Ranger privates entered saloons wearing or bearing arms while on duty, but they were usually required to leave their Colts and Winchesters behind when doing some off-duty socializing. Two of the Quanah rangers, Dennis Peale and Grude Britton, quit the service a few years later and jointly opened a saloon in the new railroad boomtown of Amarillo.[26] *Note that Company B's Irish teamster, Tom Mulhall, likes to drink. He starts pretty early in the day as well.*

Groesbeck Creek lies about four miles north of the ranger camp, a short ride. Rising in Childress County in north and south branches, bordered by riparian trees and shrubs, and once fed by strong springs, Groesbeck Creek is an important environmental resource for the Texas Rangers of Company B. Along its shady banks they gather firewood, bathe, fish, and sometimes find frolic and fun. The advent of civilization will be much less kind to the creek. Irrigators and farmers will gradually dry out and silt up most the springs. In 1890 a visitor from Kansas, James Sickler, decides North Groesbeck Creek's gypsum deposits are ideal for processing.[27] *A large industrial plant arises on the north branch of the creek at the town of Acme, Texas, a facility that will expand and contribute volumes of wastes to the declining waters.]*

APR 21, 1887 THURSDAY MORNING QUANAH

Another nice morning and every thing looks lovely. I will not go up Town till after noon. I will take a Shave and Parch coffee and clean up in general and read the Fugitive List a little and take a sleep. Well now its night and I will write a little of to days Notice. Sterling Price and his girle took a nice walk to day and went over near Wanders Creek. And I know they had a lovely time. To day has been very dul.

[The adjutant general's "List of Fugitives from Justice" or Fugitive List (called the "flist," that is "F-list" in the original) contained written descriptions of the most wanted men in Texas.[28] *It was compiled from county sheriff reports and noted the price on a man's head. Price and prestige tended to coincide. Ordinary rangers studied the list because even a casual recognition could bring a substantial reward. The Brooken Brothers, as noted earlier, were worth a cool $2,000.*

Wanderers Creek, formerly called and spelled "Wanders Creek,"[29] *was southeast of Quanah. McDonald soon dammed this creek on his ranch as an improvement. The name suggests an inclusive perception to the landscape. Situated on the level prairies of the divide, Quanah had Groesbeck Creek to the west and north and Wanderers Creek to the south and east. Both drainages were popular for fishing, spring picnics, and lovers' trysts, of course. The Texas Victorian landscape had little sense of exclusivity. People traipsed all over the place, often crossing private or state property of one kind or another. Dugouts and other dwellings were usually left unlocked—"in case a friend or stranger needed something." The temper of the times with respect to private-property rights can be gauged in the story of two riders coming on a dugout with a prominent lock on the door. Enraged that someone would not trust them, the cowboys destroyed the offensive padlock, then went on their way. When John Wesley left his small store in the early days, he left it unlocked so cowboys and nesters could get what they needed. They noted their purchases and settled their bills later.*

Many residents still remembered the great open range, even though barbed wire was acknowledged to have won the grassland war.[30] *Foreign and domestic capitalists alike were busy fencing off their new fiefdoms in the Texas Panhandle with boxcar loads of the devilish wire. Old-timers considered the new land to be an inherently open country, a quality that encouraged wandering. But the wandering of Wanders Creek is now largely behind a private-property lattice of barbed wire, sometimes penetrated by hemmed-in asphalt and dirt corridors. Perhaps the only compensation is that the flowers and forbs do better in the right-of-way than in the adjacent overgrazed pastures.*

The art of wandering in nature is still with the descendants of the pioneers, but the nets of private property have largely enclosed, walled, and finally cloistered the Rolling Plains landscape. Our wanders are more linear, circumscribed, and congested. To some degree we have fenced ourselves away from meaningful association with nature as the pioneers understood it.]

APR 22, 1887 FRIDAY MORNING QUANAH /87

Another nice morning. Cool and clear, and the wind Blowing hard. We intended going fishing to day but its too windy. Well its [Sterling] Prices night to stay at camp and I will stay with him and take a few games. I have not been up Town to day. It has been cold and windy all day. A concider-able Norther all day. [Sergeant] McNelly came home this evening from Hemphill at Scotts Company.

[Sergeant John McNelly had been dispatched to the piney woods of Hemphill in Sabine County to work the aftermath of the bloody Scotts-Conner Fight. A large force of lawmen soon captured the surviving Conners. After a well-publicized trial, Old Man Conner and his son were condemned to death. They were hanged shortly thereafter, much to the satisfaction of Texas Rangers everywhere. Two of Captain Scott's privates, John A. Brooks and John H. Rogers, survived their serious wounds and went on to become company captains themselves.

John A. Brooks had the middle two fingers of his left hand shot off, but he adapted and trained as an outstanding marksman. He also learned to fan his revolver, a useful skill in close fighting. The Conner fight taught Brooks a healthy respect for the East Texas woods and its denizens. A. Y. Baker wrote that when Brooks's company of rangers was ordered to East Texas later on, Baker was overjoyed at the thought of good East Texas cooking to replace a monotonous diet of goat and frijoles. But Captain Brooks held up his hand to demonstrate his missing fingers and said, "It may not be a picnic boys, this is what I got over there."[31]]

APR 23, 1887 SATURDAY MORNING QUANAH

Another cool, clear and a beautifull morning and everything is lovely. Well I must go up Town and see whats going on. I have met Polk Brandon and he looks as if he has not had any money in a long time. He looks like a tramp now, sais he has been sick. Well I will go and go to bed as its near 12 oclock. There were a real fine saddle raffled off at Kanes [Cain's Saloon] to night for $54.00. Mart Cunningham and McWilliams got it.

APR 25, 1887 MONDAY MORNING QUANAH

Another nice and cool morning. I will try and finish reading my Fugitive List before I enter Town. Tom and John Plat has gone after wood. Mc-[Nelly] has gone up to the shop to get the mules shewed for a trip. Well I am now at the shop with Tom Plats horse, getting him shewed and it is 5 oclock and not done yet. Tom Mulhall has the other two mules and wagon. I got my Fugitive List done about 1 oclock and took a shave and came up. Well I will go down to camp to bed as its about time. Its about 10 oclock now and I and Tom and Bradberry will go and go to bed. So good night Diary.

[The affectionate phrase returns after an absence. It was a busy day, but A. T. continues to record the opening and closing of the day. Good habits build good character. Sarge McNelly and Teamster Mulhall are busy fixing up the wagon and five mules judged "serviceable" in preparation for an extended trip by the company.[32]]

APR 26, 1887 TUESDAY MORNING QUANAH

Another beautifull morning and Brad[bury] and Ferman are going to Groesbeck [Creek] to fish to day. I expect they will have a good dinner as they went prepared to have it. Well I must stay at camp to night. Tomarrow is my Hurd day. The boys got enough fish for dinner, but did not bring but a few little ones home. This has been a beautifull day. So good-night diary.

APR 27, 1887 WEDNESDAY MORNING QUANAH

Another beautifull day we will have and its my Hurd day. [Jim] Green and the Teamster has gone after a load of wood this morning. Green got his new boots last night and real nice ones. They cost him $14.00. Oh what a beautifull day this is. The grass is so green and nice. I am sitting down on the Prarie looking at the Horses and cattle all around grazing over the nice grass. What will I be doing this time next year?

[Herd day inspires contemplation and personal reflection—the quiet pleasure of a pastoral life. Solitude and a calm, fresh, spring landscape place the diarist in an introspective mood. A year later, in fact, Private Miller will be looking for an uncooperative rustler on the distant Rocking Chair Ranche in Collingsworth County.]

APR 28, 1887 THURSDAY MORNING. QUANAH TEX 1887

A nice and clear morning and a nice time to start on our west trip. Well we have had a good day drive. We are now at a nice Spring in Childress Co. near Henry, 30 miles west of Quanah. Saw Mat Sawyer to day at Kirkland and met old Mr Coffee and wife. He is the uglist man in Texas.

[A half-dozen mounted rangers of Company B saddle up after dawn and ride out of their Quanah camp. They will make a long sweep, a "west trip" across the Texas Panhandle as per the order of Adjutant General W. H. King. Reports of troubles on big ranches, and allegations of citizens shot by lawmen had stirred King's and McMurry's interest. Handcuffs, extra clothing, camp equipment, suggans or bedrolls, and sufficient supplies are carried along in a mule-drawn wagon and possibly a pack mule. The company wagon can also be used as a prison-wagon. It will be weeks before the boys return to their base camp at Quanah. Captain McMurry is just back from a counterfeiting investigation in Fort Worth. He will catch a stagecoach in a couple of days to reach their destination.

The Quanah rangers follow the westward road of the stageline. This road runs west-northwest out of Quanah, crosses South Groesbeck Creek, and reaches a stage stand at the small town of Kirkland—or rather Old Kirkland, because R. E. Montgomery intends to move the Childress County town seven miles south to catch his new railroad. At Kirkland the diarist meets Old

Mr. Coffee, possibly the pioneer J. N. Coffee, an eighty-year-old man with a thirty-three-year-old wife. From Kirkland the stageline goes west. The rangers stop for the night at a "nice spring" near the Henry townsite, most likely at Childress Springs instead of Horsehead Lake on upper North Groesbeck Creek.[33]

The diarist continues his custom of making an early morning entry of a sentence or two, then coming back at the end of the day to add to his account. Words like "Well" often indicate a considerable lapse of time between the morning and evening entries for a day.]

APR 29, 1887 FRIDAY MORNING IN CAMP

UP IN CHILDRESS CO.

A little cloudy this morning. But a fine day to travil. Well we are over on Parker Creek in Hall Co. now in camp. We had a time crossing the Red River to day. We have passed over some beautifull country to day.

[From their morning camp at Childress Springs Company B follows the stage road northwest. After a morning ride the boys enter Hall County, Mill Iron and Shoe Bar ranch country, and advance toward the stage crossing on the Prairie Dog Town Fork of the Red River. The Prairie Dog Town Fork could be a difficult river in the spring. Bordered by extensive sand hills, the braided channel is quite wide and subject to quicksands after floods. Brine seeps and springs in western Hall County flavor the waters hereabouts.

Distant thunderstorms on the Llano Estacado, and heavy spring rains in the Palo Duro Canyon system also cause sudden rises, swirling waters that impede or stop travelers altogether. Getting their party and wagon across the Prairie Dog Town Fork is clearly an effort. Continuing a northwest course, the rangers stop for the night on Parker Creek. This small, springfed creek lies south of modern Memphis, Texas, and drains into the Prairie Dog Fork near Estelline. In this vicinity modern Texas Highway 287 approximates the old stageline. (See Map 2 for the ranger company route in the Texas Panhandle.)]

APR 30, 1887 SATURDAY MORNING IN CAMP

IN HALL CO. ON PARKER CREEK

Well I hope we will have another good day to travil as it is nice and cool. And a little cloudy. Well we got near Clarendon, Donley Co. to night and we have come over some beautifull country to day. As we crossed Buck Creek we found John Deberry there. He is selling groceries for Wood & Dixon at Quanah.

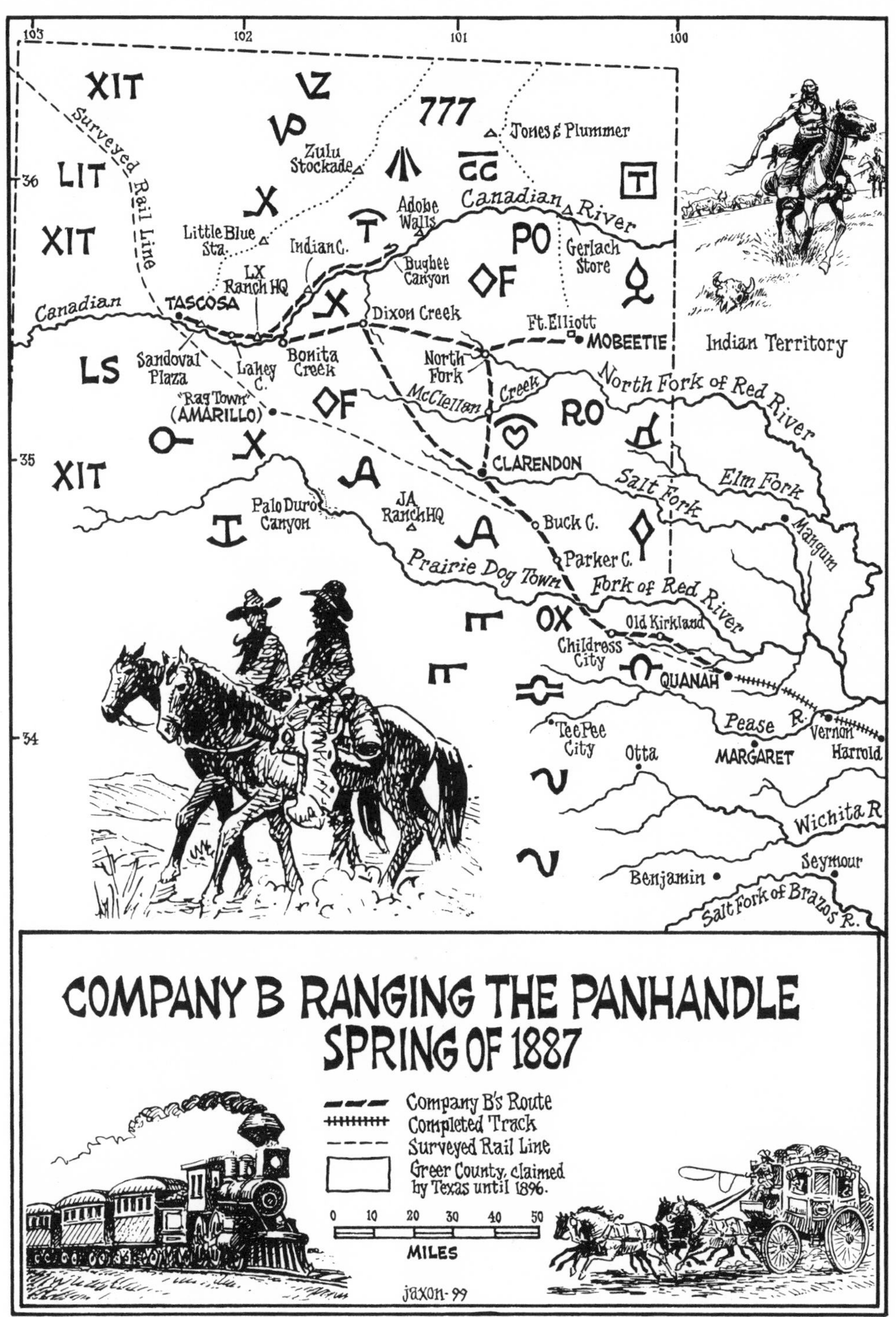

Map 2. Company B Ranging the Panhandle, Spring of 1887. Map by Jack Jackson

Carie & Jones are there now and the RR is working like rats. Tom Plat and Dennis Peal went on over to Clarendon this evening and came back to meet us at camp.

[After breakfast on Parker Creek the rangers continue northwest, climbing a low escarpment. Soon they ride upon teams of scrapers and graders working well in advance of the tracklayers. Frenetic construction crews are grading a course up the caprock and onto a spur of the High Plains in eastern Donley County. Where the line will cross upper Buck Creek, a brief tent encampment has taken hold. Buck Spring and its cool waters are nearby. A friend from Margaret, John DeBerry, has moved here temporarily. DeBerry is selling dry goods here for the Quanah mercantile house of Wood & Dixon, probably after giving up on the slow pace of business in Margaret.

With Pat Wolforth's advice, the FW&DC Railroad will soon build stock pens on its completed line at Buck Creek for shipping cattle herds to market. Around the springs and pens the 1888 townsite of Giles takes hold.[34] *The Fort Worth & Denver City Railroad had laid track beyond Quanah all spring, but they have yet to bridge the main Prairie Dog Town Fork. Dan Carey and Morgan Jones, aka Carey and Jones, were the railroad contractors who worked their men "like rats." For each mile of track laid, the railroad got $20,000 and sixteen sections of land.*

The rangers stop for the night near Clarendon, possibly at the ancient springs and wetlands of Lelia Lake.]

MAY 1, 1887 SUNDAY MORNING IN CAMP NEAR CLARENDON.

Well we must go. A nice but a cold morning. Capt [McMurry] passed while we were in camp this morning. Well we have stoped on the foot of the Plains to wait on the wagon. We came through Clarendon this morning. Its on white river in a cluster of hills, a right nice little Town. I met Mr Grant this morning. Well the stage has just passed by and Capt has gon on to Tascosa. Well we have camped on the Plains to night and its as cold as whis. We have made a good days drive and came over a beautifull country. But it has been terrible windy to day.

[After a camp breakfast on the plains and a brief word from the passing captain, Company B continues along the Dodge City–Wichita Falls stage road into historic Clarendon. The picturesque frontier town lay nestled between Eagle Hill and the confluence of Carroll Creek with the Salt Fork of the Red River. Distant salt flats, fed by brine seeps and springs that precipitated a white crust, give parts of the river the appearance of a "white river." Clarendon was the third town founded in the Panhandle, a speculative Methodist

"Christian Colony" engineered in 1878 by the Reverend Lewis H. Carhart. Carhart was an inspired preacher but an overconfident land speculator. He was in ecstasies after his 1877 tour of the eastern Panhandle—the "Paradise on Earth." Like the founders and boosters of Tascosa, Mobeetie, and Margaret, Carhart envisioned a great future metropolis.

Named for Carhart's wife, Clara, the town of Clarendon was founded on October 1, 1878. Strict Christian principles governed the community: no liquor, no gambling, no brothels, and no sin if possible. Local cowboys poked fun at the mandated morality by calling the town "Saint's Roost."[35] *Lewis Carhart's furious promotional tours across the North—and as far as Methodist meetings in England—attracted an odd but distinguished group of pioneers to Clarendon's dugouts and houses. There were engineers, retired ministers, lawyers, eager new farmers and ranchers, wives and children, a Jewish store owner, a few unemployed buffalo hunters, and dozens of other well-educated, well-intentioned newcomers. About four hundred and fifty citizens lived in Old Clarendon when the rangers of Company B rode through town. They saw the old town at its zenith.*

Old Clarendon was also in the throes of disaster that spring. The railroad planned to stay on the level divide, leaving the existing townsite a useless six or so miles in the river brakes to the north. In his environmental reveries, the Reverend Carhart had sited Clarendon for easy access to river transportation, but, alas, the steamboats that plied the Salt Fork of the Red River existed only in his imagination! Old Clarendon would have to relocate to survive in the age of steel rails. About four months after the rangers passed, the townspeople reluctantly followed the advice of merchants and moved the city to a raw tract along the new railroad.

Also in the spring of 1887 the Reverend Lewis Carhart's leveraged real estate and Texas cattle schemes began to unravel. Three years earlier, Carhart and his brother-in-law had launched a syndication scheme for the Clarendon Land Investment and Agency Company. They bought a great amount of land, including the Quarter Circle Heart brand, and they sold stock to foreign investors. Natural disasters and gross mismanagement of ranch affairs finally caused disgruntled English stockholders to send inspectors. The dreaded Count Cecil Kearney would arrive in a month's time to find a shambles of a ranch with only a few weary cattle. Shortly before he arrived, the Reverend Carhart and his brother-in-law resigned their offices and skipped out of town.[36]

Some seventy years later A. T. Miller's son-in-law, Carl Bernard Morris, lobbied state and federal authorities for a big dam on the Salt Fork of the Red River. "Cap" Morris spent considerable time refuting the notion that a dam on a "salt" river would only yield a worthless salt reservoir. His dream was finally funded and the dam built in the 1960s, but at a cost—Greenbelt Lake inundated the historic site of Old Clarendon.]

MAY 2, 1887 MONDAY MORNING ON THE PLAINS

Oh how cold. We had a Norther last night and an overcoat would feel good this morning. Well we are camped on Boneta or Vaneta creek, I dont know which is the name. And we have made a good and hard drive to day. We came by a stage stand on Dixon Creek and saw Two Ladies there, and I don't know what brought a lady in such a country as this for. We are in Carson or Potter Co. I dont know which, but I do know we are in an awful ruff county. It has been terrible since we left the Plains. We are within 35 miles of Tascosa. We met Park Gray this evening on the stage. He's traveling for Wood & Dixon at Quanah.

[The Company B Texas Rangers saw the wagon-road economy of the Texas Panhandle at its zenith, such as it was, in the spring of 1887. Freighters and bullwhackers, stagecoach drivers and stage stand operators, drummers and razzoopers, lawyers and preachers, lawmen and fugitives, all used a main network of roads to attend to their business. The old stage stands and rutted roads of the 1875–87 era are almost obliterated and forgotten today. The strings of springfed oases that linked the Panhandle frontier towns to each other, and to the commercial world of Dodge City, Kansas, are mostly dried up, silted in, or played out.

The Kansas businessman P. G. Reynolds established in the mid-1870s a lively network of freighters and stage stands from Dodge City, Kansas, into the Texas Panhandle. One road ran south from Dodge City via Fort Supply to Fort Elliott. Another stage and freight road ran from Dodge City to Beaver, Indian Territory, where two major roads diverged and ran into Texas. Freighters and stageline passengers could follow the Dodge City–Tascosa Trail, past Cator's pioneer "Zulu Stockade," to the thirsty western cowtown of Tascosa. The second wagon road, the old Jones and Plummer Trail, entered the north Panhandle, paused at a "stage ranch" on upper Wolf Creek, forded the Canadian River at Gerlach's Store, then headed south to Mobeetie.[37] From Mobeetie a further stage road ran to Clarendon, which in turn connected with distant civilization in Wichita Falls. For almost a decade travelers in the Panhandle had only the few, heavily rutted stage roads for commercial transportation.

By 1887 an important network of east-west branch roads also functioned to link Tascosa, Clarendon, and Mobeetie together [see Map 2]. At Clarendon one road followed Carroll Creek north out of town toward Mobeetie, a fifty-mile trip. Company B, however, rode west out of Clarendon on a second stage road, the old trail to Tascosa. This road traveled up the Salt Fork Valley for a spell, climbed the caprock, and continued northwest across flat Carson County. Much of the going in Carson County was on the vast, forbidding, playa-strewn plain of the eastern Llano Estacado. The Llano or "Staked Plain" was amazingly level, and therefore famed for its qualities of disorientation—"I dont know which," Miller wrote, about whether they were in Carson or Potter County.

Following the road across the Staked Plain brought the rangers to a drainage flowing north to the Canadian River. Here was the lonely Dixon Creek stage stand, some rustic dugouts and corrals on West Dixon Creek in Carson County. West Dixon Springs flowed here and provided good water for trail-weary livestock. A century later two deep pits near the depleted springs suggested former dugouts used by the stage operators.[38] *At the Dixon Creek stage stand Company B's men intersected a major east-west road, the Vanita Mail Route, which ran between Mobeetie and Tascosa. The rangers followed this dusty road westward, now off the level and grassy plains and into the "ruff" erosional brakes of the Canadian River Valley. Randolph Marcy, Josiah Gregg, James William Abert, and A. W. Whipple had passed this way some four decades earlier. These explorers had seen much cedar on the flanks of the Llano, but the big ranches and nesters alike were busy cutting them all down for fenceposts.*

Company B's destination is a beautiful former Comanche campground ahead on Bonita Creek. After a hard ride they reach the Bonita stage stand, water their horses and mules, and make camp that night under the tall cottonwoods lining the creek. They are in fact in Potter County, about nine miles northeast of present Amarillo. Miller's variant spellings—"Boneta or Vaneta creek, I dont know which is the name"—reflect a cultural reality. Lieutenant A. W. Whipple had camped on the same spot in 1853 and called the drainage "Shady Creek," but the old comanchero toponym of "Bonita" (sometimes misspelled "Bonillo") survived and became a common term in the mid-1870s. An old P. G. Reynolds's stagecoach advertisement termed the road the "Vanita and Las Vegas Mail Route," so the Anglicized "Vanita" was in use as well.[39]

Stagecoaches and new Star Route mail deliveries tried to keep regular runs between the frontier Panhandle settlements in 1887, but delays and problems were common. Floods and quicksands were troublesome. A percentage of bullwhackers and stage drivers froze to death during particularly nasty winter blizzards. Despite efforts to refine an image of crude accommodations, and some investments to remain competitive, the old stage stands looked forlorn in 1887. "Two Ladies" looked out of place, as Miller observed. The wagon-road world is obviously doomed by the coming of the railroad. It will wither for about a decade after 1888, lingering only to serve bypassed towns and ways, then quietly disappearing itself.]

MAY 3, 1887 TUESDAY MORNING ON BONETA CREEK

Another nice morning. The air is cool and Plesant and we must go on for Tascosa. This is the sixth day we have been out. Well we got into Tascosa this evening about 9 oclock. We came cross the Connadian River this morning at the LX ranch. We had to unload our wagon to cross as it had been up and was a little boggy. Went 1 ½ miles up the river to the bookkeepers house where we found a beautifull running spring and a nice little house over it and such good water. We also came by a little Mexican Town this evening. All build of Adobies. We have come over another ruff day drive but some nice vallies. We are camped in a pastur ½ mile North of Town. We came by a beautifull place this evening. Long Adobie house and a nice rowe of cottonwood trees in front and the Canadian river in front and a nice spring running through the yard.

[The Canadian River Valley was one of the most important corridors in Southwest history. Hernando de Alvarado, Juan de Padilla, Francisco Vázquez de Coronado, Juan de Oñate, Pierre and Paul Mallet, Pedro Vial, Francisco Amangual, Stephen H. Long, Randolph Marcy, James W. Abert, A. W. Whipple, and countless New Mexican ciboleros and comancheros explored and traveled along the valley. Many observers commented on the fine springs of the region, pure waters bursting from the flanks of the immense plains above and flowing down shaded creeks to the brisk Canadian River.[40]

It is apparent that two ethnic cultures reside in the 1880s Canadian Valley. The LX Ranch represents the newer Anglo-Saxon culture of Scottish capital and American great expectations. Charlie Siringo said that the parsimonious W. H. "Deacon" Bates and his fellow Boston partner Beals founded the LX in 1877.[41] *Like other first-era ranchers, Bates and Beals sold the LX for a sharp profit in 1884 to British and Scottish investors behind the quaintly named "American Pastoral Company, Ltd." The LX Ranch dominated the broken canyons of the Canadian Valley in Potter and Moore Counties in 1887. It was an impressive operation. Like the thoughtfully organized JA Ranch under Charles Goodnight, there was an organization and ecological sensibility to this large-scale ranch. Cattle—only a few years before it had been buffalo—sheltered in the valley flats over the hard winters, and then summered on the rich, flat grasslands of the High Plains above. Water was excellent due to the large number of discharge springs flowing from the untapped Ogallala Aquifer. The neighborly rival to the LX was the equally huge LS Ranch to the east.*

The second and older culture reflected the expansion of the Hispano homeland in New Mexico eastward into the Canadian River Valley of Texas.[42] *New Mexican ciboleros and comancheros had hunted and traded respectively in the Canadian River Valley for several centuries. Even before the final dissolution of the Comanchería, pastores were grazing their sheep in the area. After the removal of the last Comanche tribes in 1875, a remarkable flow of Hispano pastores and pioneers surged eastward from daughter colonies on the eastern drainages of the Rocky Mountains. From Mora County, Anton Chico, and Las Vegas, New Mexico, the pastores and their patron financiers sought the rich Panhandle grasslands for their herds.*[43] *For a brief period a number of plaza and placita settlements, anchored to sheep herding, appeared in the Canadian River Valley. The best-known of these plazas was Casimiro Romero's Atascosa in Oldham County, which dropped the "A" to become Tascosa, its new 1887 post office spelling. The Texas Rangers rode past the "little Mexican town" of Sandoval Plaza on Corsinio Creek, about seven miles east of Tascosa on the north side of the river.*[44]*]*

MAY 4, 1887 WEDNESDAY MORNING IN TASCOSA, OLDHAM CO.

Another cool nice morning. Well we have been in Tascosa to day and a Town it is. Not to be forgotten. Nearly all Adobies. The courthouse and Jaile is connected and made of stones and a nice house. The Town is on the banks of the Connadian River. I paid 10 cts for a spool of thread to day for the first time in my life.

[The cultural landscape of Tascosa shows its architectural roots in New Mexico; this was probably A. T. Miller's first encounter with a substantial town of this nature. Adobe construction was a much more refined technique of working with dirt, however, than methods used to build the leaking pioneer sod-house or troglodytic dugout. Prices for thread and everything else are high in Tascosa because almost all merchandise is freighted from distant Dodge City, Kansas. Captain McMurry, who rode the stagecoach to Tascosa ahead of his rangers, arrests Bob Briley today for stealing horses in Childress County.]

MAY 5, 1887 THURSDAY MORNING IN TASCOSA

This is another nice morning and Price is on Hurd to day. So I will go down Town and get my Horse showed on one hind foot, as it is broken. Well I paid 50 cts to have one shoe put on my Horse today, the worst I ever did. Capt Arringtons case was moved this evening to Clarendon for trial in July. Well I must go to bed.

[George Washington "Cap" Arrington (aka John C. Orrick, Jr.)—"The Iron-Handed Man of the Texas Panhandle"—was a former Mosby guerrilla and soldier of fortune turned Texas law officer.[45] *Born as John Orrick, Jr., this Confederate veteran shot a black businessman in 1867, fled to Honduras, and then resurfaced in Texas under the flattering alias of George Washington Arrington.*[46] *Despite being wanted for murder in Alabama, Arrington maintained his new identity and eventually worked his way into an enlistment in the Frontier Battalion. He saw much service with Captain Lee Hall in bloody South Texas. In 1879 the adjutant general elevated G. W. Arrington to captain, and dispatched "Cap" Arrington and his Company C rangers to the remote Texas Panhandle and South Plains. As the first ranger captain in the region he had numerous challenges, adventures, and accomplishments. Arrington was a stern man and a strict disciplinarian. He made friends and enemies easily. Walter Prescott Webb called Arrington "the first and greatest peace officer" of the Panhandle.*[47] *Arrington resigned from the ranger force in 1882 to take up ranching and serving as sheriff of Wheeler County.*

There may also have been a touch of the shootist in this former fugitive, ex-ranger, and current sheriff, an exultation in using his gun that sometimes left him a bit too trigger-happy. Arrington's "case" refers to a recent Oldham County grand jury indictment of the Wheeler County sheriff—for murder! The indictment grew out of the controversial death of a well-liked settler. One of the main reasons Company B trekked to Tascosa in force, apparently, was for the Texas Rangers to forestall any trouble—from either side—in the sensational trial of "Cap" Arrington for murder. Despite Arrington's fame and ex-ranger status, Private Miller expresses no particular admiration for him.]

MAY 6, 1887 FRIDAY MORNING TASCOSA

Another nice morning and I suppose we will have to go to day about noon as Capt Arringtons crowd has gone to Mobeetie. I dont know whether we will have to go there or not. Well we did not start to day as we expected. But we will go in the morning bright and early.

[Sheriff Arrington brought his "crowd" with him to Tascosa to face his murder charge. His lawyers did their work well the previous day. As the diarist noted on May 5, Arrington's trial for murder was moved on a change of venue to Clarendon, a much more distant and sympathetic location. Moreover the trial is put off until July, letting tempers settle down further. Arrington's business in Tascosa is thus done. The sheriff and his armed supporters take the Vanita Road to Mobeetie, back to his center of power in Wheeler County.]

MAY 7, 1887 SATURDAY MORNING TASCOSA

We have another nice morning and I think we will have a nice day to travil. Well we have camped at the Scotchmans Spring at the LX ranch, that is the bookkeepers house. This has been a terrible warm day to day, but we got here in good time. Capt [McMurry] has gone up to the house for supper and he will stay there to night I suppose.

[With Arrington's murder indictment settled for the moment, the rangers begin to pressure his critics. Company B rangers, wagon, and mules trail out of Tascosa after sunup. They head eastward on the regular stage trail along the Canadian River. After a good ride they reach the LX Ranch in Potter County. The boys stop for the night at the headquarters, camping near the pleasant bookkeeper's house on a strong spring on Pitcher Creek in the Canadian Valley.

The Scottish bookkeeper is James Wyness. Wyness's young wife, Lizzie Farris, is expecting a baby shortly, but she will die in childbirth five weeks after the rangers pass by, her infant son soon following. Their graves are in the old LX cemetery.[48] Wyness kept distant investors accurately informed, thus enabling the LX Ranch to survive the economic turbulence of the late 1880s and 1890s. Note that wherever possible Captain McMurry prefers to avail himself of more gentlemanly accommodations. Do the others quietly resent it? In any case he is doing the syndicate ranching interests a favor; they owe him a good night's sleep.]

MAY 8, 1887 SUNDAY MORNING IN CAMP

ON THE CONNADIAN RIVER AT LX RANCH.

Cloudy and looks like it will rain to day, but we must go down the River to day to Indians Canyon. Well we have had a hard days ride. We had a Pilot from the LX ranch to the canyons this evening. He got a little rattled and we did not get to Indians Canyon till about 5 oclock. Then we came on to Bugbies Canyon to the Meaks family that used to live in Hardeman Co. We took supper with them and will stay here to night and take some of the men with us tomarrow. Well its time to go to bed, so goodnight diary.

[With no other populous settlements between Mobeetie, Tascosa, and Clarendon, the Canadian River Valley was still something of a frontier in the spring of 1887. For a moment a man could still get lost in the myriad of tributary canyons downstream from Tascosa. It was also the kind of geography that outlaws preferred: lots of concealment possibilities in the brakes, good wood and water, and the ready availability of stock from nearby large ranches. After

breakfast at the LX bookkeeper's place, Company B veers off the stage road with their pilot. The men head northeast toward Indian Creek Canyon, a five-mile Canadian tributary in Northwest Potter County. Thence they have a hard ride down the Canadian Valley, crossing the river, and reaching Bugbee's Canyon.

A little farther down the Canadian River was the historic trading site of Adobe Walls. About four miles upstream of old Adobe Walls was Bugbee's Canyon. Now called Bugby Creek, it is an intermittent canyon stream some six miles northeast of Borger in Hutchinson County. Thomas and Molly Bugbee arrived here from Kansas in the fall of 1876 with a trail herd. The couple built a dugout, wintered the herd, and thus established the second large ranch in the Panhandle. Gradually they built their Quarter Circle T ranch into a small kingdom. But the aggravation and hard life got to be too much for Molly. After a spring tornado and waterspout threatened their Canadian Valley home, the Bugbees sold out to a syndicate in 1883 for $350,000 and returned to a splendid orchard on the edge of Kansas City. The call of Panhandle ranching proved irresistible though to the brilliant cattleman, Thomas Sherman Bugbee. After operating out of Old and New Clarendon for years, he will finally move his family from Kansas to Donley County.[49] *A. T. Miller and T. S. Bugbee will get to know each other in Clarendon in the 1920s.*

The Texas Rangers take most of the day to thread their way down the Canadian Valley. Their destination is the humble Meeks Place in Bugbee Canyon. What urgent state business brings them thither?]

MAY 9, 1887 MONDAY MORNING STILL IN BUGBIE CANYON.

And a beautifull morning. Well we are at the LX ranch to night. We got in about Sundown. We arrested four men at Meaks in Bugbies Canyon. Two of the Meaks and a Mr Liverton and a fellow who gives his name as Dawson. We will gard them in the office at the LX Ranch to night.

[The Company B rangers rode up to the Meek homestead at sundown on Sunday night, announced their intentions, dined with them, and spent the night. At some point they read out arrest warrants and quietly took four residents, including two adult Meek family members, into custody. Guarding their prisoners, all critics of Sheriff Arrington, they returned upriver to spend the night at the LX headquarters still some twenty miles below Tascosa. Few modern peace officers could expect to eat supper and spend the night with the families on whom they were serving arrest warrants.

The Meeks and Levertons were typical of the nesters irritating the corporate ranches. John and George Leverton, and Ike and George Meek had all cowboyed together on the Hardeman County frontier in the early 1880s. They were pals whose aspirations took them deeper into the Panhandle. But when they moved into the Canadian River Valley in the mid-1880s to operate on their own hook, they soon ran afoul of and earned the lasting enmity of existing syndicate management. In part the difference was philosophical: the corporate ranchers just did not like any nesters at all. Nesters were trouble. The LX was convinced that Ike Meek, George Meek, and the Leverton brothers were undesirables, men not above branding many a so-called "syndicate calf."

The syndicates, that is, the second-era "big ranchers" considered the Meeks and Levertons to be more than troublesome squatters. They were harbingers, likely to bring more thieving nesters onto school lands inside the ranch, and thus to cause further friction. The first-era, Anglo-Texan ranchers in the '70s had used money, the law and courts, and some intimidation to displace the Hispano sheepmen back to their New Mexico homeland. Money was tight in 1887 for syndicates, so perhaps it was more economical to harass, intimidate, and use the law to cleanse oneself of families judged undesirable, rather than to buy them out. The LX especially did not like nesters in "their" pastures, that is, on the enormous quantities of public land checkerboarded with bought or leased ranch land. The big cowmen used various stratagems to rid themselves of the first nester newcomers.

By 1887 the Canadian Valley syndicate ranchers were rather hard-pressed monopolists, savaged by blizzard and drought losses, eager to enclose public settlement lands behind their barbed wire, and not above using the law to harass suspected settlers who dared to settle on the legitimate school lands. In turn the average new settler's feelings often ran high against the syndicate ranchers. These kingdoms unto themselves broke the 1883 cowboy strike, blacklisted the strikers, rigged local elections, ended the old open-range relationships, enclosed public lands for their own use, and often subverted the democratic process. Hounded westward for decades by the ecological shock wave of small farmers and livestock raisers crunching the land behind them, the big ranchers turned defensive in the Panhandle, knowing there was no more frontier for retreat. The LX in particular disliked many of the newcomers that ran small herds.

The nesters' unfortunate problem was to operate on a different spatial scale than the big ranchers. Gus Gober, a friend of the Levertons, recalled that the winter northers would scatter the poor nester's cattle well off his small range. At roundup time in the spring the exclusive big ranchers employed an artful dodge to take advantage of the situation: they carefully branded each others calves where just and appropriate, but they left the nester's calves unbranded. When these calves were weaned they bore no brand, and thus were range mavericks, whereupon the big ranchers branded and claimed these calves for their own.[50]

Tactics and shortcuts like this had the undoubted advantage of eventually driving the little cowman off the range while increasing the syndicate balance books. Gober felt it was only fair that the nester recover his losses, declaring, "if a nester was to survive there was just one thing for him to do, go out and brand a few mavericks for himself."[51] The nester branding of syndicate calves, or its perception, is really what brought the Texas Rangers down on the heads of the Meeks, Dawson, and Leverton.

The shock of the '86 winter and drought left many parties eager to recover losses with a branding iron. Because there were only so many mavericks to go around, some Panhandle counties proved to be rough nester–syndicate ranch battlegrounds in 1887. Captain McMurry did the formalities of arrest, reading out Wheeler County warrants (probably the work of G. W. Arrington), charging George Leverton and George Meeks with "unlawful assembly," charging Ike Meeks with "carrying pistol," and charging William Dawson with "bribing witness."[52]]

MAY 10, 1887 TUESDAY MORNING AT THE LX RANCH.

Looks very much like it will rain. And we must go to Tascosa to day, it is called. 26 miles. Well we got into Tascosa this evening again about 4 oclock. We got a wagon at the LX untill we go back, as we got ours broak down yesterday on the way to the canyons.

[The boys wake up at the LX Ranch headquarters, a utilitarian cluster of buildings and corrals that constituted most of what civilization there was in early Potter County. An adobe and stone bunkhouse, storeroom, stables, wagon sheds, and blacksmith shop serve the denizens. Charlie Siringo had worked here as wagon boss, and Billy the Kid had visited the ranch in the early days of Bates and Beals. By 1887 the syndicate American Pastoral Company ran the outfit.[53] The LX headquarters was located on the north side of the Canadian River, upriver from Ranch Creek and near the spring on Pitcher Creek in northern Potter County. The first post office in the county, "Wheeler, Texas" opened here in August of 1879, and was still open in 1887.

The syndicate is happy to loan Texas Rangers an LX wagon to haul away arrested nesters. Company B loads their prisoners, hits the stage road west, passes the stage stand on Lahey Creek, and reaches Tascosa in the afternoon.]

MAY 11, 1887 WEDNESDAY MORNING IN TASCOSA

Another cloudy morning. We had a right smart wind last night but no rain. Well Liverton and the Meaks boys have got out on bale, but Dawson is still in Jaile. He thinks he can give bond, but I am afraid he cannot.

Figure 7. Headquarters of the LX Ranch, built in 1887. Courtesy Panhandle-Plains Historical Museum, Canyon, Texas

[Miller does not say which of the Leverton brothers was arrested and released on bail, but C. F. Rudolph, editor of the weekly The Tascosa Pioneer, *provides the details in the Saturday, May 14, 1887, issue: "The jail has not been so neglected this week as has been customary. Besides the man Briley, arrested some days ago for horse stealing at Quanah, the rangers Tuesday brought in George Leverton, Ike and George Meeks, and two other men named Dawson and Wallace. Leverton gave bond at once, and the remainder of the party did the same Thursday. These arrests were made in Moore and Potter counties all minor charges except one for theft."*

George Leverton had already attracted the law's attention; he had a prior arrest record, as did Ike and George Meek.[54] *But these priors likely reflected syndicate harassment. Was there a further hazing campaign? A. T. does not seem antagonistic to the prisoners; he may even be sympathetic to their plight. In any case the harassment was hardly new for George Leverton.*

A little over five months earlier Sheriff G. W. "Cap" Arrington had botched the arrest of George's brother, John Leverton. John had earlier and accidentally built his rock cabin inside the (poorly known) survey line of the LX Ranch. The *syndicate sued John Leverton, forcing him to move, and then asked for $5,000 in damages. The LX also nursed suspicions that John was branding their cattle. "Someone," historian John L. McCarty wrote, suggesting the possibility of a frame, "took an LX calfhide and hid it in a prairie-dog hole near the John Leverton home."*[55] *Eventually an arrest warrant was made out against John Leverton. Sheriff Cap Arrington joined Cape Willingham and four deputized others (the former scout Billy Dixon wisely refused to go), then all rode off to serve the warrant.*

Arrington and the others allegedly burst into John Leverton's home at dawn on December 1, 1886. Leverton's family was preparing breakfast. John Leverton was unarmed, grinding cinnamon bark with a coffee mill. Willingham, the former sheriff of Tascosa and now a syndicate superintendent, had recently accused Leverton of branding just one of his Hansford Land and Cattle Company calves. According to Charles Rudolph, editor of The Tascosa Pioneer, *"Arrington is said to have asked if this was Leverton, and upon being answered that it was, fired a shot that took effect in the man's arm. Other shots were fired, and John Leverton fell to the floor and under the edge of the bed."*[56] *Leverton's wife, "seeing that his murder was inevitable," got him a gun, but his shots were wild. Arrington and his fellow lawmen kept up a hot fire on the suspect, fatally wounding John Leverton, and setting his baby's bed on fire with their blazing, close-quarters shots. When the shooting was all over, it is said Cap Arrington walked up and coldly read out his arrest warrant for the dying Leverton.*

Mrs. Leverton saved her baby from his burning bed, the first Anglo child born in Moore County, but her husband soon died in agony from his thirteen gunshot wounds. She buried him in a homemade coffin of poplar planks. The boards had been specially carried all the way to Moore County to make a cupboard for the growing family in their Evans Canyon home.[57] *Questions abounded in the aftermath of the killing. Was John Leverton a notorious thieving rustler resisting arrest, or the brave victim of a sinister syndicate? Was Arrington a quick-witted lawman, or a boot-heeled government killer?*[58] *Needless to say, Arrington's account differed completely. He claimed that John Leverton fired twice at him, necessitating his return of fire. Arrington finally dropped Leverton as the latter was fleeing his house.*

George Leverton was convinced that a trigger-happy Arrington simply murdered his brother. He swore out a warrant against the ex-ranger, but the legal system largely dismissed his complaints. Editor Charles Rudolph was shocked initially by Dr. Croft's expertly reconstructed account of the poor man's slaying. Dr. Croft's report suggested that John Leverton had suffered a wrongful death. In the heat of the moment Rudolph wrote: "That an officer of the law

[Arrington] could so forget his duty and his manhood as to arm five deputies and then go beyond the line of his jurisdiction on an errand of deliberate and cold-blooded murder, seems incredible. But those who have had opportunity to know Arrington best pronounce his reputation in that direction an unsavory one as an officer."[59] Rudolph soon cooled in his editorials, but others took up the cause.

Walter Prescott Webb may have been enamored with George W. Arrington in the 1930s, but the historian today can be less adulatory. Arrington had a dark past, including a name change. His actions in the so-called arrest of John Leverton appear questionable if not illegal. The criminal justice system responded slowly and inadequately to George Leverton's call for an investigation into his brother's death. The same system quickly dispatched the Company B rangers to haul George in, just five months after Arrington had gunned down his brother. Conveniently, the rangers arrested George Leverton and brought him into Tascosa after "Arrington's crowd" had left town, as noted by the diarist. While the system thus backed Sheriff Arrington, other old-timers were outraged at the slaying. They saw it all as a travesty of justice for the nesters. Jim Browning had started a press campaign with a sensational open letter to Governor L. S. Ross, a letter printed in the prestigious Fort Worth Gazette.[60]

The Leverton affair was quietly handled, even hushed up a bit, and it gradually faded away. The question lingers though: did Sheriff Cap Arrington kill John Leverton without just cause?]

MAY 12, 1887 THURSDAY MORNING TASCOSA

Another nice day I think from the looks of this morning. Well all our men left for home this evening but Dawson. I think he will have to go to Mobeetie.

MAY 13, 1887 FRIDAY MORNING AT TASCOSA

Nice morning and we will start for Mobeetie to day with Dawson. Tom Plat is not able to ride his horse, so he will have to go in the wagon. Well we camped 5 miles East of Boneta Creek. Made a good 40 mile drive to day. It looks very much like it will rain to night.

[The rangers saddle up and leave Old Tascosa in the early morning, their business done and a prisoner in tow. They follow the Mobeetie-Tascosa stage road to the east, traveling along the north bank of the Canadian River. They pass the Lahey Creek stage stand, cross the wide river, and ride onward to the Bonita stage stand in eastern Potter County. Making good time, they continue east of Bonita and stop for the night along the road, near the Potter-Carson County line.]

MAY 14, 1887 (SATURDAY) IN CAMP THIS MORNING FOR MOBEETIE

Very cloudy this morning and I think we will have a good day to travil. Well we got to the stage stand on the North Fork [of Red River] 25 miles from Mobeetie. We made a good days drive to day. We came across the Plains from the stage stand on Dixon Creek to here. A big rain passed around in front of us to day. We are now in where it fell. Well the Duchman that lives here gave us two buckets of milk for supper.

[After sunup the boys eat, break camp, load their prisoner, and continue down the road. The rangers soon reach the forlorn stage stand at Dixon Creek. Here they continue along the east stage road to Mobeetie, instead of turning on the southeast road to Clarendon. They spend much of the day on "the Plains," the featureless High Plains of Carson and Gray Counties. Travelers on the Staked Plain see for many miles in all directions. It is easy to watch a thunderstorm form and boom in the distance. Near modern Pampa the road dropped off the High Plains for a stage stand on the upper North Fork of the Red River. The rangers stop and make camp at the North Fork stage stand, wrangling milk from the resident German-American operator, and finding wood and water.]

MAY 15, 1887 SUNDAY MORNING IN CAMP ON NORTH FORK (OF RED RIVER).

Cloudy this morning and cool and Plesant. I think we will have a good day to ride. Well we got in Mobeetie about 12 or 1 oclock and found a beautifull little Town. We came through Ft Elliot and that surprised me to see such a nice place all fixed up nice and kept up in good style. All nice blue box Houses. And by the way I met an old North Carolina boy, a soldier. He lacked 21 days of his time, being out of 5 years, and he sais he will go right strait home. And he dont want any more souldering in his life. So I know he is happy. Well I am on Hurd this evening and am lying down on the grass, writing. We are camped in the courthouse yard. They have a good courthouse and Jaile.

[A morning's ride down the stage road brings the boys to the pretty U.S. Army facilities at Fort Elliott in Wheeler County. A little farther away is Mobeetie, the oldest town in the Panhandle. Sheriff Arrington is friendly to the respectful Company B rangers. They camp in the convenient courthouse yard and lodge their prisoner with him. The Mobeetie jail and courthouse were indeed solid structures, built at some expense to taxpayers.]

Figure 8. Oldest jail in the Panhandle, Mobeetie, Texas. Courtesy Panhandle-Plains Historical Museum, Canyon, Texas

MAY 16, 1887 — MONDAY MORNING IN MOBEETIE

Another cloudy and warm morning. Well the Sheriff and Capt Arrington put Dawson in jaile last night and kept us from having him to gard. Well we will go over to Town to day and see what kind of a place it is. We find some right nice houses in this little Town. Well the day is passed and gone. There are 4 companies at Ft Elliot and about 30 Indians scouts. Well enough for to day, so good night diary.

[A beautiful spring day to walk the streets and observe Mobeetie at its zenith as a pioneer community. The old frontier towns had an appreciable and distinctive sociability, one that differed from the new railroad towns.

Sadly, poor Mobeetie's fate is unkind. Like the coaches and stage stands, the Dodge City freighters and Fort Elliott soldiers, the buffalo and bone-pickers, Mobeetie will be overtaken by steel rails and swept aside.]

MAY 17, 1887 — TUESDAY MORNING MOBEETIE

Cloudy and misting rain a little. It is John Platts Hurd day. So we will hold down the courthouse to day. Old Dolly Vardon and one of her girles came over to day and she is one of the largest woman I ever saw I think. Well we started for Clarendon this evening at 3 oclock and are now on North Fork [stage stand], 15 miles from Mobeetie and 25 miles from Clarendon.

[Two centers of pioneer prostitution were Mobeetie and Tascosa, serving soldiers and cowboys, respectively. That is to say, all the frontier Panhandle towns were centers of prostitution with the exception of those Methodists in Clarendon, whose moralizing and good character made them poor customers. In Millie Jones Porter's magnificent history of Wheeler County, Memory Cups of Panhandle Pioneers, *she notes obliquely that many "dance hall women" in Mobeetie were charged with vagrancy, "as an expression of disapproval of their trade." Virtually all the names appearing in the local vagrancy records from 1885 to 1890 are those of active prostitutes.*

Excluding a few male names for 1885, the county court records suggest that 1887 was the busiest year on record for arresting and fining prostitutes in Mobeetie.[61] *Indeed, the 1887 female vagrancy citations are a veritable roster of pioneer Panhandle prostitution: Lou Owens, Mable Gorman, Mamie, Minnie Palmer, Minnie Stacy, Dollie Harris, Mabel, Josephine, May Eddington, Minnie Jones, Eva Cooley, the beautiful Kittie Stein, Luvenia Booker, Lou Aiken, Lou Smith, Mary Brown, Catherine Lemley, Matilda Ware, Fannie Mansker, Emma Grant, Minnie Guy, Dollie Varden, and Jessie Sinclair.*[62] *There were undoubtedly others. But these twenty-three names suggest the scope of activity, and the nature of Varden's visit to the courthouse where the rangers were hanging around.*

Dollie Varden (Miller spelled it "Vardon") was cited annually for "vagrancy" in the criminal justice dockets from 1886 to 1890 with but one exception. She was a large woman, a well-known madam in the red-light district, and a memorable personality. Abner Miller thought her worthy of mention. Panhandle historian Millie Jones Porter recalled Dollie Varden in a sketch on frontier prostitution, "Dance Hall Women," published in her 1945 book, Memory Cups of Panhandle Pioneers. *Porter chose her euphemism with care, because "dance hall women" suggested more professionalism and less vulgarity than the offensive "prostitute" or common "whore." Porter's memory cup of Dollie Varden recalled:*

> *Dollie Varden's real name was Hattie Franklin. She was the manager of the "hall" which stood at the northwest edge of Mobeetie, and was always referred to as "Feather Hill" because two women fought over a cowboy and scattered feathers from a feather bed. . . . When a child I used to go to Mobeetie occasionally. Dance Hall women were sometimes in the stores. They were always well dressed and generally very pretty and I could not know who they were and would be looking at them with admiration in my*

> *eyes when some of my family or friends would tug me and tell me in an undertone, "Don't be looking at her, she is a Feather-Hill woman." Such a statement was enough, after that I would not have been seen looking at her for any consideration.*
>
> *Dollie Varden was not good-looking, was large and unshapely but must have had a certain charm. She is sometimes charged as Dollie Butts. She married a handsome young man named Ed Butts, and kept him well dressed and supplied with ready cash. I said she married him. He was billed for living in adultery and for vagrancy and as a professional gambler, so my informant might not have known. Dollie was accused of separating C. A. and Rachel Fenno, and many other similar crimes. She died in Shawnee, Okla.*[63]

Minnie Stacy was also in Mobeetie in 1887 and she was one of "the girls" of Feather Hill. Stacy was later the subject of Temple Houston's famous "Plea for a Fallen Woman," an extemporaneous speech made in the surprise pro bono defense of the poor prostitute, who was charged with vagrancy in Woodward and hauled into court for a heavy fine. The tall, long-haired, last son of Sam Houston was a master orator. Temple Houston was also a former resident of Mobeetie and he may have known Minnie Stacy from there. He entered the Woodward courtroom with the trial in progress, gallantly offered his services to the bewildered woman, and then delivered a sublime example of courtroom peroration. One line of argument that Temple Houston used was the sheer and hypocritical injustice of adding court fines and costs to Stacy's great shame and misery: "They wished to fine this woman and make her leave. They wish to wring from the wages of her shame the price of this meditated injustice; to take from her the little money she may have; and God knows, gentlemen, it came hard enough. The old Jewish law told you that the price of a dog or the hire of such as she should not come within the house of the Lord, and I say unto you that our justice, fitly symbolized by woman's form, does not ask that you add aught to the woes of this unhappy one, who only asks at your hands the pitiful privilege of being left alone."[64] *Temple Houston's speech swept the hard-hearted jury and judge into a paroxysm of compassion. Sobbing jurors consulted and then acquitted Minnie Stacy. The judge agreed.*

Back in Mobeetie the Company B Rangers have no more time to gawk at local women. They must hit the stage road to Clarendon that afternoon. They load up the wagon, hitch the wiry mules, and travel southwest down the stageline. After fifteen miles they stop for the night at the North Fork stage stand, a regular restover on the upper North Fork of the Red River. The distance from Feather Hill to Saint's Roost is not far, but it makes all the difference in Hell.]

MAY 18, 1887 WEDNESDAY MORNING IN CAMP.

A very heavy dew fell last night and cloudy this morning, but hope it will not rain before we get to Clarendon, for Tom Platt is quite sick. Well I am on McClelland Creek now waiting for the wagon. I killed a Prarie chicken and a Patridge this morning. We failed to get the mules that we expected to get here to day. Well we got to Clarendon this evening in good time to camp. We came over some nice country to day. On McClelland Creek there are several House dugouts &C and a Blacksmith shop. Well as the Sheriff [Al Gentry] has put our man in jaile, I will go to bed. But I must go over and se Miss M[Illegible] first.

[Tom Platt, sick as a dog, rides along anyway. The stage road from Mobeetie to Clarendon went to the North Fork, and crossed south into the pleasant McClellan Creek valley. The greater annual moisture of the eastern Panhandle gave the landscape a more fertile appearance. Prairie chickens were common in the region in the 1880s; their booming cries in the spring drew many hunters. Unfortunately, they were rather quickly hunted out. They are now an endangered species in Texas; the survivors gathered in a Gulf Coast refuge, and thereby placed in the path of an eventual hurricane.

The McClellan Creek stage stand has the usual dugouts but also an important amenity—a blacksmith shop. Blacksmiths gravitated to favorable sites on the wagon roads, and they made a good living while the roads lasted. At day's end Clarendon is a welcome stop. Sheriff Gentry locks up Bob Briley, their prisoner, sparing Miller from guard duty and freeing him for a social engagement with the Grant family.]

MAY 19, 1887 THURSDAY MORNING CLARENDON

Cool and a little cloudy this morning and I hope we will have a good day to travil. I had a real nice visit with Mr Grant and family last night. Well, we have got to Parker Creek and Capt [McMurry] is with us. We have made a good days drive to day sure. So now I must go to bed for I have to stand gard to night.

[The Company B rangers retrieve their prisoner from Clarendon's jail, load up, and head back to Quanah. They are retracing their earlier route on the old wagon-road, stopping once more on Parker Creek south of modern Memphis. The captain joins his men there.]

MAY 20, 1887 FRIDAY MORNING ON PARKER CREEK

IN HALL CO. AGAIN.

A nice morning and we will go for Childress City to day to have our Prisners trial. Well we got to Childress about 4 oclock and the young man waved his trial and we came on in about 6 miles of Kirkland. We came by the RR crossing on Red River and they had about all the piling down and some of the stringers on and the track is laid nearly up to the river. We eat dinner at 4 miles the other side or North of Childress, where the boarding car is and the Justice of the Piece. Fred Campbell came from there to Childress with us. Well I gave my measure to T. A. Williams this evening for a new per of boots.

[The railroad crossing of the Prairie Dog Town Fork of the Red River is watched with great interest not only by rangers but also by the citizens of Tascosa and Clarendon. Already it is clear the tracks will miss Old Clarendon, gleefully pronounced "that doomed village" by The Tascosa Pioneer. *A few pessimists and students of corporate behavior predict that Tascosa is gone as well—"gone where the woodbine twineth and the whang-doodle mourneth for its first-born."*[65] *The residents of Tascosa are now desperate to win the support of Grenville Dodge for their town. The railroad titan is scheduled for an upcoming inspection.*

"The Front" is now north of Childress and nearing the Prairie Dog Town Fork, the river prone to dangerous rises. On their way southeast the rangers stop again at the railroad's boarding car for a free meal. With pilings and stringers in place, and tracklayers almost at the bridge, the FW&DC will soon cross the Prairie Dog Town Fork. Once across this obstacle, construction crews can race across the graded plains at a mile and a half a day. Clarendon's fate is sealed; Tascosa's future hangs in the balance; Mobeetie's faith is in denial.]

MAY 21, 1887 SATURDAY IN CAMP NEAR KIRKLAND

IN CHILDLESS CO.

Cloudy and looks very much like it would rain to day. Well we got to Quanah about noon. Got home on our 21st day and I am glad to get back. I found they have had fine rain.

[Thus the road-weary rangers, horses, and mules of Company B return to their humble camp at Quanah. The boys are glad to be "home" after three weeks and 320 miles on the road. They lock Bob Briley, the prisoner carted along from Tascosa, in the Quanah "boos." Private Green will take Briley on to Vernon by train the next day.[66] *Spring cattle roundups are now underway in the Panhandle. Good rains seem to have ended the drought.]*

MAY 22, 1887 SUNDAY MORNING IN QUANAH

Cloudy and looks like it will rain. I must rest a while and go up Town. Well this has been a warm day. Miss Moneta Westmorland came up this evening. She looks sweet and lovely.

MAY 23, 1887 MONDAY MORNING QUANAH

Another warm morning and a little cloudy. A goodeal of wind last night but no rain. Well this has been another warm day and I feel like going to bed, so good night diary. Oh before I forget we put up a new tent this evening. And I think we will have a plesant sleep to night. And I got my new barrel for my revolver this evening and a new scabbard.

[The '87 winds shredded the older tents, so a snug new canvas tent supplied by a stingy state was something to celebrate. Texas Rangers were fond of a seven-inch barrel Colt .45, a fairly devastating weapon.]

MAY 24, 1887 TUESDAY MORNING QUANAH

Nice and cool this morning but expect it will get as warm as h— before night. Well this has been another hot day. Bob Lervin broke a billiard Q over lip to night and Dennis [Peale] arrested him. He also arrested a man for whipping his woman. I met Sam Platt to day.

[Pool hall fights and spousal abuse calls seem to form the routine of police work then and now. With the passing of horse-culture, the prevalent 1880s cultural form of directed abuse—the use of whips—may have altered to fists. Note A. T.'s reticence in writing (or presumably pronouncing) "hell."

Sam M. Platt was another of the doughty Platt brothers who became Texas Rangers. Captain Lee Hall thought Sam Platt was one of the best rangers who served under him in the Special State Police in the latter 1870s. Sam Platt, Sam McMurry, John McNelly, and G. W. Arrington rode together under Captains Hall and Oglesby. They saw a number of hot actions in the feuds, the Nueces Strip, and the border troubles.[67] *Sam Platt joined Company B and served under McMurry with distinction, rising to sergeant then lieutenant by 1885.*[68] *He resigned from the Frontier Battalion in mid-1886, but Sam loved to visit his brother and old friends. He was a favorite guest of the Company B camp.]*

MAY 25, 1887 WEDNESDAY MORNING QUANAH

Cool and Plesant when we got up but it is getting warm now. Greens Hurd to day. He has bought a new Blackening Brush and Blacking and is giving his Boots a shine. Well I have put us a carpet down and now I must go to Town. I met with old Uncle Pud [Pood] and he had a knife. A barlow and the largest one I ever saw. He has had it ever since 1848. This is my night to stay at camp. I must go to bed as tomarrow is my Hurd day.

MAY 26, 1887 THURSDAY MORNING QUANAH

This morning is warm and close. Very sultry and I think it will rain sure soon. I got breakfast this morning myself and now I must go saddle my Horse and go on hurd.

MAY 27, 1887 FRIDAY MORNING IN WILBARGER CO.

This is a very cloudy and warm morning. It rained like rip last night. We got orders yesterday evening to get up the Horses and get ready for a scout. So we started a little after dark and the rain came on us between Chillicothe and Vernon. And oh, how it did rain. Green, Price, Peal, Jno Plat, and I and the rifles went on the scout. We were met by three men at Pease River to take us in to Vernon. And there we got McDonnell and Sam Plat. We went and rounded up Spencers house and got Jim Lyons. But not the men we expected to get. We then went up Plum Creek and eat Breakfast, and went and rounded up another house on Beever Creek, and eat dinner on Beever about 3 oclock. After sleeping about two hours then we went up Beever about 6 miles and then back to [Vernon]. We got there about 10 oclock. To bed then I went.

[Sergeant McNelly and five boys move out suddenly, riding east through the monsoon night to gather at Vernon, railroad county seat of Wilbarger County. Bill McDonald is waiting for them there. He cannot resist joining a manhunt for horse thieves, if not trying to lead it. Sam Platt, ex-ranger of Company B, rides in part for the pleasure of his brothers' company.

They launch a lengthy hunt late at night, ride all over Wilbarger County, and strike at early dawn. "Rounding up" a house was best done as an applied art, not an act of terrorism. Dawn arrests are still popular with state and federal lawmen for reasons well known to the 1880s rangers. Despite the element of surprise and two roundups, they only bagged the unfortunate Jim Lyon (charged with "failing to discharge his duty as an officer") at the Spencer place. Beaver Creek drains the southern portion of Wilbarger County.]

MAY 28, 1887 SATURDAY MORNING IN VERNON

Cloudy this morning. Had a good rain last night again. Well we eat breakfast at the commercial and will start for Quanah. I met old Dr Kuyekendall and his son, Osker, at the Hotel this morning, on the River waiting for the [Illegible]. We had to go before the Grand Jury this morning before we left Vernon. Spencer came and swore we were all drunk and one down. Well we got to Quanah this evening at sundown. We came from Pease River since 2 oclock 25 miles. Found Brad[bury] and Furman at home. Good night.

[Apparently Mr. Spencer objected to the ranger search and seizure of Jim Lyon at his house, swearing that the fatigued rangers were "all drunk and one down." Spencer is no parson himself. His sworn statement sounds like a typical spurious charge against the law, was treated as such, and undoubtedly was—except for one little nagging point. In a later entry Abner Miller innocently notes rangers and local lawmen sharing some liquid courage before setting out on another night scout. Cold rain, riding all night, and looking for dangerous men might just make some lawmen want a little medicinal nip or two.]

MAY 29, 1887 SUNDAY MORNING IN QUANAH 87

Back again. And how long will we stay? Well we have a nice morning. Tom Plat has gon west to day with John Hammond and McDonald after some witnesses. I will hurd to day again. I will go out and get Old George and herd on him if I can get him. Well its now after 4 oclock and I have just eat dinner. I have Old George and he makes a good saddle mule. This will do for this time as I must go. I got a letter from Lonie [Miller] yesterday as I got home. I met Riley Wheat in Town to night and Bob Wilkinson. Well I will go to bed as its now 10 oclock.

[Bill McDonald keeps busy on Sunday. J. G. Ayers recalled later in life a distant Sunday morning when he and other pioneers had gathered—beneath a tree—for a worship service. McDonald and some Texas Rangers came riding up hard to the group. A brusque McDonald pointedly inquired about the nature of the gathering. Mr. Ayers "told him they were fixing to have church and asked if they [the Company B rangers] would join them." Ayers recalled that Bill McDonald "threw his bridle reins down on the ground, got a song book and led the singing."[69]

Rangers got to know pack mules like Old George quite well. Mules were indispensable to the operations of Company B in the field. They carried the camp tinware, making such a clatter that McDonald claimed the noise could be used to make a pack-mule charge into an outlaw camp. As Bill Jess explained, "That infernal racket seemed to jar the nerve of a criminal. . . ."[70]]

MAY 30, 1887 MONDAY MORNING IN QUANAH

A real nice and clear morning. I hope we will have a nice day. Green went down towards Vernon to day. And Tom Plat went West yesterday. John

Bland and John Coltharp came over to day. We had to arrest Dug Melton to day. He was drunk.

[May 30, 1887, is the fatidic date for Edward Bellamy's futuristic novel, Looking Backward 2000–1887. *On this day the novel's narrator, the class-conscious Julian West, falls into a 113-year-long trance. West regains consciousness on September 10, 2000, finding himself a stranger in a very different world—a metaphor for most 1880s Americans then leaving independent lifeways and entering the new world order of corporations, industry, and urbanization.*

"The thirtieth day of May, 1887, fell on a Monday," Bellamy began in chapter 2. "It was one of the annual holidays of the nation in the latter third of the nineteenth century, being set apart under the name of Decoration Day, for doing honor to the memory of the soldiers of the North who took part in the war for the preservation of the union of the States.

At dinner that evening conversation centered on the biggest social issues facing the United States—economic disparities, layoffs and labor strife, and urban violence.

"It was agreed that affairs were going from bad to worse very fast," Julian West related, "and that there was no telling what we should come to soon."[71]]

MAY 31, 1887 TUESDAY MORNING IN QUANAH

Another nice morning. After a good rain last night. Oh how the grass is growing. It is as fine as I ever saw. Well its night now and I have stayed at camp all day. I slep all evening. The last day of May. Where shall I be at this time next year? I am well and harty now. And hope I may be this time next year. I am in Henrys Saloon. The boys are all Playing Dominoes.

[Private Miller rises late, contemplates spring verdure, and ponders his fate. His fellow rangers socialize over dominoes in Dutch Henry's Saloon. What do they think of him for keeping a diary?]

JUNE 1, 1887 WEDNESDAY MORNING QUANAH 1887

Oh such a nice morning. Clear and cool and plesant. Everything around seems so lovely. The Pasenger train has just left. Well I must go up Town. Well we drawed our pay to day—$90.00 and I payed W. R. Wheat what I owed him. $16.40 the ballance on my Horse. I was around with Frank Spoon to night awhile. So I must go and go to bed.

[With his first big paycheck Private Miller pays local rancher W. R. Wheat the balance on his ranger mount. What will he do with the rest of his pay?]

JUNE 2, 1887 THURSDAY MORNING IN QUANAH

Another nice clear and warm morning. It was cool when we got up but is getting very sultry now at 10 oclock. Well the boys are all gone to Town and I must go.

I loned to Tom Platt $25.00 Twenty Five Dollars this evening. Untill next Payday or untill I need it. If he should quit before that time he is to pay me then. And when he pays me I will make a Note of it on this Page. Well everything has went on all OK to night and I will go to bed.

[The Texas Rangers were paid quarterly: March 1, June 1, September 1, and December 1. Privates got $30 a month; the captain earned a respectable $100 a month.[72] *The bonds between some Rangers might include small loans shortly after payday. Tom Platt was a good risk for such a loan, coming as he did from a solid family of Texas Rangers. Or maybe his brothers had already turned him down, and he needed a fresh face.]*

JUNE 3, 1887 FRIDAY MORNING QUANAH

Nice and clear this morning but a little warm. I will not go up Town before noon. So I will take a nap. Well I have been to Town this evening and everything went all OK.

JUNE 4, 1887 SATURDAY MORNING QUANAH

Well we have a nice morning after such a good rain yesterday evening. I had another talk with old man Taylor. He said two men passed his house this morning, inquiring the way to Greer Co. and one had a white handle Pistol. Well I slep most all evening and must go up and stir around a little. I had a talk with Sy Smith to night. He told me that Mr. Fry had indicted Lee Hickman and another man for steeling his cattle. This man was cutting the cattle for Lee Hickman.

[Talk is turning to Greer County again. Lee Hickman lived northeast of Mangum near the border with the Indian Territory. The rangers had already visited him twice that spring to pick up suspected rustlers.]

JUNE 5, 1887 SUNDAY MORNING QUANAH

This is a nice morning. I have got up and got the breakfast and fed the Horses. I must go to the Hurd as its my Hurd day. I started to camp this evening at 6 oclock. And a heavy cloud caught me just as I got there, but not much rain. Nothing more.

JUNE 6, 1887 MONDAY MORNING QUANAH TEX

Cool and plesant. Clouds flying all around. I got a letter from Thomas [Miller] last evening from California. He is in San Diego, Cal. Well we had a good rain this evening again. How the grass does grow. Tom got a telegram from Monell at or near Austin and he wants to send it to Mangum, Greer Co. to Neel Monell right away. Think he got a Negro to go. I answered Thomases letter and wrote Ed Conell to night. So Good night Diary.

JUNE 7, 1887 TUESDAY MORNING QUANAH

Cloudy and warm this morning. I think it will rain soon. Think John Platt is liable to get wet this evening as it's his hurd day. Well I must go up Town and get the shoes pulled off of my Horse. Well I am going over to Margaret this evening and see what changes over there. Well I got to Margaret about 5 ½ oclock. I found [Private] Furman there. He had went out to help attach some cattle of Jim Oats. Found everything lively as could be expected to. Crops fine and people in Good Spirits.

[On his days off A. T. is drawn to the community of Margaret. Although he does not know it yet, he is destined to settle near these good folks for over two decades.]

JUNE 8, 1887 WEDNESDAY MORNING MARGARET

Nice morning except its warm. Some clouds around. I am afraid it will rain before I get back to Quanah. I must go out and see Mr Ayres and Moore run the new reeper on Wesleys Wheat. Oh what a nice crop of wheat, oats, corne, millet, sorgrum, Johnson Grass, rye, and alfalfa that Wesley has. It is beautiful. He also has new PO [Post Office] Boxes and they show up so nice. John Cox is lying at Mr Wesleys with Pneumonia and George Burk is at old man Pruwitts up in Cottle Co. Well I must go back to Quanah this evening and I am afraid it will rain on me from the looks of the cloud now.

Well I got in camp at a little after Sundown and did not get wet. I passed Scy Smith with a hurd of cattle. Going to Dakota.

[John Wesley was not only a town promoter but also a master farmer. His Margaret fields amounted to a demonstration farm on the viability of traditional agriculture for the new area. After the "Pease City" promotion soured, he set out to build the new town of Margaret with sincere, practical, and demonstrative deliberation. After the disastrous drought of '86, the better spring rains

of '87 nourished Wesley's crops, and built the confidence of the young community. Wesley's 1887 planting of Johnson grass was consistent with the plant's Victorian use as a novel forage crop, another African sorghum. Now considered a damaging and costly invasive species, Johnson grass was then a valued component of the ecological transformation underway.

Abner's friend George Burke is off to Cottle County. His visit to Mr. Prewitt's place may not be all business, as he will marry the old man's daughter a little over a year later. "Mr. Ayres" or Nathaniel John Ayers was another 1887 pioneer of Hardeman County. Originally from Georgia, he settled his family on a place about three miles east of the county seat. The Ayers children grew up in the Old Margaret community, attending school in the jailhouse and going to church in a brush arbor on the north side of the jail—a scant distance between heaven and hell. Jesse William Moore was another Collin County pioneer farmer.[73]

"Scy" or Cy Smith was part of the declining culture of transhumance, a cattle drover in the shadow of railroad freight cars. Cowboys continued to trail herds to distant ranges, but the difficulties and costs soon ended the trail drive.]

JUNE 9, 1887 THURSDAY MORNING QUANAH

Warm and cloudy this morning. I have fed and got the most of the Breakfast this morning. Price will make a big pot of soop so I will not go up Town before noon.

Well we had another good rain this evening. Sterling Buster and two of his sisters came up on the train this evening. Bradbury and Furman has gone fishing to day on Groesbeck Creek. Well its time I go to bed as I have a big Boil under my arme. We had a nice mess of fish for supper.

[One cannot help noticing that the rangers of Company B are catching far more unarmed fish from Groesbeck Creek than they are armed members of the Brooken gang. But camp meals were often monotonous, and so the thought of a slow simmered soup and a fresh mess of fried perch for supper was enough to enliven the spirits for all. Meal times were also prime centers of sociability, a gathering and a communion of sorts. Captain McMurry left the previous day for Central Texas to track down a supposed train robber.]

JUNE 10, 1887 FRIDAY MORNING QUANAH

Another warm and cloudy morning. I think it will rain to day again. Well I will go up Town now and see what is going on. And its nearly elevin oclock Well this day is passed and gone. And it will be remembered. A little shooting affray came up this evening, or rather noon between a

White man and a Negro—Ben Tuck [Tutt] and Negro Dug. Ben got in only one shot and Dug 5 or 6. Nothing hurt but a good many scared. Green and I was about first to the House. Well we all got there about the same time except the [Illegible] and he did not get there at all.

[This eyewitness account of an interracial "shooting affray" creates more questions than it answers. We do not know why Ben Tutt and Bob Douglas (Negro Dug) draw their pistols. The flurry of shots naturally brings the rangers on a run to the scene. Jim Green and A. T. Miller arrive early at the house. The neighborhood is in panic, with frightened residents all around—"a good many scared," in his laconic expression. While it is not clear what precipitated the exchange of gunfire, it seems clear the rangers exercise colorblind justice: Private Green arrests Bob Douglas and Private Platt arrests Ben Tutt. Both men are charged with "Assault to murder" and thrown in jail. Bob Douglas makes bond on Monday, June 13. Ben Tutt will make bond as well.[74] They will go to court in the fall.]

JUNE 11, 1887 SATURDAY MORNING QUANAH

We had a nice little rain last night and it is cool and cloudy this morning and very plesant. Well I must go up Town and see whats going on. Green got breakfast and fed this morning. He is gone up Town now. Well this day has passed off quiet. Our new Constable was in Town this evening and gave every body orders to close up Tomarrow. His name is Akin. The clouds were very threatening this evening, but no rain here more than a sprinkle.

JUNE 12, 1887 SUNDAY MORNING - QUANAH

Cloudy and warm and looks as we will have some rain this evening. McDonnell went off somewhere to day and got Tom's winchester. Well I went to church this evening at 4 and at night and we had a nice talk. McDonald came back about 3 oclock. He found only one hide cut up. Price got a letter from Grude Britton telling him that Capt had Enlistd him in the company. I got a letter this evening from T. A. Williams saying to send the price of my boots by Registered Mail and he would forward the boots. But I did not do so and am not liable to before I get the boots. The business Houses kept shut to day.

[The contrast in temperaments between Private Miller and Deputy McDonald is apparent. It is a fine Sunday. It is the monsoon season in the Rolling Plains, when brilliant evening storms sweep over the landscape. A. T. prefers the genteel sociability of church and camp. Bill McDonald, on the other hand,

prefers to borrow a Winchester rifle from Tom Plat and go manhunting on the Lord's day. Is he an avenging angel? He finds one hide with the tell-tale brand cut away. McDonald excelled at the detection of altered brands and hides, approaching it as a deductive challenge to his mind.

The assertion of authority is furthered by Constable Akin's closure of the "business Houses" that Sunday, especially the dance halls and saloons. Akin made the announcement on Saturday, and, sure enough, the owners went along with him the next morning. The loose ways of the town are now being choked off by the Victorians—specifically through greater government intervention. It is the order behind law and order that now merits attention.]

JUNE 13, 1887 MONDAY MORNING QUANAH

A nice cool morning but cloudy. This is my hurd day and I must go and see the Horses and put some ointment on Johnys horse as he got down last night and cut himself right bad. Well everything all OK to day. Negro Dug got out on bond to day. (I believe the Brookin Gang were in Town to night from all manners. We all was on the wach untill 9 oclock, but no catch-Em.) I Got Two Hawk eggs this evening. They are about the size of a hens egg. The first I ever saw.

[A big payroll is headed to Quanah. Rumors of the Brooken gang are starting to percolate again. The rangers show some extra vigilance and interest.]

JUNE 14, 1887 TUESDAY MORNING QUANAH

A nice morning. We got up late as we went to bed late last night. I will not go up Town untill after noon. Well I am about ready to go up Town now. It's about 9 oclock and is very warm indeed. The pay train came up to day 14th. McDonald arrested Porter Drace to night and Mr Furman arrested Harry Scott and hit him across the head with his six shooter. There were several horses drove away last night. The Brookin Gang were run last Sunday and one horse killed. Three of them and four officers.

[Bill McDonald is really getting into his work now, although it involves arresting well-known locals and friends of A. T. like the bon vivant Porter Drace. The exuberant Drace keeps getting in trouble, and now there is nothing left to do but ride to Margaret for a courthouse trial. Because he knew virtually the entire community there, he could expect at least to be judged by sympathetic peers.

Would Private Furman's pistol-whipping of citizen Harry Scott constitute police brutality today? Or was violence responding to violence? Scott was thrown into jail on a charge of aggravated assault and battery. Captain Sam "Soft Voice" McMurry seems more distant, less involved, and certainly less thirsting for local action. He traveled a lot. He had gone to Taylor in Williamson County looking for a man named Barnes, suspected in a recent robbery of the Fort Worth & Denver Railroad. The Taylor sheriff assured him that the suspect was in Travis County, so Captain McMurry went to Austin, got Sheriff Hornesby's support, and after several days of hard riding brought in the suspect. All this work came to naught when the critical witness, "a passenger who was on the train[,] failed to identify Barnes as the proper party."[75]

In McMurry's absence Bill McDonald is beginning to dominate the town, not the captain. In another dramatic episode, the Brookens and a gang associate escape and outrun other lawmen, apparently on Sunday June 12. It was a narrow escape for the fugitives.]

JUNE 15, 1887 WEDNESDAY MORNING QUANAH

Another nice morning. I think it will be a nice day to day. McDonald took Porter Drace over to Margaret to day and came back. News came in tonight that a mesenger was on the way here for us to go out near the line of New Mexico and get some men. Eight thieves were steeling Horses, and they sent word to the Sheriff where they were and that they would not be arrested. Suppose we will have to go when Capt gets Home.

JUNE 16, 1887 THURSDAY MORNING QUANAH

Another nice morning, a little windy. Green and I got breakfast and now I must go and get my Horse shewed. For we are liable to have to go at any time.

Mr Akin our new constable arrested about four men for getting drunk this evening. Ones fine was $7.55 and costs altogether.

[A night's spree thus cost a week's pay.]

JUNE 17, 1887 FRIDAY MORNING QUANAH

Plesant morning but a little cloudy. Well we got our Photographs last night and I want to send them off to day. $8.00 for 24. He came down as he got the negative broken. He was to charge $12.00. Tom Plat was sick last night but is better this morning. Capt got home this evening. I wrote a letter to Thomas and one to Lonie to day. Old man Wilson and wife came down to camp this evening. He has a young and good looking wife.

JUNE 18, 1887 SATURDAY MORNING QUANAH

Another nice and clear morning. I think we will have some dry weather now. Furmans Hurd day. Well I believe I will go up Town. This has been a nice day but warm. Mr [Marshall] Hankins came in on the train this evening. I got a card from T. A. Williams saying he would make and send my boots when ever I write for them.

[The speed, comfort, and connections of the railroad are challenging the old order of Hardeman County. County Attorney Hankins and other officials have to go to Quanah anyway now. Why not move the county business there as well?]

JUNE 19, 1887 SUNDAY MORNING QUANAH

Nice and clear this morning but warm. Price started for Weatherford this morning to be gone three days. Grude Britton came up this evening. He enlisted at Ft Worth last week.

[A new recruit arrived for Company B, Frontier Battalion. Captain Sam McMurry carefully interviewed and enlisted James Magruder "Grude" Britton during one of his trips back east. The camp knew he was coming from Britton's letter to Sterling Price, noted in the diary on June 12. A new recruit was sure to be made welcome, although the boys loved to josh and create practical jokes as well. Grude Britton will prove to be an outstanding Texas Ranger.]

JUNE 20, 1887 MONDAY MORNING QUANAH

Another clear and nice morning. My Hurd day to day. I have helped to get Breakfast and will go and see where my Horses are. I will go up to Town when I eat my dinner and see Logan and Smith as they are in Town. George Brandt is in Town to night and says Johnie is getting along all OK. McDonald pulled all the Prostitutes to day and made them pay a fine.

[Quanah probably has three or four houses of ill repute with perhaps a score of "dance hall women" or "soiled doves," as the expression went.[76] *McDonald was just the kind of deputy sheriff to "pull" all the prostitutes as part of a sudden but not entirely unexpected routine. It is likely that they were charged with vagrancy.*[77] *Revenues were thus shared with the local government, and the law asserted its ultimate authority. Is it a coincidence that McDonald "pulled" the courtesans on a Monday, that is, just after a weekend of peak earnings following the pay train and big railroad payroll mentioned on June 14? Share and share alike.*

Unlike Mobeetie (soldiers) and Tascosa (cowboys), Quanah's bagnios served the railroad community. One of the few pioneers to write of the early railroad-town prostitutes was Judge James D. Hamlin of Amarillo. Judge Hamlin's candid memoirs noted that many were well-mannered women, who for one reason or another were working their way through a difficult life. Putting a positive spin on their plight, he reported: "I knew a number of men of different stations of life who married girls of the red-light district. In most cases they made good and faithful wives. There seemed to be a tendency for the most sensitive prostitutes, after enduring a season of the rudeness and vulgarity which invariably accompanied commercial promiscuity, to eagerly accept a proposal which offered monogamy and security."[78]

Judge Hamlin also provides some background to railroad-town prostitutes in his affectionate memoir of the pseudonymous "Ella Hill," a prominent madam of 1890s Amarillo. In straitened circumstances as a young woman in the '80s, Ella Hill placed her two children with a respectable couple in Fort Worth. She set out for Henrietta where she got a job as a railroad-town cafe waitress. As the Fort Worth & Denver Railroad advanced westward, she moved with it as a waitress. Somewhere in or beyond Wichita Falls her one-quarter Cherokee blood and attractive features made her too popular. Her career altered, and she became a prostitute in new towns like Quanah. As she advanced economically, it was said Ella Hill dispatched sufficient funds to ensure that her children were well educated and launched on a respectable course in life.[79]*]*

JUNE 21, 1887 TUESDAY MORNING QUANAH

Another beautifull morning. Dennis is on Hurd duty to day. We had a good dinner to day. Had milk, butter, potatoes, onions, ham, and good bread &c. I gave [Marshall] Hankins a letter and some bur seeds for Mrs Wesley to day. Capt [McMurry] went to Henrietta this morning and think he will come home to night. Bradberry and Furman went out to the Front this evening and Tom Platt will go Tomarrow. Two train loads of cattle came in from the East to day. Dr Sumpter gave me two nice shirts to day.

[Privates Bradbury and Furman catch the next train to the end of the track, "the Front," where trouble is brewing.]

JUNE 22, 1887 WEDNESDAY MORNING QUANAH

Nice and clear but warm this morning. Well I must go up Town and see whats going on. John Platt hurds to day on Old George. Well the longest day in the year is gone and we have a nice cool night. But it's cloudy and threatening rain. John Davidson and his gang is on the war path to night. I bought me a new valice this evening for $2.50.

[Despite Company B's spring roundup of outlaws and reprobates, the forces of disorder blow strong as summer begins. The railroad contractors are con-

Figure 9. Street scene in Quanah, Ft. W. & D. C. R. R. From Texas Live Stock Journal *(Oct., 1887).*

tributing to the workload. Worried about labor unrest and a threatening crowd in Tent City, Morgan Jones and Dan Carey had requested McMurry's help on June 20. He dispatched a detachment of rangers to the "Front" on the 21st, "there being a hard gang of thieves & cut-throats hanging around the saloons."[80]

On the longest day of the year Private Miller hears the distant thunder of a drunken "warpath," as Deputy John Davidson, brother Sid Davidson, and their rowdy friends drink with abandon in the Quanah saloons. The Davidsons drink with relief. The law rides for the Brookens, not them—and Bill and Bood are still free. But this night's spree will cost Deputy Davidson of Wilbarger County more than the mere price of whiskey. It will cost him his honor.]

Chapter 3

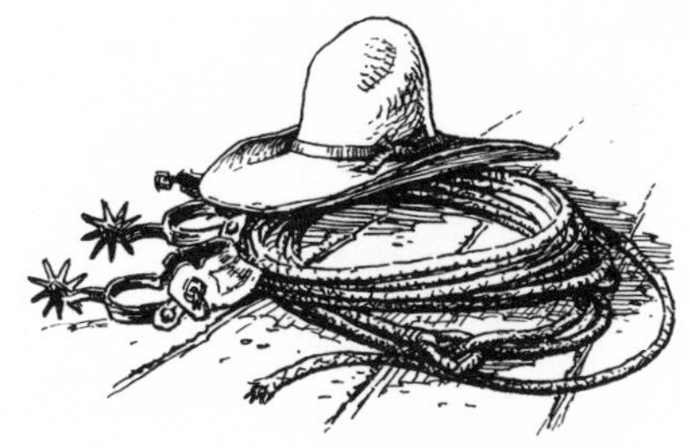

Distant Thunder

SUMMER OF 1887

I found it impossible to convince my friends that [Texas Ranger] camp life could be attractive, and they could not understand how I could be content to live in a tent . . . Living close to nature had its pleasures and benefits that far outweighed the privations.

—*Mrs. Lou Conway Roberts,* A Woman's Reminiscences of Six Years in Camp with the Texas Rangers

Not so many years ago the Pan-handle was distinctly a world apart, and a new one. With No-man's Land on the north, Indian Territory on the east and New Mexico on the west, civilization could only come from the south, and it did not come very fast.

—*Albert Bigelow Paine,* Captain Bill McDonald, Texas Ranger

The building of the pioneering Fort Worth & Denver City Railroad and the rival Atchison, Topeka & Santa Fe Railroad was the most important factor in developing the Texas Panhandle, North Rolling Plains, and Southwest Oklahoma in the late 1880s. Western peace officers were central for the security of capitalists financing and managing these transport and commerce corridors. One of the primary missions of Company B was to be the locomotive of justice, to implement the rule of law along the FW&DC right-of-way. The Texas Ranger force was also establishing a reputation as strikebreakers. The very appearance of armed rangers patrolling company business was a form of intimidation to "dynamiters and anarchists" (in the words of Company B's later Sergeant W. J. L. Sullivan), that is, any workers contemplating labor strife. Captain McMurry regularly dispatched trusted men up to "the Front" just to keep an eye on things; he also responded with alacrity to the special requests of railroad officials.

"The Front" was the current railhead of the Fort Worth & Denver City Railroad. This noisy industrial community, largely on wheels, had laid track across most of the Rolling Plains by 1886.[1] *Continuing its pattern of corporate economic conquest, FW&DC townsite developer Robert Montgomery had ignored the existing '86 Hardeman County hamlet called Quanah. He planned instead to move the raw, rude town to his company's right-of-way. He did this principally by the rule of law, following an obscure legal feint that qualified a male voter anyplace in the county where his laundry was done for six consecutive weeks. Naturally in October and November of 1886 railroad men all had their laundry washed at Montgomery's townsite of Quanah. Their votes swamped the called election and the railroad townsite of Quanah prevailed.*[2] *Montgomery sold the first Quanah town lots on December 1, 1886, although company officials did not accept the finished line to Quanah, at Milepost 193.3 from Fort Worth, until February 1, 1887.*

The chief executive of the FW&DC Railroad made the decisions to penetrate the rest of the Panhandle hinterland beyond Quanah in late 1886. On November 22, 1886, the Welsh-born Fort Worth capitalist Morgan Jones signed an important contract with the newly organized Panhandle Construction Company, the construction firm headed by the mighty Grenville M. Dodge. This contract provided for the further construction of a railroad from Milepost 200 (some six miles west of Quanah) northwest across the Panhandle to the distant Canadian River in Oldham County. Dodge's Panhandle Construction Company would earn $16,000 in bonds and $20,000 in stock for each mile of accepted track.[3] *By June of 1887 the tracklayers were deep into the Panhandle, requiring Company B rangers to ride long shuttle trains to the Front.*

The progress of the railroad across the plains and the sweeping changes in social geography that accompanied its steel rails are amply documented in the Miller diaries and "Monthly Reports" filed by Captain McMurry. The FW&DC Railroad was the corporate inheritor of the legendary rail wars between northern and southern capital, each side poised to exploit or block the potentially rich traffic and colonization of the Texas Panhandle. An acute spate of labor strife from the Knights of Labor in 1885, directed largely against Jay Gould's Texas & Pacific line, caused great anxiety among other railroad exec-

utives. The presence of Company B at the Front was thus a show of state force to intimidate immoderate organized labor or angry local citizens confronted with the legal but ruthless ways of monopoly capitalism. Captain S. A. McMurry had an instinctive bias against agitatory labor and in favor of management. He was not a ranger captain for nothing.

The railroad advanced in tightly coordinated stages. Mysterious surveyors and railroad officials first appeared to examine and plot the right-of-way. Next Dan Carey's grading crews arrived to rough out the surveyed line, usually many miles in advance of the railhead itself. Behind Carey's mules and men were the noisy mechanical pile-drivers and gangs of tracklayers. The latter lived in a small rolling city of their own. Dormitory and kitchen cars provided shelter and food. Nearby was "Tent City"—the convenient tent camps and hovels that provided more shelter, periodic drink, and even some of the ruder social pleasures. With adequate supplies on hand, experienced men could lay a mile of steel rails a day. But the work was brutal as the summer heat intensified toward its August peak.

Summer of 1887

JUNE 23, 1887 — THURSDAY MORNING QUANAH

A nice morning again. This is Grude Brittons first day on Hurd. Well I understand John Davidson knocked a young man down with his Sixshooter last night. Tom and Capt got in to night and Tom and I have to go back tomarrow and take Brad[bury']s and Furmans Horses. McDonald and wife [Rhoda] got in this evening.

[Deputy Davidson of Vernon had been "on the warpath" in Quanah saloons, the diarist noted in his previous entry. It is not clear if the deputy considered himself to be on or off-duty because he had a gun. At some point this bully used his weapon to pistol-whip a youthful patron.

Captain McMurry returns to Quanah after assessing for himself the trouble at the end of the track. It is nothing very serious, but requires watching. He dispatches Tom Platt and Abner Miller to the Front.]

JUNE 24, 1887 — FRIDAY MORNING QUANAH

Another nice morning. We got up this morning at 4 oclock to go to the Front. Well, we got out at the Boarding car at about 12 or 1 oclock and found the boys there. And a lot of Drunk Irish. We had a good dinner and stayed around all evening, and got supper and came back to night. We got

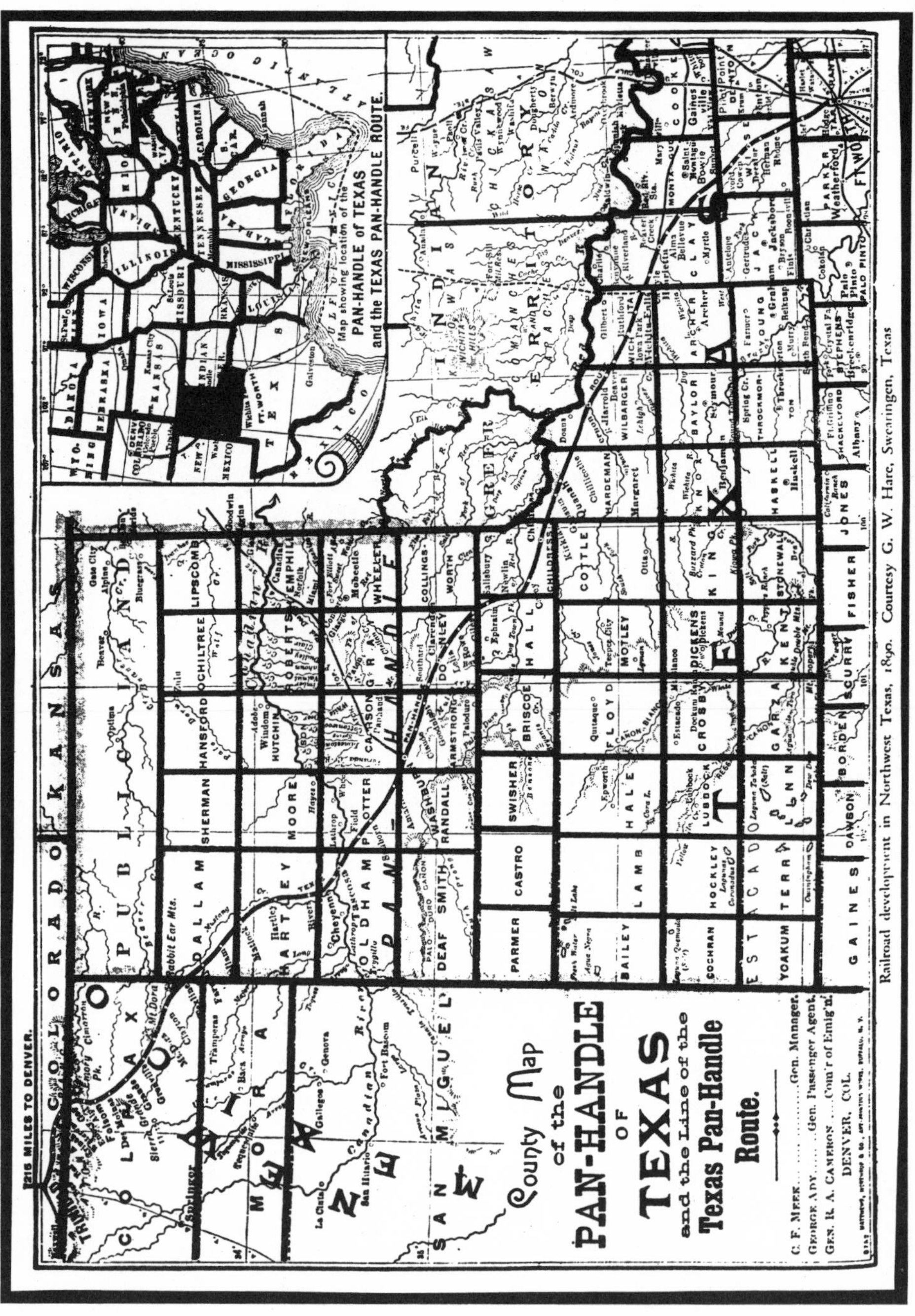

Map 3. Texas Pan-Handle Route. Fort Worth & Denver City Railroad Map, 1887. Courtesy Lewis Buttery, Lampasas, Texas

in about 12. Dr Christen road in the car with me from Henry to Red River. He was going to pull some teeth for Mrs Ashburn. I saw a little file out at the Boarding car to day. When we left it was raining out at the Front.

[Hundreds of men labored at the Front, the FW&DC railhead on the plains. The Front had crossed the Red River and was nearing Clarendon. Nearby was the mobile village called "Tent City," a large canvas community that periodically relocated to keep abreast with the men working on railroad. Tent City had a vigorous life, a communal spirit, and a variety of denizens. A large number of women and children also lived in "Tent City," sharing the toil, the '87 winds and rains, the relocation caravans, and the occupational risks.[4] *The work was hard at the Front, as was the drinking. Some drinkers were locked up for a spell at the Front, apparently in an FW&DC boxcar, which the rangers maintained as a temporary jail. This explains Miller's professional interest in spying—and presumably confiscating—a "little file," a useful instrument for a breakout attempt.]*

JUNE 25, 1887 SATURDAY MORNING QUANAH

Another clear and warm morning. Well I got in in time to Hurd to day and its time I am going out. I understand Coldwell arrested John Davidson in Vernon yesterday evening and brought him back to Quanah for striking those boys with his Pistol night before last. Davidson was put under $500 Dollar bond. And Jimmie [Davidson] was arrested for taking their money. Well this has been a nice hot day. I fear the Hot winds is going to get in. I met Joe Beverly in Town to night. John Hammond came in this evening. Price sais Gov. Ross has issued a proclamation ordering Capt McMurrays company to Vernon.

[While on his liquid "warpath" in Quanah, Deputy John Davidson of Vernon apparently pistol-whipped several young thrill-seekers. He has crossed a line this time. His brother Jimmie Davidson allegedly relieved the unfortunate youths of their cash. Deputy Pink Coldwell of Hardeman County travels over to Vernon, arrests Deputy John Davidson, and hauls him back to Quanah by train. This arrest is notice served that adjacent officers of the law are not going to tolerate this kind of thuggish behavior.]

JUNE 26, 1887 SUNDAY MORNING QUANAH

Another clear and hot morning. I got breakfast this morning. No one to eat with me but L. Carr. Well it clouded up about 10 oclock and looked very much like it would rain, but not much apperrance to night. Well I did not go up Town untill night. I had to take a sleep this evening.

JUNE 27, 1887 MONDAY MORNING QUANAH

Clear and Plesant this morning. Oh how I would like to se a good rain. Everthing is beginning to need it very much. Well everything has went off all OK to day. John Darnell and Billie Key was about to have a fus last night. John DeBerry came in last night from Margarett with [Attorney Marshall M.] Hankins and his wife. It clouded up to day and to night but no rain.

[DeBerry had last been seen selling dry goods for Wood & Dixon at the railroad grader's camp near Buck Spring in Donley County.]

JUNE 28, 1887 TUESDAY MORNING QUANAH

Well its now about 12 oclock and is very warm and cloudy. Hope it will rain. This morning was nice and cool. Justice court is to day. Jimmie Davidson [is in court] for taking those young mens money. And John Davidson for hitting them. Dont know how they will come out yet. Well the [Davidson] Trial has been going on all day and is not done yet.

I met Rollie Vaughn and Jones. To night for the first in a long time. Said they were going to open up the mines again on a small scale. Got a letter from Ed Hay and one from S. S. Steele. Telling me of a good many deaths, Lyla Deaton among the rest.

JUNE 29, 1887 WEDNESDAY MORNING QUANAH

Another clear and warm morning. No hope or prospects of rain. Well theres a large circle around the moon to night and I hope it will rain soon. John Davidson was bound over to District court under 200 Dollar bond I was told to night.

[Therefore Deputy John Davidson of Vernon could not clear himself in Quanah's court of the charge against him. After hearing the testimony, the justice of the peace felt obliged to bound him over for district trial. At the same time the J. P. helpfully reduced his bond to a more manageable figure. Davidson's brother Sid has his own legal troubles. Inevitably, Deputy John Davidson of Wilbarger County will have to choose between his new career as a law officer and his old friends who had followed other career paths. Around the end of June Davidson decided to give up his old friends. Telling the story to his biographer years later, McDonald said that Deputy Davidson quietly contacted him. Davidson offered insider information on the Brooken gang dugout-hideout

deep in the Wichita Brakes. Bill and Bood would be there, he assured McDonald. In return, John Davidson demanded that the indictments against him be dismissed.[5] *McDonald and Sheriff Barker of Wilbarger County quietly began to make some arrangements.]*

JUNE 30, 1887 THURSDAY MORNING QUANAH

Cloudy and looks like it may rain. Oh how I hope it will. I dont believe I'll go to Town this morning. But stay and shave and read some. Well we had a fine rain this evening and the glad harts it did make. John Coltharp came over to day. And Billie Bales of Seymour. John Coltharp sais there will be a Picnic on next Monday the 4th of July.

JULY 1, 1887 FRIDAY MORNING QUANAH/87

This is the first day of July and a plesant morning it is. Tom Platt and Grude Britton went out to the Front to day, and Capt [McMurry] I suppose. Well this has been a long day. I have not been well. My bowells is out of fix. Well I am good deal better to night and find the heat was up to 102 in the shade to day.

[The boys will draw routine assignments to the FW&DC Front during its advance across the plains. Dan Carey's crews were drawing near Clarendon now, although it was abundantly clear that they would bypass "Saint's Roost." As state peace officers entitled to operate beyond confining county lines, Texas Rangers were ideal for railroad security interests. Well-armed Tom and Grude rode out to the railhead on the convenient supply and freight work trains. They left their horses behind for A. T. to herd.]

JULY 2, 1887 SATURDAY MORNING QUANAH

Nice and clear this morning and I am glad of it as I have to Hurd to day. The horses hasnt been any trouble to me to day. A big crowd in Town to night. Louie the Night Watchman and I caught Two women under a box car to night, one watching her Husband to se if he went to the Notch house. Furman came down this evening from the Front.

[The "Notch House" was a brothel in Quanah's red-light area. A. T. and Louie must have wondered why two women were hiding under a boxcar. Who had more explaining to do at bedtime—husband or wife?]

JULY 3, 1887 SUNDAY MORNING QUANAH

Nice and cool this morning. And I know Dennis is glad for he is on hurd to day. Well the day has went off all right, but a little bussel to night. One man hit a couple of others and John Platt arrested him. But Platt let him go as he could not get the boos key. I went around to church a little while to night. A very good crowd out.

[The "boos key" is the skeleton key for the lock to the "caliboos," a distinctive Southwestern adoption of the Spanish term for jail—"calabozo." Apparently this assaulter walked free when the rangers could not locate the jail key.]

JULY 4, 1887 MONDAY MORNING QUANAH

Nice and cool this morning. A little cloudy. It rained good somewhere last night. Well who did I meet this morning but Mrs Hawkins and Mrs Minnie Latham. Who I havent saw in a long time. This day has passed and gone and everything went off nice. A nice Mother Hubbard ball at Carry Wilsons and a supper at Cunninghams, but I did not get to the supper. I got my money from Dr Anderson this evening and got me a pair of boots to night from Wood & Dixon at $6.00. A very good boot.

[The traditional July Fourth celebrations bring old friends to Quanah. A Mother Hubbard Ball was an inexpensive party thrown by lively folk with limited resources. Mart Cunningham's "supper" was our version of a party with lots of rich food and convivial company. An erased sentence follows this entry that notes, "A very Hard Wind storm came up to night but no rain."]

JULY 5, 1887 TUESDAY MORNING QUANAH

Another nice cool morning after a hard wind storm last night. But no rain except a sprinkle. Jim Allee was in Town yesterday and last night. I had a good talk with a young man from McKinney. He has some fine Saddles here for sale. The [saddles] is of Stovalls make and worth $40, 50, 60 Dollars apiece.

[These Stovall saddles are too expensive for a private, but a better-off cowman—in town after the July Fourth celebrations—might take the plunge.]

JULY 6, 1887 WEDNESDAY MORNING QUANAH

A very nice morning. This has been a very Hot Day. The heat has been to 108° to day. Billie Agely was in Town to day. Capt [McMurry] and Tom Platt came in this evening. I eat some fine cak to day that was baked at [Mart] Cunninghams.

JULY 7, 1887 THURSDAY MORNING QUANAH

We will have another hot day from the apperance now. Capt and [Jim] Green went to Vernon today. Dennis [Peale] has been garding Jo Littleton ever since night before last. He was arrested by a tilagram from Ft Worth. I have been on hurd to day as Green had to go to Vernon. Mr Crews comenced his Singing School last night here and has one at Margaret. I learned to day that Miss Bettie Crossland died and her grave is being dug today. Capt came back this evening but Green did not come.

[Singing schools were old but still popular entertainments in Texas. Parents enrolled their children, and young people signed up for the amusement and company. A traveling musician like Mr. Crews advertised in advance, arrived in a town with popular songs and sheet music, and demonstrated good cheer in the face of the musically challenged. He also performed, collected student fees, and conducted the locals in intensive singing lessons and demonstrations.]

JULY 8, 1887 FRIDAY MORNING QUANAH

Another clear and hot morning. We garded Joe Littleton last night. And the Sheriff and his Deputy took him to Ft. Worth this morning. They came up yesterday evening. Well this day has passed and gone.

JULY 9, 1887 SATURDAY MORNING QUANAH

Nice and cool this morning. I went up to the train to see that Jimmie Davidson did not com on the train as he is under bond. Mr and Mrs Wesley came over to day. She had some teeth drawn. Got one broke off. Green came up last night about 1 oclock. Capt and Jim Wilson had a few [angry] words last night. Dennis threw Jim down, then made the boys take him and put him to bed. Two of Cap Arringtons men came down from Clarendon to night and sais Cap came out all OK. The jurors did not stay out but a very short time. Green, Price, John Platt, Grude Britton, and John Hammond left to night on a scout. They went S. E. Sucess to them is my wishes. They have a beautiful night to start.

[Sheriff "Cap" Arrington's murder trial was moved, of course, from Tascosa to Clarendon on a change of venue. As anticipated, the Clarendon jury cleared him of any official charges in the killing of John Leverton. But this verdict did not erase the cloud of suspicion around his methodology. McMurry and Wilson's fight in the ranger camp left some tension.

The Davidson brothers, John and Jimmie, are both in trouble. But John has been talking, supposedly to Bill McDonald, about the location of the Brookens' secret hideout in the Wichita Brakes. Perhaps as a direct consequence, most of the boys ride southeast on a scout toward Baylor County. The name of John Hammond turns up more and more in the diary. McMurry's monthly reports soon mention a "Private Hammond" as well, so perhaps this Wilbarger deputy joins the company in some capacity.]

JULY 10, 1887 SUNDAY MORNING QUANAH

Cloudy and sprinklin rain this morning. I would like to know where the boys is at this morning. I got a presant of a nice Silk Handkerchief last night.

JULY 11, 1887 MONDAY MORNING QUANAH

Warm and a few Thunderheads around this morning. I hope it will rain. My Hurd day again as the boys is gone. I met Jones Vaughn this evening. He is right bad. Had a couple of Ribs cracked. I lossed my watch this evening. $60 gone if I cant find it. Jones Vaughn is as full as a tick. Walcott left to day some time for Childress I suppose.

[The seasonal shift from spring rains to summer convective thunderstorms increases the speculation on rain chances. Miller's numerous wishes and incantations for rain reflect the social pressures accompanying primary economic expansion toward the 100th meridian, that is into the semi-arid plains after the '86 drought. The sound of distant thunder rolls over the hot plains from time to time, tolling the promise of random rain for a thirsty and still poorly known land.]

JULY 12, 1887 TUESDAY MORNING QUANAH

Still warm and a little hope of rain. A big cloud came up last night but it did not rain any. Tom and Capt went down to Vernon this morning. I had the good luck to find my watch this morning, and nothing broke as I can se, but it is not running. So something is rong in the inside. So I will go up and have it fixed. My watch cost me $2.50 owe and of Pimit [payment] on the balance. Wheel was hurt so he had to put in a new one. The boys got home this evening. [They] got to se Pet[e] Rose but did not get clost to him. They had them well located if some of the men had not flickered.

[Rangers Jim Green and Ed Furman, Sheriff W. N. Barker and some deputies, and most likely Bill McDonald himself had sallied forth on Sunday, July 10, to arrest Bill Brooken and accomplice Pete Rose. They rode toward an outlaw hideout in the Wichita Brakes of Baylor County, near Seymour. Apparently, while carrying out surveillance the next day—and sneaking up close enough to recognize Pete Rose—some of Barker's men "flickered," betraying their presence and alerting the outlaws, who promptly fled the scene. Green and Furman, no doubt tired and frustrated, got back to camp on Tuesday evening after riding some 150 miles.

This incident strongly resembles the anecdotal account given later by Bill McDonald of a foiled attempt to arrest the Brookens. In Paine's biography of McDonald, chapter 4 opens with an undated story, "The Brookens Don't Wait for Callers," in which McDonald, Sheriff Barker, and "two rangers from Quanah," draw near the Brooken dugout. McDonald wants to charge the hideout right away, but Barker counsels caution, noting that Bill Jess's big white hat would give them away before a charge could be effective. Barker instead sends two of his men forward to reconnoiter. As the remaining lawmen watch from a distance, two other men—outlaw lookouts?—are seen riding up to the dugout, which soon erupts with wanted men riding away. McDonald again wants to charge, but Barker waits until his men return, announcing that the Brookens are getting away. McDonald explodes: "Of course they're getting away. Do you suppose they are going to wait and hold an afternoon tea when we arrived?"[6]

McDonald, accompanied by one of the rangers—perhaps Green or Furman—races after the disappearing fugitives, but with no luck. In his biography McDonald claimed that it was this frustrating incident that caused him to resolve "to hunt on his own hook," that is, to seek a commission as a Special Texas Ranger from Captain McMurry.]

JULY 13, 1887 WEDNESDAY MORNING QUANAH

Clear and warm this morning and not much hopes of any rain. Well its now after noon and I believe I'll go up town. A good many clouds around and I hope it will rain. A good cloud came up tonight but no rain. The Sheriff of Young Co. and a Indianna man came in Town tonight with two men wanted in Indianna. One was a man about 6 ft tall with light complection. He had killed a Lady after caducing her. And the other was a low fello. Looks as he has had his back broken. All drawned up and he has larg pop eyes. McDonald came up this evening. The thermometer stood at 107° this evening at 3 and 4 oclock.

[Sheriff Marion D. Wallace worked out of Graham in Young County. He had less than a year and half to live before receiving a fatal wound during Boone Marlow's gun battle with a deputy. Intent on avenging Sheriff Wallace's death, a dirty lynch mob—in cahoots with the authorities—ambushed four other Marlow brothers on the night of January 19, 1889. The prisoners were in transport and supposedly under federal custody. The manacled but alert Marlows surprised their foes, obtained or wrested weapons away, and fought back with desperation that night on Dry Creek. Two brothers died, each chained to a survivor. The two living brothers found a knife and freed themselves from the

leg irons attached to the corpses by sawing off the ankles. Hollywood fictionalized and adapted the story into the classic John Wayne and Dean Martin 1965 film, The Sons of Katie Elder.[7]*]*

JULY 14, 1887 THURSDAY MORNING QUANAH

Nice and cool this morning. Tom and I got up soon, as we slept at the caliboos to gard those two men. We were paid a $1.00 a piece for sleeping there last night. A big Tourniment and picnic and dinner and Dance etc at Childress to day. But I cant go. The Heat was at 105° this evening again. News came in this evening that Charles Kinzy was run over by the cars and will have to have his legs taken off. The Dr thinks he will die.

[The voters of Childress County had organized on April 11, of course, and they had gleefully snubbed Montgomery's townsite of Henry for the new county seat. R. E. Montgomery coolly gave the entire county ninety days to change its mind. He refused even to consider building a depot at the rival Childress City, despite the hasty construction of a courthouse there. He applied pressure, made offers, subverted, tempted, and schemed until the voters did indeed realize the error of their ways in opposing the almighty railroad.

Three months later, on July 11, 1887, a second election relocated the county seat to Montgomery's preferred location. A big picnic was ordered to celebrate the citizens' wiser choice. As per his agreement Montgomery changed the town name from Henry to Childress, exchanged lots freely between the two towns, and built a depot and a hotel. In turn almost all the buildings of Childress City were soon loaded on skids, hitched to teams, and dragged four miles east. Round two went to Bob Montgomery, captain of capitalism. The fight was over.]

JULY 15, 1887 FRIDAY MORNING QUANAH

Plesant this morning. A little cloudy. News came in this morning that Charles Kinzy died last night at one oclock. The Pasenger [train] brought Charleys Father and Mother this evening. And the fraight [train] from the Front brought in Charley. He looks very Naturel. [Sheriff] Barker and [Deputy] Coldwell came up and said the mare that the boy found on the Wichita scout was Jim Allees, and he has got her. George Brandt brought in 160 head of Beef steers and will ship them tomorrow to Chicago. And Joe Brown will go with him. Yesterday was a good day at Childress. Bill Tilson won the $60 Saddle. 11 rings won it. 5 rings was up 160 yards. Time was 12 sec. One made it in 7 sec. It was Charley Swearingen. Second best was 9 rings.

[The Childress tournament was some kind of manly West Texas contest and public entertainment, one that involved rings, time, and distance, perhaps an early form of the rodeo. The town itself was a recent creation of the railroad. The FW&DC prided itself on the lack of passenger accidents, but beginning in 1885 various employees lost their lives in railroad construction and operation.[8] *The trains that brought expectant newcomers west, sometimes carried a few others homeward in coffins.]*

JULY 16, 1887 SATURDAY MORNING QUANAH

Cool and Plesant this morning. A cloud last night but no rain. Charley [Kinsey] was taken off this morning to be buried East somewhere. At Decatur I think.

JULY 17, 1887 SUNDAY MORNING QUANAH

Tis a plesant morning and my Hurd day. Green came down and told me they wanted the Horses and I drew them up and he got John Platts Horse to help me pen them. The Horse fell with him and sprained his rist. He went to Vernon and John Platt and Price went with him to stay a while. Kid took the wagon but will be back tomorrow. I went to church to night and heard a nice talk. I dont know the man who preached. Parson [James] Hosmer was here too.

[Men's values required them to render social as well as physical assistance to one of their own when hurt. It was the concept of company *(as in keeping company) that led Platt and Price to accompany Private Green to Vernon "to stay a while." With no else to care, the boys looked after each other in sickness and health.]*

JULY 18, 1887 MONDAY MORNING QUANAH

This is a very warm morning. Tom Platt hurds to day. I parched coffee this morning and now I must go and take my close [clothes] to Indian Kates and go up Town. This has been an awful hot day. The heat was up to 109°. At one time 110°.

[Hot enough to force a man into a saloon.]

JULY 19, 1887 TUESDAY MORNING QUANAH

Another awful hot morning. I dread the day. Grude will have a hot day to hurd. Grude lossed three horses. Toms, Dennises, and mine. Tis been an awful hot day. Heat was at 111°. Shenolt [Chenault] wrote J. N. Coleman a letter to day about steeling his vest. Kelly told me where Jink Williamson was. Hes between Red River and Clarendon. I collected $186 off H. Lyster and gave it to Rollie Vaughn for [John] Wesley.

JULY 20, 1887 WEDNESDAY MORNING QUANAH

Another hot morning. I and Tom Platt went to hunt the horses. Tom found them not far. I was at J. Y. Hendersons and Hutchesons places this morning. I met Mr Forbs to night. The first time since he was married. He came down and went back to night. McDonald arrested Jink Williamson to day again up at Red River. Lon Akin arrested a little negro for steeling a watch. Mart Cunningham was on a bust to night and broke a buggie up bad. He and Bob Boyce and Bill Ross was in it. Mart had his pistol and got it taken from him.

[Private Miller likely communicated his information on Jenk Williamson's whereabouts to Bill McDonald the previous day. McDonald then rides off, finds Jenk in Hall County, and brings him back on Wednesday. Mart Cunningham was a colorful character, even in early Quanah. He ran a popular dance hall establishment and was generous in his habits. He worked hard and apparently partied hard as well. His kind still live in West Texas, and sometimes they bust up their Ford or Chevy pickups.]

JULY 21, 1887 THURSDAY MORNING QUANAH

Clear and hot again to day. I did not get up until about 9 oclock. The Brookin boys was at Wichita Falls yesterday morning. Everything has went off all OK to day. Jim Allee came over this evening. Said he was going to get his two gray horses at Burk below Harrold. He informed me that old man Doolin and Dikens was married. The heat was at 110° this evening.

[Sheriff Allee was traveling to Burk Station, a Fort Worth & Denver switch and tiny community in western Wichita County.]

JULY 22, 1887 FRIDAY MORNING QUANAH

I did not get up untill about 11 oclock and it is hot as ever. I must write some Discriptions to day. This has been a more plesant day than for some days passed. Not so hot as it has been. I got a letter from Mrs Wesley to day. Bradbury came down to night with Ben Tut[t] and Duch [Dutchie]. McDonald and Dennis put a drunk man in the boos to night and Tom Platt put one in this morning. The boys were a little Rolicke to night but no harm done.

[Bill McDonald and his fellow rangers clean up the town after a rollicking night. Miller maintained noticeable correspondence habits while rangering. A veteran postmistress, Mary Wesley, kindly nurtured the young ranger's connection to the Margaret community with friendly letters.]

JULY 23, 1887 SATURDAY MORNING QUANAH

Cool and nice this morning. Cloud in the west and wind from the East. I hope it will rain. Well I got breakfast this morning and fed and than parched coffee. So now I must go over to old Kates after my close. This has been the coolest day we have had in some time. Capt came home this evening. There was a man knocked down to night, and Dick Bates was arrested and put under bond. Will Rambo and Steve Roberts is here to night. The first time I have seen them in a long time.

This book I commenced Jan 1st while in Gainesville and closed July 23rd/87.

[With this notice the red diary ceases its daily entries. From the frigid winter northers to the hellish days of summer heat, the daily entries cover the criminal justice apprenticeship of a new ranger on the last Texas frontier. After the sparse initial hesitations, A. T. Miller advanced as a diarist, developing intimacy with his "good night diary." As his new life took him far and away, out at day and night, he began to record one man's vision of the New West.

The remaining three pages of the red diary contain notes and meticulous entries on Miller's various financial transactions and miscellanea. Although small loans were made on the strength of an individual's name, this wise man noted the date, person, and amount of any loan of any size. Selected items from these notes are found in Appendix A.

The daily entries now begin without break in the second or black diary, containing an ownership signature of "A. T. Miller/Quanah Texas/July 24th 1887." At the top of each page in the black diary is the heading "1887."]

JULY 24, 1887 SUNDAY MORNING QUANAH

Nice and cool this morning. And I am glad of it for it is my Hurd day. Tom Platt and Capt [McMurry] went to Vernon this morning.

Dept Sheriff of Donley came down this [evening] with Bob Murray and a Negro. Going to the pen with them and will keep them here to night. I was at J. Y. Henderson's for Dinner to day. We had a nice dinner. I found a nice Gold Pen and a photograph and letter and two pencils to day. But I think they belong to Furman.

JULY 25, 1887 MONDAY MORNING QUANAH

Very plesant this morning. Hope we will have a nice day. Well I went over to Margaret to day for McDonald and took Ben Tut[t] to Jaile. And Jink Williamson and [County Attorney] Hankins came back with me. [Sheriff] Allee let Jink out to have his bond filled. I brought him over and turned him over to McDonald, and he got his bond filled and signed and was going to se if the J. P. would approve it or not, and Jink struck him [McDonald] and ran off from him and got away. Mc[Donald] and Jim Housal shot several times but no catch him.

[According to McMurry's "Record of Scouts" for July, 1887, which may be inaccurate, Private Miller arrested the alleged horse thief Jenk Williamson on July 23 in Hall County. Miller then delivered Jenk to the Hardeman County authorities. According to Miller on July 25 he escorted and guarded Jenk's return from Margaret to Quanah, where he turned him over to McDonald.

How interesting that Jenk escapes while in the custody of Special Texas Ranger and Deputy Sheriff Bill McDonald! The Miller diaries attest that McDonald was a strong-minded and competent lawman, but hardly the infallible figure of legend and myth. Another story relates a prisoner escaping McDonald by throwing whiskey in his eyes. Jenk Williamson certainly ran a risk when he braved the gunfire. McDonald prided himself on his marksmanship.]

JULY 26, 1887 TUESDAY MORNING QUANAH

Another very nice and plesant morning. Bob Murray and the Negro went down the road to the pen yesterday morning. [Co. B teamster] Tom Mulhall went to Vernon yesterday to take some things to the boys and he brought Mays Horse back with him and he has an awful back on him. I brought Logans watch over with me to have it fixed. So I must go up Town and have it done. It has been a nice day and everything went off all OK. It has been very warm to day. Nothing of interest I believe.

JULY 27, 1887 WEDNESDAY MORNING QUANAH

Well this has been a hot day. It is now about ½ past 4 and I havent been up Town to day for I have not been well. I took some medicine to day or last night and have been trotting to day. But I am feeling better now, and must go and meet the train. Everything has gone off all OK to day. [J. G.] Witherspoon loaded 16 car loads of cattle to ship to night and has two to go tomorrow morning.

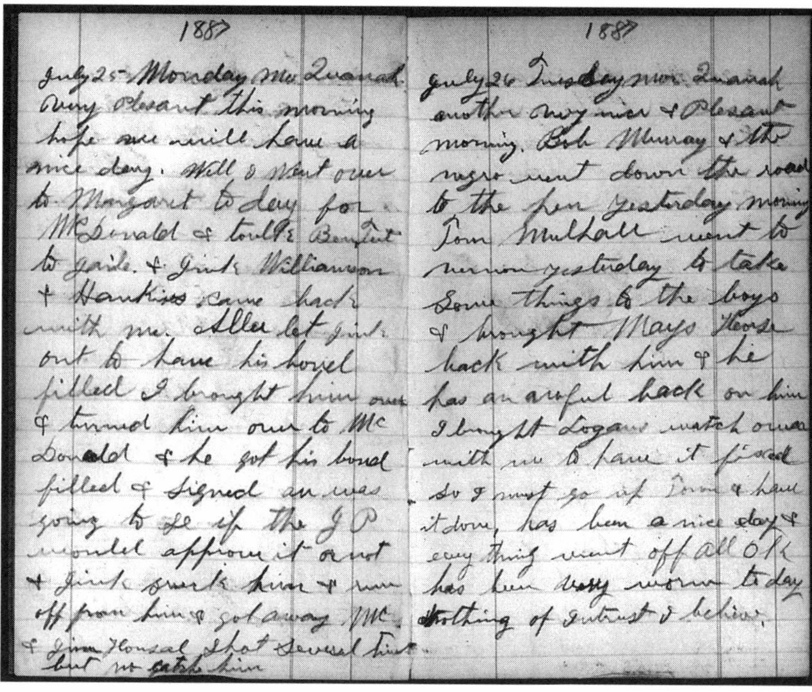

1887

July 25 Monday mo Quanah
Very Plesant this morning
hope we will have a
nice day. Well I went over
to Margaret to day for
McDonald & took E Benfit
to jail. & Jink Williamson
& Hankins came back
with me. Allen let Jink
out to have his bond
filled I brought him over
& turned him over to Mc
Donald & he got his bond
filled & signed an was
going to see if the J P
would approve it or not
& Jink struck him & run
off from him & got away. Mc
& Jim Hounsel shot several times
but no catch him

1887

July 26 Tuesday mor Quanah
another very nice & Plesant
morning. Bob Murray & the
negro went down the road
to the pen yesterday morning
Tom Mulhall went to
Vernon yesterday to take
some things to the boys
& brought Mays Horse
back with him & he
has an awful back on him
I brought Logans watch over
with me to have it fixed
so I must go up Town & have
it done, has been a nice day &
every thing went off all OK
has been very warm to day
nothing of interest & believe.

Figure 10. July 25–26 diary pages

JULY 28, 1887 THURSDAY MORNING QUANAH

Very Plesant this morning and I am so glad for its my Hurd day. Well I was riding around with Frank Spoon after some of his horses. And we found them near Wanders [Creek]. I now must go to Town and deliver a deck of cards to a lady who asked me to get some for her. Well I got those cards but will not deliver them untill sometime to day when I have a good chance to put in a word. I delivered those cards and they were very thankfully received. Every thing has went on all OK to day.

JULY 29, 1887 FRIDAY MORNING QUANAH 1887

This is a very plesant morning and I hope will be a nice day. There were 2 Horses rode in Town this evening that I do not know the brands of. One Brown branded PU on left shoulder and one KY on left thigh. A good crowd of boys in Town to night. Terrible warm to night.

[Cowmen liked Quanah and it quickly became a major shipping terminus for their herds. Timing their arrivals for the weekend made lots of social sense as well. Greer County herds were frequently driven across the Prairie Dog

Town Fork of Red River in the morning, reached Groesbeck Creek for a noon rest and watering, then trailed into the Quanah shipping pens before evening.]

JULY 30, 1887 SATURDAY MORNING QUANAH

I did not get up untill about 8 or 9 oclock. It is very warm. A good cloud in the South and I hope it will rain soon. I think [Sergeant] McNelly went down the rode this morning and I hope he will never come back. *[Outlined in Black:]* Well I received some very sad news this evening. I got a letter from Adda telling me that Thomas [Miller] is dead. He died on 22nd July 1887. He was sick just one week. He and Dr. Landis was out in the country looking out a place and he took sick, the 15th [of July], and was sick one week. Poor boy. I hope he is in a better place than me.

[Adda's letter brings terrible news—the death of their brother. The eldest of the Miller brothers, Thomas Aushine Miller, was born on September 22, 1856. He died in San Diego, California, at the age of thirty-one.]

JULY 31, 1887 SUNDAY MORNING QUANAH/87

Cloudy this morning and I hope it will rain. It is so warm. I got a letter from Johnie yesterday evening. And wrote him last night and sent him $10. I also wrote Lonie and A. L. Steele and Lucius. I have been at camp all day untill train time, then went up and eat supper with L. Can, at Levies. Well everything has been quiet to day. July 31/87 Sent John $10.00.

[A. T. stays in camp and pours his grief into letters.]

AUGUST 1, 1887 MONDAY MORNING QUANAH/87

Clear and very plesant this morning. I hope it will not be hot as it is my Hurd day. [Private] Furman came down last night. He is not looking well. He has been sick.

[The summer heat may be affecting the water and food; some rangers are trotting and others look poorly.]

AUGUST 2, 1887 TUESDAY MORNING QUANAH

Nice and clear and warm and my birth day to day and I have to go to Vernon. So goodby Diary. Well we got to Vernon about 2 oclock. And found the boys all looking for us. We made them feel good by taking them some whisky. Well we started that night for Wichita Brakes and [we] road all night. We got in about 8 miles of where we were going, which was Bill Brookens.

[After assembling in Vernon, the Quanah rangers share some liquid courage—they are after a desperate man—and ride southward into the coolness of a summer night. They head for the distant Wichita Brakes, the rough, cedar-clad country along the Wichita River and its tributaries. This area, mostly in North Baylor County, has man-made lakes and weekend cabins now. In 1887 the Wichita Brakes were remote and difficult to search.

After a hard night ride lit by moonlight the scouts stop and make camp a safe distance away from their quarry. They are near or over the Baylor County line now, but county lines are never a problem for Texas Rangers.]

AUGUST 3, 1887 WEDNESDAY MORNING NEAR WICHITA BRAKES

We have camped near a mile by here to day and go to his house to night. Its a clear morning but awful warm. I se there has been a fine rain down here.

[Deep in the Wichita Brakes, far from prying eyes, Bill Brooken has built a utilitarian dugout and refuge from the long arm of the law. It is supposed to be a secret, but his former buddy John Davidson has been in some recent trouble with the law. On Wednesday the rangers rest, sneak a little closer to Bill's dugout, and prepare for a special night ride and visit. For special cases like Bill and his associates, Company B manhunting employed numbers, caution, and surprise if possible.]

AUG 4, 1887 THURSDAY MORNING ON WICHITA
AT BILL (BROOKEN'S) HOUSE.

But he is not here. We road most all last night getting here. Yesterday was warm. This looks like it will be a nice day.

[The Quanah rangers ride much of Wednesday night to reach Bill's secluded—but empty—dugout near the Wichita River. Had their caution or surveillance on the way alerted someone?

Texas Rangers were noted stylists in the terseness of their reports. Writing a few words in his diary that morning, Miller summarized a complex but futile arrest attempt in his heading and understated irony. "But he is not here," is in the best of the laconic ranger report tradition.

From Bill Brooken's hideout on the Wichita the rangers turn northward on a fast scout that takes them past Beaver Creek, the principal drainage in southern Wilbarger County, all the way back to Vernon after dark.]

AUG 5, 1887 FRIDAY MORNING VERNON

Warm and cloudy this morning. We stoped on Beaver [Creek] for dinner yesterday at about 4 oclock near Mr Bracks, a Duchman. We got in here last night at 10 oclock. We were met by a man telling us that the Ft. Worth & Denver train robbers were near Spencers, so we started for them as soon as we could give our horses some water. Spencer reported that 5 men and 15 head of Horses were camped near his house. We found where they had been but no men. We rode untill near one [1 A.M.] and John Platt, Price, and myself came back on down river [with the] horses, and Green and Peal went on with the other men and trailed the horses near Beever [Creek], and lossed the trail and came back. They got in after noon.

[Barely are the five rangers back in Vernon before they must turn around and ride to Spencer's place on the lookout for armed train robbers. Fresh sign points to Beaver Creek in the south, but Jim and Dennis lose the tracks there.]

AUG 6, 1887 SATURDAY MORNING VERNON

The wind is high this morning. Mr Caughn [Kahn?] has come around for one of us to go help him with a Horse thief on Beever Creek. Green has just come and I have to go.

[Jim Green had just gotten back from his own scout to Beaver Creek, so the new job goes to a slightly more rested ranger.]

AUG 7, 1887 SUNDAY MORNING ON BEEVER (CREEK)

Nice morning. We got to Mr Pullimans yesterday for dinner and he came down to help us to get the man. His name is Pinto Spradly from Collin [County] on Rowlet Creek. He gave us the dog yesterday and we lay for him last night, but he left in the night for Wichita Falls so said. So I will go to Harrold and tiligraph the sheriff to meet him there and Caughn [Kahn?] will go down Beever [Creek].

AUG 8, 1887 MONDAY NEAR VERNON

Nice morning. I got in yesterday about 9 oclock. Had a terrible hot ride yesterday. I got to Harrold just in time for the sheriff to come and I met him at the train. He missed getting his man and came back. I got breakfast and fed my Horse at Harrold yesterday which was the first time I ever was in that place. I saw Rollie Vaughn at the train going East. Frank Spoon and Mrs [Harriett C.] Witherspoon came to Town yesterday. Frank came and took supper with us.

[Harrold, Texas, was a rip-roaring 1885 Fort Worth & Denver Railroad promotion town in eastern Wilbarger County. A. T. and the other rangers are kept busy during their sojourn in Vernon, with detachments going hither and

yon. The outlaws are kept busy as well. For dash-and-color friends like Frank Spoon sometimes dined with the rangers. After their weekend scouts, the captain orders the men back to the Quanah camp on Monday. They set out that afternoon.]

AUG 9, 1887 TUESDAY MORNING QUANAH

Back to Quanah once more. Cloudy and warm this morning. We got a telagram to come to Quanah yesterday about 2 oclock and started about three and got here at 10 last night. Well I have cleaned our guns and my revolver to day. So now I will go up Town for its after noon now. I got my watch this evening and I hope it will keep better time. I got $1.85 from Holly. Left by Rolley Vaughn. I wrote Sister Adda and Mr Wesley to night.

AUG 10, 1887 WEDNESDAY MORNING QUANAH

This is a very plesant morning and am glad of it for its my Hurd day. So I must go and put the Horses on Spring Creek. Every thing has went off all right to day.

[Spring Creek, a northern tributary of the Pease River, lay southwest of the ranger camp.]

AUG 11, 1887 THURSDAY MORNING QUANAH

Another warm morning. And I know we will have a hot day again. Well I must go up Town.

[That night a ranger detachment with Private Miller leaves for Vernon.]

AUG 12, 1887 FRIDAY MORNING VERNON

Nice and clear this morning and we will start towards the Navajo Mountain after some Horse thieves, if we can find them. We came down here last night. We got here at 12 oclock.

[From Vernon the lawmen ride north, cross the Red River, and head into southeastern Greer County (see Map 4). They are on an interdiction scout along the troubled, disputed borderland between Texas and Indian Territory. The Navajo Mountains are a cluster of large granite outcroppings at a bend in the North Fork of the Red River, just across from the Kiowa Reservation. The place was said to be the site of a Comanche defeat of a far-flung Navajo war party.[9]

Only a few years before the five Marlow brothers had filed a claim and ranched in the vicinity of the Navajo Mountains. But Boone Marlow shot a man, reportedly in self-defense, over near Vernon in Wilbarger County, so the Marlows moved on to Colorado for a spell. By the time of Company B's 1887 scouts, however, the hard-working clan had returned and resettled nearby, over around Fort Sill. Preoccupied with "legitimate" thieves and rustlers in the border area, the rangers have nothing against the family. Federal authorities, however, will swear out questionable warrants and arrest the Marlow brothers a year later, in August of 1888, inaugurating a tragic chain of events.[10]*]*

AUG 13, 1887 SATURDAY MORNING IN GREER CO

NEAR THE NAVAJO MOUNTAIN

We camped at a nice valley near North Fork [of Red River]. We got some nice milk and butter yesterday evening at Mr Morrises near Red River.

[Only a year earlier W. H. Acres and H. P. Dale had started the community of "Navajoe" the second town of any consequence in Greer County after Mangum. The Dodge City or Western Trail ran a few miles to the west. There were rumors of lost mines in the granite mountains of the area. Long a ghost town, Navajoe attracted a picturesque crowd in its day, including gold-seekers and the alcoholic wayward brother of Supreme Court Justice John Harlan.[11]*]*

AUG 14, 1887 SUNDAY MORNING IN GREER CO

BETWEEN WICHITA MOUNTAIN AND MANGUM.

At a good spring. We came by old man Suttles, an old Buffalo Hunter who lives now on North Fork at Suttles mountain. Also by Harts Ranch. Very fine country. We met old Mr Dale up there cutting hay. Or fixing to cut. We will go to Mangum this morning and back to Quanah. Corwin Doan was at Suttles while we were there. We came on by a little store at the trail crossing near the mouth of Elm [Fork of Red River].

[Company B's detachment has made a grand sweep along the North Fork border between Greer County and the Indian Nation. Along the way they encounter true pioneers of "Old Greer." The old-timer B. F. Suttles settled on an outcropping along the North Fork between Navajoe and Mangum. H. P. Dale was a co-founder and postmaster of the Navajoe, Texas, community. And Corwin F. Doan was a direct and eloquent witness to the epic cattle drive era.

In 1879 Corwin Doan joined two family members in running Doan's Store, a major frontier entrepôt in Wilbarger County. Doan's Store was set in a grove of hackberries and cottonwoods at a point where the great Western or Dodge

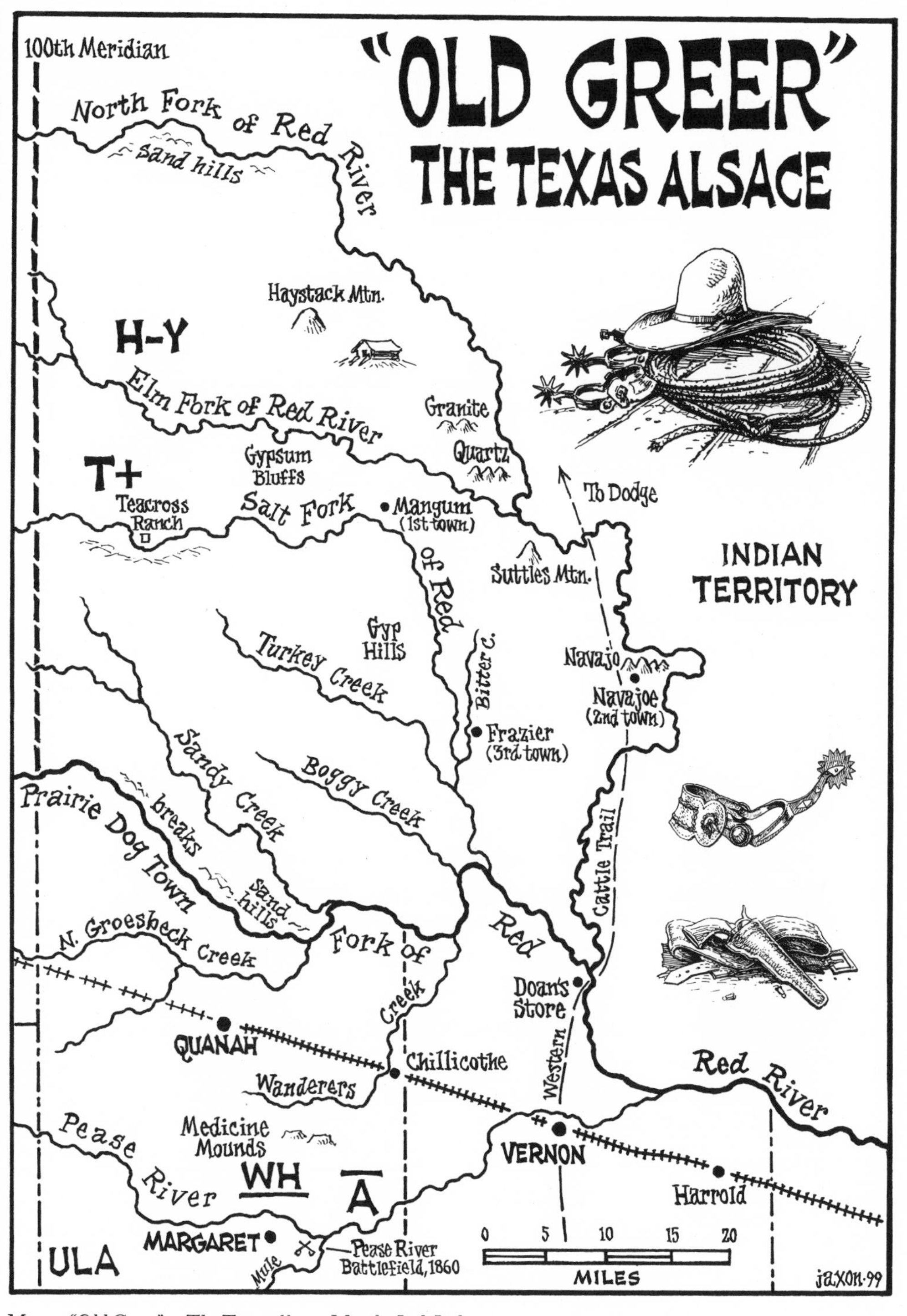

Map 4. "Old Greer"—The Texas Alsace. Map by Jack Jackson

City Trail crossed the Red River. Corwin saw millions of cattle and horses trailed north at Doan's Crossing. But the FW&DC railroad ignored and missed the bustling Doan's community in 1885, and thereafter Corwin's town played out. He continued to live in the old house, recalling as a seventy-four-year-old: "Here, my old adobe house and I sit beside the old trail and dream away the days thinking of the stirring scenes enacted when it seemed an endless procession of cattle and horses passed, followed by men of grim visage but of cheerful mien, who sang the 'Dying Cowboy' and 'Bury Me Not on the Lone Prairie' and other cheerful tunes as they bedded the cattle or when in a lighter mood danced with the belles of Doan's or took it straight over the bar of the old Cow Boy saloon."[12]]

AUG 15, 1887 MONDAY MORNING QUANAH

We got back to Quanah about 9 oclock. We left camp this morning 9 miles the other side of the Dugout, 15 miles North of this in Greer Co at daylight. This is a very warm morning. Cap and Tom Platt has gone to the Front.

[After seeing much of eastern Greer County and its border, the scouts return to the amenities, such as they are, of their Quanah camp. Captain McMurry and Tom are on the track of alleged train robbers.]

AUG 16, 1887 TUESDAY MORNING QUANAH

Cloudy and warm and looks as it might rain. It rained a little last night. We had to gard two men last night. Arrested by Capt and Tom and Henderson, the Dept Sheriff of Hood Co., for the train robbers of Gordon in Palo Pinto Co. Capt and Tom went to Ft Worth this morning with the prisners. Pink Coldwell and George Ranes [Raines] came up this evening.

[Next entry outlined in pencil ticks:]

AUG 17, 1887 WEDNESDAY MORNING QUANAH

Cloudy and looks very much like it will rain. Dennis went to Margaret to take a cow thief. August 17 1887. This is one day I will always remember well.

[But why?]

AUG 18, 1887 THURSDAY MORNING QUANAH

A very nice and clear morning and I am glad of it for I have to hurd. It has been a warm day but every thing went off all O.K.

AUG 19, 1887 FRIDAY MORNING QUANAH

This is a terrible warm morning. I think it will rain soon. There will be a Supper at the schoolhouse to night, but dont know whether I can go or not. Tom Platt and Grude will go to the Front to day.

[By mid-August the FW&DC construction crews were laying track into Potter County. As work crews sweated in the heat, Texas Rangers watched over the fortunes of the company.]

AUG 20, 1887 SATURDAY MORNING QUANAH

Another nice clear morning and no hopes of rain. My hurd day and I must go and se about the horses. I went to the festival last night and had a real nice time. About $200 made up. One cake sold for $30. For Miss Alice Jones and Miss Wood. I was with Mrs Randolph. She and Mr Wilkinson gave Music with violen and organ.

[Miller spends leisure time with Mr. and Mrs. Randolph, whose company and culture he seems to enjoy. S. D. Randolph was a pioneer Quanah merchant, selling groceries, hardware, and agricultural implements from his downtown store.]

AUG 21, 1887 SUNDAY MORNING QUANAH

Another warm morning. I am glad I dont have to hurd to day. Tom Boon came down last night from Tascosa. $220.00 taken in the night of the festival net profit.

AUG 22, 1887 MONDAY MORNING QUANAH

Cloudy and looks very much like it will rain. I do hope it may. My hurd day again and Dennis [Peale] is gone to the Front. So I am afraid I will have to hurd tomarrow again.

AUG 22, 1887 TUESDAY MORNING QUANAH

Cool and plesant this morning. Feels like a fall morning. Good many in Town last night, but no racket though I thought there would be. Dennis did not go to the Front yesterday. He went to Kirkland to Summons a witness to Ark. But think its the rong man. I went to Charley Ashfords to night to hear Mrs Randolph play some on the pianno. Had a very nice time.

AUG 24, 1887 WEDNESDAY MORNING QUANAH

Another cool morning. Very much like fall but no hopes of any rain yet. My hurd day again and I must go to the horses for its now about 10 oclock. I have had a good day to hurd. And have read my book about half through. *It's a Mad Love.* And it is splendid. I got a letter from Lonie this evening. No news of importance. She was writing me for the first time about Thomas [Miller] and wife. Since his death.

AUG 25, 1887 THURSDAY MORNING QUANAH

Cloudy and raining this morning. We had a fine rain last night for the first time in a long time and I know theres many a glad hart this morning. I have fixed up the dugout this morning to keep it from falling in. And cleaned it up as I often do. Tom [Platt] and Grude [Britton] got in this evening from Henrietta.

[Cool mornings and cold rains have reminded Abner Miller to start fixing up the dugout in anticipation of winter.]

AUGUST 26, 1887 FRIDAY MORNING QUANAH

Very cloudy this morning again and misting rain and I have to hurd to day. I had a real good time last night again. W. D. Dunn and J. D. Collins have come over with some beef steers to ship.

[W. T. Dunn was an 1880 pioneer and close friend of John Wesley. D. J. Collins also led a colorful life. Born in Alabama, he enlisted and survived the Civil War, then moved west to Texas in 1867. In the mid-1870s he joined Captain George Stephen's company of Texas Rangers. Ranger Collins rode some hard trails—from the town of Decatur to the Davis Mountains—during his stint in the service.[13]]

AUG 27, 1887 SATURDAY MORNING QUANAH

Warm and a little cloudy to day. I did not get up untill about noon and was very warm at that time.

AUG 28, 1887 SUNDAY MORNING QUANAH

Nice and cool this morning and no hopes of any more rain for some time to come. Tom Platt Hurds to day for the first time in some time. Well. Well. Green and John Platt and Price got back from Vernon to day, and such happy boys as they were. To get back to Quanah. Very cloudy and looks like it may rain. I got a letter from Johnnie [Miller] and one from J. S. Kerr this evening. No news of importance.

AUG 29, 1887 MONDAY MORNING QUANAH

Another cloudy and damp morning. Grude [Britton] will hurd to day and I expect he will get wet. Dennis [Peale] went to the Front yesterday evening, going to Ammerias for the election tomarrow. I had a nice little talk with Mrs Wyet to day. She is very Plesant. Gene Wicker was in Town tonight making some of his threats. He is the man Sam Platt shot through the shoulder at Wichita Falls for shooting up the Town as he ran out.

[Gene Wicker should keep his mouth shut, what with two of Sam Platt's brothers and their clannish ranger companions all around. Sam Platt shot Gene Wicker in the course of a tumultuous, alcohol-fueled spree by the latter in booming Wichita Falls around 1885.

In keeping with their state peace-keeper role, Dennis Peale is dispatched for the important Potter County organization and election on August 30 at "Ammerias" or "Amorilla," better known today as Amarillo.[14] *Near the halfway point between Clarendon and Tascosa was an otherwise insignificant drainage named "Amarillas Creek." The name was an old comanchero toponym for the bright yellow loess soils exposed in the upper drainage. As Dan Carey's grading gangs passed through Potter County that summer, Tascosa's saloon-keeper Jesse Jenkins had the presence of mind to file on a speculative section of land along the line. Aware that Tascosa's days might be numbered, Jenkins was one of many mercantile pioneers who sought the main chance. He readily tolerated a rude tent city that sprang up along the right-of-way, not far from the north shores of Wildhorse Lake. Carey's construction foremen called it "Amorilla Village," but it was really a whiskey stop and temporary railroad camp.*[15] *The zephyrs and seasons of the High Plains soon shredded many tents. The wind-whipped tatters and camp laundry gave the small community a distinctive appearance. The inhabitants derisively called the place "Rag Town" for its bedraggled and tattered appearance.*

Jenkins and everyone else was aware that while the Fort Worth & Denver was building from southeast to northwest, the powerful Santa Fe Railroad was dissecting the Panhandle from northeast to southwest. Stalled at Panhandle City, the Santa Fe would someday intersect the Fort Worth & Denver. The junction of the two lines was certainly a strategic piece of real estate, as it was widely predicted to grow into a great metropolis. It made good sense to Jenkins that his "Amorilla City" tent town on Section No. 22 near Wildhorse Lake should win the election for county seat, then become the junction point. He ran his site in the county seat election under the marketing name of "Odessa."

Unsure of the outcome, most of the denizens of Jenkins's Amorilla kept their temporary living quarters but prepared to move wherever fate—or big capital—directed.

Jess Jenkins's make-do or subsistence capitalism was no match for the better-organized mercantile capitalists of distant Colorado City in Mitchell County. Accustomed to dominating trade with the South Plains and points north, the merchant princes now realized that they had better open new outlets in the Panhandle. They worked with Colonel J. T. Berry, an experienced and professional townsite planner from Abilene, to plan their commercial penetration. Colonel Berry had organized townsites in the early 1880s for the Texas & Pacific Railroad. He made his own investigation in April, 1887, and selected Section No. 188. Berry's Public School land section had the benefit of containing Wildhorse Lake, one of the best water features of the county next to the railroad. Berry skillfully orchestrated a campaign to win the upcoming county election for his "Oneida" townsite.

There was a third candidate as well, also representing a shock wave of capitalism. "Plains City" on Section No. 156 was the unloved creation of the brilliant Henry B. Sanborn, co-owner of the local Frying Pan Ranch in Potter and Randall Counties. Sanborn was an industrial capitalist, making a fortune with his partner Joseph Glidden in the manufacture and sale of barbed wire. Sanborn and Glidden bought the 120,000 acre Frying Pan Ranch in 1881, and fenced the spread with their wire the next year. When the railroad built alongside his ranch in the summer of 1887, the scheming Henry Sanborn saw no reason for the county seat not to be on his section of land.[16]

Voters were scarce enough in the new county to make bribery both feasible and practical. Colonel Berry enlisted the largest block of voters by talking to the foreman and promising a business and a residential lot to each cowboy of the LX Ranch. Consequently Berry's Oneida townsite handily won the election supervised by Private Dennis Peale the next day, August 30. Of fifty-three votes cast, the LX cowboys voted together with thirty-eight votes.[17] *Each LX cowboy duly received his new townsite lots. Berry's maneuvering allowed firms like the Ware Bros. to open new stores quickly at Oneida, which was soon renamed Amarillo and granted a post office in November of 1887. Sanborn's forlorn site on Section No. 156 had the fewest votes, but big capital was prepared to take on the mercantilists in other fashions.*

Henry Sanborn coolly initiated and persisted in machinations against Berry's townsite in favor of his section. Wildhorse Lake, swollen with rain, inconveniently flooded the Berry townsite, just as Sanborn's long-term manipulations (and more generous bribery) proved overwhelming. Within a few years the original mercantilists all gave up and moved to Sanborn's Amarillo, dragging their houses and buildings on sleds to the new site. Colonel Berry enjoyed the joke on Jess Jenkins, but Henry Sanborn had the last laugh.[18]*]*

AUG 30, 1887 TUESDAY MORNING QUANAH

Another cloudy damp morning and looks as it shurley will rain soon. Green hurds to day and I will hurd tomarrow I suppose. I got up and fed and got breakfast before any one got up but John Platt, and he went to Town as soon as he got up.

AUG 31, 1887 WEDNESDAY MORNING QUANAH

Another cloudy and drisly morning and I have to hurd to day. Tom the Kid gave McNelly a cussing last night for every thing he could.

[Sergeant John McNelly was in an uncomfortable position. Ranger records show that Sam McMurry granted him an honorable discharge on this day. After some four years as sergeant, August 31 was his last day of service in Company B. Abner Miller certainly disliked him.[19]*]*

SEPT 1, 1887 THURSDAY MORNING QUANAH TEX

A very prettie morning except a little ting of cloud around. The boys will all be in this morning to reinlist to day. Dennis and Brad will come from the Front. They would of been here last night but there was a reck on Red River and the train is to be here at 6 oclock this morning. I bought me a new pair of pants the other day and will put them on this morning for the first [time]. They cost me $5.00.

[Reenlisting was a renewal of vows and personal commitments, both to the service and to each other. The boys of Company B preferred to do it together whenever possible. In addition to payday, this date was a red-letter day for Tom Platt. Captain McMurry intended to promote Tom as sergeant to replace the departing John McNelly.[20]*]*

SEPT 2, 1887 FRIDAY MORNING QUANAH

Nice and cool and Plesant this morning. Dennis and Brad[bury] came home to inlist to day. John Platt lost the horses yesterday but found them this morning. I deposited $75.00 Seventy five Dollars with W. E. Johnson last night. Well its most night. And I se Tom coming with the horses and I must get some supper.

[W. E. Johnson and Colonel J. L. Elbert ran promotional and real estate interests in early Quanah as the Johnson & Elbert firm. Their office safe stored

various sums from rich and poor alike. Charles Goodnight and Burk Burnett patronized the back office—and its liquid hospitality. Tom Platt spent part of his day arresting the popular Mart Cunningham on a preliminary charge of assault with intent to murder.[21]*]*

SEPT 3, 1887 SATURDAY MORNING QUANAH

Clear and warm this morning and no hopes of any rains. [Jim] Green, Dennis [Peale], and [Grude] Britton started to Vernon this morning to go on a scout to Wichita Brakes. [Sterling] Price is sick this morning and I will have to hurd for him.

[The three rangers are scouting the Wichita Brakes for the Brooken gang.]

SEPT 4, 1887 SUNDAY MORNING QUANAH

A very plesant morning but am afraid all the rain is gone. I think McNelly is gone this morning and I hope he is. Tom Platt was full as a Tick last night. I had my horse shewed yesterday evening. Mart Cunningham cut a Rail Road mans throat yesterday evening, but not cerious I dont think. Bradbury went back to the Front last night. John Platt is on hurd to day. He has just gone up Town to get Price some ice. He is sick.

[Sergeant McNelly was unpopular with enlisted privates like Miller. In any case he is leaving the camp forever. Mart Cunningham's arrest doubtless arose from his bloody handling of a reckless drinker in his dance hall. A plea of self-defense would be in order. Sergeant Tom Platt celebrates his new status with a Saturday night spree. Young John Platt takes a turn in looking after the sick Sterling Price.]

SEPT 5, 1887 MONDAY MORNING QUANAH

Plesant and nice this morning. There were a good many clouds around yesterday but no rain. I went up this [morning] and shiped a sack of corne to Green at Vernon. Jack Brown was arrested last night for fighting.

SEPT 6, 1887 TUESDAY MORNING QUANAH

Clear and nice this morning. I have to hurd to day. Price is right sick this morning. I am afraid he is taking the fever. [Ed] Furman went to the Front this morning.

Well I must go to the hurd. I went up and helped Mr Randolph put his pianno in the house last night, and Mrs Randolph said it was the first house keeping she ever done. I went to Red River last night, but was told I couldnt swim so I came back.

SEPT 7, 1887 WEDNESDAY MORNING QUANAH

Clear and Plesant this morning. Still no hopes of rain. Louie Cone, the R.R. Night Watchman, knocked Dr Sumpter down last night. Dr [Sumpter] was drunk and cussing. Tom O'Hare is Teamster now. Capt hired him yesterday.

[Tom O'Hare's nickname was "Red," a reference to the flaming color of his hair. Captain McMurry hired Red as the new teamster or "muleskinner" on September 5, 1887. His Irish wit and helpfulness around the camp will be appreciated by the boys.]

SEPT 8, 1887 THURSDAY MORNING QUANAH

Clear and warm this morning. Tom Platt hurds to day. Tom Davis of Gainesville came in yesterday evening. Dr Sumpter made another brake at Louie last night, but nothing done. McDonald took a pistol from a boy last night with a wooden barrell.

[Quanah's gun-control laws gave Bill McDonald lots of practice in disarming suspects. He perfected the removal of another's weapons into a noted skill.]

SEPT 9, 1887 FRIDAY MORNING QUANAH

Clear and warm this morning again. McDonald, Tom Platt, and I put a fellow in the boos last night, and he was hell to handle. He did not want to go atal. I have to hurd to day and I must go to the Hurd now. I sent a letter to Green and one to Dennis by last mail, that is I put it in the office last night.

[Three rangers to subdue one rowdy is not the kind of mythology typically associated with "One Riot—One Ranger" McDonald. But then some bad boys are just "hell to handle" while others go quietly.]

SEPT 10, 1887 SATURDAY MORNING QUANAH

Cool and a little cloudy this morning as we had a little rain last night. Just about enough to lay the dust. I had a talk with Walcott last night and night before. He is on his way back to McKinney with his saddles. I must go up and get my watch from Hotch. Well it is about night now and we have had a fine rain. Sure it rained very hard this evening for something like two hours.

[The first of the fall rains soaks the Rolling Plains and refills the tanks and waterholes. July and August had scorched many parts of the plains, causing hardship and distress to ranchers. The September rains and floods marked the end of the summer dearth of rainfall.]

SEPT 11, 1887 SUNDAY MORNING QUANAH

Very plesant this morning after a hard rain yesterday evening. Tom Platt hurds to day and John [Platt] went out with Mr. Hallaran to look at the country. He is just in from Cleveland, Ohio, or some place up there, and he is a very plesant man. He came with Claud Ayers. A Tilagram came this evening to Cap [McMurry]—for a young Man, about 20 years old and light complection, light hare, and a small Mustache. Tom Platt and I got him. And turned him loos again. Jim Merrick, who sent the Dispatch, came and we got him [the suspect] again, and he was the right one. His name is Joe Johnson as he gives it. Than I got another [man] supposed to be his partner. Joe had left some money and checks at Henrys saloon. Cap went to the Front this morning.

[A. T. and Tom arrest Joe Johnson and Hugh Hudgins for theft of money at Clarendon in Donley County. Captain McMurry continues traveling, taking a return train to Dallas on the 11th to see the U.S. Marshal there, "in regard to horse thieves in Indian T[erritor]y."[22] This federal concern about horse thieves eventually ensnares the innocent Marlow brothers. McMurry will not return to Quanah until September 14.]

SEPT 12, 1887 MONDAY MORNING QUANAH

Nice and clear this morning and I am glad as its my hurd day. Now about 1 and I have just eat dinner. I went to se the R.R. man put a flat car on the track that fell over the cole shoot. The boys got home to day. That is Green, Dennis, and Grude. And John Hammond and McDonald with them.

[Privates Jim Green, Dennis Peale, Grude Britton, and John Hammond left camp on September 10 to join Bill McDonald on a manhunt. They traveled some seventy-five miles into the Cottle County ranch country looking for a dangerous suspect, William "Billie" Trumble. An accused horse thief and murderer, Billie Trumble was also suspected of wire-cutting incidents against syndicate interests.]

SEPT 13, 1887 TUESDAY MORNING QUANAH

Clear and warm this morning. We will move Furman and Brad[bury']s tent to day and put it down besides ours. Capt came in this evening and we have to ride tomarrow.

SEPT 14, 1887 WEDNESDAY MORNING QUANAH

A nice morning and I am glad, for Green and McDonald and I have to ride to day, though it is cool this evening. We will go up Town and get breakfast.

SEPT 15, 1887 THURSDAY MORNING QUANAH

Cloudy, wet, and sloppy. We got home last night about 1 oclock and it comenced to rain as we were unsaddling. We got wet before we got in, and such a rain as we did have all night long. The tank is most full. We went to McLellands for dinner yesterday and waited for him to come back from old man Lyons. And we started at 2 for Lyons and got there just before sundown. We got supper and came back and waited on the roadside to se if any one was with old man [Lyons] as he came home. He had a young man with him, but not Lee Hickman the man we was after. Old man Lyons lives right on Red River, four or five miles below the mouth of Groesbeck [Creek]. We got lost as we came home and came near Chillicothe. We saw some nice turkey, but could not shoot at them as we were slipping [up] on Lyons house. McDonald killed a duck on the creek on Red hollow.

[A cold front drenches the Rolling Plains. Privates Green and Miller provide backup to Special Ranger Bill McDonald in a search for suspected rustler Lee Hickman. Riding through inclement weather the trio conduct a sweep over 120 miles. The fact that they do not catch anyone is only a temporary problem. McDonald is studying the landscape and its residents, absorbing useful local news and gossip. Bill McDonald will "keep a coming." His dogged persistence and stealthy tactics are the real secret of his success, not his feisty marksmanship or braggadocio. McDonald enjoys shooting at game from horseback. His proficiency at picking off prairie dogs and birds is notable.]

SEPT 16, 1887 FRIDAY MORNING QUANAH

Still cloudy and damp and muddy. I think we will have plenty of rain now before it stops. Jim Allee, Hankins, Darby, and J. C. Roberts came over day before yesterday evening. And they are still here. The R.R. Bridge across Pease River washed away just after the Pasenger [train] crossed yesterday eve.

[Heavy upstream rains created a major rise on the Pease River. A westward FW&DC passenger train barely escaped disaster. Nevertheless, with the bridge washed away just west of Vernon, Quanah is now cut off from railroad civilization and the train is stranded.]

SEPT 17, 1887 SATURDAY MORNING QUANAH

Cloudy and misty this morning. I got up this morning and helped feed and get breckfast. 3 oclock. And we have just eat dinner. We have a new man in the company. His name is Beashop [Bishop]. He came yesterday eve from Gonzallas Co. McDonald and Harvy Husher had a little fus last night, but it did not amount to any thing. McDonald sold a mule to day. By exicution. By old man Crossland. Young Wilcox of McKinnie came in Town yesterday evening from Clarendon. Allee, Hankins, and Roberts went back to Margaret to day. The [Pease] River is still up and the R.R. cannot be fixed. Pasenger [train is] still here.

[Captain McMurry enlisted James R. Bishop into Company B on September 15, 1887.[23] *Gonzales County is on the South Texas coastal plain, a fertile farm and ranch country along the lower San Marcos and Guadalupe Rivers. Like the other boys, Jim Bishop will have to furnish his own horse and gun.]*

SEPT 18, 1887 SUNDAY MORNING QUANAH

Clouds all around this morning. And warm. Such a rain as we did have last night I never did se. The tank is most full this morning. I never saw water stand on the ground as it did last night. Grass will grow in a hurry now.

SEPT 19, 1887 MONDAY MORNING QUANAH

Cloudy and damp this morning and we want to fix our dugout to day. And Dennis has to hurd. 3 oclock and I have just shaved and will go to Town. We got our dugout fixed right well.

SEPT 20, 1887 TUESDAY MORNING QUANAH

Nice and clear this morning. Hope it will not rain to day. Now about 3 oclock and must go up Town again and get my boots. I am having new heals put on them. Old Indian Kate sent us a nice basket of dinner. Jelly, Cake, Pies, butter, beef, &c. Twas a real nice dinner, one to be remembered, by the old woman and her girl, Coody. That is the place I have my washing done.

[Old Indian Kate knows the way to a ranger camp's heart as well as its pocketbook. This enterprising businesswoman played a gregarious role in the Quanah community, although she is otherwise lost to history.]

SEPT 21, 1887 WEDNESDAY MORNING QUANAH

Another nice and cool morning, though a little cloudy and very good for [a hunt]. Britton, Peal, O'Hare, and I am going hunting to day.

[Hunting was not only recreational—it supplemented the pot, provided a spell of firearms practice, and reinforced feelings of camaraderie.]

SEPT 22, 1887 THURSDAY MORNING QUANAH

Cloudy and threatning rain. Warm. We had a nice time hunting yesterday. Got a good many birds and severel Rabbits. We had a nice fry this morning and will have a pie for dinner. Both Pasengers came in last night. The bridge across Pease is fixed so they can run over. Green and I went to a nice supper last night. It was for the schoolhouse. The people of Quanah had a supper and ball for the schoolhouse.

[Communitarian values strongly supported the commingling of sociability with fund-raising. The building of the public schoolhouse inaugurated the cultural growth of the town, as the bourgeois community established the need and confidence of imparting its values to the next generation. After the rampaging Pease River washed out the railroad's first bridge, the FW&DC rebridged the treacherous watercourse, and Quanah rejoined civilization.]

SEPT 23, 1887 FRIDAY MORNING QUANAH

Cloudy and cool this morning. Right smart Norther came up last night. Well we have devided up our mess this morning. Bishop the new man is on hurd to day, and he bought him a horse yesterday from Akin for $50.00. Yesterday was the first regular mail since the washout on Pease River.

[The thunder of the next wave of cold fronts sweeps across the Rolling Plains on the last day of summer. From drought to flood, the rangers have weathered the extremes of summer. The rigors of the fall may prove even more trying.]

CHAPTER 4

The Locomotive of Justice

AUTUMN OF 1887

The bandit gangs and stage robbers that had thrived in west-central Texas west of the farm line were fast disappearing. Crime itself would never be ended, because crime was a part of civilization itself—but significantly, throughout much of Texas, men were beginning to put their old pistols away.

—*T. R. Fehrenbach,* Lone Star, A History of Texas and the Texans

Company B emerged from an important 1881 reorganization of the Frontier Battalion. Formerly deployed as a mobile counter-terrorist force, principally against Mexican bandits and Indian raiders, by the early 1880s the company mission shifted to the steel spearheads of commerce and capital signified by the almighty railroads. Lieutenant Samuel A. McMurry was promoted to captain of the reorganized company in August of 1881. This industrious and patient lawman took charge of his force in Colorado City, a terminal boomtown in distant Mitchell County. McMurry's rangers concentrated mostly on Anglo-American rustlers, thieves, feudists, and fugitives who threatened the interests of the newer settlers and older property owners. As post-Reconstruction railroads further penetrated the vast ranges, a series of dramatic terminus boomtowns sprang up. Pioneer mercantilists rushed to these termini, hoping to claim vast hinterland trade. The arrival of quantities of goods, new sources and circulations of capital, diverse personalities and occupations, and large quantities of alcohol fueled all kinds of trouble in the new towns. Crimes against livestock and property claimed attention, but there were shootings and old-fashioned southern feuds as well.

Company B cleaned out Colorado City for a time before relocating to the boomtowns of the Texas & Pacific Railroad under construction in West Texas. From there the rangers rode northeast in 1885 to the new railheads of the Fort Worth & Denver City Railroad. Sam McMurry's men worked Wichita Falls, Vernon, and Harrold before arriving in Quanah at the end of 1886. Thus, Captain McMurry and his ranger force had considerable experience in implementing state law into communities of frontier individualists. The reputed lawlessness of the frontier was both exaggerated and accurate. Revisionist historians like to point out that murder rates were much worse in New York City than many western counties full of decent people trying to get ahead. True enough, but the frontier nevertheless had its criminal ways. People mired in a stressed primary economy were conditioned by subsistence thinking and acquisition to a certain degree.

Many decent but poor folk thought little about grazing grass, perhaps branding a maverick, or certainly cutting posts from the holdings of large-scale feudal ranches. They were accustomed to helping themselves from the land. Aggravating the situation was a national crisis in American society between capital and labor, a clash and struggle also played out in the vast enclosure movement on the Great Plains. The arrival of railroads catalyzed both sides into further economic transformations, upheavals, and complaints about the nature of justice in regulating this process.

There is little doubt that the initial enclosure movement adversely affected small-scale settlers. Railroads and freighters erected miles of barbed-wire fences on the Texas ranges during the 1880s, precipitating a minor class war. A whole generation of westering pioneers, accustomed to the economic freedoms and appropriations of an advancing frontier, found that the removal of Indians and Hispanos principally benefited the corporate interests that bought out the bright promised land before them. Perhaps some had distant class memories of the expropriation and subdivision of the English commons, when parliamentary Acts of Enclosure destroyed and parceled out the public pasturelands, often to large and monied interests.

Like the lost commons of the English landscape, the open ranges of Texas were closing with each boxcar of "Bob" wire. Prairie Luddites throughout West Texas resorted to terror and wire-cutting to counter the Western enclosure movement. They were incensed that syndicate ranches often fenced off scarce water resources and school settlement lands from the reach of the small man's herd or plow. Winter storms scattered and mixed their stock; many animals piled up on the big ranch drift fences and died. Feudal-like ranches controlled by distant capital often dominated local elections, tax appraisals, and development property interests. Although many of the ranchers proved reasonably hospitable to the hungry and poor newcomers, others dreaded the drain on their resources and the threat that the nesters posed. Inevitably there were accusations on both sides of property appropriation.

The railroads brought more than merchandise and passengers. They also brought new ways of thinking and new perceptions of what behavior was no longer permissible. In particular the old piratical and subsistence economics had to be set aside. Small folk, seeking economic recovery or subsistence through opportunistic theft from the despised syndicates, found that the railroads and rangers carried stricter regard for property ownership. Certain families—like the Marlows, some said falsely—found this transformation too stifling. Some families did emerge as clannish horseback gangs with strong anti-government attitudes.

Outlawry's nemesis was Captain McMurry and his men. Texas Ranger teams proved particularly deft in establishing order in railroad boomtowns. By breaking certain key elements, and then making slow and thoroughly legal examples of them, a larger issue of impermissible behavior was addressed in the whole pioneer community. Each criminal was thus publicly prosecuted, notifying the community—and those not yet caught—which way the wind was now blowing.

Fall of 1887

SEPT 24, 1887 SATURDAY MORNING QUANAH

A nice and cool morning. We have had a couple of very cold nights. Feels very much like winter is coming. I eat dinner with Guss Abbott at Mrs Youngs to day. He has to go to Benjamin on the Gordon & Nolan Trial. And sais he is afraid Billie Trumble will give him some Trouble. Green went out to Clarendon last night and caught a boy with a six shooter. Capt and Green went back to Clarendon this evening on some business.

[A. T.'s good friend Guss Abbott was likely a subpoenaed witness in the "Gordon & Nolan Trial," the resolution of a mysterious 1887 homicide in Margaret, Texas. W. L. Gordon was the first county judge when Hardeman County was formed in 1884. Three years later, he and George Newlin (spelled "Nolan" by the diarist) had an angry confrontation; Newlin pulled his gun and mortally shot Judge Gordon in downtown Margaret. On a change of venue Newlin's trial was moved to Benjamin in Knox County; amazingly, his stead-

fast plea of self-defense in the shooting of a county judge was accepted by Benjamin's jurors, and he was acquitted.

Guss Abbott was worried about William Trumble for a reason: Trumble had gunned down Guss's brother, John Abbott, the year before in the cowtown of Otta. Billie Trumble also claimed self-defense. After some indecision a grand jury disagreed and placed him under a warrant charging him with murder. Because Billie disagreed with this outcome he stayed clear of lawmen. The authorities will catch William Trumble soon enough. Captain McMurry and Jim Green kept going all the way to Tascosa in Oldham County.]

SEPT 25, 1887 SUNDAY MORNING QUANAH

Cloudy and cool this morning and a few drops of rain is falling. Its my hurd day and I must be agoing. Mart & Frouie Cunningham brought us a nice cake and a shoulder of Pork yesterday evening.

[Mart Cunningham is showing that he has no hard feelings after the rangers recently arrested him for assault to murder. He will plead self-defense against a drunk and abusive customer.]

SEPT 26, 1887 MONDAY MORNING QUANAH

Cool and nice this morning. Dennis [Peale] and Tom Platt was on a big drunk last night, and Dennis knocked old Carry Wilson down. And such a time I never saw. Elliot of Vernon came down last night. He and others has been on a hunt out west and killed a large black bare and a goodeal of other game.

[Dennis and Tom waited until Captain McMurry left for the Potter County frontier on September 25 before they started their "big drunk." Off-duty and inebriated Texas Rangers beating up a well-known local was definitely not good public relations. Nor were all citizen charges of excessive force or misconduct by rangers mistaken. Captain McMurry was preoccupied in arresting several Panhandle residents while on the road.[1]

R. P. Elliott of Vernon was a distinguished Kentucky lawyer who settled on the Wilbarger frontier in 1884. He made good money in real estate and was elected county attorney in 1886.[2] *Black bears could still be found in the Palo Duro, Mulberry Creek, and other canyonlands to the west, but the bruins were fast disappearing.]*

SEPT 27, 1887 TUESDAY MORNING QUANAH

Clear and cool and very blustry this morning. Price and I went after some poles to fix the dugout and to make a saddle rack, and Dennis, Grude, and

I put it up. And now I must go up Town and se what is going on up there. Sheriff Barker came in last night from the West, and said Green and Capt went on to Tascosa the night before. Dr Gearhart from Harrold came in yesterday eve and was on a big drunk last night.

[A cold front blows in and reminds the rangers to get their dugout in better shape. Another doctor with a drinking problem.]

SEPT 28, 1887 WEDNESDAY MORNING QUANAH

A little cloudy and cold and blustry to day. Am afraid we will have a cold rain and we will have to ride in it. Capt and Green will be in this evening with some prisners and Ben Cabble will be in from the East to take a trip with us in the Nation. I have wrote a couple of letters for Harry Heucher to his Lady in Austin. He will marry her the first of next month.

[Abner Miller's penchant for writing and correspondence is known to more people than his ranger friends.]

SEPT 29, 1887 THURSDAY MORNING QUANAH

Beautifull and clear this morning. We are looking for Capt [McMurry] in on every train with four or five men with him. Price on hurd to day and such a nice day for him.

[Sam McMurry returned on this day with prisoners Bob Dilworth (forfeiture of bond in Nolan County), Jack Horbeck (assault to murder in Bosque County), and Luther Dean (carrying pistol in Donley County).]

SEPT 30, 1887 FRIDAY MORNING QUANAH

Nice and clear this morning. We had our first little Frost last night. Very light. Well we have to start on a scout after dinner to Greer Co. For George Damron, Henry Smith, Jo Lowry, and a Negro for steeling cattle. Tom Platt, Dennis, Grude, and I will go.

[The cold fronts are getting stronger. Friday evening four Quanah rangers ride north into lower Greer County, once again on a scout against suspected rustlers. They make camp on Turkey Creek, a drainage flowing through the southern interior of Greer County and joining the Red River near the Hardeman-Wilbarger County line.]

OCT 1ST, 1887 SATURDAY MORNING ON TURKEY CREEK

GREER CO.

We got to the creek last night about 9 oclock. This morning being a clear and beautiful morning we went down about 4 or 5 miles to Eddlemons ranch for those boys. But they were not there, so we came back to Quanah. We went down to the mouth of the creek where it runs into Salt Fork, about 15 miles above Dones [Doan's] Store on Red River. Dennis killes a cattamount as we came home this [day]. The Pasenger train went thrugh to Clarendon yesterday evening for the first time. Green went up this evening.

[The Quanah rangers follow Turkey Creek southeast to the Eddlemon Ranch, find no suspects there, and continue to the creek's confluence with the Red River. Downstream is Doan's Store, the fading, bypassed, old adobe entrepôt located near an excellent ford of the Red River north of Vernon. A catamount is a pioneer term for our wildcat or puma.

The first passenger train arrives at the raw railroad townsite of New Clarendon. Old Clarendon is in the throes of crisis. Reverend Carhart's existing Carroll Creek–Salt Fork location of the town clearly had never been a factor in the thinking of FW&DC officials. Surveyors and graders readily bypassed the town earlier that summer. The tracklayers who followed set their steel rails some five and a half miles south of the existing town, way out on a gentle spur of the Llano Estacado. Employing their customary tactics, railroad officials convince the civic leaders of Old Clarendon to move lock, stock, and barrel to a planned New Clarendon townsite. R. E. Montgomery, townsite agent and son-in-law of Grenville Dodge, recently met with Clarendon merchants and leading citizens to plan the relocation.

Old Clarendon begins to dismantle in the fall and relocate. Historian Fred Rathjen, whose father ran a prominent store in the new town, notes, "Not only the location but also the character of Clarendon changed."[3] The arrival of the railroad brings new faces and forces that transform the original Methodist vision of the community. This change is especially visible when J. F. Cain eventually opens the first saloon in New Clarendon.]

OCT 2ND, 1887 SUNDAY MORNING QUANAH

Another beautiful morning. And John Platt is on hurd. Mr Furman came down this morning. And Green too. Furman has come to make out the monthly reports.

[Apparently Private Ed Furman gathered data and drafted the company's "Monthly Report" for the adjutant general's office. He did a good job, writing a fairly detailed chronology. A busy Captain McMurry probably reviewed the report, signed the paperwork, and dispatched it to Austin.]

OCT 3RD, 1887 MONDAY MORNING QUANAH

Clear and beautiful this morning and hope we will have a nice day. John Hammond and George Coldwell came up last night. Fixing I think for a scout. John went to Kansas for Wiley Bell and got him and 42 head of Stolen cattle and now wants nine more.

[John Hammond, a popular county deputy and future Vernon sheriff, may be working for the Company B rangers as well. State records show "Private Hammond" pursued Wiley Bell all the way to Kansas. After some five hundred miles of travel he dutifully searched, found his man, arrested him, and brought Wiley all the way back to Vernon to face charges of cattle theft. McMurry reported sixty-six head of cattle recovered.[4] It was an impressive demonstration of the long arm of the law.]

OCT 4, 1887 TUESDAY MORNING QUANAH

Clear and beautiful this morning. Price is going after a load of wood this morning and will go and get Paul Edwards, one of those men John Hammond wants in Wilbarger Co. Price got Paul and brought him to camp. He is, like all the rest, an inncent man.

[This is the practical side of manhunting. Dividing up the chase and bringing in all those "inncent" men. Paul Edwards is charged with theft of horses in Wilbarger County.]

OCT 5, 1887 WEDNESDAY MOR QUANAH

Clear and cool this morning and think we will have a nice day. Tom Platt took our man to the train to meet John Hammond. And he confessed to having baught a mare from the boys accused of being in with him, Sid Davidson and Fant Channing.

[Paul Edwards's implication of Sid Davidson in horse theft will be duly handled on October 20 by the Texas Rangers. The confession plays neatly into the Quanah lawmen's plan to purge both Sid and John Davidson, who are proving too great an irritation to the new bearers of law.]

OCT 6, 1887 THURSDAY MORNING QUANAH

A very plesant morning, but a ting of cloud all about and the wind is blowing a goodeal. I have to hurd to day and must go and se where the horses is at. The mules did not come up last night. The stage was robed last Monday night again, right when it was robed a few nights ago by one man. Near Bawlenger [Ballinger] in some of the lower counties. Mr May told me yesterday evening that Mr Kelly and wife had parted. Poor man. He has Two Wives living now. One in Town.

[Private Miller knew well enough that the wind shift and "ting of cloud" overhead might indicate a fall weather problem. The high clouds were likely altocumulus, harbingers of a major cold front on the way. At the end of a blustery hurd day there is only a little town gossip for news. There was one small sign on October 6 of reversing the tides of livestock theft on the Texas-Oklahoma border: Private Hammond arrests Wes Gibson for stealing horses from the Indian Territory.]

OCT 7, 1887 FRIDAY MORNING QUANAH

Raining and looks as it will rain all day. It is now after 11 oclock and just raining right down. We got breakfast about 9 and had pancakes and steak, bread and coffee, and I just dont know what all. Mart Cunninghams Dans Hall Burned down last night, and he is gone to Tascosa. Town is dying fast. I went to take a letter to Mrs Edwards yesterday evening. Old man Taylor got his mare and mule back after being rode most to death. Got them in Greer Co. Hobbled.

[A mature wave cyclone is developing overhead, drenching Quanah in heavy rains. The railroad economic boom has rolled past Quanah by now, just as it did past Decatur, Henrietta, Wichita Falls, Harrold, and Vernon. Some of the fast-buck Quanah boomers like Mart Cunningham and Big Bill Williams are moving on, or thinking about it. Other more stolid civic leaders like N. L. Jones and Colonel Elbert are still conjuring visions of Quanah as the next Chicago.

Quanah must essentially switch regional development gears, from rapid or divergent growth to more steady-state trade expansion and gradual development. The Quanah economy chronicled in the diaries readily exhibits the three transforming shock waves of closing frontier capitalism. The first or subsistence wave of the late 1870s and early 1880s is highly individualistic, anti-statist, mobile, resource extractive, and of course picturesque. Many of these survival-oriented pioneers did no more or no less rustling than their neighbors, or the many Texas cattle drives to Kansas that arrived with hundreds more cattle than when they started. Gradually informal networks arose. These networks involved the exchange, handling, care, brand alterations, pasturing, transport, removal, and sale of stolen livestock in the subsistence wave of capitalism.

Though the trade in liberated livestock was obviously illicit, some Texans were just too tempted to avoid this primitive form of capital accumulation.

Nevertheless, the rules had changed for men and their sons by the mid-1880s. The boys of Company B and the Panhandle criminal justice system were in the process of smashing older networks and strangling the conduits of stolen beef and horses between Texas and Oklahoma. The frequency of ranger scouts to Greer County, and their identification and pursuit of these pirates of the plains, were all part of the new order.

The second or mercantile wave of capitalism was more complex and therefore more organized. Merchants maintained some mobility. Mercantile capitalists had learned a lot in their commercial penetration of West Texas. "Terminal merchants" like Mart Cunningham understood completely that the new action was now shifting to Clarendon, Jess Jenkins's Ragtown, and beyond. When Cunningham's dance hall burned down, it may have seemed logical and timely to make the next move. Already the clever terminal merchants of Colorado City in Mitchell County, including the Ware mercantile firm, were eyeing and laying plans for the commercial conquest of the Panhandle. New spatial linkages like the FW&DC Railroad were crucial for the terminal merchant penetration of the last big Texas hinterland.

After the easy boom money, however, many mercantilists themselves were soon confronted by a third and powerful wave of monopoly capitalism. Large syndicates, ruthless railroad interests, and powerful outside capital interests actually owned most of the Panhandle hinterland. Where necessary, these overlord capitalists simply shoved aside both the pioneers and the terminal merchants, although the latter often put up a good political fight. In contrast to the old-timers, the monopolists were corporate, pro-statist, less mobile, and burdened by increased and fixed capital investment in buildings, equipment, fencing, water tanks, windmills, new improvements, and personnel.[5]

By the end of 1888 Quanah must forge a new community vision and begin reorganizing the town's economic foundations.]

OCT 8, 1887 SATURDAY MORNING QUANAH

Cloudy and wet this morning after another very hard rain last night and yesterday evening. Yesterday was a Terrible stormy day. It rained all day. The tank is fuller than ever I saw. Five Bents of the Pease River Bridge was washed away yesterday eve again and havent hurd this morning. Dennis and I and Red [Tom O'Hare] haulled a load of wood this morning, so I must go to town now. I baught me a Slicker and par of gloves yesterday evening for $4.75.

[In meteorological terms, the wave cyclone of October 7–9 developed into a "cold-type occluded front" on top of the Rolling Plains. The cold front first

glimpsed as altocumulus, a "ting of clouds," arrived in force on Friday. Its low pressure and cyclonic circulation trapped and uplifted massive quantities of moist fall air. Cumulonimbus clouds converted this heat and moisture to heavy downpours. A key word for this storm is occlusion. Occluded fronts travel slowly, seem to stall and linger, and dump maximum rainfalls. They bring a storm's greatest fury to bear on the land below. The torrential rains of Friday and Saturday were the result. The Pease River railroad bridge is washed away. Quanah, Clarendon, and Childress are cut off from Fort Worth. The drouth of the 1950s also ended in heavy rains and floods that did much damage.]

OCT 9, 1887 SUNDAY MORNING QUANAH

Very cloudy and raining and wind from the North, and for the cold everything is sloppy and wet. Claud Ayers was in Town last night. Going to Clarendon to se after his cattle. He came over the bridge yesterday evening and said Seven Bents was gone. That is too bad.

OCT 10, 1887 MONDAY MORNING QUANAH

Another cool, cloudy, damp, and watery looking morning. And Price has to hurd. Dennis and Bishop has to go to New Tascosa or Camp No 1 on first train. Yesterday was another cold and damp day all day. Well I must fix our Tent.

[Although the business practice seems cruel, grading crews for the FW&DC followed a surveyed course that bypassed the famed and well-known pioneer town of Tascosa by a mile and a half—and south of the Canadian River at that. Tascosans were asked to raise the funds to route the railroad through their city, but the sum was so deliberately large that the "little men" mercantile interests could not do so. They watched helplessly that fall as the railroad prepared to construct a new station, the so-called New Tascosa.

Never a success, New Tascosa and the subsequent railroad town of Cheyenne amounted to little more than a raw grab for the existing commerce and settlement. Most remaining residents, including the gifted editor of the Tascosa Pioneer, *watched with horror over the next two years as Old Tascosa withered away. Dennis Peale and Jim Bishop were dispatched to New Tascosa to keep an eye on things during the tense period when the existing mercantilists sought court injunctions and other remedies to avoid economic strangulation.*

Miller is spending time fixing his tent for a good reason. McMurry's October inventory of ranger property shows seven tents were "Good" and ten tents were "Worthless."]

OCT 11, 1887 TUESDAY MORNING QUANAH

Clear and nice this morning, but cool and chillie. Well this has been a real nice day. J. Y. Henderson came down and eat dinner with me to day. Dennis and Bishop got off last night.

OCT 12, 1887 WEDNESDAY MORNING QUANAH

Another nice clear and cool morning and my hurd day. I arrested an old Irishman last night for cutting Charley Smith, an Ingineur, and locked him up. He was drunk. Had $11.90 on him. And I turned him loos this morning.

[Apparently the Irishman was never formally charged with disorderly conduct or assault. No ranger record of the arrest appears.]

OCT 13, 1887 THURSDAY MORNING QUANAH

Nice and clear this morning. And cool. We had a nice piece of venison this morning off a Black tail Deer. Mart Cunningham killed it out at the Palladora [Palo Duro] canyon. I learned the other night that Jones Vaughn once went under severel different names. I had a talk with Mr Kelly last night for the first time since he and wife parted.

OCT 14, 1887 FRIDAY MORNING QUANAH

Clear and cool this morning. Prices hurd day. So I will go up Town and not come back before night.

OCT 15, 1887 SATURDAY MORNING QUANAH

Clear and cool this morning, and I have to hurd to day as Grude and Capt had to go to Clarendon last night, to se a man that was arrested on suspison of Train Robery. He was the rong man.

[McMurry's cool head often freed a "suspicious stranger" arrested by locals. It was his second train trip of the month after an urban fugitive that involved a wrong man. Part of being a great lawman is knowing when not to arrest someone.]

OCT 16, 1887 SUNDAY MORNING QUANAH

Nice and clear this morning. I am glad for I have to go after wood. I wrote C. Askew last night and EK about our land Tax Receipts. I have them from '83 '84 '85 & '86 so there is no going back on them. We went over near Pease River after a load of cedar wood. Got in about 4 oclock. I reckon we will have to go on a scout tomarrow from what Red told me.

[With colder weather coming, wood for the ranger camp becomes a priority. Private Miller and a companion take the wagon about fifteen miles south and spend the middle of the day as cedar-choppers.]

OCT 17, 1887 MONDAY MORNING QUANAH

Clear and cool this morning. We will not go off to day as I thought we would have to do. Grude and Johnnie had a little shooting scrape last night with a cople of boys. As they ran out of Town. And one [boy] came back and they got him. Grude and the constable has gone out to get the other one. On Groesbeck [Creek]. If they can find him.

[Again there are no ranger arrest records for the two juveniles or young men. Small fry did not count apparently.]

OCT 18, 1887 TUESDAY MORNING QUANAH

Clear cool and a nice morning. Price hurds to day and I know he is glad. Capt has gone out to Tascosa to look [at] a place for the winter, or that is what the boys say, and I hope he has. Jim Allee was in Town last night. I did not speak to him. I got a letter from [Sister] Adda last night, and she wants us to come out to California. Charley Bingham died this morning down at Carry Wilsons, with congestion, and his sister in Kansas has been Tilagraphed. She wants his remains sent to her.

[Abner and Johnnie's sister hoped to reunite the family in balmy southern California. He could have escaped a dreadful winter—and pesky Texas descendants—had he gone. McMurry apparently saw no advantages to relocating the company to the dying town of Tascosa.]

OCT 19, 1887 WEDNESDAY MORNING QUANAH

Nice clear and cool this morning. I must go up Town and se what is going on up there, and se what was done with Charley Bingham. I got up and fed and got my breakfast, and Price and [Constable] Akin has just gone to the Dugout, and Ed [Furman] hasnt got up yet. I got three teeth filled to day. Cost me Two Dollars $2.00 as one was to refill. John May, a brother to the man Price killed, was in Town last night. But he was very Quiet. Price got his new suit of close that he had made to order at Henrietta.

OCT 20, 1887 THURSDAY MORNING QUANAH

Another beautifull morning. And my hurd day so I am Glad. A conciderable wind from the North last night. But not very cold this morning as I expected it would be. I wrote Johnnie and sent him Lonies and Addas letter yesterday. The Grass is very fine yet, and plenty of water all over the Prairie, and a good many ducks on the little ponds. The Tank is falling fast.

OCT 21, 1887 FRIDAY MORNING QUANAH

Nice and clear this morning. We are having some real nice weather now. Everything is lovely. I went to the concert last night. Had a very nice time. Price went to Clarendon yesterday evening and came back this morning.

OCT 22, 1887 SATURDAY MORNING QUANAH

Clear and cool but windy this morning. I got a letter from Willie Steele last night for the first time in life. He told me of some things that had Happened in the last year that I never expected to hear of. One thing was that Sis R or C had a babie in 7 months after she was Married. And I know she was a good Girle. Capt Tilagraped Tom yesterday that he would be here this morning, but he did not come.

[Willie Steele was a candid maternal relative of Miller, writing about family back in North Carolina.]

OCT 23, 1887 SUNDAY MORNING QUANAH

Cool and nice, but a thin sight of clouds all around. I am afraid of falling weather soon. I wrote S. S. Steele & W. C. Steele yesterday. I saw a Six wheeled Engine night before last for the first time in life. Drivin wheels.

[Miller forecasts another cold front from reading the sky.]

OCT 24, 1887 MONDAY MORNING IN CAMP UP PEASE RIVER IN THE BRAKES.

And it is a rainy and cold day. We came up yesterday evening and got six Turkeys last night and I got one this morning. Wagner got five and I got two. Harry Miller, Red [Tom O'Hare], Wagner, and I went.

[Autumn is a temperate, lovely, and happy season on the Rolling Plains—unless you are a turkey. A fall hunting party travels about sixteen miles southwest of Quanah, camping along the Pease River upstream from Margaret. The Pease Brakes have some good cedar timber, revived creeks, and active game. This cold front is wet but bearable, with earlier light frosts creating spectacular foliage patterns. The nations of geese and ducks are migrating down the plains on the Great American Flyway. Men turn to cleaning guns and thinking of fat game.]

OCT 25, 1887 TUESDAY MORNING QUANAH

Cloudy and looks like rain and cold. And I have to hurd. We got home yesterday about Twelve oclock. Wet and cold. With six Turkeys and Two Patridges. And had a good dinner. And a good breakfast this morning.

OCT 26, 1887 WEDNESDAY MORNING QUANAH

Cloudy and cold and looks like rain. We must haul a load of wood. I killed a nice mallard Duck yesterday and we eat it for breakfast. It was fine and fat. A croud of Roudies in Town last night, but no harm done.

OCT 27, 1887 THURSDAY MORNING QUANAH

Clear and beautifull this morning. Some of the boys wants to go hunting this evening. Dont know whether I will go or not. Another Six driving wheel Engine just gone by with 20 carloads.

OCT 28, 1887 FRIDAY MORNING QUANAH

Another beautifull morning. I got up and fed just as the sun was rising. Billie Keys, John Darnell, old man Pace, Skin, and Ed Miller all went in a hack Turkey hunting last night. And they had a beautifull night for it. I saw the first repeeting shot gun this morning I ever saw. Lewis Cone the night wachman had it. It belongs to Mims the comissary man. I must go over to old Aunt Kates after my coat. She is fixing it for me.

[A bright harvest moon lights Friday night.]

OCT 29, 1887 SATURDAY MORNING QUANAH

Another nice morning. And looks as we will have a few more nice days. We are having som as nice weather as I ever saw. We had to gard Sid Davidson last night. Tom and Grude arrested him last night. They will take him to Vernon to day to make a bond. John and Red went after a load of wood to day. Kelly and Ashford went to Margaret last evening. Capt went up the road yesterday evening.

[According to the "Monthly Report," a report probably drafted by Ed Furman and signed by the captain, Tom Platt arrested Sid Davidson in Quanah on October 20, 1887. Sid was charged with horse theft in Wilbarger County.[6] *The lawmen are closing the circle on the Davidsons.]*

OCT 30, 1887 SUNDAY MORNING QUANAH

Another nice morning and I am glad for I have to hurd to day. I got up and fed and got the breakfast this morning. The boys took Sid Davidson to Vernon yesterday and he gave a $500.00 bond and came back. I got a letter from Johnnie last night. I wrote one to Lucius yesterday to Maiden, Montana. J. Y. Henderson and George Abbott and George Benton made start for Benjamin this morning. Prof. Westmorland and Joe Westmorland is lying in jaile at Benjamin awaiting trial. In the school land bisiness.

OCT 31, 1887 MONDAY MORNING QUANAH

Another nice morning and the last day of October. This has been a very nice month. Some very cold weather and a greatdeal of nice weather. I got up and got breakfast this morning and have to go after a load of wood. I got a letter from C. Askin that our land [in North Carolina] is all OK.

[October ends with pleasant Indian Summer weather. "Greatdeal," "goodeal," "goodmany," "somekind," "atal" [at all] and so on are typical Millerisms reflecting the speech patterns or parole of the Texas Victorian frontier. Note no mention of Halloween festivities.]

NOV 1ST, 1887 TUESDAY MORNING QUANAH

A beautifull morning and the first day of Nov/87. What kind of a month shall we have? Capt and Grude went to Clarendon last evening to se Mr Furman. He is lying low, not expected to live. Now I must get to the train and se if he comes down. Charley Smith, Engineer, took Morphine last night and killed himself. It is not known whether he did it intensionly or not. He was taken to Ft Worth this morning.

[Poor Charly Smith was cut up in a barroom brawl only a few weeks earlier. A. T. Miller had arrested an Irishman for the offense. Now a depressing drug overdose claims Charly's life. Drugs were apparently a much larger problem on the frontier that our happier legends suggest.]

NOV 2ND, 1887 WEDNESDAY MORNING QUANAH

Another fine morning. Oh what nice weather we are having now. [A] Mr Furman went by this morning on his way to Ft Worth. He is very sick and will never come back in the sunrise again, I dont think. Dennis came down this morning and will go back this eve. He had a man in charge for imbezzlement. His name is Frost, Ex President of the Frankland Land & Cattle Co. Tom and Grude went on to Wichita Falls with Furman and him.

[Dennis Peale traveled all the way to Tascosa to arrest, according to records, a "V. G. Frost." Frost was charged with embezzlement in Parker County. Pos-

sibly this man was Frederick de P. Frost, an otherwise prominent capitalist and powerful trustee steering British bondholders into control of the Franklyn Land and Cattle Company. Operating out of New York, Dodge City, and now Texas, Frost may have been in Tascosa in connection with the liquidation of local Franklyn pasture interests. There were various legal charges and actions connected to Frost during the hard times besetting the English syndicate. Any charges against de P. Frost apparently did not prove serious.[7]]

NOV 3, 1887 THURSDAY MORNING QUANAH

Another beautifull morning. Tom got a Tilagram from Capt to arrest W A Cone and hold him untill he comes home. I suppose he [Capt McMurry] will be here to day or tomarrow. John and [illegible] went up to Clarendon yesterday with Dennis. They will come down this morning I suppose. I was told this evening by Randolph that F. J. and J. W. Westmorland casses were dismissed at Benjamin.

[The Westmorelands were indicted for possible involvement in fraudulent school-land sales, but they convinced a judge of their innocence.]

NOV 4, 1887 FRIDAY MORNING QUANAH

Another clear and a beautifull morning. I am glad of it for I have to hurd to day. Dick Browley came and slept with me last night. He gave me a great many pointers of which I was glad to know. John Platt went to Clarendon last night to meet Capt. Capt and John came down at 11 with a prisner wanted in Houston for imbezzlement and we will have to gard him to night.

[McMurry arrested fugitive W. A. Cone in the Panhandle hinterland at Tascosa. Cone was wanted in a major embezzlement case in Harris County. A significant share of McMurry's work consisted of arresting urban fugitives trying to lose themselves in the rural frontier. This flow of gateway city crime into the mostly peaceable farm and ranch communities contributed to the frontier image of lawlessness.]

NOV 5TH, 1887 SATURDAY NEAR QUANAH

Another beautifull morning and I have just come from Town and eat dinner. I got up at 10 oclock. And went up Town and found Mr Campbell lying in the Depot with the Doctor working with him to pump the Morphine out of him. But they failed to do so and he died about ½ past 11 oclock. He leaves a wife and two or three little children. He was the Tilagraph opperrator.

[Mr. Campbell's death—accidental overdose or suicide?—is the second morphine death within five days. The arrival of railroad civilization clearly brings new social issues to the closing frontier.]

NOV 6, 1887 SUNDAY MORNING QUANAH

Another nice morning. We still have our prisner in charge yet and will have untill tomarrow I suppose. Mr Campbell was buried to day about ½ past 11. Mr Moore stayed here last night with me.

NOV 7, 1887 MONDAY MORNING QUANAH

Another nice morning and looks as we will have the same for some time. The Sheriff of Harris Co of Houston Tex came up yesterday eve. He will take our prisner [W. A. Cone] this morning. He and Capt was here a few minutes ago.

NOV 8, 1887 TUESDAY MORNING QUANAH

Another nice morning, but not as I expected, as it was cloudy last night conciderably and cool. Well, the Sheriff of Houston left yesterday morning with our prisner, Mr Cone. Boniy Tucker of Ft Worth was killed last night at 1:30 in Gainesville by Assistant City Marshall Bozzell. He shot him three times and every ball went through his boddie.

[Coming from Gainesville himself, the diarist may have known the assistant city marshal. Certainly Private Miller admired the deadly accuracy of the law officer's shooting.]

NOV 9, 1887 WEDNESDAY MORNING QUANAH

It clouded up last night and I thought it would be a raining by the morning, but it is not although its very cloudy and threatening this morning. And I have to hurd. I got up and Red and I fed and I got breakfast. McDonald went to Wichita Falls yesterday and left Greens horse here, and I will have to hurd him to day.

NOV 10, 1887 THURSDAY MORNING QUANAH

A little cloudy again this morning, and cool, and looks as it may rain or have somekind of falling weather. Mrs Campbells babie isnt expected to live. The widow of the man that comitted Suiside the other day. I got up and fed and got most of the breakfast and now I must shave and go to Town. *[Added sentence:]* Mrs Campbells little Girle died this evening at 7 oclock.

NOV 11, 1887 FRIDAY MORNING QUANAH

Again a thin Ting of clouds are around, and is very cool, and looks as if we may have somekind of falling weather. Capt and Price went to Clarendon yesterday. I sent my watch to Ft Worth by Claud Ayres to day to have it Regulated. Rally Ryne [Rolla Ryan] came in to day and will have a performance here tomarrow night. Tom Latham and Kirk McGee came in Town this evening. They have a hurd of beeves near Town.

["Falling weather" refers to the drop or fall of barometric pressure, indicating the possible arrival of another mid-latitude cyclone. Miller's "ting of clouds" was likely a sighting of high cirrus clouds, the kind that precede a warm front, which in turn occludes and gives way to a cold front.]

NOV 12, 1887 SATURDAY MORNING QUANAH

Warm and cloudy this morning and I look for rain soon. Price on hurd to day. Four of the Anarchist were hanged yesterday at 11 oclock. Poor fellows. Gone to H— I suppose. Grude gave me a report yesterday that is of a great benafit.

[On May 4, 1886, Chicago police opened fire on striking workers. During a confrontation the next day with police at Haymarket Square, someone threw a crude bomb that exploded and instantly killed a policeman. A number of people were killed in the panic, melee, and indiscriminate police fire that followed. Authorities arrested eight dreaded anarchists, mostly German-born workers. A biased judge, reactionary system, and hostile jury sped four of the arrested men to the hangman's gallows on November 11, 1887.[8] *Most bourgeois citizens regarded anarchists with horror. But, in time, the Haymarket Massacre also came to stand for capital's brutal repression of labor. Whether their destination was hell or heaven, the four hanged anarchists became martyrs to many.]*

NOV 13, 1887 SUNDAY MORNING QUANAH

Cloudy and a Norther coming up and looks and feels as it is going to be cold. Prices Trial comes up this week. So he and all the boys nearly has to go to Margaret tomarrow. I went to hear Rolla Ryan last night and was good.

[Sterling Price has to face the district court over his shooting of John May's brother. The other boys will turn up in support of his case.]

NOV 14, 1887 MONDAY MORNING QUANAH

Another nice clear morning and the boys all have to go to Margaret. I eat a good dinner at old Indian Kates yesterday. For the first time in my life to eat with an Indian. Priv[ate] Price came up yesterday evening. Lee Hickman camped near here last night on the bank of the Tank.

[Sterling Price tracked down Lee Hickman and Ed Barton on this day; he arrested both men on charges of horse theft, lodged them in the boos, then rode off to Margaret for his own trial.]

NOV 15, 1887 TUESDAY MORNING QUANAH

Nice and clear this morning. I will go up Town and se what is going on. [At] noon the boys started to Margaret. Tom Platt and Private Price and Tom Mulhall went in the wagon. J. Cheek was in Town this evening. And said Johnie [Miller] would be here this evening. Most every body is having to go to Margarett.

[The rangers went to Margaret, ostensibly at the request of Judge Cockrell to provide security as additional peace officers during district court. It had only been a year since Judge Gordon was shot and killed in Margaret. Captain McMurry and another ranger followed a day later.]

NOV 16, 1887 WEDNESDAY MORNING QUANAH

Clear and as the wind has got in the North its a little cool. It looks as we will have a Norther to day. Johnnie came over last night. He is going home [to North Carolina] this winter, and how I wish I could go. Capt has gone to Margarett to day. I loaned $5.00 to a fellow to day for a watch as a bond. He is to send it back in Ten Days. His Name is J. A. Laseter, Colorado City Tx. But he has been working on X.I.T. Ranch near New Mexico, Blackwater or Spring Lake, and near Big Salt Lake, N.M. in the Sindicate pasture.

[Lasater is working in the southern pasturelands of the famous XIT, at the head of Blackwater Draw and around the large saline lakes of the Texas–New Mexico border. Another Lasater worked on the JA Ranch around the same time. Company B rangers like Ed "Big Ed" Connell will spend considerable time in the XIT pastures in the 1890s serving as protection men.]

NOV 17, 1887 THURSDAY MORNING QUANAH

Another clear, cool, nice morning and I have to hurd to day. Price came over last night. I dont know what for. I understand his jurors was set yesterday evening. The Man Laseter I talked with yesterday evening put me on to some things, and sais he will put me on more. John Arnold has a big black horse belongs to the Widow Carter at Vernon.

NOV 18, 1887 FRIDAY MORNING MARGARET

Another nice morning and we are in Margaret. We came over yesterday evening. Price, Grude, and I. Red came with the wagon and went back this morning. I suppose we will stay here untill court is over. Price came out of his case without any trouble. His jurors was only out about 15 minits. They were on Billie Trumbles case of cutting wire.

[Sterling Price's shooting of Mr. May is therefore ruled self-defense. Captain McMurry had just visited Margaret and spoken with the authorities. The arrival of more Texas Rangers, and their presence in the courtroom, demonstrated company interest in the verdict of the jury, which proves amenable. Does the prosecution have enough evidence to convict William Trumble?]

NOV 19, 1887 SATURDAY MORNING MARGARET

Another nice morning and we are now just getting breakfast. I went down to se Mrs Wesley last night. She was very sick and I did not stay. The jurors hung on Billie Trumbles case. I went out and took dinner with Miss Kittie Morrow yesterday. McDonald left this morning for Chillicothe or Quanah, and dont know when he will be back. He sais Tom Platt will be here to day or tomarrow.

NOV 20, 1887 SUNDAY MORNING MARGARET

Another nice morning and we are still in Margaret. I went to se Mrs Wesley last night and found her a goodeal better than the night before. Such another talk that is going on now. In the Sunnyais room in the Jail of the County of Hardeman.

[A prisoner hurls abuse at the world from his cell in the Margaret Jail.]

NOV 21, 1887 MONDAY MORNING MARGARET

Another nice morning but a little blustery and dusty. I was at a little Singing at Enoch Borens last night. And we had some good singing sure. Mrs Crutcher bed. [unclear sentence]

NOV 22, 1887 TUESDAY MORNING MARGARET

Another nice morning, but still a little blustery and dusty. I was at Mrs Morrows last night and the old man was not at home. I had a real nice time for a few hours. Dennis Peal came over last night, and Green and Frank Boushar came over. Tom and Capt came in this morning. Tom brought my watch.

[Private Miller liked Miss Kittie Morrow of Margaret, soon to be fifteen

years old. He certainly enjoyed her family's hospitality more when Mr. Morrow, "the old man," was not at home.]

NOV 23, 1887 WEDNESDAY MORNING MARGARET

A little cloudy this morning, and cool and looks as we will have some falling weather before long. The wagon brought some food and girle to day, and went back. And Dennis went too.

[A manly ranger camp attracted the interest and curiosity of some women.]

NOV 24, 1887 THURSDAY MORNING MARGARET

Cloudy and misting rain and frosting, and I am afraid it is going to be bad before any better. Allees case was desided to day in favor of him. There is ice all over the Tank, and pools around, and has been for some days.

NOV 25, 1887 FRIDAY MORNING MARGARET

Another drizzly morning, and looks as we will have a big rain before it clears away. The Jurors was discharged this morning and suppose the court will soon be over. Mat Swearingen came over this morning. I think I will sell a couple of my lots, No 13 and 14 in block 8, I believe. I can rent my house at $7 per month, but would rather sell. L. A. or Lou Caruth was arrested Wednesday evening for cow steeling in Denton Co. Sheriff Sparks came and got him this evening.

[Once again Sterling Price made the arrest. District court sessions were popular events on the frontier. They were often well attended due to their serious and dramaturgical nature. Parties and even families would arrive from all over, often to set up camp and socialize among themselves for days. Like present encounter or tabloid TV shows, public trials bared it all to the western bourgeois, providing inexpensive and often sensational entertainment. Speculation on outcomes was rife. Jury verdicts and trial proceedings were experienced virtually, impressing upon young and old alike where the lines of unacceptable behavior were now positioned. At the end of court session the county-seat town of Margaret emptied out noticeably now. Farmers and ranchers returned home, and far too many county residents headed back for Quanah and its mighty link to a larger world.]

NOV 26, 1887 SATURDAY MORNING MARGARET

Another cloudy and drizzly morning. I was at Mr Wesleys last night. Grand Jurors Adjurned this morning with 23 bills found. Billie Trumbles case was Moved to Anson, Jones Co. Ben Tut[t] was fined $25 and cost. Negro Dug was fined $25.00 and cost. We expect to start for Quanah tomarrow morning by daylight. But as a big Norther has just blown up, I am afraid we cannot go soon.

[After their gunfight on June 10, Ben Tutt and Bob Douglas have the final resolution of their "little shooting affray" held on the streets of Quanah. Each man is held to blame and both are fined and released equally. "No harm done," as Miller liked to comment. Court is adjourned and citizens scatter or hunker down in the teeth of another norther.]

NOV 27, 1887 SUNDAY MORNING MARGARET

Cold as whis this morning, and we will not get off to Quanah before noon. Now 1 oclock and we are about ready to start to Quanah. I took dinner with Mr Coltharp and his wife and Mrs Wesley for the last time for some time I am afraid. We got in Quanah about train time, and had a right cold ride, but not as cold as we expected we would have. The [Pease] River was frozed over as we came over to day.

NOV 28, 1887 MONDAY MORNING QUANAH

Another clear and cold morning, but not so cold as yesterday was at Margaret. Allee left this morning with Billie Trumble, and Tom Platt and Capt went with him. He was going to Abilene by rail, and [then] take the stage to Anson where his trial comes off in February. I have been over to Old Kates to get my washing this morning. And saw her other girle. She looks very much like Coodie. Well I must take a shave now and put on some clean close and get up Town.

[William or "Billie" Trumble was headed for his murder trial in Anson, Jones County. He was considered dangerous, and therefore Sheriff Allee sought an experienced and additional peace officer, Tom Platt, to accompany the prisoner. Guarding a man like Billie Trumble was a serious business.]

NOV 29, 1887 TUESDAY MORNING QUANAH

Cool and a good many clouds around though the sun is shining. My hurd day and I must go to the horses. I got up and fed and made a fire and helped get breakfast. Noon Bill Baker and Jim Donnaly and Bob Colyer and another man eat dinner with us to day. Night. Capt and Furman and McDonald came from Vernon this evening, and reports a good many in Jaile. Spencer and Billie Bell among them. I paid Claud

Ayers $1.50 for repair of my watch this eve. Grude went to Tascosa this evening.

[There is a fall roundup underway, and illicit livestock networks operating in Wilbarger County are being smashed to pieces. On November 21, 1887, Private Hammond arrests Joe Martin in Donley County for cattle rustling near Vernon. Two days later Hammond and local lawmen suddenly descend on nearby "Chouning's Camp," where they arrest locals Yank Chouning for horse theft and Fred Mallory for cattle rustling. Tom Platt and Deputy Sheriff J. T. Conn surprise and arrest A. L. Spencer for cattle theft in Wilbarger County on November 26, 1887, while Dennis Peale and a second ranger arrest John West and J. L. Williams for horse theft activities from New Mexico to Vernon, recovering nine stolen head on November 28, 1887. The next day McMurry dispatches Grude Britton for a trip to distant Dallam County to track down rustler Bogs Campbell. As Billie Bell has been in jail awhile, he can tell the crowding newcomers what to expect.[9]]

NOV 30, 1887 WEDNESDAY MORNING QUANAH

Cold and cloudy and I have to go for a load of wood this morning. McDonald is here and wants Price to go and bring Pall [Paul] Edwards to the Train, as he has an Attachment for him to go to Vernon. W. T. Dunn was over yesterday and said Standlers safe was broken open and De Stephens and Joe Nelson was under arrest for it. No loss as he had taken his mony out before hand. About 2 oclock and we have got back with a good load of roots, and it looks as we may have snow soon. Heavy cloud in the South.

[Of necessity and opportunity crime is moving out of the plains and brakes and into the new towns, settlements, and safes of North Texas. As bankrobber Willie Horton maintained, "That's where the money is." A. T. and the teamster go for more wood, grubbing up mesquite roots, and bringing back a wagon load.]

DEC 1ST, 1887 THURSDAY MORNING QUANAH

A cloudy drizzly Morning and I hope we will not have such weather all the month. Red hurds for us to day and he will have a bad day. Professor Westmoreland and Mr Thacker and wife passed through here yesterday evening, going to Childress to se the Town. I bought an over shirt from Louie Cone last night for $2.20. A Note of our supplies. About 75 # [lbs.] of flour on hand, something near 25 # bacon, coffee near 8 or 10 #, corne something near a sack, sugar not 5 #, potatoes none, onions none, rice 4 or 5 #, and other things in proportion and about the same way Sept 1st.

DEC 2ND, 1887 FRIDAY MORNING QUANAH

This is the first clear morning we have had in some time. As it was very foggy last night I did not look for such a nice morning. About 3 oclock last night it was very clear all around, and at 5 it was cloudy and then clear this morning. Price and I was to have gone to Childress last night, but the train did not come. We was going after Mike Swain for cow steeling in Denton Co. Capt and McDonald and severel others were playing poker last night. Lan Akin, John Darimer, and Tom Shoemate were all playing.

[A warm air mass is overrunning the cold earth, triggering advection fogs the night before. Note that outlaw Swain followed a similar migrational path (from Denton and Collin County to Hardeman County and beyond) as did many of the pioneer settlers. Bill McDonald and Sam McMurry were both avid small-stakes gamblers, a ranger obsession of courting the sense of personal luck while enjoying the fickle play of fate. In the course of field trips with the 1930s Texas Rangers, Dr. Walter Prescott Webb was "compelled" to play many a hand of poker with the officers, but he learned enough to win regularly against J. Frank Dobie and Roy Bedichek.]

DEC 3, 1887 SATURDAY MORNING CHILDRESS

Another nice, clear morning. Price and I came up here yesterday evening for Mike Swain for cow steeling, and got him this morning. He is wanted in Denton Co. We expected a big danse here last night but did not have it. I met a lot of my old Friends.

[Sterling and A. T. arrested Mike Swain without incident at Childress. They traveled back to Vernon, lodged him in the Wilbarger jail, and then telegraphed the sheriff of Denton County that the suspect was available.]

DEC 4, 1887 SUNDAY MORNING QUANAH

Another beautiful morning but right cool. I got up this morning and fed and got my breakfast. Made a fire. Capt and Price took Swain on to Vernon and put him in jaile. And Dennis came back with him. I bought me a Good Holtar [halter] last night for $1.25.

DEC 5, 1887 MONDAY MORNING QUANAH

Another beautiful morning. Cool and plesant. I and Grude saw an order last night written thus: "Mr Mims please pay to J. F. Cane $50.00 Fifty

Dollars and charge to acct." And signed S. A. McMurray. And I know he has been playing poker for the last night or two and in day time too. Well I have to hurd today and I must go and se where the horses is. And go up Town and get my Voucher cashed and put the money away.

[The moralist in Private Miller does not approve of his boss's gambling streak, playing all night at Cain's Saloon, "and in day time too." McMurry and McDonald's poker game started on Thursday night, and by Sunday it seemed to be over. Ranger privates were not permitted to gamble in camp, but there were local outlets of course. There were also friendly horse races and shooting contests with small wagering. McMurry's losses may be considerable, but they are within his means.]

DEC 6, 1887 TUESDAY MORNING QUANAH

Another beautiful morning and Grude has to hurd as Tom Platt has to go up the Road this evening with Capt. I got a nice pair of cuff buttons yesterday and a collar button, all for $2.00, but the collar button was thrown in. Price goes down the Road this morning to Weatherford, to be gone 5 or 6 days. Furman and Bishop went up the road this evening to Tascosa. I had my boots halfsoled this evening.

[Ed Furman and Jim Bishop were assigned to deterrence duty at Tascosa. On November 19 the Fort Worth & Denver City Railroad bridged the Canadian River four miles west of the cowtown. By early December, Irish work gangs were advancing along Oldham County's High Plains toward the far New Mexican border.]

DEC 7, 1887 WEDNESDAY MORNING QUANAH

Cloudy but from the looks in the Northwest, it will clear off. The clouds were very dence and heavy last night. John Platt came up last night and went back this morning. Tom Platt was going down to Ft Worth to day, and was going to take some prisners from Vernon. There was a real nice dance at Mr Louies to night and an oyster supper at Carters Hotel. I did not take any part in it atal. I got to speak to Miss Moneta [Westmoreland] for the first time in a long time.

[The rangers are now operating a prisoner shuttle from the migrational hinterland back to the heartland. Criminals often availed themselves of the same diffusion routes followed by settlers. Tom Platt and a second ranger took four men on the train to Fort Worth to place them in the state-of-the-art Tarrant County Jail.]

DEC 8, 1887 THURSDAY MORNING QUANAH

Tis another real nice day again. I did not get up untill about 11 oclock. And would not of got up just then, had Mr Lously [not] came after one of us to go with him to se a calf, or some parties that had just caught [one] over on Groesbeck [Creek]. They was making a fire and he thought they were going to kill it. The parties was Guss Abbot, Mr Neely, and hair-liped Tom that is running Jes Carpenters ranch over on Arkansaw flat on Pease River.

[A false alarm but a chance to see an old friend, Guss Abbott.]

DEC 9, 1887 FRIDAY MORNING QUANAH

Cloudy and cold this morning. And Smoky looking. It feels very much like we would have some falling weather soon. Grude has to hurd to day. I had a Sick horse last night, but is well apperently this morning. I gave him Spirits of Nitra and than got a bottle of Wizzard oil and gave him about ⅓ one third of it, and it seem to eas him at once. Dennis and Johnie came up to day from Vernon. I got a letter from J. A. Laseter this evening in regard to his watch. I have loaned him $5 on it. He wants me to send it to Colorado City Tx.

[Because rangers furnished their own horses, it was in their interest to keep the animals healthy. Private Miller administered two popular remedies to the sick horse: first, "spirits of nitra" or nitrous ether (a solution of ethyl nitrate in alcohol, used as a diuretic and diaphoretic); and second, Hamlin's Wizard Oil, a very popular patent medicine used for a variety of ailments.[10] John Platt and Dennis Peale return to camp after helping to guard the extra prisoners at the Vernon jail.]

DEC 10, 1887 SATURDAY MORNING QUANAH

A very plesant morning and I am glad to se it as I have to hurd to day. And I have some big boils on my leg. Some thin clouds around and in the NW, and looks as it may rain, or do something else soon. Capt came up yesterday evening. Mrs Wyet left yesterday morning for Galveston she said. I handed C. Coldwell my Voucher yesterday morning, and he gave me credit for it on his book. 60 odd bills [of indictment] found at Vernon court this last session, and all for theft. Seven against old Spencer and about that many for Wiley Bell and old man Bink.

[Three score of indictments is a sign of punishing enforcement against the old-time livestock liberationists, A. L. Spencer, Wiley Bell, and Old Man Bink. "Old" was a relative term, as high birth rates and youthful migrants

lowered the average age of citizens. A man in his forties or certainly fifties might be called "Old Man" so-and-so.]

DEC 11, 1887 SUNDAY MORNING QUANAH

Cloudy and cold this morning and John Platt has to hurd. I got a letter from Lucius [Miller] last night for the first time in a long time. He is still in Montanna, in a logging camp I think. Well I must take a bathe, and go over after my close, and pay up my wash account to old Indian Kate. [Evening entry?] I got a letter from Lucius the last day or so for the first in severel months. He is at Lancy, Jefferson Co., Montana TY.[Territory] in a logging camp.

DEC 12, 1887 MONDAY MORNING QUANAH

A beautifull morning again but right cold. Price came back yesterday evening and Dennis went back to the front. I and Grude went to Church last night, but did not here a very good surmon. But as there was such a small congragation, I dont blame the old preacher for not preaching. He just made a talk. Price and Britton started for Benjamin this evening about 2 oclock by the way of Margaret.

DEC 13, 1887 TUESDAY MORNING QUANAH

Real nice and clear but cool this Morning. The wind is strong from the south. Capt and Tom Platt went to the Front this evening and will go on to Cheyenne to attend the Sales on the 15th. Capt left me in charge for the first time since I have been here.

["The Front" of the Fort Worth & Denver City Railroad reached Oldham County in the early fall of 1887. But Dan Carey's grading crews stayed high on the south side of the Canadian River that September, effectively bypassing the shocked and hysterical community of Tascosa on the north side. Not until some three or so miles beyond the historic town, did Carey's Irishmen turn north, cross the wide river, and advance onto the High Plains along Cheyenne Creek. The tracklayers followed in October.

Under the maximizing corporate management of Grenville Dodge, railroad officials preferred for existing frontier towns to pay heavily for favorable routes, or even better for whole towns to give up and move to their site. All the historic Panhandle towns were slated for economic destruction in 1887–88 by big capital. The roster of bypassed communities included Doan's Store, Margaret, Kirkland, Clarendon, Mobeetie, and Tascosa. Clarendon sensibly surrendered and moved, but diluted her cultural vision and moral dreams in the process of becoming just another railroad town. Tascosa's financial inability to meet exorbitant railroad demands, her tradition of populist challenge to big capital, and her high-minded mercantilist agitation all played directly into the hands of the railroad's own townsite developers.[11]

It is also true that the London-Chicago syndicate behind the XIT wanted to strangle the populist upstarts at Tascosa. They deliberately encouraged the FW&DC to bypass the mercantile town to stifle the competition. Boyce and other XIT managers had their own townsite dreams to promote in Dallam and Hartley Counties.[12]

Populist leaders in Tascosa, inflamed by the brilliant pen of editor Charles Francis Rudolph, lashed out at the railroad with legal action, optimistic editorials, and merchant prayers. The projected town of New Tascosa, near the former Hispano sheepmen's ruins of Borregos Plaza, saw a small spate of land speculation but no real development. Having already alienated the Farwell and XIT syndicate interests, the desperate citizens of Tascosa finally pushed big capital too far in 1886. Using their county seat powers and pioneer political machine, Tascosa officials voted to raise taxes sharply on the syndicate interests and big ranch outfits.

The funds were to pay for a contracted $22,000 iron wagon bridge, a public improvement designed to link Old Tascosa with the projected New Tascosa railroad station across the river. Local officials backed off a bit, but did authorize and build an $18,000 wooden bridge that year, a structure that dared the Canadian River, and worse, dared the wrath of stockmen. The legendary capitalist W. M. D. Lee, owner of the vast LS Ranch in Oldham County, strongly objected to higher taxes and new roads affecting his fiefdom. He saw the project as a white elephant, a so-called "public" improvement designed to bail out private Tascosa merchants. Lee also intensely disliked the pro-nester regional growth that the merchants desired. All these improvements could only lead to new settlers and farmers clamoring to destroy the power of the big ranchers.

When "little men" W. A. Dunn and Jess Jenkins rounded up enough votes to pass new county taxes over his strenuous objection in 1886, W. M. D. Lee decided that the best way to choke out Old Tascosa involved a new commercial rival, but one more amenable to LS interests. In September of 1887 Lee discreetly met Robert Montgomery, chief townsite agent of the FW&DC, at Tascosa.[13] *The two men agreed on a suitable plan to destroy Tascosa.*

Lee donated a nice tract of LS land along the Cheyenne Creek right-of-way to the railroad. Montgomery then surveyed, platted, and heavily promoted this "Cheyenne, Texas" townsite. Cheyenne was located along the tall cottonwoods in Cheyenne Arroyo about three miles above Tascosa. Montgomery's Texas

Townsite Company widely advertised the coming new town in late November and December of 1887. Desperate Tascosa merchants meanwhile sought a court injunction to force the railroad to build a station near their town.]

DEC 14, 1887 WEDNESDAY MORNING QUANAH

Cloudy and cold. J. Y. Henderson stayed with us last night. My and Capt horses were out last night, but Red [Tom O'Hare] got them this morning. About 9 oclock and it [is] raining and sleeting and snowing.

DEC 15, 1887 THURSDAY MORNING QUANAH

A good Snow on the Ground this Morning. Maby 2 inches on an average. The ground was to wet to ly, as it rained at the first of the storm. Rains and sleet all day yesterday. Had not the ground been wet we would of had 4 inches of snow this morning. The Excursion train went by last night. Connected with the Pasenger only 8 Extra coaches. Sam Davis, Saul Stanbury, John Darnell, and Ben Watkin the R.R. Swichman was all drunk last night. A letter from Bradberry to Capt saing he will quit to day.

[The excursion train carried eight coaches of potential lot buyers through the Llano night. They were bound for the great Cheyenne Town Lot Sale, a public auction of new townsite lots held on this day by the Texas Townsite Company. Turnout was good, as some five hundred excursionists showed up for the hoopla. At one in the afternoon J. H. Hosack started the bidding. Montgomery offered easy terms and arranged a good sale, supposedly disposing of two hundred lots and raising $20,000 from sales to the gullible. The citizens of Tascosa maintained an overwhelming revulsion and repugnance toward the spoiler railroad town. Texas Rangers provided security, "after several clashes between Tascosans and railroad officials and workers."[14] The FW&DC desired a ranger presence rather more to protect themselves from outraged local interests—pioneers being "downsized" by big outsider corporations—than to intimidate outlaws and excursionist pickpockets.

Cheyenne, renamed Magenta a year later, flickered into a depressing life for several seasons. There was a two-story hotel, depot, saloon, stockpens, and a few lonely homes. Editor Charles Rudolph at Tascosa called the Cheyenne Town Lot Sale an orchestrated railroad swindle, one stemming from "the direct outcome of a [W. M. D. Lee] spleen that found its opportunity to dictate conditions there and to vent itself here."[15] Mutually despised as neighbors, both Tascosa and Cheyenne disintegrated as other railroad towns boomed. At least the departing Tascosans enjoyed the view of the railroad rival succumbing first. A new golden railroad town, named Amarillo, claimed many of the survivors.

Private Bradbury's resignation, noted as "Discharged J. M. Bradbury Dec 15th," was the first sign that the tight-knit Quanah boys of 1887 were slowly dissolving. But who can blame Jim Bradbury for avoiding a winter ranger camp? Texas Rangers were often hired away by large firms for their above-average qualities, and other privates thought they saw a good opportunity elsewhere and took it. Arctic storms now break across the landscape with increasing ferocity, driving citizens into Quanah's well-stocked saloons.]

DEC 16, 1887 FRIDAY MORNING QUANAH

Cloudy and looks as we will have more falling weather. I am expecting to have to go down to Ft Worth or Vernon to day. Dont know untill I go up Town and se if Capt has Tilagraphed us. As I sent him a Message last night.

DEC 17, 1887 SATURDAY MORNING QUANAH

This is a beautifull morning, clear and nice but Muddy on the ground. I got up and fed and helped to get breakfast after making a fire. I and John Platt has to go to Wichita Falls to day to Meet [Sheriff] W. N. Barker.

DEC 18, 1887 SUNDAY MORNING VERNON

Another very nice morning. Little ting of clouds around. John Platt and I went to Wichita Falls yesterday to meet old man W. N. Barker, Sheriff of Wilbarger Co, with Bood and Bill Brooken in charge. And loged him in Jaile for to give bond, but I dont believe he can. We will board with George McTaylor untill farther orders. I look for Capt to day or to Marrow. To give us different instrctions. Capt came on the noon train. And left orders what to do.

[The capture of the Brooken brothers was a spectacular feat for "Old Man" W. N. Barker. The harassing scouts of Company B kept the gang in motion and on the defensive, while the law chipped away at their members, friends, and contacts. With the late November roundup of other thieves and rustlers, the law was at last getting the upper hand. The old era of country trade in stolen stock between Hardeman County, Greer County, and Wilbarger County—with connections from Mexico to Kansas and points east and west—was drawing to a close. The piratical ways of frontier capital accumulation were ending.

New barbed-wire fencing blocked trails; railroads and telegraphs shuttled lawmen around rapidly; and syndicates and new settlers enforced claims to most of the best land and water. By their very success the Texas Rangers were changing the nature of their future work in the Panhandle. The Panhandle and Greer County were not cleaned up yet, but McMurry and McDonald worked out the means and methodology in the late 1880s. Among the means was the habitual loaning of Texas Rangers to county sheriffs. The additional and trusty firepower encouraged sheriffs to take action.

Miller and John Platt got a good look at Bill and Bood Brooken at Vernon. They personally guarded Bood Brooken on the train to Wichita Falls. The outlaws were not half as impressive as myth and blame had imagined them. Both were typical, young, white male delinquents, inclined to the easy-going, independent ways of livestock thievery and local heists. Gang members enjoyed a peculiar sociability: the excitement of their work, high-spirited companions, and the dime-novel drama of their local reputations. Like the railroad Irish, frontier doctor, and a "goodmany" rangers, outlaw drugs of choice were alcohol and nicotine. Now confronted with the powerful organization and close confinement systems of the western peace officers, the brothers wilted as do roaming bedouins locked in town stockades.]

DEC 19, 1887 MONDAY MORNING VERNON

Another nice cool and clear morning. I went to church last night and heard a Camelite [Campbellite] preach. There was a good croud out. I am expecting to go to Ft Worth to day to take Bood and Bill Brooken back to jaile. Dont know before train time. If W. N. Barker takes him and Capt or Tom dont come down we will go. In Ft Worth to night. We got in about 730 oclock. Sheriff Barker, John Platt, and I came down with Bood Brooken. And went into the jail and saw one of the best jailes I ever saw in my life.

[McMurry detailed Private Miller and John Platt to accompany Sheriff Barker to Fort Worth, "to assist in guarding Bood Brooken to Vernon and Habius Corpus trial."[16] Bood was unable to post bond on a writ of habeas corpus at Vernon's lower court; therefore, Barker's party traveled to Fort Worth—with Miller and Platt continuing as guards—to lodge the defendant in the fancy big-city jail while awaiting district trial. The two rangers returned to Quanah the next day after traveling some 380 miles.

Followers of Alexander Campbell, who envisioned restoring Christianity to a purer, more fundamental state, were called "Campbellites." The proper term today is Disciples of Christ.]

DEC 20, 1887 TUESDAY MORNING FT WORTH

Another clear but cold morning, as a Blue Norther came up last night and is getting colder all the time. John and I stayed at the Mansion [Hotel] last night. We met a goodmany that we knew. I met Willie Lowrance for the first time in nine or ten years. He is in the Pacific Xpress office. Back to Quanah at seven oclock and got three letters, one from Uncle A. L. Steele and one from Frank Twlyfild, and one from Dr Landis of San Diego California, telling me that Adda died Nov 29/87 leaving a little Girle 5 days old.

[The mortality of the Millers in California is tragic. Brother Thomas is dead. Now A. T.'s beloved sister Adda dies days after giving birth. There is nothing one can do. After a giddy prior evening of urban splendor at the Mansion Hotel in Fort Worth, Miller goes back to a darkened winter camp. It is a cold world.]

DEC 21, 1887 WEDNESDAY MORNING QUANAH

Another cold morning. The coldest we have had. Everything is frozed up tite. I have got up and fed and made a fire and am now melting some ice to get breakfast with. John Platt and I had a nice trip to Ft Worth yesterday. Yesterday Morning was a nice Morning but cold. And before 9 oclock it was snowing a little. We eat dinner at Mrs Collins at Wichita Falls last Saturday, Monday and Tuesday. And a nice dinner it was at 25 cts. I got a nice Lunch Tuesday for Mrs Chynaworth and little boy. She was on her way home. Had been visiting her Pa at San Antonia.

DEC 22, 1887 THURSDAY MORNING QUANAH

This is a nice clear and plesant Morning. The Norther has ceased at last and I hope we will have some nice weather now. I did not get up untill after 10 oclock and fed all but the mules and helped make fire and get breakfast. I wrote to Dr Landis, Louie, and A. L. Steele yesterday evening. I have to hurd to day and its now about 12 oclock. I had better saddle up and go and se where the Horses is.

[On this winter solstice day Abner Miller sleeps in, gets some routine camp chores done, herds the remuda, and answers his correspondence. A solemn letter to Dr. Landis on sister Adda's unfortunate death in childbirth is in order. There is no thought of reuniting the family in beautiful Southern California now. He must make a destiny where he is.

The autumn of 1887 was productive for "Soft Voice" McMurry and the boys of Company B. From September 1 to December 22 they made thirty-one

Figure 11. A view of Quanah, Texas, 1890, by Thaddeus M. Fowler. Courtesy Amon Carter Museum, Fort Worth, Texas.

recorded arrests, including three men wanted for assault to murder, eight men indicted for horse theft, six men arrested for cattle theft, two more men sought for embezzlement, three men charged with disorderly conduct, and eight other men wanted for miscellaneous offenses (fighting, carrying pistol, theft, and jumping bail). These were only the official arrests, small-fry incidents were often not included, as the diaries attest. The boys made or assisted county lawmen in other arrests in Quanah and elsewhere.[17] *The courts and jails are undoubtedly busy from their labors. Congratulations are in order.*

Nevertheless, the coming winter of '87–'88 would be a bitter season in many respects. The privates are cooped up in camp, often cold, dispersed hither and yon, and considered corporate hirelings by some citizens. Sterling Price, Grude Britton, Ed Furman, Jim Green, Tom Platt, John Platt, Dennis Peale, Jim Bishop, John Hammond, and A. T. Miller have also made enough fuss and local arrests to have some enemies by now. Most will sensibly quit within a few years. Too many of those who stay in law enforcement—Jim Green and John Hammond have only a few more years—will die on the job from gunshots. Abner Miller and the other privates of Company B could at least look forward to the coming Christmas holidays. Or could they? Signs of tension and stress are showing in the ranger camp that winter.]

CHAPTER 5

"Cold As Whis"

WINTER OF 1888

As she turned toward the north, she saw a puny cloud, slight and fragile, touching the prairie's rim, a white, feathery nothing, like a ball of thistledown floating along the ground. But as she looked, it grew and darkened. Swiftly it spread over the sky until it blotted out the blue, till it hung, a black pall, over the wide heavens. It happened so quickly, with such incredible rapidity that Letty could scarcely believe it, even while her eyes watched it.

—*Dorothy Scarborough,* The Wind

Old-timers in the Panhandle will tell you to-day that it never was a bad country, that its citizens held a high average of character. This is beyond question true. The incidental lawlessness was much less than that which obtained at the same time in the neighboring territory of New Mexico. What was characteristic of the Panhandle as to its long struggle for the rights of property in live stock applied also to most of that part of the state from the water shed of the Brazos west.

—*William MacLeod Raine and Will C. Barnes,*
Cattle, Cowboys, and Rangers

For years pioneers spoke of nature's cruelties with the winters of the '80s. A truly massive arctic front slammed into Texas on January 7, 1886. Blizzards over the following two winters added to the losses. The destruction of livestock was sometimes appalling as fierce winds drove cattle against the new drift fences of barbed wire. The Miller diary records the experience, beginning with the bitter and windy '87 winter detailed in chapter 1. Now in chapter 5, Company B, Frontier Battalion at Quanah—the northernmost rangers—tough out a second season of uncommon cold. Many of these winter days were "cold as whis," writes the diarist, where "whis" or "whiz" is slang for the extraordinary, the unusual, the notable. The lost word comes down to us only in a lingering American colloquialism—the mild exclamation of surprise in "gee whiz!" or "Gee-whilikens!"

There is a general retreat from the adventuresome phases of manhunting as storms break repeatedly over the land. Far safer to comb the new upstart railroad towns and assist local law enforcement in catching hapless fugitives. Crime and punishment has its seasonality too. Life is cold in the ranger dugouts. Christmas is memorable for its cruelty. Going "up Town" is more than a spell of duty now, it is social therapy and body warmth. Gathering around the Pullman stove at the depot, socializing with townsfolk, and possibly taking a nip are ways to keep warm and pass time. The railroad is a crucial spatial link to the outside world. Captain Sam McMurry uses it freely.

There is an gritty ordinariness to this winter of ranger discontent. After a year on the trail Miller is no longer the new kid. Nor is he so sure that ranger camp life is his lifelong destiny. What kind of life was it, after all, living out a winter in a dugout like a prairie dog, consorting with manacled criminals and livestock for long, monotonous stretches, often sick, and poorly paid at that? At times gripes and complaints penetrate Miller's otherwise stoically optimistic and sociable nature.

Of special interest are the intimate glimpses into his companions' personalities. A darker side to almost all "the boys" emerges. The life of a ranger has been so glamorized by myth and media, that some of these entries may shock the tender sentimentalist. But the lawman's struggle with loneliness, boredom, depression, violence, alcoholism, and fear is the mental challenge of the profession, a challenge often as tough and relentless as the worst outlaw who refuses to die and keeps a coming. There are also other career temptations, the new opportunities that a closing frontier offers men of caliber and ambition.

Ultimately it was the mental and physical challenges, contrasted with tempting opportunities elsewhere, that led to resignations from the company force. One of the oldest Texas Rangers traditions is the honorable discharge by request. By the time the Miller diaries cease the following summer, many of the Company B rangers had quit or showed other clear signs of stress, depression, and sickness. Some of the boys wandered off, while a few others obtained better jobs nearby. McMurry fired one teamster for drinking. The turnover rate in ranger privates was perhaps higher than commonly thought. The lack of training, crude camp conditions, and ceaseless troubles in handling armed citizens and belligerent alcoholics also contributed to burnouts and resignations.

With the start of a new year, the Texas Panhandle continued a profound settlement transformation, a massive change in its social and economic geography marked by the arrival of two railroad lines. Industrial capitalism arrived in a big way. Maps of this last frontier, such as Cram's 1887 map or Randall's 1888 map, show this rapid advance and linear dissection of the great ranch region. From a meager population of stockmen—numbering some thirteen hundred souls in the official 1880 census—a large wave of westering folk are now pouring into the railroad growth corridors.

Many of the region's largest towns for the next century—and beyond—are in place by winter's end. Into these new towns poured passengers, ideas, pastimes, vices, machines, domesticates, and bloodstocks of a new order. The diarist buys his first patent razor, watches baseball games, and takes a railroad excursion to scenic Colorado. Judge Nelson of Panhandle City brings in carloads of Hereford bulls to revolutionize the area stock herds. Trail drives are foreshortened trips to the nearest railroad stockpens and switches, like Giles, Rowe, Quanah, and Amarillo. Big ranches have a few more decades of glory before succumbing to a wave of agrarian colonization after 1905.

The sociospatial dimensions of the region are being recast. Communities keyed to cattle, creeks, and rivers—water resources—give way to flat, empty, abstract sites, engineered places keyed to economic determinations. Nature bows before commerce. The colorful original settlements, such as Clarendon and Kirkland, that served the open range must dismantle and relocate for economic survival. Those communities unable or unwilling to relocate, like the adobe Tascosa and the clapboard Mobeetie, can only launch uphill and entirely futile struggles against the bright railroad townsites. It was a brave new world unfolding. Over it all towered the Fort Worth & Denver City and the Panhandle & Santa Fe Railroads.

Winter of 1888

DEC 23, 1887 FRIDAY MORNING QUANAH

Another nice clear morning but cool. The ice is seen every where. I have to haul a load of wood to day, and I must go and get back to go up Town to the sale. The Copper Mines sells a lot of stuff today. Well I went to the sale this evening and saw the things was going very low, but did not buy anything atal.

[The last of the late George McClellan's disgraceful mining promotion was thus liquidated. Among the big losers in the Grand Belt Copper Company were Henry and "Baby Doe" Tabor, and John Forbes, Jr. Wooden-frame mine buildings and some scrap machinery still remained. Farmers would disassemble or haul the buildings away over the years ahead. The old mine site was inundated in the 1990s by the brackish waters of Crowell Brine Lake, a subcomponent of the federal Red River Chloride Control Project.]

DEC 24, 1887 SATURDAY MORNING QUANAH

Another beautifull morning and Tom has to hurd. Pat Westmorland came down and wanted me to buy a nice cake and come up to a Christmass dinner tomarrow. The boys gave me the Laugh on it. And I know I will get fits when I go up Town. The sale will continue to day and I must go up Town and se what is sold.

[The Westmorelands were a socially prominent family.]

DEC 25, 1887 SUNDAY MORNING QUANAH

One more Christmas has come and still I am in no better circumstance than ever. Tis a cloudy morning and looks as we may have some falling weather. The boys has all gon up Town to get a free drink this morning and I will get breakfast myself I reckon. Tom Platt got full and came to camp last night, and got hot and killed both dogs, or at least killed the slut and shot the pup and left him for dead. And he [the pup] went down near the tank and lay there all night. Red went down and shot him this morning. I got some Eggnog at John Darnells this morning and a nice dinner at Mr Randolphs. We had a nice Turkey and cake. Boiled custard &c.

[Few western artists would want to portray the Company B ranger Christmas of '88. Abner Miller is plainly depressed. Two of the boys, Green and Bradbury, had already resigned, received discharges, and left the camp. Other rangers are irritable. Fueled by alcohol, Sergeant Tom Platt flies into a rage, pulls his pistol and shoots two camp dogs. No modern peace officer would want to face an animal cruelty charge on Christmas Sunday. Tom O'Hare's first pistol duty with Company B consists of executing a dying dog. Miller takes the saner winter course by availing himself of family dinners with merchant S. D. Randolph instead of free drinks at the saloons. Fighting the holiday blues with turkey and boiled custard is an excellent idea.]

DEC 26, 1887 MONDAY MORNING QUANAH

This is a very nice morning but cold. I must go over and take my washing to Kates. Noon. I went to Kates this Morning and she and Coody said they had a notion of pulling my ears for not coming to eat Christmas dinner there yesterday. I told them I would eat it to day and have an eggnogg too. So I will go back at 4 oclock with Roleigh Vaughn, [Deputy] Pink Coldwell and have a Eggnog and nice dinner. I surely ought to have enjoyed yesterday. Got up at 10 oclock and eat four times, once in camp, and dinner at Randolphs, and supper at Harpers, and Lunch at Shephards.

[Traces of a page—with writing on both sides—remain from the next leaf in the bound diary. The original entries for the next two days, December 27 and 28, were torn away, discarded by the diarist, and replaced with new entries.]

DEC 27, 1887 TUESDAY MORNING QUANAH

Oh how cold this morning and I have to hurd to day. Well we had a real nice time at old Aunt Kates last night. We had a nice Eggnog and a real nice supper. Mrs Randolph had a 10# boy last night and not a very good night for boys eather. I run a very narrow escape there as I eat dinner there yesterday. Well, I have just got in off a cold ride to day and have lossed the horses. I will have to ride tomarrow.

DEC 28, 1887 WEDNESDAY MOR. QUANAH

Another cold morning but not as cold as yesterday. It is clear and looks as we may have a nice day yet. I have to hunt the horses to day, but Red [Tom O'Hare] will help me. Well I got in about dark and got the horses way south of McDonalds [ranch]. I had a right cold ride to day again but not as cold as yesterday.

DEC 29, 1887 THURSDAY MORNING QUANAH

Windy and a little cloudy this morning and right cold. Luther Clark came this morning with Greens horse. He has bought him and Saddle at $100. He said he cost him about a $100 in a traid. We got 5 bales of hay this morning for the first time since I have been in the company. I have been working all day at the dugout, a cleaning it out and putting in some other posts as its about to break in. I got a letter from E. L. Co[nnell] this morning. It came last evening.

[Hay was a luxury, given low state appropriations for the Frontier Battalion. Instead of a poor ranger's being delegated to ride herd all day in the cold, the boys could keep the animals at the camp and feed them.]

DEC 30, 1887 FRIDAY MORNING QUANAH

Not so cold as has been but cloudy and threatening falling weather. Toms hurd day and we keep the horses tied again and feed them hay. Some one sent Capt a new overcoat on yesterdays train from Schwartz Bros. in Ft Worth. Roleigh, Pink [Coldwell], John Platt and I had a nice oyster fry last night at Shephards [Restaurant]. Louie Cahn sais he and Frank Sheffield will start to Greer Co. on a hunt to day. Tom Platt fed the horses this morning for the first time I have ever knew to.

[The division of camp chores clearly falls heavier on some rangers than others. Trouble-shooting veterans like Tom Platt and Sterling Price were in great demand and on frequent assignments entailing their absence. The novelty of herd duty, dugout repair, and outfitting the camp had long worn off them in any case. Newer and younger recruits found themselves handling proportionally more camp duties.]

DEC 31, 1887 SATURDAY MORNING QUANAH

The last day of 1887 and a cloudy morning. And cold too as a Norther blew up last night. [Private Jim] Bishop came down yesterday on his way to Gonzallas Co. to court. He has a terrible time with his little spell. John and Tom Platt got a nice box of cakes and pies and a ham from there parrants at Austin. A big croud of the Matador boys are in Town. They are shipping about 2000 head of cattle. And it is getting late to ship. Some for beeves and some to Henrietta I believe. About year olds [yearlings]. [Sheriff] Jim Allee and [County Attorney] Hankins came over yesterday evening and went up to Childress. They got Joe Nelson and brought him down to day to give a new bond. As his bondsmen has give him up for his apperiance in next court, for trial of breaking open Standlers Safe. I may get something else to put in this before night, as this is the last day of the year.

JAN 1ST/1888 SUNDAY MORNING QUANAH

I did not get up untill about 10 oclock and found a beautifull day. Clear and plesant as can be. Its now about ½ past four oclock. I am at Indian Kates and they are having dinner. She made me a nice toddy as I have a bad cold and am feeling very bad. I was at a big dance last night at Miss C. W.s. And such a lot of drunk boys and such a time as they did have. Well I must go up town and se who comes up on the train. Tom Platt went down the Road to day. Capt came in this morning.

[Matador Ranch cowboys, Quanah townsmen, and homesick rangers party

hard on New Year's Eve at Miss C. W.'s dance. Some drink like fish, and most sleep in late the next day. New Year's Day has changed little as adults cope with and continue their dissipations.]

JAN 2ND, 1888 MONDAY MORNING QUANAH

Another beautiful morning for the 2nd Morning of 88 and I hope we will have such weather all through this month. I have just got up and its about 11 oclock. I have not got over my bad cold. Tom O'Hair, or Red as we call him, inlisted to day in the Ranger Servis. Mike Cahill takes his place as Teamster.

["Red" is the red-haired Irishman Thomas M. O'Hare. This son of Eire started with Company B as a lowly teamster or "muleskinner." He persevered with his duties and proved affable enough in camp life. McMurry now gives him a chance, enlisting Red as a Texas Ranger. Thomas O'Hare will demonstrate endurance as a ranger. He will stay with Company B until the end of 1893, almost six years of service. His willingness to help A. T. find lost horses commended him for camaraderie, an important factor in ranger camps. Now Red is truly one of the boys.]

JAN 3RD, 1888 TUESDAY MORNING QUANAH

Another real nice morning. Realy lovely. Just as clear and pleasant as can be. Two of the Girles cut up H— last night. Ray & Kate. They got good drunk and started back holering and cussing. We went down to lock them up and Capt came along. He told us to take them down home. And we done so. Ray was to carry but Kate could walk. A Mexican came here last night with two horses that was stolen from the X.I.T Ranch. He was taken up and the thief caught at Vernon some time ago. The horses will be shipped from here to Tascosa. The Mexican cant speak a word of Inglish.

["The girls" are two of Quanah's regular prostitutes. Curiously, the law shows its merciful side when Rae and Kate create a nuisance and disturb the peace. Miller and some other rangers function literally, as they should, by taking the offenders to the "Boos." Why then does McMurry overrule his subordinates, ordering his men to assist and carry the rollicking twosome home? No harm done.

The closing of the frontier has dire spatial consequences for traditional criminal enterprise. Both the theft and transport of stolen stock is becoming increasingly difficult as networks of law officers move rapidly to intercept contraband. The frontier's freedom of action is fading as railroads carve and partition the lawlessness.]

JAN 4TH, 1888 WEDNESDAY MORNING QUANAH

Another prettie morning and I hope it will be so for some time. Old Man Holland died last night. Evening. It has been clouding up a little this evening and getting warm. It looks as we may have some rain. Sam Tylor and a Lady went up on the train this evening. Suppose he has Maud. I put $75. Dollars in W. E. Johnson safe to day. And I sent one dollar to the N.C. [North Carolina] Lottary. A strange insadence happened to night. We saw a Metear fall and then Thunder after a few minuets. Me, Robyn Vaughn, Price, and Red.

[Only a few meteors or bolides are large enough to create a sonic boom. This rare fireball was possibly from the Quadrantid meteor shower in early January, named for its radiant point in the Quadrans Muralis of the old Boötes constellation. The accompanying sonic boom or "thunder" is an excellent indicator that the fireball survived its passage through the atmosphere and landed on the nearby Rolling Plains as a meteorite. The smooth surface of the plains was a favored location for finding meteorites. As early as 1809 Anthony Glass risked his life to journey into the Comanchería plains to steal a sacred meteorite, a large metallic mass he mistakenly thought was platinum.]

JAN 5, 1888 THURSDAY MORNING QUANAH

Warm and cloudy this morning. It looks as if we may have some rain soon. My hurd day and I must go and se about the stock. At noon Mr Fletcher & Adamson came down and took the dugouts and us boys photoes. Just after we all eat dinner. They got here to eat with us. Red bought him a horse from Pat Doland for $45-. Dollars to day. Governor [Grover] Clevaland issued a proclimation. Dec 29/87 ordering us not to sell or buy or ocupy lands in Greer Co.

[Company B Texas Rangers enjoyed publicity and were aware of their media image. They certainly posed at some point for Fletcher's camera, using a typical scenic backdrop as seen in their surviving group photo.[1] *The location of this original photograph is unknown, but the Moody Library has an excellent reproduction in the photo collection assembled by Manuel T. "Lone Wolf" Gonzaullas. Gonzaullas made copies of rare Texas Ranger photographs for his collection. The entry implies that other photos of the Quanah rangers and their camp were taken and may exist. Note that after Tom "Red" O'Hare enlists, he has to switch from using free state mules to buying his own private-sector horse as a ranger.*

President Cleveland's proclamation was a particularly serious blow to the claims of Texas settlers on Greer County lands. In 1881 the Texas legislature had authorized the issuance of land certificates for indigent Texas veterans of the war with Mexico. Texas officials allowed these certificates to be used and sold in Greer County, a practice that encouraged settlement and related squatter activities by Anglo Texans expanding their homeland. State and federal officials attempted to resolve the boundary controversy in 1885, but after the talks stalemated, both sides retrenched to their hard-line positions.

When the Mangum post office first opened in 1886, U.S. Post Office records listed it in "Greer County, Texas." By the beginning of 1887 federal officials changed their records to reflect a different perspective: "Greer County, Indian Territory." That same year the Texas Supreme Court ruled against the issuance of land certificates in Greer County on a technicality overlooked earlier by the state legislature. By the end of the year President Cleveland signed his official proclamation. It reasserted the full federal claim of the United States to Greer County, and it warned one and all about attempting to acquire legitimate title to the lands therein.[2]

The uncertainty of land titles, the dugouts, the weather, and other vicissitudes of life in Greer County all made their appearance in a new traveling folk song. Called "The Greer County Bachelor," the song's chorus spoke for many Texas settlers of Greer:

"Hurrah for Greer County! The land of the free,
The land of the grasshopper, bedbug, and flea.
I'll sing of its praises and tell of its fame
And starve plumb to death on my government claim."[3]*]*

JAN 6TH, 1888 FRIDAY MORNING QUANAH

Heavy fog this morning and day. And right cool as the wind is in the North. Mr and Mrs Backus came in Town this morning and I had a good talk with them. Mr Lewis and Gene in the Hardware Store. And Joe Speck & Smith & Mr Walthall & I all was in Lewis Room last night. We drank a Gallon of wine and eat a fine cake. And we got a little tipsy.

JAN 7, 1888 SATURDAY MORNING QUANAH TX

I did not get up untill about 11 oclock and found Ice and sleet all over the ground and cold as whis. Now about 5 oclock and I have just wrote Johnnie a letter to Mt Mourne [Iredell County] N.C. I must go and get some dinner. Capt and Furman came down to day. I had a nice time to night playing Polker at W. E. Johnsons with John Combs and Smith and Gene. I played a very good game. I learned a goodeal about it.

[Only a week into the new year and Abner Miller is drinking on Friday night and playing cards on Saturday. Are the rangers improving or disintegrating his moral character? Will he make church on Sunday morning? Captain McMurry returns from Tascosa with witnesses for district court trial in Vernon.]

JAN 8, 1888 SUNDAY MORNING QUANAH

Still very cold this morning and I did not get up untill 11 oclock. Now its about ½ past 8 to night and cold oh my. It has been the coldest day we have had this winter. The Thermometer stood at 15° above Zero at ½ past 3 this evening. Dr Anderson said it was down to 10° before night. I think it must be nearly down to zero now.

JAN 9, 1888 MONDAY MORNING QUANAH

I did not get up untill 11 oclock this morning and found it considerably moderated. It is not near so cold as has been for some days. I hope it will thaw now for awhile. I helped to eat another nice cake to night at W. E. Johnsons. It was Joe Specks and was baked by Miss Harper.

[W. E. Johnson's downtown store was a popular place. He was the "wholesale and retail grocer, forwarding, and commission merchant" for 1888 Quanah.[4] *His store cashed state pay vouchers, served sweets to law enforcement officers, and ran a community center of sorts, including poker therapy.]*

JAN 10, 1888 TUESDAY MORNING QUANAH

Well it has moderated a goodeal this morning. We are glad as we have to fix up our wind brake for our horses to day. Capt showed me papers for severel men.

Paul Zweibig. Ples Sanders
Castillo. Thomas.
2 Tate boys for cow steeling.

[Ples Sanders was an '87 acquaintance of Private Miller. He ran an early boomtown saloon in Quanah. Poor Ples. Legal trouble is only a part of his problem. He will be murdered in six weeks.]

JAN 11, 1888 WEDNESDAY MORNING QUANAH

Another cloudy morning and not so cold. We must finish our wind brake for the Horses. John Platt will help us to day. He tended bar for Bob Bose yesterday. While he [Bose] was attending Mrs Baties babies funeral. Capt and Tom went up the road this evening.

[Captain McMurry and Tom Platt went to O. H. Nelson's "Panhandle City." A second major railroad, the Panhandle & Santa Fe (Southern Kansas) Railroad, was also penetrating the Panhandle, in this case from northeast to southwest. Rivals to the FW&DC, the Southern Kansas Railroad tracklayers reached Panhandle City in late December of 1888. This Finch, Lord, and Nelson townsite was the most recent terminus after the establishment of Higgins, Canadian, and Miami. The first train pulled into Panhandle City on January 1, 1888.[5] Railroad workers and rowdies flocked to the whiskey men, risky women, and boisterous action there. Company B rangers also ran security for Judge White's court session in the new town. A violent storm erupts over the plains that evening.]

JAN 12, 1888 THURSDAY MORNING QUANAH

Snow this morning all over the ground. But it is not very cold as the wind is from the S.W. Such a stormy night as we had last night. It rained and sleeted and hailed and snowed. Thundered and lightened and I dont know what all it didnt do. I had a nice time playing cards in Lewis room last night with Fred Rips, Gene, & Mr Lewis. I had a plug taken out of one of my teeth this morning.

[It is all those cakes that lead to "plugs." When will the rangers switch to donuts like the urban constabulary? Private Miller plays off-duty poker with locals like Fred Rip, "manufacturer of Texas and California saddles."[6] Another severe arctic front is heading their way. January's weather is a violent collision of arctic and maritime air masses.]

JAN 13, 1888 FRIDAY MORNING QUANAH

Another nice morning but I am still suffering with my Teeth. I am about half sick and I must go up Town and get something done. I went up to day and had another plug taken out of my tooth and something put in it an it is a goodeal better. And I got a bottel of Tom Scantlens medison and took a dose about ½ past 2 oclock. So I will not go to Town any more this night.

JAN 14, 1888 SATURDAY MORNING QUANAH

Oh my. This is one of the coldest mornings we have had this [winter]. The wind is in the North and the ground is covered with a thin shift of sleet and snow. One oclock and Red and Mike [Cahill] has just gone to the commissary after some hay. Red went after beef and said the Thermometer was 6° below Zero.

JAN 15, 1888 SUNDAY MORNING QUANAH

Still it's cold a fury this morning. I learn the Thermometer was at 11° below zero this morning. I did not go up Town to day untill about train time and it was cold as cuss. I left all the boys in Town, and Pink Coldwell came down with me. I got a letter from Lonie last night. Said all was well and Johnnie was having a fine time at home. Now about 10 oclock and Red and Mike is as drunk as H—. They dont know nothing.

["Cold a fury" and "cold as cuss" take the wind chill into account. Mike Cahill, the new company teamster, and Tom "Red" O'Hare tie one on.]

JAN 16, 1888 MONDAY MORNING QUANAH

It isnt quite so cold as has been and looks like we will have a right nice day to day. Mike [Cahill] is on another drunk to day. Bill Cain has severel men down at the Tank this evening. They are cutting Ice to put up.

[Cain's saloon in Quanah will use this ice when the heat returns.]

JAN 17, 1888 TUESDAY MORNING QUANAH

Well it has moderated a little and I am glad of it. [Sterling] Price came down this morning and fed the horses for the first time in his life. He went and got his breakfast and went in Town. I watered my horse and then took my vest to Kates to have it fixed. I got a letter from E. L. Conell last night.

JAN 18, 1888 WEDNESDAY MORNING QUANAH

A real plesant morning and hope we will have some nice weather now. I must go over to Kates and take my coat to get it lined. Night and time to go to bed. I am feeling bad as I have had a tooth pulled to day and one root broken off. It had three large roots to it. I had two teeth filled and they all cost me $4.00. John Platt and Price started for Panhandle City this evening. I dont know how long they will have to stay.

[Sterling Price and John Platt were dispatched to the rollicking terminus of Panhandle City. They were to restrain the "disorderly elements congregated there."[7] These elements thrived on the town's recent status as a terminus for the Panhandle & Santa Fe (Southern Kansas) Railroad.]

JAN 19, 1888 THURSDAY MORNING QUANAH

Another real nice morning and I am glad as I have to hurd to day. My mouth will be sore as I had my tooth pulled yesterday. I must go over to Kates and get my coat and vest to day. I suppose they are done. I went over to Kates and found my coat and vest were not done. I went up Town and stayed till 1 oclock. And then came down and watered the horses and went back to Town and stayed until about night. J. Y. Henderson came down with me. He has been selling Sorgum at $8 per Ton.

I went up Town to night for the first time in a week.

[Miller's attention to his clothing was reflective of new times for the rangers. As late as the 1870s Texas Rangers had commonly dressed down. A decade later most privates had expensive "Sunday" suits, used a laundress like Kate, and commonly dressed up—at their own expense. It was part of a new, more restrained, and more professional image. Captain McMurry encouraged a western-flavored bourgeois appearance.]

JAN 20, 1888 FRIDAY MORNING QUANAH

A stiff Norther came up last night and it is cold and snowing this morning and cold, oh hush. I went to Kates this morning and got my coat and vest. I found Roleigh Vaughn eating breakfast. He and Pink [Coldwell] and Jones and Red and Bob Boze had a big spell of fun and drinking last night. I have been up Town all day and sick with newralgia and toothache. Its now 4 oclock and I must go to camp and stay there to night.

[Tom "Red" O'Hare is drinking rather steadily with each norther. Miller is no purist teetotaler, but he likely thought the red-haired Irishman drank too freely. Tom Platt and two other rangers are busy in Wilbarger County, guarding prisoners and assisting district court.]

JAN 21, 1888 SATURDAY MORNING QUANAH

Another nice morning and hope we will have a nice day. Well I wrote a letter to C. Askew [in North Carolina] and sent him $3.00 to pay our [Property] Tax, and the Reg. fee and all was $3.14.

I also wrote Lonie a letter, and would of written more but I was feeling so bad I could not. I have had the toothache and newralgia. Jim Allee came over to day and will go to Childress this evening for John Edge. Allee wants me to take him [Edge] to Margaret to Jail. I heard that a man was killed near Childress or Giles last night but no certanty of it.

JAN 22, 1888 SUNDAY MORNING QUANAH

Another delightfull morning and hope it will continue so if I have to go to Margaret to day. [Now] 1 oclock and I dont have to go to Margaret to day as Jim Allee took John Edge on to Vernon, and will go to Margaret from there. He also arrested Mat Chalk and he gave two bonds and will go to Vernon tomarrrow to Allee. Capt sais he wants me to go to Clarendon this evening.

[McMurry arrested Matt Chalk for theft of horses in Lampasas County and lodged him in the Margaret jail. There Matt has time to consider his future. On the 26th the captain took the train to Fort Worth to discuss the Fort Worth & Denver City train robbers with Superintendent Duncan.[8]]

JAN 23, 1888 CLARENDON MONDAY MORNING

Cool but not daylight yet. I cannot se what kind of a day it will be. I will go to Vernon to day with Bill Mankin or Comanche Bill. I got to Quanah all Ok and Capt and Tom went on to Vernon. They took another man they got at Quanah here by the name of Ward. Frank Drace shot and killed Mose Hockie the other day for playing with his wife. Dept Sheriff Harrison of Crosby Co came down to day with John Arnald going to Vernon as witness.

[Private Miller caught a train for Clarendon, where he found and arrested Bill "Comanche Bill" Mankin for forfeiture of bond in Wilbarger County. He accompanied the prisoner back to Quanah, where Mankin was joined by A. B. Ward (wanted for theft in Stephens County). Miller then escorted both prisoners to Vernon.]

JAN 24, 1888 TUESDAY MORNING QUANAH

Cloudy this morning and looks as we will have some falling weather soon. Well I got a letter from Johnnie [Miller] this evening and he sais he will start back in March he thinks. I got a shave to day for the first time in 3 weeks.

[In the melodramatic television series "Walker, Texas Ranger" actor Chuck Norris sports an anachronistic scraggly beard. Mustaches were common in the 1880s, but ranger beards were out of fashion then—and they are not allowed on the Texas Ranger force of today.]

JAN 25, 1888 WEDNESDAY MORNING QUANAH

Another beautiful Morning. I will go out with Mike for a load of wood and to exchange some coffee to Blain Hendersons wife for some butter. Well we got two # of butter.

[Ranger camps significantly improved their fare by trading state-supplied staples for fresh local produce, milk, and eggs. Miller obviously had an arrangement with the nearby J. Y. Henderson farm family.]

JAN 26, 1888 THURSDAY MORNING QUANAH

Another fine morning and I am glad as I have to go to Vernon to day. Dennis and I will take Tom Platts horse and Capt & Mine and a pack. Bill Tudwell or Davis left on the train yesterday evening for the west. This is Tom Platts 30th Birth day. And he is not well. We got to Vernon by 4 oclock. Spencer got 5 years in the pen to day and he has 5 more cases.

[The armed Quanah rangers are providing a little extra security for Wilbarger County court proceedings. After the outdoor scouts and fall harvest of suspects, some rangers at least get to spend time indoors during the winter trials. Poor Bill Tudwell will not get far enough west—at least not far enough to save his life. A. L. Spencer will have plenty of time in East Texas to contemplate the error of his western ways.]

JAN 27, 1888 FRIDAY MORNING VERNON

Another lovely morning and the birds are singing like spring. Well I will go over to the courthouse and se who will be sent to the pen to day. Well, J. Y. Burk was sent to the pen to day for two years for cow steeling. The main witness was Sid Davidson and Berry Hightower. Capt did not come down to day as I understand he went to Ft. Worth to day.

[Captain McMurry caught a train to Fort Worth. He will meet again Panhandle Route Superintendent R. J. Duncan, a Jay Gould man, to discuss the FW&DC "train robbers." Dennis Peale and A. T. Miller stay over in Vernon, likely lodging at McTaylor's boarding house. They will guard the Brooken gangsters and run security for a crowded district court. These courthouse duties were congenial alternatives to cold scouts, but the work was serious. Emotions over verdicts and testimony often ran high. Worried defendants and freshly convicted felons thought often of escape; they watched closely for a single lapse by their guards. The thought of a smuggled gun made judges, prosecutors, and attorneys nervous.]

JAN 28, 1888 SATURDAY MORNING VERNON

Cloudy and warm this morning and looks as we may have some rain. There will be no court to day as it aujurned untill Monday morning. Night and still its cloudy and warm. John Wesley came down this evening after Abners Toombstone and some lumber and oats etc. Jim Alee, [Marshall] Hankins, [Sterling P.] Furgeson, Roberts, Logan, Doolen, and old man Anderson came down on Masonic business.

John Davidson and John Arnell had a little dispute at the Depot this evening on some old thing.

[John Davidson is still the deputy of Wilbarger County. His propensity for troubled public relations seems unabated.]

JAN 29, 1888 SUNDAY MORNING VERNON

Still cloudy and warm. It was reported last night that Bill Brooken had 16 men out on Beever Creek. But no one showed up last night and I dont think they will.

[Bood Brooken cannot raise bail, much less a mounted rescue party of sixteen gang members led by Bill, his fugitive brother. Public rumors show more imagination and numbers than hard-pressed, stressed-out outlaws can muster.]

JAN 30, 1888 MONDAY MORNING VERNON

Another warm morning and I think it will rain soon. I will go over and se who will go the pen to day. Bood Brooken was tried to day and acquitted. Capt and Furman went to Quanah this evening and one will go on to Clarendon. As Bill Tudwell died up there and has to be attended to.

[Bood shakes one charge—but there are others. Tudwell fled Quanah on Thursday but meets his maker in Clarendon over the weekend.]

JAN 31, 1888 TUESDAY MORNING VERNON

A heavy fog this morning and getting cool. [Bood] Brooken has another case to come up this morning. His lawyers are Col. McCall of Weatherford and [D. R.] Britt of Vernon.

[The defendant has excellent counsel. Britt and McCall were outstanding attorneys.]

FEB 1ST, 1888 WEDNESDAY MORNING VERNON

Another foggy morning and damp and warm. Brookens case yesterday was continued. Wiley Bills case comes up to day, and I wander what will be done with it. I dont se any salvation for him as they have good evidence against him. John Hammond and Jarrett, U.S. Marshall of Colwell Ka [Caldwell, Kansas], is witness.

FEB 2ND, 1888 THURSDAY MORNING VERNON

Not so foggy as last two mornings but still warm and a little fog. Wiley Bill got three years in the pen last night. To day I suppose nothing will be done but motions for new trials. ½ past 3 and court is over. All today was taken up by motions for new trials. Red Gates got a new trial. He is the only one. [J. Y.] Burk Appealed. [A. L.] Spencer goes for five years for horse steeling. B. Tompson got two years for cow steeling. Wiley Bill got three years for cow steeling.

[Greer County could be attached to Wilbarger County for judicial purposes. Therefore, rustlers operating in the disputed land might receive their justice in Vernon's Texas courts.]

FEB 3RD, 1888 FRIDAY MORNING VERNON

Still it's warm and damp and still drizzly. James Lunsford was arrested last night for swindlin in Bell Co, and he told us that John Barber that killed the Sheriff of Williamson Co was here yesterday evening, and that he [Barber] was to meet the [outlaw] Boys at the 9 mile Springs by noon to day. Tom, Dennis, John Davidson, and John Allen went up last night about eleven oclock to go after them. Well the boys has come in at 4 oclock. Done no good. Dispasch from Bell Co to hold Lunsford at all hazzard and the Sheriff will be on 1st train.

[After Company B rangers apply some skillful interrogation on Lunsford, they get an interesting new lead. Two Quanah rangers and two Wilbarger deputies make a night ride in the hope of intercepting this killer. John Barber, who shot the sheriff and was charged with robbing the train, eluded the lawmen and fled into Greer County.[9]]

FEB 4, 1888 SATURDAY MORNING VERNON

Still cloudy and raining. It comenced to rain about 6 oclock and looks as it will rain all day. Well Barker and the boys will go to Ft Worth with some prisners to day. I expect to go to Quanah with the horses. Well I went to the train and saw Cap and he sais not to go to Quanah to day as it is raining. Well I met Capt at the train at 4:00 oclock and he sais come on tomarrow. They took Bood Brookin, and Spencer. And Wiley Bill, J. Y. Burk, and the two Arazona Kids. Still it rains. We have had a fine rain sure.

[Here is a rogues' gallery of a half-dozen Texhoma outlaws. Bood has had his walk on the wild side. Now he shambles in chains through the Quanah depot, fighting legal battles mostly to reduce the number and severity of the various charges against him. A. L. Spencer has his own problems addressing a conviction of horse theft. Wily Bill, aka "Comanche Bill," obviously cannot conform to the stricter standards diffusing along the railroad corridors. This brood of bad guys has little chance of escape with Sheriff W. N. Barker, Tom Platt, and three other Company B guards along for the ride from Vernon to the Fort Worth jail.]

FEB 5, 1888 SUNDAY MORNING VERNON

Cold this morning. I se it sleeted last night and will have a cold ride to day. I have to go to Quanah to day with the horses. I did not go yesterday as it was raining. Well I got in Quanah about 5 oclock and had a very good day to come. I found Red [Tom O'Hare] sick when I got here.

FEB 6, 1888 MONDAY MORNING QUANAH

Right prettie day to day. I got up at 11 oclock. I got a letter from Dr. Landis last night as I got home.

FEB 7, 1888 TUESDAY MORNING QUANAH

Another foggy morning. I got up soon this morning. As I was up severel times last night with my bowels. Tom Platt went up the road last night and got Charley Spiers, in Clarendon. He is charged with horse steeling near Abilene.

[Red was down on Sunday and Abner gets the trots on Monday. "Charley Spiers" is an alias. McMurry's later report shows that Tom Platt arrested one "Jno Frye" on February 6 for horse theft in Taylor County.[10]]

FEB 8, 1888 WEDNESDAY MORNING QUANAH

A little cloudy this morning and damp. Dennis went to Childress last night and got [J. B.] McClure and brought him to camp about 2 oclock and we shackeled him and Spiers [John Frye] together. I had shackeled Spiers to a post about 8 oclock. McClure is wanted at Mangum. I have to go to Vernon to day with Spiers. I got to Vernon with my man Spiers or Frye, which ever his name is. All OK. He I expect is the rong man, and McClure, the man for Mangum, is charged with burglery.

FEB 9, 1888 THURSDAY MORNING QUANAH

Cold as whis and sleeting and snowing a little. Tom has to go to Margaret to day with a man [Porter Barr] for carrying a sixshooter. Capt arrested him yesterday evening as he was on the street with it in his hand. He is from Greer Co. L[ouie] Can went on over to old man Taylors last night with Joestine in the back, and suppose he was glad the fellow was arrested. I took a watch for J. S. Long and one for myself to Vernon yesterday to have them fixed.

[A. T. Miller was noted for keeping his possessions in good repair. His diary records solid personal habits of clothing, tool, camp, and horse maintenance.]

FEB 10, 1888 FRIDAY MORNING QUANAH

Another cold cloudy morning. Everything looks as if frozen. The mist is sticking to everything as it falls and a cold looking day. Tom Platt did not come back last night. East bound fraight train was recked yesterday just below Chillicothe and 4 cars thrown off by a Bull. So the pasengers had to meet there and transfur, and it was very late on that account. Al Gentry, Sheriff of Donley Co., passed by this morning going to Ft Worth.

[Grude Britton also sets off on the 10th to distant Dallam County. He carries a murder warrant for Jim Jones. Jones had been there but fled to Arizona to avoid prosecution.[11]]

[Later blue-ink inscription:] I inlisted Feb 11- 1887 at Quanah Tex. as Ranger.

FEB 11, 1888 SATURDAY MORNING QUANAH

A nice morning one more time. Am glad for I and Mike [Cahill] will go to J. Y. Hendersons to get some butter and Eggs if we can. One year to day since I Enlisted in the Ranger company and expect I will be here one year from this if I live and get along well.

We went to Hendersons but got no butter as they were out. Got 4 doz eggs. Got back about 9 oclock. I halled som rock to fix the steps and halled a bbl [barrel] of water.

FEB 12, 1888 SUNDAY MORNING QUANAH

Another beautifull morning and I did not get to camp untill after 6 oclock this morning. I was to se Dora last night and stayed untill 6 oclock. And I had a real nice time. E[noch] Boren, John Bland, and Darby was in Town last night. And Boren told me that Kittie Morrow was married to Dug Dunham. Got a letter from C. Askew this evening sending me our receipt with 70 cts cost added to it for our land down east.

[Enoch Boren and his brothers ranched and ran a livery stable in Margaret. At the tender age of fifteen Miss Kittie Morrow married Richard Douglas Dunham on February 8. The young couple had their first child a year later. Kittie and Doug Dunham moved to Quanah about 1890 and eventually opened the Dunham Confectionery on Main Street.[12]]

FEB 13, 1888 MONDAY MORNING QUANAH

Another beautifull morning and I am glad of it for I have to hurd to day. 2 oclock and I and Mike [Cahill] went to Sam Harpers [blacksmith] shop and ground our axes and got a shoe put on my horse. Price, John, and

Grude got home this morning from the front. And reports every thing quiet.

FEB 14, 1888 TUESDAY MORNING QUANAH

A stiff Norther blew up last night and cold as whis this morning. The train is late this morning about 20 minuits. This has been a very cold day all day. Capt came up this evening and the Sheriff of Decatur.

FEB 15, 1888 WEDNESDAY MORNING QUANAH

Still is cold this morning and as cloudy as last night. The Sheriff of Decatur was down there this morning. He and Furman will go to Mangum this evening. Mike and I went to the commissary this morning and got hay, oats, potatoes, salt, spice & pepper and came back and halled a bbl of water. Got our dinners and had nice fryed pies.

[McMurry assigned Ed Furman to accompany Sheriff Bill Mann of Decatur. Furman knew the Greer County trails quite well by now. The two lawmen were riding for the Campbellite preacher, J. B. Duncan. This Disciple of Christ was charged with appropriating more cattle for himself than souls for the Lord.[13]]

FEB 16, 1888 THURSDAY MORNING QUANAH

A very plesant morning. Pink [Coldwell] and I were at Kates last night awhile and played a few games of cards. I got my watch to day from Vernon and it is in nice fix. The silver watch I got by loaning $5.00 to J. A. Lasater. I had took it and J. S. Longs to Vernon to have them fixed. To night is very foggy and looks like rain. The [Fort Worth] Gazett says this evening that four men robed the Cisco Bank yesterday of $6000. Six Thousand Dollars.

[The 1887 Cisco Bank robbery was notable. Four outlaws made off in a day with more money than Company B's privates earned in a year. Cisco's real fame in banking-crime circles, however, came four decades later. Near Christmas of 1927, four men—"Santa Claus and three helpers"—robbed the First National Bank of Cisco.[14] They completely bungled the job—seven people died during its course and aftermath, and several desperate robbers continued to elude local posses and lawmen. Two legendary Texas Rangers, Captain Tom Hickman and Sergeant Manuel T. "Lone Wolf" Gonzaullas, arrived to restore order and organize the captures.]

FEB 17, 1888 FRIDAY MORNING QUANAH

Cloudy a little this morning but the sun is peeping out and think we will have a nice day. Furman and Bill Mann Sheriff of Wise Co got in this evening with Mr Duncan, the Camelite [Campbellite] preacher, and we will have him to gard to night. Its cloudy and looks as it will rain before morning. Guss Abbott got back from court at Anson and brought the news that Billie Trumble got 99 ninety nine years in the penitensuary for killing John Abbott at Otta in '86. Mat Chalk got away from Allee at Abilene last night.

[The wheels of justice turn slowly on the frontier, but Miller's friend Guss Abbot has the satisfaction of seeing his brother's killer get ninety-nine years in the pen. Otta, Texas, was a nester settlement in Cottle County just west of Margaret.[15] *Prisoner Mat Chalk breaks away from Sheriff Allee and escapes.]*

FEB 18, 1888 SATURDAY MORNING QUANAH

A little rain last night but not very much. Mr Mann, Sheriff of Wise Co, and his prisner is here this morning. They will start for Decatur to day at 11–5. Grude [Britton] hurds to day for the first time in a long time. This has been a very windy day.

FEB 19, 1888 SUNDAY MORNING QUANAH

Well a real nice morning and I am glad as its my hurd day. Red was out of pocket, but I think I know where he was. Mike and I both stayed at camp last night. Capt J. S. Longs crew of surveying party got in yesterday eve. Kates folks came to day.

[Was Red in the saloon? Was he drinking while on the job? Is alcohol the dirty little secret for some of the boys of Company B?]

FEB 20, 1888 MONDAY MORNING QUANAH

Another beautifull morning and hope we will have some nice weather for awhile. I and Pink [Coldwell] was at Kates last night. Dr Sumpter came over with Coody from church and old Kate raised H— with her.

FEB 21, 1888 TUESDAY MORNING QUANAH

Another beautifull morning. Capt arrested Bill Clark last night on suspicion of a Austin murderer. I was wakened at 2 oclock by Grude to go on gard. The first I knew of it. There was to be a dance at Kates last night. But for some reson they did not have it.

FEB 22, 1888 WEDNESDAY MORNING QUANAH

Cloudy and raining this morning. We still have Clark under arrest and have been garding him every night. I was at a dance at old Kates last night. And danced with her for the first time I ever danced with an Indian. Well its now after 8 oclock and I am in W. E. Johnsons [mercantile] house writing this days observation. A letter came this evening in regard to Clark and he is turned loos. Capt went to Clarendon to night.

[McMurry arrested William Clark the day before on a homicide charge from Travis County. The letter convinced him that an innocent man was lodged in jail instead of a murderer. Captain McMurry continued on from Clarendon to Panhandle City. Clamorous citizens there were demanding rangers.[16]]

FEB 23, 1888 THURSDAY MORNING QUANAH

Cloudy again this morning and cold. Expect we will have some bad weather before it clears up. I and Mike got breakfast and fed this morning. Price has to hurd to day. 2 oclock and I have just wrote a letter to Aunt Zou.

FEB 24, 1888 FRIDAY MORNING QUANAH

Another beautifull morning I and Mike got breakfast and I must go to Town. Well we had a nice morning, but a cold, cloudy, and windy evening. I took Tom Williams over to Claud Ayres but I dont think they will be Tried.

FEB 25, 1888 SATURDAY MORN QUANAH

Another nice morning but it may turn out like yesterday, cold and bad. I hope not as I am on hurd to day. I and Mike fed and got breakfast this morning as usual. 1 oclock and I have been to Town and around the Horses etc. Capt came down this morning. I will have to get Claud Ayres another man. Guss Abbott payed me the money back to day. He borrowed of me some time ago $20.00.

[Captain McMurry arrived back in Quanah from several days of assessing Panhandle City. There were the usual troublemakers in this new terminus town.]

FEB 26, 1888 SUNDAY MORNING QUANAH

Another nice morning and am glad to se it. 3 oclock and the boys have just gone on a scout to Greer Co. Tom Platt and John, Price, Grude, and Red went. And Furman goes to Panhandle City this evening. Capt told me yesterday evening that he had ordered Dennis and outfit there already.

Dan Carey's outfit got in this morning with his mules &c. Grading outfit. The last few days has been the most changeable I ever saw. This is a nice bright night.

[Tom Platt and his privates rode into Greer County to arrest Tom Hickman, an associate of the Brooken gang. They got their man, charged him with rustling, and returned with him on the 28th for a total scout of 270 miles. This arrest will have important ramifications.[17]

Panhandle City was the 1887 terminus town of the Panhandle & Santa Fe (Southern Kansas) Railroad during its construction across the Texas Panhandle. Officially platted only a few weeks earlier in January, 1888, it had three saloons to serve the adjacent huge ranches and hired hands. An election was soon held to organize Carson County; railroad officials naturally selected Panhandle City as the county seat. As always there was trouble over the location. Captain McMurry and his rangers rode into the raw town that February, "at the request of citizens to assist in keeping order."[18] *The captain left Private Peale in charge of a small detachment.]*

FEB 27, 1888 MONDAY MORNING QUANAH

Cool and a little cloudy but think we will have a nice day. Mike has gone to haul a load of wood to Pats house. A letter from Johnnie and answered this evening. Jim Cain hit Ples Sanders this evening on the head with his six shooter, and he will die to night I expect. Dpt U.S. Marshall and Frank James killed each other at Wichita Falls to night. And a man was killed to day at Clarendon. I have learned that Frank James the cowboy assisted of the Desparado.

[Four homicides or shootings occur during one winter day—including a lawman. It seems excessive. Does the railroad increase violence, spread drug use, and cause a higher death rate for the new counties? The Wichita Falls gunfight in February was a violent affair. Before succumbing to "lead poisoning," Bob James severely wounded Deputy U.S. Marshal Edward W. Johnson. Ed Johnson's right arm had to be amputated after the fight, but the deputy marshal lived and learned to use his left hand.

Johnson continued service as a federal peace officer. His judgment may have been clouded though. In any case, in August of 1888, some five months later, Ed Johnson will make an infamous name for himself by trumping up charges against the Marlow brothers near Fort Sill. Johnson and his associates will arrest four brothers under deceptive conditions, and haul the unfortunate siblings off to jail in Young County. The saga of "the fighting Marlows" will take a decisive turn after the turn of the year.[19]*]*

FEB 28, 1888 TUESDAY MORNING QUANAH

Cloudy and cool and stormy like this morning. Well. Well. Well. The like of killing that was last night. Ples Sanders died about 6 oclock this morning. His skull was broken. His family is taken it very hard. Cain cannot be found. Capt came down this morning. The Brooken gang was caught yesterday. And taken to Vernon. Dr Dickey came up last night for Ples benefit. [Sheriff] Jim Allee and [County Attorney] Hankins came over to night to try and work up something to get Cain.

[Alas, the death of Ples Sanders, a genial acquaintance of Miller in early-day Quanah. Now Jim Cain truly has the mark on him for killing and fleeing. Tom Platt's detachment to Greer County accomplished more than the arrest of Tom Hickman, alleged cattle rustler—for Hickman wilted under interrogation and gave away his leader's hideout. Using this information lawmen at last arrest the notorious William "Bill" Brooken and take him to Vernon for safe-keeping. Brother Bood is convicted and already headed to prison; now Bill is under arrest and confinement. The favorite gangsters of Quanah gossips are out of action.

McDonald's biographer tells a different, more grandiloquent story. Albert Bigelow Paine wrote in 1909 that Bill McDonald "went after the Brooken gang forthwith," relentlessly following the Brookens, "like a hound on the trail." A determined McDonald "brought in Bood Brooken at last and got him sentenced to five years," while, "Bill Brooken himself escaped to Mexico, was captured there, brought back and sentenced for one hundred and twenty-seven years."[20]

This account is almost certainly a distortion of the actual events. The Miller diaries draw no connections between Bill McDonald and the capture of either of the Brookens. Paine's version of the end of the Brooken gang is exceedingly scanty in details but large in crediting Bill McDonald with the personal destruction of the gang: "The life work of the boy [McDonald] who long ago had begun it by hunting slaves in the swamps of Mississippi was well started, now; his name as a thief-catcher was beginning to be known, and honored, and feared."[21] *It is more likely that Sheriff Barker and Captain McMurry provided the resolve and forces that finally terminated the Brooken gang—not Bill McDonald.]*

FEB 29, 1888 WEDNESDAY MORN QUANAH

Cloudy and raining a little this morning. The boys got in last night with Tom Hickman. I understand that Bill Brookin was the one that was caught of his gang. A one-eyed Mexican and a Duchman and the Duchy

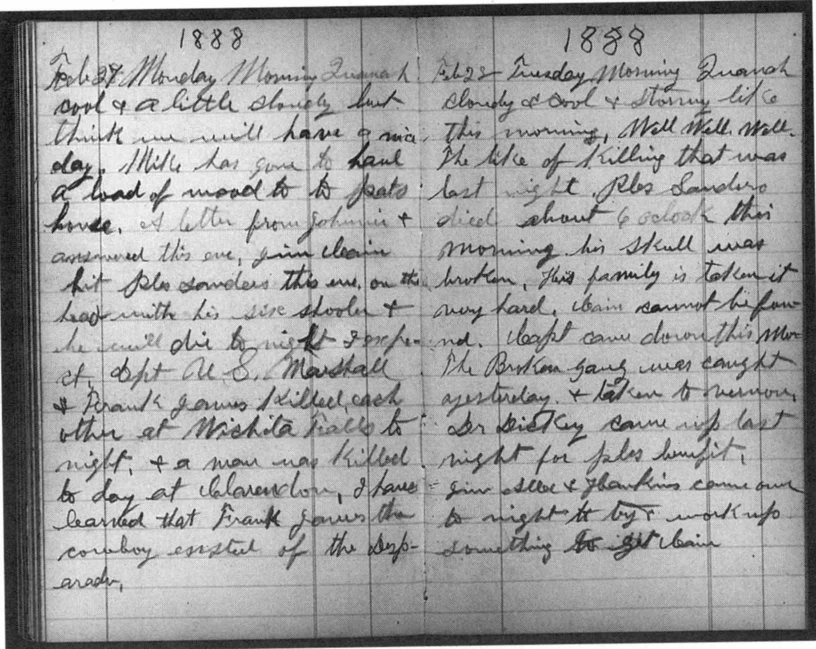

1888
Feb 27 Monday Morning Quanah
cool & a little cloudy but
think we will have a nice
day. Mike has gone to haul
a load of wood to to Platts
house. A letter from Johnnie &
answered this eve, Jim Cain
hit Ples Sanders this eve. on the
head with his sixe shooter &
he will die to night I expect, Dept U.S. Marshall
& Frank James Killed each
other at Wichita Falls to
night; & a man was Killed
to day at Clarendon, I have
learned that Frank James the
cowboy [illegible] of the Desparado,

1888
Feb 28 Tuesday Morning Quanah
cloudy & cool & stormy like
this morning, Well Well Well.
The like of Killing that was
last night, Ples Sanders
died about 6 oclock this
morning his skull was
broken, His family is takin it
very hard, Cain cannot be found. Capt came down this Mor-
The Brooken gang was caught
yesterday. & taken to Vernon,
Dr Dickey came up last
night for Ples benefit,
Jim Allee & Hankins came over
to night to try & work up
something to get Cain

Figure 12. February 27–28 diary pages

[Dutchman] was turned loose. No word from Cain yet. Tom Hickman give Brookin away. About 1 oclock and the sun has come out real nice and looks as we will have a nice day after all. I and [Constable] Akin arrested Jim Cheek last night. Well Furman will be in tomarrow with Jim Cain from Clarendon.

[Company B is busy on leap day. Back in Quanah Tom Platt arrests Frank Barley for disorderly conduct, and A. T. Miller arrests Mr. Cheek for disturbing the peace. Miller confides to his diary that it was Tom Hickman who betrayed Bill Brooken. In Panhandle City, Private Hammond has already arrested "Sailor Bob" and Jim Wilson for fighting. While prowling in Clarendon, Private Ed Furman spots the fugitive Jim Cain. He arrests him for the murder of Ples Sanders.

January storms obviously kept the company close to home; Captain McMurry reported only four arrests for the month. But by the end of February Company B had made fourteen arrests. Captain McMurry's tactics of dispersal and small detachments on the move are proving effective, capable of rounding up wanted men in a dragnet stretching from Tascosa and Clarendon to Greer County and Vernon. On March 1, McMurry reenlists Tom Platt as company sergeant.]

MARCH 1ST, 1888 THURSDAY MORNING QUANAH

A very nice morning again. I will go up Town and se [Jim] Cain come in. 3 oclock. Well Cain was brought down to day. He is having a preleminary trial now at the J. P. office. Furmans brother Henry is here to defend Cain. The J. P. granted him bond at $21000. And came down to $15000, and Cain went to Mobeetie this evening to a District Judge to have it reduced. Sheriff Jim Allee and Henry Furman went with him. I bought a new pair of shopmade boots this eve at $11.00. A nice supper in Town to night.

MARCH 2ND, 1888 FRIDAY MORNING QUANAH

One more beautifull morning but we did not get up untill noon. Mike fed & he & I got breakfast. [Private] Furman has quit. He sais as soon as he gets the books straitened out he will leave. Beason, the man who killed those young Ladies in Gainesville last spring, jumped off the train and is dead. And the man Foresythe, who killed the co[unty] tresurer in S.E. co[unty], was hanged after his confession. We got our Norther to day. I saw a race to day by Miss Easley and a cow.

[Ed Furman's impending departure from the Texas Rangers was not unexpected. The glamour of the ranger force in the 1880s only partially offset the realities of a dangerous job. There was also the question of "burnout." Once the novelty value wore off—probably in a year or two—ranger life began to look rough, dirty, dangerous, and poorly paid. Perhaps Ed Furman felt that the job stress was more than the money was worth. He would still work a hard month in March, traveling to Panhandle City, thence to Canadian, Texas, and arresting four men to prove his grit.[22]

Beason was a Texas Victorian serial killer in Gainesville, who managed to precede—but not exceed—London's notorious Jack-the-Ripper. Beason's attempted escape or remorseful suicide spared him either way from a hangman's noose. Jack-the-Ripper's reign of terror was just about to begin—and he was never caught for his murders of London prostitutes in 1888.]

MARCH 3, 1888 SATURDAY MORNING QUANAH

Snow. Snow. Another snowy morning and cold morning. It thundered and stormed teribly last night. Tom Platt payed me $5.00, the last he owes me this morning. Cain gets out at $5000 bond. Guss Abbott and [I] goes into a barber business together on the halves. I furnish half the money and get half that is taken in. I received my first copy of the Landmark this evening.

MAR 4, 1888 SUNDAY MORNING QUANAH

Cloudy and the snow is still on the ground and looks as if we will have some bad weather. Now about dark. Capt went up the road this evening. I was told to day by Flint that Lawyer Spartman at Vernon died yesterday with a fit, and if so it was from too much whiskey. Saul Stansbury came into Town to day from the West.

MAR 5, 1888 MONDAY MORNING QUANAH

Another cloudy morning, and cold, and my hurd day. Night and the day has been right cold all day with a little drift of snow falling. A new man Enlisted in the company. George Adamson. Furman has concluded to stay awhile longer. John Hammond came up this evening and says we will have to go on a scout to Greer Co tomarrow.

[George R. Adamson enlisted on March 1. He was a well-built young man in his mid-twenties with an accent. Originally a citizen from Canada, he enlisted in Company B at Quanah on March 3, 1888. George (or "Geo" in Miller's diary shorthand) quickly began establishing enterprising and financial ties to the community, much as A. T. Miller did while a Texas Ranger.[23]]

MARCH 6, 1888 TUESDAY MORNING QUANAH

Still its cloudy and looks like rain. Red has to hurd to day. Now 5 oclock and we have just eat a fine pot of soop. Tom Platt and John, Grude, Red, and George Adamson has gone on a scout. They got a lat start this evening. Also, John Hammond went with them.

[Sergeant Platt's detachment is off to Greer County in pursuit of John Grooms, a killer wanted in Dallas County. In Clarendon, Dennis Peale arrests L. D. Addis, charged with "Seduction" at Mobeetie.]

MARCH 7, 1888 WEDNESDAY MORN QUANAH

Still cloudy but looks as we may have a nice day after awhile. I have to go to Jim Wilsons to day to serve a citation on him for [Constable] Akin and will get the [serving] fees. He [Akin] and Capt went to Mangum.

MAR 8, 1888 THURSDAY MORNING QUANAH

Cloudy and windy this morning and I have to hurd to day. I had a trip to Jim Wilsons yesterday to serve a citation in a civil suit. I saw about 20 or more cattle dead on my road yesterday. And saw a nice bunch of Antilope also. Came home with Dr. Tye. He was down at the Lyons place to see severel of the family. I got a card from E. L. C[onnell]. on my arrival. To day I had a shoe put on a my horse. And I took a Note from Guss Abbott for $19.60 for three months with Shaws name to it.

[The late northers and snows of March finish off some winter-weakened cattle. Pronghorn antelope often piled up against the new wire fences—something for which nature had not prepared the species—and they died in frozen drifts by the hundreds.]

MARC 9, 1888 FRIDAY MORNING QUANAH

Another blustry and a little cloudy day. Yesterday and to day has been terrible Windy. Price went out to se Bill McDonald this morning when he saddled up to hurd. The boys and Capt came in this evening about night from Mangum. I put in the safe at W. E. Johnsons to night $70.00 in Greenback & $19.60 in a Note on Gus Abbott and due out $5.00.

[Sergeant Platt's scouting party tracked down John Grooms. Their numbers and force overwhelmed the desperate man. The boys arrested Grooms, charged him with murder, locked him up in the Mangum jail, and wired the sheriff of Dallas County to pick him up.[24]]

MARCH 10, 1888 SATURDAY MORNING QUANAH

Another blustry morning and right cool. My hurd day but I think I will go to Margaret to day if I can get off. I will go up and se Capt. Yes I have seen Capt and I am going to Margaret to day. J. H. Kelly will go over with me. He is just in from Mexico [Missouri].

MARCH 11, 1888 SUNDAY MORNING MARGARET

Oh such a nice morning and I have to get up early. A real nice frost last night and its right cool this morning. I got over here about 5 oclock yesterday evening. I brought the return papers of Jim Wilsons to Allee. I will get $2.00 for serving them. I found all of Mr Wesley['s family] well and Mrs [Frank] Sheffield here.

MARCH 12, 1888 MONDAY MORNING QUANAH

Another beautifull morning. I got back from Margaret about dark last night and had a nice visit. Went over to Kates this morning and got my washing and payed her what I owed her. Then I went up Town and saw the first Brass Band ever came in Quanah. A little show in Town to night. It is McCoys Novelty show. I bought a patent razor yesterday at Margaret from Robert Henry for $2.50 that I cant cut myself with. Oh it is a fine thing.

[The safety razor soon made it more convenient to adopt the clean-shaven lawman look, an image enforced by the modern Texas Rangers.]

MARCH 13, 1888 TUESDAY MORNING QUANAH

Another beautifull morning and I am glad as I am on hurd to day. I went to the show last night and had a very nice time. Night and this has been one of the loveliest days we have had this spring. Jim Witherspoon came over to night and he is going to Vernon tomarrow. Show in Town to night again.

[McMurry travels the same day to Gainesville for a meeting of the Northwest Texas Cattle Raisers Association, precursor to the important Texas and Southwestern Cattle Raisers Association.[25] Charles Goodnight is there, complaining of rustlers, and the captain gathers other news for further Panhandle investigations.]

MARCH 14, 1887 WEDNESDAY MORNING QUANAH

Another beautifull morning and looks so much like spring. Summer will soon be here and what a nice thing it will be. I bought a nice suit of close to day at $24.00 off Coldwell. Well this has been another beautifull day and I hope we will have such for awhile. I sent my silver watch to Vernon to day with Witherspoon to have it put in good running order.

MARCH 15, 1888 THURSDAY MORNING QUANAH

Another nice morning and I must go up Town and get some money and pay Coldwell for my suit I bought yesterday. 2 oclock and I have just got through eating my dinner. I payed Coldwell to day $24.00 for my suit.

[Some rangers spent a good share of their pay on better duds.]

MARC 16, 1888 FRIDAY MORNING QUANAH

Another beautiful morning. [Private Sterling] Price and Tom Ferguson had some trouble last night and Price shot at Tom. But no harm done. Capt put Price under arrest untill he made an investigation and turned him loose. So every thing is nice and quiet. And a fine warm day. Capt came up last night.

[Miller is wrong about the Price-Ferguson outcome. To be sure Sterling Price was exonerated by Captain McMurry's investigation of the shooting incident. But there was significant psychological damage done to Tom Ferguson in the incident, damage that is going to explode in the near future. Harm was done.

There is no mention of this serious incident in McMurry's "Monthly Return" for March, 1888. McMurry's arrest of Sterling Price was perhaps more for public consumption than official inquiry, as no paperwork was recorded for it or the investigation. McMurry likely "arrested" Sterling, heard a satisfactory version of the incident, and told him to go back to work.]

MARCH 17, 1888 SATURDAY MORN QUANAH

Another nice morning and hope it will be so today. McDonald got back yesterday eve. Dr Sumpter was on a drunk last night. The boys all have green ribbons on and even on the Engine as its St Patricks Day.

[Dr. Sumpter appears to have a substance abuse problem. Festive Irish green decorates both train engines and state lawmen on St. Patrick's Day. Bill McDonald returns, no doubt sporting a green ribbon and imbibing a friendly drink.]

MARCH 18, 1888 SUNDAY MORNING QUANAH

Cloudy and sprinkling to day. Now about 1 oclock and it has rained considerable amount to day. Mike [Cahill] is prettie full this morning. And I am afraid he will get drunk before he lets up.

[Captain McMurry discharges Mike Cahill on April 14, 1888—presumably for one too many drunks. Red, the former teamster, drinks as well, but he apparently does a better job of separating it from the job.]

MARCH 19, 1888 MONDAY MORNING QUANAH

Cloudy and cold this morning and as blustry as get out. Night and oh what a day. This has been the windiest day we have had in a long, long, time. Capt went up the road this evening. I think and hope we will have a nice day tomarrow.

[Captain McMurry traveled to Collingsworth County and then on to Mobeetie in Wheeler County. His aim was to investigate the loud complaints of cattle theft from large ranches, especially the Rocking Chair Ranche. He spent five days on the stage roads and traveled 320 miles. After a brief return to Quanah on March 25, "by permission of Genl King" he will catch the new train to Denver, Colorado, the next day.[26]]

MARCH 20, 1888 TUESDAY MORNING QUANAH

Well. This is quite different morning to yesterday. Tis so nice spring like looking day. Night. Well we have had a real nice day. I played the first game of base ball this eve I ever did. Everything quiet.

MARCH 21, 1888 WEDNESDAY MORNING QUANAH

Another cloudy and windy day. We did not get up untill about 10 oclock. Little Timmie came to deliver a dispach and woak us. [The dispatch was] from John Hammond at Vernon that he was in Trouble.

MARC 22, 1888 THURSDAY MORNING QUANAH

Another right nice day. We were late about getting up again. The Steel Gang beet the Picked Nine playing base ball this evening. Right windy again this evening. Mike was on another drunk last night but all O.K. now.

[The diffusion of popular culture greatly facilitated the social transformation of the closing frontier. The railroad brought more than commodities; it also brought new ideas on social behavior, like brass band concerts ("McCoys Novelty Show") or playing the organized sport of "base ball." The New York Knickerbocker Club version of a bat-and-ball game spread widely in the East after 1845, but this fashionable Northern team game was largely spurned in antebellum Texas. Yankee soldier teams played the game some during Reconstruction. The adoption of the sport by the urban middle-class of Texas in the '70s and '80s finally converted a Northern popular culture influence into a national pastime.

The arrival of baseball to the West Texas frontier is interesting. It was readily taken up by these notorious individualists. "I played the first game of base ball this eve I ever did," wrote Miller. Even though it was a heavily ruled team sport, it featured individuals prominently and frequently. From the Scotch-Irish point of view, it also offered foot races, some physical contact, and frenetic chases. The arrival of the railroad was often the precipitating factor in the formation of a local baseball club.[27] *Railroad teams like the "Steel Gang" challenged local young men (Quanah's "Picked Nine") and thus diffused the sport into frontier town society. The healthful game certainly fostered a sense of community.]*

MAR 23, 1888 FRIDAY MORNING QUANAH

We got up about 10 this morning again and considerable clouds around indicating wind to day again. I saw in yesterdays [Fort Worth] Gazett that the capitol at Washington D.C. was struck by lightening on the 21st. No damage. I had a nice game of cards with Mr Lewis and Two Drummers last night. [The salesmen were] by the name of Messrs Dennie & Shoister. I have been reading the History of U.S. to day.

MAR 24, 1888 SATURDAY MORNING QUANAH

Another nice morning though a little clouds around and I think the wind will rise to day. Night and every thing quiet to day. Johnnie [Miller] came back from North Carolina this evening, and Walter Johnson came with him. Johnnie got $35.00 from S. S. Steele for our last years [farm] rent. And he gave me mine and Louis part to keep. Dick Coffee attacked Cains bar keeper for Hill Co this eve. And he will go tomarrow.

MARC 25, 1888 SUNDAY MORNING QUANAH

Another nice morning but a little cloudy againe. My hurd day. I am now sitting writing on the prairie and it is 2 oclock. And I must go. I se the horses not far off. The base ball club will play this eve. And I must go to se them.

[Railroad and town promoters considered leisure culture directly in their interests. Organized leisure activities channeled the aggressions of the young men into civic boosterism and outdoor exercise. Baseball led to interurban games and civic rivalry, which sold more railroad tickets, filled hotels and cafes, and earned bragging rights!

Spectators represented a cross section of society, mingling and conversing, and cheering to the democratic betterment of all. Playing baseball as spring began in 1888 was perhaps a less violent form of competition for many Texans than poker, drinking, or whoring—the traditional low pursuits of towns.

With this entry the black diary comes to an end. On the remaining pages are notes and enumerations on ranger camp supplies found in Appendix B.]

CHAPTER 6

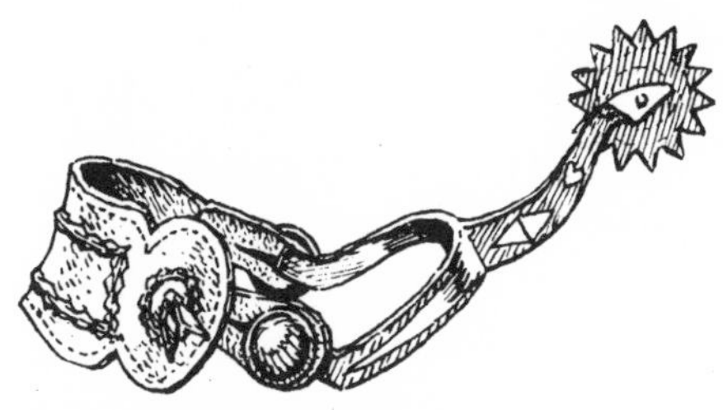

The Maroon Diary

SPRING AND SUMMER OF 1888

Conditions have changed. We still revel in Wild West literature, but there is little of the wild left in the West of to-day, little of the old lawlessness. The most lawless time of America is to-day, but the most lawless parts of America are the most highly civilized parts. The most dangerous section of America is not the West, but the East.

—*Emerson Hough,* The Story of the Outlaw *(1907)*

Here begins the maroon diary of Private Abner Theophilus Miller, the last of his ranger diaries. After forty-two pages of entries Miller abandons his work. No reason is given, but he also resigns from the ranger service at the end of this summer payroll period. Written on the front flyleaf are several ranger notes:

J. E. White Alies [alias] James Sexton
John T. Oliver Sheriff Georgetown Tex Williamson Co.
Joe Kerby wants 2–10 in plow points. Norwegin

He wrote on the reverse of the flyleaf:

G. W. Copeland
a right black Negro at Shephards old Lunch Stand
About 6 ft high & about 160 or 170 #.

Like his fellow rangers, Private Miller badly needs a vacation after a grinding year on the job. He gets a spectacular one. Captain Sam McMurry and many of the boys start the new spring with a historic railroad excursion to

Denver, Colorado. The final tracks of the Fort Worth & Denver City Railroad were joined ceremonially at Union Park on March 14, 1888. Regular passenger service between Fort Worth and Denver would commence in a little more than three weeks. But to inaugurate the line's completion, company and municipal officials planned the grandest excursion of the year between the two cities for the last week of March. Starting on Monday, March 26, and ending on Saturday, March 31, Denver was ablaze with light, filled with sound, and thronged with celebrants. To mark the completion of the Gulf-to-Rockies route, company officials in Fort Worth offered special excursion fares, sold hundreds of tickets, arranged for local publicity, and coordinated the arrival of excursionists from throughout Texas.

Five hundred eager travelers arrived at the Fort Worth depot alone, requiring four sections of FW&DC excursion trains. Each section had fresh-painted coaches, Pullman cars with names like "Kashmier," "Germanic," and "Morelia," and of course a well-stocked dining car. The first section train, trailing banners and cheers, left the crowded Fort Worth depot at 7:30 in the morning in fair weather. A decorated baggage car at the front was heaped with bananas and fruits, symbolizing the miraculous transport of tropical foods from the Gulf of Mexico to the Rocky Mountains. The train skirted the Trinity River and steamed northwest. It was bound for Denver on the fresh steel rails of the "Great Panhandle Route." The historic occasion was suitably reported.[1] *The other section trains followed shortly thereafter, with the last one leaving at 9 A.M.*

Reporters noted with favor that large crowds turned out all along the way to wave on the lucky excursionists. Waving hats and handkerchiefs from the trains at well-wishers became a ritual. Pulling into Wichita Falls around two o'clock, the horde of excursionists found ample meals, including a generous country dinner at the depot cooked and served by the Episcopal Ladies' Society.[2] *From Wichita Falls the trains rolled through Harrold, Vernon, and Chillicothe before reaching the Quanah depot. There Captain McMurry, Abner Miller, the Platt brothers, and other ranger companions boarded one of the excursion sections for the trip to the mountains. Privates Ed Furman and Dennis Peale were left behind to maintain the camp and to lock up the most disorderly drunks.*[3]

In the coaches and Pullmans steaming toward Denver rode a fabulous assemblage of Lone Star cattlemen, investors, brokers, real estate men, contractors, delegates, and journalists. Many of the dignitaries were accompanied by their wives. Among the legendary cattlemen present were Charles Goodnight, Samuel Burk Burnett, Dan Waggoner, S. W. Lomax, Elisha Floyd Ikard,

William Benjamin Worsham (who had coined the derisive term "nesters"), George W. Littlefield, and Ben White Chamberlain.[4] *Rich Texas bankers were a dime a dozen. These men and their wives occupied the better accommodations. The cattle kings—and Mrs. Mabel Day, a cattle queen—were also attending the International Range Association convention held in Denver at the same time.*

The citizens of Denver prepared a glittering "Grand Jubilee" to celebrate the completion of the line. The whole town erupted in festivities the last week of March. Visitors and tourists arrived and scouted the attractions of the metropolis. Elaborate decorations appeared on streets and at the depot itself. Merchants draped their stores with bunting. "Everywhere flags wave in the breeze," a local reporter noted, "while numerous firms have adorned their buildings with crayon drawings. . . ."[5] *Dazzling electric light arches illuminated the city at night. Plans were made for a grand parade, grand ball, and further lavish events.*

Denver's newspaper had great hopes for the new line, the most important event "since the completion of the Denver Pacific in 1870."[6] *Addressing the Denver Chamber of Commerce on the evening of March 27, 1888, Governor John Evans carefully described the geographic and economic advantages that would accrue to the city and Centennial State. The railway linked Denver to more than Fort Worth; indeed, it linked Denver directly to the Gulf of Mexico via Galveston and New Orleans. This piece of economic geography suddenly placed the city within competitive reach of cheap ocean-going transport. Denver's distribution capacity could now conveniently reach the Atlantic trade. With her existing links to the Pacific trade, the governor noted, the metropolis was poised for further expansion and had passed a crisis. Moreover, Colorado's great resources could now flow southeast from the Rockies toward the Gulf.*[7]

The movement of merchandise, capital, and resources between Texas and Colorado vastly stimulated the economic geography of the Texas Panhandle and Rolling Plains. Anticipating the new opportunities, the Rocky Mountain News *printed a special illustrated section, "Through the Panhandle," on Thursday, March 29, 1888. This guide to the new Panhandle counties and towns extolled their "wonderful future," because the existing reality was so slender.*[8] *Soon enough though quantities of coal from Trinidad, Colorado, poured into the Panhandle. Coal fueled the transformative machines coming to the plains from Eastern factories.*

Together the new resources, settlers, and technologies fused in the 1890s and launched a major era of industrialization and urbanization for North Texas after 1900. Steam tractors to plow under the big ranches could not be far behind. Extensive railroad advertising campaigns began to tout the virtues of Panhandle lands and settlement. New systems of environmental perception arose to recast a harsh frontier into a populous granary and irrigated garden of earthly delights. There were demands for even more railroads, warehouses, stockpens, facilities, hotels, and services for people on the move across the region. A new era was dawning.[9]

Spring of 1888

MARCH 26, 1888 MONDAY MORNING QUANAH

A nice but cool morning. I will go to Denver, Colorado on an excursion trip. For $10 and return. I anticipate a good time. We got to Clarendon about 9 oclock and saw a nice crowd. And I met Miss Mamie Grant. She looked lovely.

[Clarendon's depot was equally full of well-wishers. The FW&DC excursion trains were loaded with passengers now, who paused to disembark, stretch their legs, and eat a hearty supper served in town. Charles and Mary Goodnight, who had more memories of Colorado than most Texans, joined the excursion here. A strong norther blew in that afternoon. Increasing snowfalls began to hinder progress after the trains pulled out of Clarendon.[10]*]*

MAR 27, 1888 TUESDAY MORNING CLAYTON N.M.

The ground is covered with snow. We got in the snow as we crossed the plains last night. And cold, cold. We expect to get to Denva to night.

[The engines fought through the snow on the Panhandle and New Mexico tracks without trouble, but the drag delayed the excursion schedule. Only at Trinidad, Colorado, the next afternoon did the travelers stop for a free repast served up by the local townspeople. Pushing on through the cold weather, they reached the Pueblo depot around midnight. There a Denver welcoming committee boarded the train—bearing enough liquor to ply the passengers for the last stretch. A free drink usually made Charles Goodnight feel welcome. The diarist spells Denver as "Denva," a likely phonetic rendering of the town in a southern accent.]

MAR 28, 1888 WEDNESDAY MOR(NING) DENVA COL(ORADO)

A real nice morning. Cool and bracing this morning. We got here last night or this morning at 4 and stoped at the Markam Hotel.

[The first train arrived around 2:40 A.M. with the other sections following thereafter. Noisy band music and salutes from the Rocky Mountain Phantom artillery greeted the Lone Star visitors. Denver had started her own celebrations the day before. Tuesday night Governor John Evans had delivered a keynote address to a packed Chamber of Commerce on the historic significance of the Gulf-to-Rockies route.[11] *Accommodations were tight in the city with all the celebrants arriving.*

A special morning edition of the Rocky Mountain News *greeted the arriving Texans. There were illustrated stories of the new railroad, its leading officials, and everyone's predictions of great success. Denver's buildings bore banners and welcoming mottoes everywhere. City officials had recently erected multicolored arc lights on arches across many downtown streets. The bright lights of the big city greatly impressed Abner Miller and other visitors from the darker hinterland. Wednesday night thousands gathered around the downtown courthouse for a giant outdoor concert by the Cowboy Band of Dodge City, Kansas.*[12]*]*

MAR 29, 1888 THURSDAY MORNING DENVA COL.

Another beautifull morning and a magnificent city this is. We went to se the Battle of Gettisburge to day and a grand site. It is one of the best paintings I ever saw. I bought a nice Diamond pinn to day. Was in a fine Dog show to day. Was at the Grand Ball to night and oh such a crowd. Went to the Court House and saw all over the town.

[Jubilee festivities of all kinds continued on Thursday. Bands roamed and enlivened the streets by day. That night a Grand Jubilee Ball for over four thousand guests was held at the Tabor Grand Opera House—"One of the Greatest Social Receptions in the West." Governor Evans, Mayor Lee, Townsite Agent Robert Montgomery, and many other dignitaries joined the whirl. Carpenters had laid down an enormous dance floor in the opera house, but the immense crush of guests forced an overflow dance at the Chamber of Commerce.

"Looking upon the scene from the top gallery, the sight was as brilliant as a thousand meteors and as intoxicating in its giddy whirl as the first kiss of a sixteen-year-old girl," enthused a local reporter.[13] *The Denver Courthouse was also illuminated at night "from basement to dome." From its upper stories, Abner Miller's view of Denver's crowded streets, fireworks, bands, and electric arches was fabulous.]*

MAR 30, 1888 FRIDAY MORNING DENVA COL

Another nice morning and I am at the European Hotel. Well we went to se the Smelter and a grate many other things to day. Well we surely have had one of the nicest times we ever had. The boys all left last night—but Holly and I. The band went to se the 1st train off and will go to all. As they met us as we came up at Pueblo [Colorado].

[After a visit to the U.S. Denver Mint or "Smelter," the big event of the day was a "Grand Parade" that afternoon. Several miles of bands, dignitaries, and marchers wound their way through Denver, past the reviewing stand, and on to the armory. Along the way men and boys set off Roman candles. At the end there was an exhibit of fireworks, a "grand pyrotechnic display" that duly impressed the Texas contingent.[14]*]*

MAR 31, 1888 SATURDAY MORNING DENVA COL-

Another nice morning and we, that is Holly and I, will go out to se some real estate to day with Major Brown of Alabama. Which I will wright more about after I come back.

[The celebrations ended that morning with a "Grand Old Fashioned Western Barbecue" at the large Denver stockyards. Thousands turned out for the barbecued beef, possum, and mutton. Like other Southerners, Miller could not suppress an interest in the economic opportunities of this dazzling city. Compared to the paltry growth of Margaret, Denver was clearly in the big leagues. The first return trains left that day for Fort Worth.]

APRIL 1ST, 1888 SUNDAY MORNING DENVA COL-

Another nice morning and we will start for Texas this morning. We will go by way of Colorado Springs and take the excursion for Manitou Springs. [Now at] Manitou Iron springs and 3 oclock. And oh what a magnificent place it is, and Colorado Springs also. Colorado Springs has about 5000 inhabitance and Manitou 1000 or 1500. I bought me a nice ring and a nice pin for Lonni and will send it to her. Iron, sulphur, soda, and other waters here.

[The completion of the Gulf-to-Rockies railroad opened the eyes and minds of hundreds of influential Texans to the grandeurs of Colorado. It was suddenly practical for bourgeois Texans by the carload to enjoy "mountain glory"—the cool affinities of Rocky Mountain tourism. The foundation of today's rush and crush of sightseeing Texans in the Rocky Mountains, both summer and winter, began in 1888. Many of the Texas excursionists specifically lingered for the touristic side trip on the Colorado Midland Railroad. They wanted to witness and drink from the famous mineralized springs at Manitou. This classic Anglo-Victorian spa still harvests the summer Texans.]

APR 2, 1888 MONDAY MORNING FOLSOM N M

A beautifull morning and a nice cenery but a little place only a few tents. I met John Davidson here.

[Folsom was a new railroad townsite near Capulin, fashionably named after Frances Folsom, President Grover Cleveland's recent twenty-two-year-old bride.[15] A few weeks before, dignitaries and officials had driven in the last spike north of Folsom to complete the route. Regularly scheduled train service between Fort Worth and Denver began after the first week in April.]

APR 3RD, 1888 TUESDAY MORNING QUANAH TX

A little cloudy and rainy like this morning. We got back last night about 12 oclock and can say we had a fine trip to Denva, Col. I met old Green at Clarendon last night. Capt stayed there and will come on to day I expect.

["Old Green" is Miller's youthful former companion in Company B, James F. "Jim" Green. Jim Green resigned from Company B, possibly to work security for the railroad, but he soon settles in Clarendon and takes a position as a Donley County deputy.]

APR 4, 1888 WEDNESDAY MORNING QUANAH

Another very nice morning and the grass is looking fine. Tom tells me I have to go to Greer Co for a man Friday on the T+ ranch. He is an attach[ed] witness.

[For almost a decade Panhandle cattlemen slipped back and forth over the 100th meridian to avail themselves of the free grass of Greer County. Some new arrivals, like Sam and Joe White of Brady, Texas, even bought a headquarters section near the 100th meridian. The White brothers got good legal title to a section in eastern Collingsworth County, whence they grazed eastward into the disputed grasslands of western Greer. The Rocking Chair Ranche bought out the Whites' OM brand in 1883.

Texas officials took note, considered the unregulated practice, and in 1885 the state began leasing the disputed public lands of Greer at six cents an acre. It was not a lot of money, but then Uncle Sam got nothing and he claimed to be the real owner of the grass. The cattleman Sam White entered southwest Greer (modern Harmon County, Oklahoma), acquired grazing leases, and ran the Teacross Ranch west of Mangum.[16]]

APR 5, 1888 THURSDAY MORNING QUANAH

Right cloudy this morning. I will start for Greer Co this Morning for Hubbard Mathison to Attach him for a witness in the Will Suddith case in Ft [Worth?]. He killed a man below Ft this winter.

[The Lone Ranger rides north from Quanah into Old Greer County. Captain McMurry meanwhile catches a hack from Clarendon to Mobeetie to attend the last meeting of the Panhandle Stock Association. Organized by Charles Goodnight in 1880 to fight rampant rustling, the Panhandle Stock Association in the past had dispatched John Poe to rid Texas of Billy the Kid, built a two-hundred-mile-long drift fence, established the "Winchester Quarantine," and in general made life miserable for cattle thieves tempted by the association members' large herds. Charles Goodnight's spectacular 1886 defection to the Northwest Texas Cattle Raisers Association marked the rapid decline of the Panhandle Stock Association. It disbanded a year later.[17]]

APR 6, 1888 FRIDAY MORNING GREER CO

I left Quanah yesterday thinking it was Friday insted of this. I missed the way yesterday evening and came down here at Mr Guthries on the head of Turkey Creek. Daylight [now] and at the T+ [Teacross Ranch] at last. I got here at day light. And its very cloudy and looks as it will rain soon. Well, Mathison is gone to the H—Y pastur to se about the Horses. So I will go over there and se if I can get him.

[Teacross cowboys direct the private's attention to the northwest. The H Bar Y was a big cattle spread in western Greer. Miller rides most of the day, visiting the H Bar Y and Jay Buckle pastures, but to no avail. He finally turns around, rides back to the Teacross Ranch headquarters, and spends the night.]

APR 7, 1888 SATURDAY MORNING GREER CO TEX

Another rainy like looking morning and I am at the T+. I failed to get Mathison yesterday. Went to the H—Y and the J Buckles and had a hard ride and done no good. So I will start for Quanah to day.

[The daily heading unthinkingly considers Greer County to be a part of Texas. Miller's search for Mathison is complicated by the clannish nature of the denizens of Greer County. News that a single Texas Ranger was looking for someone often reached the concerned individual well before the lawman rode up. The H Bar Y and Jay Buckle were early ranch brands acquired by the Day Land and Cattle Company. J. M. "Doc" Day of Austin, Texas, was the principal.[18]]

APR 8, 1888 SUNDAY MORNING QUANAH

Cloudy and will rain to day I think as it rained some yesterday evening. I got in last night about dark. Tired and wore out. Night and oh what a good rain we had to day.

APR 9, 1888 MONDAY MORNING QUANAH

Another cloudy and rainy like morning. My man did not come in yesterday eve as I thought he might do. Night and every thing quiet. I se Joe Speck is very sick with Inflomation of the bowels.

APR 10, 1888 TUESDAY MORNING QUANAH

A real nice morning and every thing looks so well and growing like. The first through trains started on the Ft. Worth & Denver yesterday. And the South bound is 7 hours late to day. Capt and Furman went up the road this evening.

[Governor John Evans of Colorado launched the first southbound train from Denver.[19]*]*

APR 11, 1888 WEDNESDAY MORNING QUANAH

Cloudy this morning and I have to hurd today. The boys have gone fishing to day on Groesbeck [Creek]. I have just eat dinner and am writing up my diary. Since this day [a] week [has passed], so I may make some mistakes as I have not had time to write before. Now nearly 2 oclock and the train has just passed going South. Well I must go and se about the horses.

APRIL 12, 1888 THURSDAY MORNING QUANAH

Another fine morning after a big rain last night. Everything looks flourishing this morning. I was envited to a big dance at Chillicothe to night, but dont know whether I can go or not.

APRIL 13, 1888 FRIDAY MORNING QUANAH

Another beautifull morning and the birds are singing sweetly and the are is cool and bracing. Capt came down on the 8 oclock train. Dan Careys men and construction trains came in last night and a whole lot of drunk Irish last night.

[McMurry returned from supervising the strategic new link between Washburn and Panhandle City. Dan Carey's construction men had been working hard in building a Denver Road spur reaching out from Washburn toward

the Panhandle City terminus of the Southern Kansas railroad. On April 9 at 7:40 in the evening the two lines were joined.[20]

For a short time Washburn assumed tremendous importance as the intersection of the Southern Kansas with the Fort Worth & Denver. Wise men predicted Washburn's future as a great metropolis. Confident of their geographic position, town officials neglected to offset Henry Sanborn's considerable bribe in 1891. Sanborn intended to claim the final and lasting strategic intersection for his own Glidden and Sanborn townsite at Amarillo. Sanborn's bribe was an action that ensured boom and decades of growth for Amarillo, while Washburn remained an insignificant switch and historical footnote.]

APR 14, 1888 SATURDAY MORNING QUANAH

I dont remember everything that passed. As I am writing on the 19th. Sam Harper, Gene Stevens, and Joe Rucker went a fishing on G. B. [Groesbeck Creek].

[Private Miller is breaking his daily entry habits now, attempting to catch up when he falls behind. Sam Harper was Quanah's blacksmith.]

APR 15, 1888 SUNDAY MORNING QUANAH

A real nice morning and I will go to church to day. Night and I heard a good Surmond to day by Mr Hi[gh]tower. A good croud out. Tom Platt and John and Price started on a scout by Vernon this evening. Capt went down the road to day.

[Sergeant Platt's detachment rode to Seymour at the request of Vernon's Sheriff Barker. Captain McMurry stayed in Vernon on business until the 17th.[21]*]*

APR 16, 1888 MONDAY MORNING QUANAH

Another nice morning and I have gone over to Kates to take my pants. I went to church last night and heard a splended Surmond. I met Mrs Husband to day. Tom Gerin U.S. Marshall or Dpt. Arrested a Negro here this evening that broke Jaile in Ft. Smith ARK.

APR 17, 1888 TUESDAY MORNING QUANAH

Another nice day and I have to hurd to day and must get to se where the horses are. Night and I am all alone, as Grude and Red and George went off to Vernon to join John Hammond and go to Greer Co.

Tom, Grude and Capt went to Clarendon to night after a man for opening Henry Ramseys mail and getting his Louisiana Lotery ticket for $2000.

[Grude Britton's detachment rode into Greer County looking for Ben Wooten and his unsavory associates.]

APR 18, 1888 WEDNESDAY MORNING QUANAH

Another nice morning and the Negro the Dpt marshall left in my charge is in the Boos. O.K. They expect to be down to day. Night and still got the Negro. As Capt and the Marshall did not come down.

APR 19, 1888 THURSDAY MORNING QUANAH

Another plesant morning and still got my Negro and think I will get shed of him to day as Capt and Tom and Green will be down to day. Night and I am free as the Dpt Marshall came by today and got the Negro. Capt went by going on to Ft Worth with the Marshall. They had in charge Mr Barney, the man who got Ramseys Ticket. Old man John Wilson from San Antonia. He sais he is going to stay at camp with us. Well, I must go up Town and se that everything is quiet.

APR 20, 1888 FRIDAY MORNING QUANAH

Another plesant morning but already every thing went off quiet last night for the times now. Good many boys in Town, and drinkin some but all peasable. 1 oclock and got a dispach from Capt that he is in Ft Worth and will come up tomarrow.

APRIL 21, 1888 SATURDAY MORNING QUANAH

Another plesant morning but cloudy. Word came in yesterday evening that a large stud at McCullas ranch was stolen, but it was a mistake. He was found in the pastur last night.

APRIL 22, 1888 SUNDAY MORNING QUANAH

Another plesant morning. Tom, John, and Price got in yesterday evening from Seymour and Vernon. I went out yesterday and killed nine birds and we will have a nice stew to day. Night and I am going to the singing to night.

APRIL 23, 1888 MONDAY MORNING QUANAH

Cloudy and rainy like. Grude, Red and George came in this morning with a Negro. Also John Hammond. 10 oclock and has been raining like smoke and I have to gard the boy that the boys brought in. Night and we have Two Negros in charge, [one accused] of steeling and a witness Jef Organ from Greer Co. I think for witness in U.S. court. And George Copeland here for steeling some money, and I think he is wanted somewhere else.

[As detachments return to Quanah, the wanted men pile up in the boos. Private Britton arrested Jeff Organ for cattle theft in the Indian Territory and a Charles Coupland for theft of money.[22]]

APR 24, 1888 TUESDAY MORNING QUANAH

A cloudy and Muddy Morning. It looks as if we will have a big rain as the clouds are very heavy. Dispach this morning from Capt to bring Jef Organ to Vernon. Mart Cunningham and family came down yesterday evening. He is going down the road to day to buy cattle and mares. To go to raising stock out near the Paladora Canion.

["Paladora Canion" is Palo Duro Canyon. This magnificent sixty-mile-long canyon system lies well west of Quanah. Charles Goodnight was known as its Anglo pioneer, but restless Mart Cunningham thought he still saw advantages a decade later. Cunningham stayed in the Panhandle into the 1890s, participating in the Digger-Kickapoo political controversy in Roberts County.]

APRIL 25, 1888 WEDNESDAY MORN QUANAH

A right plesant morning and I am glad of it for we have to go on a scout to day. Grude Britton, Red and I have to go. We have to go after Joe Creswell at Sam Whites ranch. And Capt sais to follow him if we can get any trace of him. As far as we can.

[Privates Britton, O'Hare, and Miller are given orders to bring in Joe Creswell, wanted in McCullough County for cattle rustling—and suspected of the same activity in the Panhandle. After breakfast in Quanah the three scouts head out, cross the Red River, enter Greer County, and ride north for the next branch of the Red River. About twelve miles west of Mangum, G. S. "Sam" White ran the Teacross Ranch among the sand hills and arroyos along the Salt Fork of the Red River.

At the Teacross Ranch headquarters, near a bend in the Salt Fork branch,

Grude, Red, and A. T. make inquiries and determine that Creswell has moved on. The three rangers advance up the Salt Fork of the Red River until nightfall. This stretch of country is characterized by rough terrain and colorful ravines. They camp for the night on the Salt Fork of the Red River very near the 100th meridian.]

APRIL 26, 1888 THURSDAY MORNING GREER CO

Right cloudy this morning. We are in camp 7 miles from the T+ ranch on Salty Fork [of Red River]. We got here last night about dark.

[After breakfast the boys continue the search on Thursday, going well beyond the 100th meridian and entering the big ranch country of the eastern Panhandle. After trailing along the Salt Fork a bit, the scouts turn north and ride through spring rains for the Elm Creek drainages. They spend most of the day in Collingsworth County (spelled correctly by the diarist in the next entry's heading; a state clerk's earlier error led to the irreversible addition of a "g"). In 1888 most of the county belonged to the "Rockers," the famed Rocking Chair Ranche. Anxious to get rich in Texas cattle, English investors in the 1880s had bought large amounts of land in the Texas Panhandle. The boys camp that night along the South Elm Creek of the Red River, not far from the H Bar Y pasture over in Greer County.]

APRIL 27, 1888 FRIDAY MORNING COLLINSWORTH CO

On Elm creek near H—Y pastur. We got here last night about dark after a hard ride and in the rain apart of the time. And it is raining this morning and the rain run us up last night. Joe Creswell is in this pastur somewhere.

[The boys are combing the pasture of the Rocking Chair Ranche Company, Ltd., an English "estate" encompassing some 300,000 acres of the eastern Panhandle. The brand had a lineage going back to the 1860s, but by 1888 it was J. John Drew's syndicated promotion owned by two wealthy and titled English investors: Sir Edward Majoribanks, Baron of Tweedsmouth, and his brother-in-law, John Campbell Hamilton Gordon, Earl of Aberdeen and later governor-general of Canada.

The co-owners of "Nobility's Ranche" dispatched Sir Edward's younger brother, Archibald John Majoribanks, to serve as bookkeeper and to co-manage syndicate affairs with John Drew. But "Archie" or "Marshie" offended many Texans with his high-handed ways and snobbish behavior. Refusing to socially mingle with the locals, he drank and gambled in Mobeetie, rode to the hounds across the ranch, and shut himself up in headquarters to write long letters.[23]

Continuing north in the course of the day, the rangers ride from South Elm Creek to North Elm Creek. After a short ride they find the old ranch headquarters along North Elm Creek, a set of impressive buildings located not far from the Wheeler County line. A year later the Rocking Chair Ranche headquarters moved to the new townsite of Aberdeen, near the center of the ranch.]

APRIL 28, 1888 SATURDAY MORN AND AT DREWS RANCH

At the Rockenchars Headquarters. It is a nice morning. A heavy dew last night. We will go over on Salt Fork to day to old man Smedleys, where we think Joe is.

[Co-manager John Drew was the effective boss at headquarters as per the diary heading "Drews Ranch." Despite—or because of—Drew's care the Rockers suffered high depredations on their cattle. Cresswell may have been attracted to the ranch because of the double standard that many Texans adopted when it came to English capitalists. Locals considered it very bad to steal a fellow Texan's cattle; they cared less when it came to liberations of an English syndicate's property.

After their inquiries at ranch headquarters, McMurry's men decide to visit Mr. Smedley on the southern border of the Rocking Chair Ranche. They spend much of the day riding south, recrossing the mighty ranch in a fruitless search for Joe Creswell. Failing to catch him, they turn homeward and spend the night at the southern division headquarters of the Rocking Chairs—the "Salt Fork Camp" also called the "Hay Camp."

Despite further capital outlays and better weather, the Rocking Chair Ranche began to lose money heavily after 1888. John Drew blamed local nesters, a claim backed by Amarillo historian Laura Hamner, who noted simply: "Everybody mavericked from the Rocking Chairs."[24] *But among the settlers there were scurrilous whispers that Drew shipped off a hundred ranch cattle on his own hook from "Nobility's Ranche" for every beef illegally taken by a poor nester. When the two titled co-owners arrived to pay a surprise inspection visit, Drew indeed bamboozled the lords by driving the same Rockers herd round and round a hill for an exaggerated cattle tally. This expedient sufficed for only a while. Eventually Texas Rangers from Company B were called in to settle the question of the mysterious cattle thieves of Collingsworth County.*

In April of 1892 Corporal W. J. L. Sullivan and Private Madkins of Company B moved to the new town of Aberdeen, the relocated headquarters of the Rocking Chair Ranche. Both the state and the ranch owners paid a salary to the two rangers. For four months John Sullivan and Madkins lived and boarded at the new ranch townsite of Aberdeen. They also ran an investigation.[25] *W. J. L. Sullivan concluded that the neighbors were far less responsible for any losses than the superintendent, John Drew. Indeed, the worst criminal type he encountered in his sojourn was Mrs. Drew. Dressed in finery and diamonds, the superintendent's wife matter-of-factly solicited Sullivan and Madkins as hired killers. She offered $2,000 apiece for the scalps of seven nesters. "She said she had the money ready to pay for their scalps," Sullivan wrote, "as soon as they were turned over to her."*[26] *A furious Corporal Sullivan correctly tried to set up a sting operation against her (for solicitation of murder), but local officials discouraged and dissuaded him. He continued to think that Mrs. Drew's proper place was a Texas penitentiary.*

By 1892 most of the damage to the ranch had been done anyway. Drew was soon fired and G. W. "Cap" Arrington, nearby rancher and former Texas Ranger captain, took over the operation in mid-1893. Rustling ceased with Arrington in charge, but there was little left to guard.[27]*]*

APRIL 29, 1888 — SUNDAY MORNING ON SALT FORK

At the Rockenchars headquarters at South End of the pastur. And a right nice but very cold morning. We failed to run on Joe [Cresswell] yesterday.

[Old-timers called this line rider camp the "Hay Camp" because its improvements dated back to the HAY Ranch. James R. Haynie had moved a herd here, and he had legally bought a well-watered school section—only he chose his section to be just barely west of the 100th meridian! Haynie therefore turned his HAY herds west into (undisputed) Collingsworth County, and then east into the (disputed) grasslands of Greer County. He made the most of the unusual situation. In December, 1883, the English syndicate behind the Rocking Chair Ranche bought out Haynie. The new owners recast his HAY Camp as the "Salt Fork Camp," the main line rider camp for the company's southern operations.[28]

The Salt Fork Camp indeed anchored the southern end of the Rockers. The Salt Fork branch of the Red River flowed nearby, a decent freshwater river despite its misnomer. Rocking Chair Ranche line riders were based at the camp, and cowboys rode in and out at all hours. A substantial frame house with large kitchen and living room was at the center of the camp. Ranch employees lived here who resupplied and often boarded the line riders and passing cowboys. The Texas Rangers likely slept in the camp as did ordinary cowboys, availing themselves of water and possibly a meal. The community of Dodsonville was established not far away in 1910.

Joe Cresswell eluded the rangers for only a short while. Less than a month later, one of the three scouts, Private Tom "Red" O'Hare, had the satisfaction of arresting Joe in Childress. Red escorted him to the Vernon jail for further disposition. Joe Cresswell could disappear in the ranch pastures, but not in the railroad towns.]

APR 30, 1888 MONDAY MORNING QUANAH

A nice morning and back to Quanah again. Cap and Tom is gone up the road. We will have a horse race tomarrow by Tom Williams and Maldwin.

[Sergeant Tom Platt headed for Tascosa on the track of horse thieves.]

MAY 1, 1888 TUESDAY MORNING QUANAH

Another nice morning and we will go out to se the race near Carrie Wilsons. $10 on the side. Noon and the race come off, and the Horse of Maldwins beat the mare.

MAY 2ND, 1888 WEDNESDAY MORNING QUANAH

Another nice morning. We expected a big rain last night by the clouds but did not have any. Fred Rips came in from Trinadad [Colorado] yesterday evening. He bought some more lots for himself and brother.

[Quanah's saddle merchant, Fred Rips, is speculating in FW&DC townsite real estate in Colorado.]

MAY 3RD, 1888 THURSDAY MORNING QUANAH

Another nice morning and am glad of it as I have to hurd to day. Night. Capt and Tom came down to day. Also Mrs Kelly and Mr Saterwhite, and she went out to his camp last night.

[McMurry returned from business in Mobeetie while Tom Platt, failing to get his man, rode the train back from Tascosa. Mrs. Kelly, of course, had separated recently from a distraught Mr. Kelly. Her arrival with Mr. Saterwhite at the depot and her overnight visit to Saterwhite's camp did not go unnoticed in Quanah.]

MAY 4, 1888 FRIDAY MORNING QUANAH

Another beautifull morning and I will go after wood and milk at old man [J. Y.] Hendersons.

MAY 5, 1888 SATURDAY MORNING QUANAH

A plesant but cloudy morning. I got a letter from Dr Landis of California informing me that my little Niece and Thomas' little babies death came on April 29th /88. Now Thomas and all his family is gone to rest together. So I answered his and a letter from Lucius and Johnnie last night. Capt leaves this morning for Ft Worth and told me to let the mules go if Hutchison came. A good many cow men in Town.

[More sad news from Dr. Landis: all of Thomas Miller's children are now dead.]

MAY 6, 1888 SUNDAY MONDAY MORNING

And just after a terrible big rain last night. It rained so hard I did not go to Town. The Tank is most full this morning. I heard yesterday Mrs Wesley has another Girle baby. Mrs Hawkins has one. Ada and the old Lady will have one soon. The Pease River Bridge is washed away.

[Brother Thomas's children die, while other infants enter the world. Heavy spring storms and tornadoes batter the Rolling Plains. The Pease River turns into a raging torrent. The citizens of Margaret go down to gaze at the awful rampage.

Washouts along the FW&DC tracks caused extensive delays. The Pease River floodwaters quickly smashed the initial railroad bridge and washed its remains far downstream. Captain McMurry had just gone to Fort Worth on May 5 to receive five state mules being transferred from Company D. He is forced to wait in Fort Worth for almost a week, not returning to Quanah until May 12.[29] *Railroad officials must rethink their engineering for bridging the Pease and other rivers of the plains.]*

MAY 7, 1888 MONDAY MORNING QUANAH

Another beautifull morning after another rain last night. Grude and Akin arrested a Negro last night for making a sixshooter play on Bamhill.

MAY 8, 1888 TUESDAY MORNING QUANAH

Another dreary, muddy morning and looks as it will be for some time. I wrote Cowan Steele and E. L. Conell both to day. There will be a picnic down on Groesbeck [Creek] on next Friday and a dance that night at Good & Golstons Store House.

MAY 9, 1888 WEDNESDAY MORNING QUANAH

Another cloudy morning but I dont think it will rain from the looks of the clouds to day. And I hope it wont as I have to hurd.

MAY 10, 1888 THURSDAY MORNING QUANAH TEX

A nice clear morning and warm as summer time. Capt wired to day that the mules was shiped to day for Quanah.

[Mules ride the railroad too. Although transportation habits were expanding, Company B maintained its traditional use of these intelligent animals. Personally chosen by Captain McMurry, these new mules would uphold old ranger traditions. They were frequently used as pack animals to accompany ranger horsemen moving over difficult terrain. Historian Frederick Wilkins notes that mules became an essential part of the folklore of the Frontier Battalion: "The mules, carefully selected and smaller than most of their breed, had impressive endurance and made possible the long scouts that became a Ranger trademark . . . Brave as they were, the feature that most impressed those who wrote about the mules was their sense of the ludicrous. They were animal comedians which, unless confined, wandered through the camps taking food from the Rangers. They delighted in frightening wagon trains by spooking other mules or horses hauling freight."[30]]

MAY 11, 1888 FRIDAY MORNING QUANAH

Stormy this morning. T,is very windy and cloudy and I am afraid it will be a bad day for the picnic. The mules was to be here to day at about 3 or 4 oclock but did not come.

MAY 12, 1888 SATURDAY MORNING QUANAH

A real nice clear morning after a fine dance last night. I had the best time I have had in a long time. The mules came about 3 ½ oclock this morning and Red and Osker drove them to camp at 7 or 8. Nice mules.

[The Friday night dance at Good & Gholston's store is a success. FW&DC workers build a temporary bridge across the Pease River to resume service. McMurry and the mules arrive in Quanah on the train from Fort Worth. Oscar Zollicoffer is the new teamster and future private.]

MAY 13, 1888 SUNDAY MORNING QUANAH

Another beautifull morning. Tom Platt started for Austin this morning to the Dedication of the New Capitol. The Excursion [train] will be along this evening about night. Capt did not go, but suppose he will tomarrow or next day.

[Sergeant Platt worked hard. His excursion to Austin for the dedication of the new Capitol building was a welcome opportunity to rest, recuperate, visit

his retired parents, and enjoy the festivities. From May 14–19 Austin made merry with parades, bands, nightly fireworks, and marching drill teams at Camp Mabry. The City of Austin erected triumphal arches; colored lights lit up the dome; barrooms were crowded; and flags waved everywhere. Twenty thousand people, including Tom Platt, watched the formal parade, speeches, and dedication on May 16. A favorite son of the Panhandle, Temple Lea Houston made the main address, accepting the building on behalf of the citizens of Texas.[31]

The monumental new Capitol was made possible of course by the generous conveyance of three million acres of public domain in the Texas Panhandle to John and Charles Farwell and to other interests of Chicago-London capitalism. In return for the land empire assembled into the XIT domain, the Farwells funded the expensive, pink granite structure that boosted the real estate ambitions and economy of Austin.]

MAY 14, 1888 MONDAY MORNING QUANAH

Another beautifull morning and Grude hurds to day. I went to church last night and heard the Rev Mr Vanenmons Preach. He called on us to take up a collection at the end of the Surmond. Dept Sheriff of Greer Co., Mr Barr, was down to dinner to day with us.

[May 15–19 represents an unprecedented break of five days. Miller's attention and daily interest in the diary are beginning to wane. Has the diary already served its purpose? Grude Britton leads a scout into Greer County to arrest John Chalk for cattle theft, while McMurry travels to Wichita Falls to look after stolen cattle.[32]*]*

MAY 20TH, 1888 SUNDAY MORNING QUANAH

A beautifull morning and we have to go to Vernon to day, i.e. Price and I. Severel days has elapsed since I have written. Not since the 14th. We got to Vernon about 5 this eve on the freight. And had a nice ride. I am to stay here untill Dennis comes down and then go back.

[Sheriff Barker requested two rangers to guard the Vernon jail and attend district court. Privates Sterling Price and Abner Miller are dispatched by train for the job.]

MAY 21ST, 1888 MONDAY MORNING VERNON

Another nice morning and court is to comence to day. The civil docket is to come up first.

[Due to the spring roundup of delinquents, there are now numerous cases coming up in district court. These dockets will keep several rangers busy with court duties for a spell. Duties included screening visitors for guns, guarding and escorting prisoners, and maintaining order.]

MAY 22ND, 1888 TUESDAY MORNING VERNON

Another nice morning but a little cloudy and warm. We look for Capt to day. I hope he will come down and tell us how everything is going on.

[Captain McMurry came down from Quanah on the train, gave instructions to his men, and returned the same day. The following day he rode to Margaret's court session for the same purpose.[33] *Private Miller catches a train back to Quanah. A squall line thunderstorm breaks over the ranger canvas tents Tuesday night.]*

MAY 23RD, 1888 WEDNESDAY MORNING QUANAH

Well a plesant morning after such a storm last night. I never saw as much lightening in my life and a goodeal of hail and a big rain. Well this has been a plesant day. Price was wired by Cap to come to Quanah at once and bring his gun and blankets.

[Miller leaves a storm-lashed camp to resume court duties in Vernon. Sterling Price is recalled from Vernon.]

MAY 24TH, 1888 THURSDAY MORNING VERNON

Another plesant morning. John Hammond tells me that Capt and the company is ordered to Hempstead Waller Co. And the boys went yesterday eve with the horses, and Cap and Price will go to day. Well Price came on the train and got Dennis to go in his place. Tom and John Platt. George Adamson and Grude went yesterday eve with the horses. And Dennis and Cap went today.

[Adjutant General W. H. King ordered McMurry and five men to Hempstead, Texas, to help control the "threatening elements" in Waller County. In particular McMurry's men were to provide security for the preliminary trial of two dangerous toughs, Dick Springfield and Jack McDade.[34] *The railroad made this rapid deployment between population centers possible, as horses and rangers alike were loaded on board and shipped through the night.*

Note that Sterling Price talks Dennis Peale into going in his place, thus leaving Price behind. This substitution will have fateful consequences for Private Price.]

MAY 25, 1888 FRIDAY MORNING VERNON

Another nice morning and hope it will be a nice day. Court is still going on. I understand about 8 bills has been found.

[Privates Price and Miller continue their Vernon court duties.]

MAY 26, 1888 SATURDAY MORN VERNON

Another nice morning after a stormy night. Price went to Quanah to night again. I had an attachment served on me this evening by Sheriff Barker to go to Margaret to attend [Jim] Cains case.

[Sterling Price finishes court duty and catches a train to Quanah. He will be lucky to live out the night.]

MAY 27, 1888 SUNDAY MORNING VERNON

A clear nice morning and every thing nice and plesant. 9 oclock and Harry Edwards and I are out riding and came by the Depot and I got a dispach from [Sterling] Price telling me that he could not come down as he and [Jim] Green had killed Tom Ferguson. So he will have another Trouble. Grigsby the J. P. at Childress came down last night with one of the Creswell boys. And says he has the other one there. Red came down on the train this evening and brought Joe Creswell and I got the peticulars of the killing of Tom Ferguson. When he [Tom Ferguson] found that Price was there he got his winchester and went in, and when Green asked him what he had his gun for, he than shot at Price and than all three shot. Green shot him through the heart. Price shot him in the arm.

[Price and Ferguson had tangled before, as Miller noted in his "no harm done" entry for March 12. Strangely, in that entry he wrote that Price had taken a shot without mentioning whether Tom Ferguson had fired first or even back. In any case the shooting affray in Vernon festered for two and a half months in Ferguson's troubled mind. He finally reached the conclusion that only Price's blood could erase the insult. On Saturday night a brooding and purposeful Tom Ferguson walked into a Quanah saloon armed with a Winchester.

Sterling Price was there, as expected, and ex-ranger Jim Green had joined him. There were some quick words. According to the "Monthly Return," Private Price attempted to arrest Ferguson "for disturbing the peace and carrying unlawful weapons."[35] *It is doubtful that Price had that kind of time. Ferguson's Winchester, while a deadly weapon, is certainly not the ideal gun for a close-quarters shoot-out with two trained lawmen, both aware that the approaching man harbors a nasty grudge against one of the boys. Jim Green's alertness, spoken query, and his fatal shot through Tom Ferguson's heart likely saved Price's life. It was in any event a close call.]*

MAY 28, 1888 MONDAY MORNING VERNON

Oh what a nice morning. Clear and cool and such a plesant morning. Sam Platt came up from Austin yesterday evening. I am glad for I have to go to Margaret to day as witness. Well, I got to Margaret after dark and found the boys all right and not in jail.

[Miller travels to Margaret as a witness in Jim Cain's trial for the murder of Ples Sanders. Price and Green are there of course to account to the court for their shooting of Tom Ferguson. With eyewitness testimony available to exculpate them, neither are jailed in Margaret on a charge of murder.]

MAY 29, 1888 TUESDAY MORNING MARGARET

A real nice morning and I hope it will continue so during court. I am at Mr Wesleys and will go up and se what is going on. Well, Davenport was convicted to day for burglery and sent for two years. He also has to answer a charge for horsesteeling in Wilbarger Co. Price and Green went to Quanah this evening and will be back tomarrow.

MAY 30, 1888 WEDNESDAY MORNING MARGARET

Another nice day. J. R. Cains case comes up to day, and Prices and Greens [case comes up] tomarrow. I intended going to Vernon to day but will stay untill the boys case comes off. Well, I went a fishing with Sam Platt and Ed Furman and Price and [we] caught a few little perch. When we came back, or rather before we went, we found out that Cains case is continued. The boys came in this evening. John Wesley is cutting rye and he has as fine a crop of wheat, oats, rye, and barly as I ever saw.

[John Wesley raised many a fine crop in his remaining years. According to local farmer Tom Smith, in his old age "Mr. Wesley" loved to tell stories of his pioneer days in Hardeman County (now Foard County). One of his last appearances was at the Crowell, Texas, schoolhouse, where he enthralled the Depression-era students with his amusing stories and personal optimism.[36]

John Wesley lies buried not far away from his favorite townsite of Old Margaret. Starting from the 1936 state marker of the Old Margaret townsite, the visitor travels east along a dirt road for a mile or so, turning north at a field boundary. A bumpy two-lane farm lane leads along a field edge before turning west. This is the secret location of the Margaret Cemetery. Locals somehow manage to mow the historic cemetery, so it appears clean and serene. Just to the left after the entrance is the Wesley family plot. Here John Wesley, Mary Wesley, and a child rest forever in the land they loved deeply.]

MAY 31, 1888 THURSDAY MORNING MARGARET

Oh what a fine morning and I am glad. I will go up Town and se what will be done with Price and Green. Noon, well the Boys case was continued untill next court. So I will go to Vernon in the morning. There was a cutting scrape in Quanah last night by some con men.

[Miller hangs around the Margaret courthouse, providing company for Price and Green and demonstrating support for their cause in the Ferguson shooting. This case also gets a continuance.]

JUNE 1ST, 1888 FRIDAY MORNING MARGARET

Another nice morning and I will go down to Vernon to day. The crops from here to Vernon and around here and Vernon is as fine as I ever saw in my life. Its something I will remember a long time. I get in Vernon at ½ past 10. [Temple Lea] Houston, [Attorney] Hankins, and another man came on the hack. Green and Price came down on the train. I learn [A. L.] Spencer has got 2 more years. And Bill Brookin was convicted to day and sent for seven years. And [J. Y.] Burks case is started. The Jurors is set and one witness examined which is Sid Davidson.

[The diffusion of farming along the railroad corridor created new landscapes of breathtaking fecundity. With decent moisture, recently turned virgin soil often produced magnificent crops on the Rolling Plains. Agriculture was possible but hardly economical until railroads penetrated the ranchlands. Cattle could walk to market and eat free along the way, but crops demanded storage, transport, and commodity markets. Once the railroad passed through, farmers moved in quickly and planted bonanza crops all along the line for convenient sale and export.

Miller's vision of these great fields of crops did indeed stir his agrarian soul. Within a few years the visions turned him to a new destiny: farming near the Old Margaret community. He became a granger, a nester, a hoeman—a farmer. John Wesley was a great influence in this direction, as he "proved" that good crops were regularly possible and profitable in the area.

It is the end of the outlaw trail for Bill Brooken, facing seven years in prison. County Attorney Hankins and defense attorney Temple Lea Houston arrive for court. The flamboyant youngest son of Sam Houston, Temple Houston was a familiar figure in early criminal justice for the Northwest Frontier. After two terms in the Texas legislature and fresh from his May 16, 1888, dedication speech at Austin's new Capitol, Houston was at the top of his oratorical form. Edna Ferber fictionalized his character as Yancey Cravat in the novel and movie Cimarron.[37]*]*

JUNE 2ND, 1888 SATURDAY MORNING VERNON

A real nice and cool morning and the court is still Grinding on Burks case. But I dont believe he will go this time. The jurors will hang or acquit according to my notion. I will so state by night. Now 2:50 oclock and the jurors are out on Burks case. After the prosicution attorney spoke 1 hour and 12 minutes after noon with the closing speach.

[J. Y. Burk got two years for "cow steeling" back on January 28 in Vernon's court. Things look a little better for him now. The prosecution's current case looks weak even to Private Miller.]

JUNE 3RD, 1888 SUNDAY MORNING VERNON TEXAS

I have just got up and find a cloudy and sultry day this morning. The Jurors have hung on Burks case and are still together. I understand there are 7 con[vict] to 5 clear.

JUNE 4, 1888 MONDAY MORNING VERNON

Another nice morning and we are still here yet. The Jurors came in at 8 oclock and say they agree to disagree. So another of Burks cases will come up this morning. I met Mrs Baker this morning of Dallas. She is going to [Frank] Sheffields.

JUNE 5, 1888 TUESDAY MORNING VERNON

A cloudy and warm morning but I am thinking we will have another blustry day like yesterday and day before. Not very much done in court yesterday. We came near having a fight yesterday evening by Marian Molett and Hamilton near Doans Store. I gave Al Bateman the brands of our Mules this morning, and he will sure get them if he runs across them. I also met with Tom Baxter this morning for the first time in a couple of years.

JUNE 6, 1888 WEDNESDAY MORNING VERNON

Clear and warm this morning. Price went to Quanah yesterday eve and will be back to day I suppose. Another prisner came to Jaile last night.

From Benjamin and he is going on to Huntsville. Dr Keller is here on his way to Galveston to live. Buckskin Joe is in Town. Wicker brought Indian Jim in to day.

JUNE 7, 1888 THURSDAY MORNING VERNON

Warm and clear this morning and looks as it may rain and I am in hopes it will for its very dry and dusty. 1 oclock and the clouds are very heavy and looks as it may rain at any minit. Price came back to day. He has gone to Quanah for the last two nights. We have had a real good rain to day and now its nice and clear again and about dusk. Price tells me that Green has quit the Engine and gone to working for Al Gentry at $75.00 pr mo.

[The boys were naturally interested in the pay scales and job opportunities of the closing frontier. Private Jim Green followed an old ranger tradition when he quit the force. He only made $30 a month as a Texas Ranger. Presumably the railroad ("the Engine") paid him more as a guard, and then of course he advanced to $75 a month as a deputy sheriff for Donley County. Surely his new job seemed a safer and steadier course of action. How could Deputy Green know that instead it would be his last job?

Jim Green went to work for Albert L. Gentry, the talented sheriff of Donley County at Clarendon, Texas. Raised in a refined and cultivated Tennessee home, Al Gentry joined the Confederate Army, survived the Civil War, and turned West for fortune. His refinement and steady nerves served him well on the frontier. In Abilene, Kansas, he even turned the tables on Wild Bill Hickock. Hickock encountered the well-dressed youth in a saloon and sportingly called for Gentry to dance to his music, firing shots near his feet to test his nerve. Gentry endured the poor jest stoically, without flinching or responding. When Hickock came forward to express admiration, Al pulled his own gun, threw down on Wild Bill, and called in a menacing voice for Hickock to dance or die. Covered unexpectedly by Gentry's gun, Wild Bill Hickock, the Prince of Pistoleers, gamely danced away to everyone's bemused satisfaction.

Albert Gentry drifted into the Panhandle in the early 1880s and settled in Carhart's colony of Clarendon. He worked on the Quarter Circle Heart Ranch but found himself winning the first election as county sheriff of newly organized Donley County in 1882. A gifted peace officer, Al Gentry managed the law and order of "Saint's Roost" for a crucial decade from 1882 to 1892. He avoided creating trouble if possible, but was personally courageous, intrepid, and effective as sheriff. A calm man with a receding hairline and bushy mustache, Gentry married Sella Phillips, the sociable daughter of the White House Hotel proprietor, J. C. White. The popular couple resided in Old Clarendon, then moved to the new townsite with the arrival of the railroad.[38] *Jim Green, the new deputy, soon became a good friend to Al and Sella Gentry.]*

JUNE 8TH, 1888 FRIDAY MORNING QUANAH

Cloudy and warm this morning and looks as it may rain to day again. I was at the Depot at 1100 as the train came in, and five men came down to comence on the train, [that is] to comence work on the R.R. Bridge. It will be an Iron bridge.

JUNE 9TH, 1888 SATURDAY MORNING VERNON

Warm and sultry and feels very much like rain this morning. Tom Platt came up yesterday evening with a new man. And Capt will be up this evening I expect.

[L. E. Delfraisse enlisted on June 5, but the captain discharged him on July 27, 1888.[39] *Delfraisse is never mentioned again in the diaries, perhaps a reflection that he soon failed to fit into the force and quit.]*

JUNE 10, 1888 SUNDAY MORNING VERNON

A nice clear cool morning after such a storm and rain last night. The awning of Dr Edwards Store and the north side of the Hardware Store blew down and we had a very hard rain. Paradise Creek is out of its banks this morning. About 1 oclock and I have had dinner, and a good dinner it was. Chicken, beans, cabbage &c &c. [Sheriff] Jim Allee came down on the train and brought Moore Davidson as a witness. George Benton of Quanah came down and said Dennis [Peale] had come and brought the Horses back. Capt will be up this evening.

[After reining in Waller County, transferring two dangerous prisoners to Brenham, and making some incidental arrests in Hempstead the first part of June, the assigned Company B rangers return by train to Quanah. Dennis Peale was given charge of shipping the horses and outfit back. Captain McMurry stopped over in Austin on June 6 to report personally to Adjutant General King on the "condition of affairs."[40]*]*

JUNE 11, 1888 MONDAY MORNING VERNON

Warm but clear this morning. But feels like rain. Jim Allee slept with me last night. Price went to Quanah yesterday evening. The Judge and [Prosecution] Attorney and Lawyers came in yesterday evening. And everyone is ready for court this morning. Capt did not come yesterday eve as expected. I went to church last night for the first time in a long time. Dan Careys night watchman in Quanah shot himself last night.

[Another suicide. Was this Miller's friend, Louie, the regular night watchman for the railroad? Suicide was considered a crime, thus inviting official interest, although it was obviously difficult to punish the perpetrator. A new man, John W. Bracken, enlisted in Company B and joined the camp. He would become a life-long friend of the Platt brothers.]

JUNE 12, 1888 TUESDAY MORNING VERNON

Cool and plesant this morning and I hope we will have some good harvesting weather for awhile as it is gratly needed. John Platt went up on the train yesterday eve and said Capt was in Ft Worth sick. I have just brought Spencer to the court house to try and have his case carred to the court of appeals I suppose. Also Bill Brooken is over here too. Court is About done. Furman went to Ft Worth to day to make out Reports and Vouchers.

[On his way from Austin back to Quanah, Sam McMurry fell sick in Fort Worth on June 7. The illness turned serious. Private Ed Furman has to take over the captain's paperwork.]

JUNE 13, 1888 WEDNESDAY MORNING VERNON

Another real nice and cool morning. Plesant as it can be. Spencer is still sick of the diarea. He and Bill Brookin got 7 years apiece and will have to go I suppose right soon. If they dont carry their cases to the Court of Appeals.

[Is it the stress of sentencing or the prison food that is getting to the convicted horsethief A. L. Spencer? Neither of the gang members has money for an expensive appeal. What can they do instead?]

JUNE 14, 1888 THURSDAY MORNING VERNON

Cool and plesant but a little cloudy this morning. Court Adjurned yesterday at 10 oclock untill Noon. I was at the train this eve and saw Capt Long and he said Capt [McMurry] would be up tomarrow evening. And then Price and I went to the Lake and went in Bathing. Also Dr Dickey and John Williams was there, besides a lot of Kids.

["Capt Long" refers to Captain Ira Long, a respected veteran of the Frontier Battalion. Ira Long's distinguished service earned him the command of Company A in 1875. Long thus witnessed a major transition for the Texas

Rangers: old rangers rode from settlements against hostile natives, new rangers rode into settlements against hostile whites. Long resigned the service in September, 1876, but returned briefly in 1880 when he was appointed the Company B commander. Captain Long of Company B had excellent officers, including Lieutenant Sam McMurry, a friend, and Sergeant Dick Ware, the man said to have fatally wounded Sam Bass.

Historian Frederick Wilkins calls Captain Long "an interesting character, big, strong, bold, fearless and a superior scout leader. Shortly after his assumption of command, he received a new recruit, Jeff Milton, who was sworn into Ranger service at Swenson's Pasture outside Austin on July 27, 1880."[41]

The other lawman of note mentioned is John T. Williams. Johnny Williams arrived in Wilbarger County in 1882. He turned to law enforcement in the late 1880s, serving as a deputy to Sheriff J. T. Conn. In the early 1890s he was appointed city marshal of Vernon. He was a fair and respected man who earned the trust of the community. The citizens went on to elect Johnny Williams as sheriff of Wilbarger County for five consecutive terms.[42]*]*

JUNE 15, 1888 FRIDAY MORNING VERNON

Another cool and plesant morning. We searched the Jail yesterday evening and got four little saws or one broke in four pieces. The Prisners had comenced to cut out of the top of the cell.

[Company B rangers not only provide security during district court in Vernon, they also search cells and thwart escape attempts by men not optimistic about their chances or lawyers. Bill Brooken and A. L. Spencer will have to go to the state penitentiary in Huntsville after all it seems. McDonald's biographer, as noted earlier, said that Bill Brooken had fled to Mexico, was arrested there, and was extradited back to Texas where he was sentenced to 127 years.[43] *The Miller diary provides a realistic time and place for Bill's captivity. It also provides little support for extravagant claims by either McDonald or his biographer about his role in the destruction of the gang.*

The modern economy of Vernon derives significant income from its nearby major prison and state institution. "Bad Boys, Bad Boys" are shipped from larger urban realms into the Vernon state facilities to serve out their time in the country. Some Texas towns even compete for new prison site locations, just for the local jobs that go with state incarceration. In Vernon the descendants of cowboys and nesters now walk herd on a different kind of stray—state inmates.]

JUNE 16, 1888 SATURDAY MORNING VERNON

A clear and warm morning and the young people of Vernon is glad as they are going fishing over in the Nation. About twenty-four is going. Well, Well. Frank Turbifill came in yesterday evening from San Diego California and Washington T[erritor]y, Utaw, Col[orado]—&c. He was with Thomas [Miller] when he died and told me all about it. So it was a good satisfaction to me. A party of 28 left this morning to fish on Otta [Otter] Creek in the Nation.

JUNE 17, 1888 SUNDAY MORNING VERNON

Another nice clear but very warm morning. This has been a very warm day and now is cool and nice as we had a sprinkle this evening and must of been a good rain somewhere. News came this evening that the Train was Robed near Muskoga, I. T. and only got $8. But killed one man and cripled the News boy and the Mesenger.

[The Muskogee Train Robbery of 1888 was as senseless as current murders of store clerks and customers over small amounts. Muskogee, Indian Territory, was a troubled railroad town on the Missouri, Kansas & Texas Railroad. Historian Glenn Shirley noted that, despite Congressional action to establish a federal court at Muskogee the following March, "banditry still reigned in Indian Territory. Bank and train robberies occurred more frequently than the change of the moon."[44]]

JUNE 18, 1888 MONDAY MORNING VERNON

Cloudy and warm this morning, and looks and feels very much like it will rain soon. News came in last night that the horse case of Spencers was affirmed. So he is ready for the pen now. Old Man Barker started for Bell Co on business yesterday morning.

[Justice was hardly swift. A. L. Spencer's cases have been in the courts for months. But now the convicted horsethief has exhausted his legal remedies and must go to Huntsville. "Old Man Barker" is Sheriff W. N. Barker of Vernon, Texas.]

JUNE 19, 1888 TUESDAY MORNING VERNON

Very cloudy and warm this morning and looks and feels very much like rain. I think the fishing croud will get scared of the cloud and come in to day. This has been a very warm day. I se in the gazette this evening that Peet McMurray & Dick Ware of Colorado City, Texas shot a man in the act of steeling a saddle. After they [the outlaws] had stold Two Horses. Capt did not come up this evening as expected.

[Dick Ware had been just another 1870s Texas Ranger private—until July 19, 1878. While getting a shave in Round Rock that Friday afternoon of 1878, a raging gunbattle broke out. He rushed out—with barber's lather still on his face—joined the battle, cut down outlaw Seaborn Barnes with a bullet to the head, and probably was the one who mortally wounded the notorious outlaw Sam Bass. Official reports credited another ranger, George Herold, for shooting the famous outlaw, but many revisionist historians now recognize Ware for the pistol shot that proved fatal to Bass.

Dick Ware rode west to enlist in Company B, Frontier Battalion, under the doughty Captain Ira Long. While stationed at the Hackberry Springs ranger camp of Company B in 1881, Dick Ware was elected the first sheriff of Mitchell County—by one vote. His disgruntled opponent carried a grudge that later got him shot by another Texas Ranger. Ware made numerous arrests and delivered periodic shootings in his 1880s campaign to clean out Mitchell County and bring Colorado City under control. All the action brought him further press and notoriety.

The "Peet" McMurry referred to by Miller was possibly Douglas McMurry, the half-brother of Captain Sam McMurry. Another veteran of Company B, Douglas McMurry resigned in 1886 to become deputy sheriff under Dick Ware. In 1892 he ran against his boss in the Mitchell County election for sheriff and won by one vote. President Grover Cleveland appointed Dick Ware as U.S. Marshal for the Western District of Texas in 1893.[45]]

JUNE 20, 1888 WEDNESDAY MORNING VERNON

Clear and warm this morning and I know we will have a hot day. Sheriff Barker got in from Bell Co last evening. The Thurmometer stood at 99° about 9 oclock this evening. Capt is still sick in Ft Worth and I am told getting poor all the time. Everything quiet tò day.

[Captain McMurry has been out of action since June 7. His recuperation in Fort Worth was uneven and slow.[46]]

JUNE 21, 1888 THURSDAY MORNING VERNON

Clear and warm this morning. News came in last evening that two of those train robbers near Muscoga was caught. George McTaylor sold his Restaurant yesterday to Mr Murphy. The heat was up to 98 to day again. A heavy cloud to night as it may rain to night. Hura [Hurrah] for Frank Witherspoon. He came in with his new wife this evening. He married

Miss Keys of Dallas yesterday. Mrs J. G. Witherspoon is with them. Two nice hurd of cattle passed through Town to day. One for the East and the other for Greer Co.

[J. G. and Harriet C. Witherspoon were pioneer Hardeman County ranchers. Their large ULA Ranch is now part of the Halsell Ranch. Miss Keys has made a good marriage. After the heady days of razzoopers and outlaws, Quanah is settling down as a friendly cowtown.]

Summer of 1888

JUNE 22ND, 1888 FRIDAY MORNING VERNON

Cloudy and warm this morning. The wind is rising so I am afraid it will blow the rain all away. Old Man Caps and severel others went out on Boggy [Creek in Greer County] saneing [seining] yesterday evening and got a nice lot of fish. Well we got back to Quanah this eve on the train.

[Concluding a lengthy spell of Vernon court duties, the boys return to their Quanah camp. Company B Texas Rangers were active over much of the Panhandle during spring and summer. Tom Platt was a regular in Tascosa, Tom O'Hare worked Clarendon and Quanah, Abner Miller knew the Margaret and Vernon courtrooms, and Ed Furman and Jim Bishop made a number of arrests in Panhandle City in May and June.]

JUNE 23, 1888 SATURDAY MORNING QUANAH

Another cloudy morning and back to Quanah once more. We have been gone nearly five weeks. I have just packed the Trunk to send to Lonie.

JUNE 24, 1888 SUNDAY MORNING QUANAH

A little cloudy and warm this morning Well, Capt came in last night. Also the Sheriff for the boy we have under arrest for Kansas.

[Captain McMurry, barely recovered from his illness, traveled to Clarendon and back on the track of B. L. Dunlap, a forger wanted in Wise County. Dunlap had already "left the country."[47]]

JUNE 25, 1888 MONDAY MORNING QUANAH

Warm and clear this morning and we will have a hot time putting up our Tent. I was at church last night, but it was so crouded we could not get in. Capt and Furman went west this evening.

JUNE 26, 1888 TUESDAY MORNING QUANAH

Cloudy and Raining this morning. Right smart cloud and wind came up last night. But not very much rain. I saw Frank Spoon in Town last night.

JULY 20, 1888 WEDNESDAY MORNING QUANAH

Price quit the Ranger [Company] about the first of this month and is gone to Weatherford. Furman has quit also and gone. I suppose to M.O.[Missouri?] to work for Dan Carey. Severel of the boys has gone out to Mexico since the last of last month and nothing heard of them since.

[The resignations of Sterling Price and Ed Furman, discharged at their requests, created summer personnel problems for Captain McMurry. Both men were experienced and trusted rangers. The diarist suggests that railroad contractor Dan Carey hired them as company security guards, possibly on a construction job at Mexico, Missouri. Price's resignation is more a leave of absence, as he departs on good terms and plans to ranger some more. Indeed, he reenlists on September 3. Ed Furman, the diarist earlier informed us, had been in the habit of writing up the monthly reports for the company; now the captain will likely do so briefly.[48]

A. T. Miller's habit of daily entries has ended. There are no entries from June 27 to July 19, perhaps a reflection of other concerns or the demoralizing resignations of his companions. It is becoming harder to stay faithful to his sweet diary.]

JULY 20TH, 1888 FRIDAY MORNING QUANAH

Plesant this morning. A little ting of clouds around. I have not wrote any since June 26th. And we have had some terrible hot weather. Last Sunday the 15th was the hottest day we have had. The thermometer stood at 109° at Cains saloon. And it has been to 104° and 100° severel days before and since. I was at a barbecue and dance on the 4th [of July] and had a nice time. Also was at Childress night before last, the 18th, at a big dance. Johnnie [Miller] came over and went with me. I and him bought 4 lots in Childress while we were there for $60. And I sent $62 yesterday evening for the lots and Recording of them. Billie Smith Engineer and his fireman Jim Wilson was killed on the R.R. on the night of the 14th last Saturday night near Tascosa. Tom and John Platt starts to Austin to day to meet a brother they havent seen in a long time.

[Heavy rains the week before led to flooding and a washout on Sierrita de la Cruz ("Sweetly Cruze") Creek between Tascosa and Amarillo. The flood waters weakened the crossing, which collapsed in the night just as a FW&DC

freight train was edging its way across. Billy Smith and Jim Wilson were crushed to death in the wreckage.[49]

As Christmas is to winter, so the Fourth of July is to summer. The Independence Day celebrations that summer included an early and organized Texas rodeo, a public event sponsored by the Santa Fe Railroad at Canadian, Texas.[50] *Cowboys hanging around the new railroad stockpens had taken to informal competitions in bronc busting and roping. Spectators sat on fences and watched the action. Organizing this activity into a two-day event at Canadian, inviting cowboys from area ranches to compete, and offering traditional cowboy "tournament" races, prizes, and the like, proved to be exceedingly popular entertainment. New traditions are being forged.]*

JULY 21, 1888 SATURDAY MORNING QUANAH

Clear and nice this morning and looks like we will have a nice day. This has been a nice day and we have had a good time. Very little rain, not enough to keep us in.

JULY 22, 1888 SUNDAY MORNING QUANAH

A little rain this morning but not very much. Johnnie [Miller] and Walter has gone up Town and is going to church I believe.

JULY 23, 1888 MONDAY MORNING QUANAH

Another nice clear morning and as lovely as can be. I was at church last night and went home with Mrs Randolph. Johnnie [Miller] left this morning for the ranch about 10 oclock. And left his coat.

[With the note of his brother's coat left behind, A. T. Miller ceased his journal at the bottom of page 40 of the maroon diary. He never wrote another word on his service in the Texas Rangers. The chronicle ends at this point, although there was once a following page 41–42, a page that was carefully trimmed from the diary. Whatever content was on this following page is now gone. Was there a humiliation or hot words exchanged with someone? A resolve to do better in life than guard hapless locals?

There are further accounts, notes, and even some genealogical comments scattered throughout the remaining pages of the diary, but most concern Miller's later business affairs. As former diarists can swear, one day we start a diary, and one day—sooner or later—we stop making entries. What triggers the first lapses, then finally the total abandonment, or when does approach become avoidance?

A. T. Miller started the diary with timid winter entries that swelled with diligence and hope as the frontier opened his mind to new experience, opportunity, and learning. He grew attached to his daily tally sheet, even bidding it adieu at night. He kept the diary near him and wrote of friends, family, and the pivotal events transforming the Panhandle and Rolling Plains. But after a year and a half he ended it in laconic passages drawn from the sweltering heat of the closing frontier. The novelty or shock value of the plains was an important education, but the shock was fading. Now it was the farming frontier that increasingly drew Miller's attention. The railroad made getting rich in farming a viable prospect.

While some pioneers were drawn to ranching and animals, and others preferred the hunt of humans, Abner Miller found all his old North Carolina Anglo-German farming instincts aroused by the promise of the nearby fertile prairies. Miller lasted little longer in the company than Jim Green or Ed Furman. State adjutant records show that Private Abner Theophilus Miller voluntarily left his service in Company B, Frontier Battalion, on August 31, 1888—only thirty-nine days after his last entry. He would plunge into the regional boom to make his own way. He turned his eyes toward Margaret, Texas.

Epilogue

THE BOYS OF COMPANY B

He [Captain Hall] called his troops his "boys," as he had his Rangers.
—*Dora N. Raymond,* Captain Lee Hall of Texas

A real Southwestern man, I soon learned, had to be big in all things. He had to stick to his friends through thick and thin. He should always be generous and sociable to a fault, always ready to make sacrifices for his town and country and stand prepared to defend his honor with fist or sixshooter.
—*Harry Koch, editor, Quanah* Tribune-Chief

That sooner or later . . . somewhere . . . somehow . . . we must settle with the world and make payment for what we have taken. That all things change but truth, and that truth alone, lives on forever.
—*Fran Striker, "Lone Ranger Creed"*

It was an old ranger custom for a company commander to call his men "boys." Captain Lee Hall, Captain Dan Roberts, and Captain Sam McMurry all used the term as an affectionate diminutive. The boys of Company B continued to ride under Captain McMurry for almost two and a half more years. The rangers often shuttled around on trains now, but they remembered the old ways. They found these ways still useful in manhunting, as the taking of desperate fugitives encouraged conservative thinking and approaches. Some of the Quanah boys found fame, some grew up and married, a few were shot to death, and others largely disappeared from view. There were various personnel changes after the summer of 1888, but in significant ways there was a continuity of Company B spirit.

The continued success of the company owed much to Captain McMurry. There were always more applicants than positions in the service, but by September of 1888 the captain reviewed applications to fill his depleted ranks. As the Panhandle rapidly developed under two new railroads, demands on McMurry's law enforcement services were increasing as well. New towns like Panhandle City and Amarillo preferred a state-paid ranger inside and outside every saloon. The captain had a few stalwarts in Sergeant Tom Platt, his brother John, Grude Britton, John Hammond, and Sterling Price. Their experience and leadership would be invaluable to leaven new recruits. He also had the recently enlisted rangers George Adamson, Tom O'Hare, and John R. Bishop. They were able and gaining experience. John W. Bracken and L. E. Delfraisse enlisted in June, but the latter had not worked out and was discharged on July 27. McMurry clearly needed more men to handle the demands on his company. Accordingly, the captain interviewed and hired a new group of company rangers at the end of summer: W. M. Breshauer, Arthur Terrell, A. Lewis, A. Young, and T. C. Gentry. Some lasted only a few months while others needed extra discipline and training.[1] Oscar Zollicoffer rose from company teamster to enlisted private in October, 1888. McMurry enlisted Tom Hickman in November and A. A. Neeley in December. John L. Sullivan was added to the company roster on April 16, 1889, at Thurber, Texas, proving to be an outstanding if temperamental ranger.[2]

It was really the beginning of a new phase for the Company B rangers. If the last Texas frontier was now pierced and broken, the rush of settlers and opportunists were creating fresh opportunities for imposing law and order. The new towns proved demanding, the big ranches complained of depredations, and gateway city crime continued into the region. McMurry's attention was often drawn to management, official business, and supervision in the process. The old ranger traditions lingered, but there was a new, more civilized Texas to tame. The new "frontier" was in railroad towns and cities such as Amarillo.

A fair number of the original Quanah rangers were still in the service by early 1891. Grude Britton and Tom O'Hare stayed on, Sterling Price returned for a spell, and the Platt brothers and George Adamson started the year. Captain Sam McMurry had hired other good men from 1888 to 1890, trained and governed them well, and he watched with satisfaction as many of them graduated from Company B into other important careers in Texas law enforcement. A roster of McMurry's distinguished graduates includes W. John L. Sullivan, Ed Britton, Frank Hoffer, and John W. Bracken.

Periodically the Quanah-based company was assigned to troubleshoot or suppress a hot spot in another part of Texas. Most of the Company B rangers traveled to Thurber in 1889–90 to settle alleged coal mine labor violence. They were expected to out-intimidate the intimidators. Thurber was a company town halfway between Abilene and Fort Worth in northern Erath County. It had decent housing but the atmosphere was repressive. Labor recruiters had gathered a polyglot, multinational group of miners to work there. The anti-unionist Robert Dickey Hunter ruled Thurber in such a manner that he was soon clamoring to state officials for the services of the Texas Rangers. Hunter got Company B for a crucial spell. He then hired armed guards, including ex-rangers, to enforce his will. Company B evolved therefore from service against Indian and bandit raids in the 1870s, through the 1880s—when it adapted to law enforcement on the passing frontier—into labor suppression for anti-union capitalists by the early 1890s.

A major change for the company took place in early 1891 when Bill Jess McDonald took over the captaincy from Sam McMurry. McDonald joined his men at Quanah, kept them busy that year, and then oversaw the company relocation to new headquarters in Amarillo in late 1891. Amarillo was a growing cowtown and strategic railroad junction. It had known Texas Rangers since its founding, but McDonald's men would enhance and elaborate the ranger legacy while stationed there. Henry Sanborn's new city was chosen for its rapid growth and central-place logic to law enforcement in the Panhandle. Although Sanborn had lost the county seat election in 1888, he had masterfully manipulated capital and events in 1889 until the merchants finally gave up. The defeated mercantilists loaded their houses and businesses on skids, and moved lock, stock, and barrel to Sanborn's nearby Glidden and Sanborn section.

The original courthouse stayed forlornly behind, compelling county officials and rangers to walk a mile outside of the new town to the building. On the way they often admired the mirages of lakes, forests, and towns that appeared out of the ether. Captain McDonald settled in Amarillo to run his company, but he continued to visit Quanah, a town he loved

Figure 13. Captain Sam McMurry's Texas Rangers, Company B, Thurber, Texas, 1888. Courtesy Texas Ranger Hall of Fame and Museum, Waco

and one in which he did business for his nearby ranch. In Amarillo, McDonald was often imperious and publicity-hungry. He was also very skillful, experienced, and courageous. The first sheriff of Potter County, Gus Gober, recalled that the change in leadership in Company B was quite noticeable if not abrupt: "McDonald was altogether a different character than McMurray. McDonald was seeking a reputation as a notorious general and hero and was somewhat boastful of his adventures in capturing or killing outlaws, but he seemed to be friendly with me. However, I noticed that he and [Sheriff] Criswell were together often, and it was not unusual to see them playing faro or monte at the same table."[3]

McDonald likewise employed and trained a new generation of lawmen. Dudley S. Barker, for instance, started as a lowly Company B teamster in Amarillo in February, 1896. He quickly moved into the ranks as a private in July. This former Company B teamster served by the side of John Sullivan at San Saba, where both won distinction against the "Buzzard's Hole mob."[4] Dud Barker was taken seriously after a San Saba mob tough, vowing to kill one of the interfering rangers that day, picked on him as the youngest and most inexperienced. "Aiming his rifle at the ranger," wrote Robert Stephens, the wannabe killer "was unable to fire a shot before Barker's six-shooter was in action and he had fatally shot his assailant five times."[5] Barker went on to survive almost two decades as sheriff of Pecos County. The unfortunates who fell before his guns were said to have been "Barkerized."

Figure 14. Company B Texas Rangers in Amarillo. Left to right: *J. W. Bracken, F. H. Martin, Tom O'Hare, J. M. Britton, A. A. Neely, Tom Platt "Sergeant," "Little Mac" [the mule], J. R. Bishop, J. R. Platt, P. Hoffer, and J. W. Murphy. Courtesy Panhandle-Plains Historical Museum Archives, Canyon, Texas*

Joe Britton, Ed Connell, Forest Edwards, and Ollie Perry were further graduates of Company B. Captain McDonald polished each of them well. He often relied upon his new sergeant, W. John L. Sullivan, a colorful character and dangerous foe to an outlaw antagonist. There was also the brave William J. "Billy" McCauley, McDonald's nephew. The issue of nepotism was moot because this company recruit had thoroughly proved his mettle at San Saba, Amarillo, the Red River, Alice, and elsewhere.[6] Rangers Sullivan and McCauley were both in the posse that tracked down and killed the renegade ex-lawman Joe Beckham, former sheriff of Motley County.[7]

Company B, Frontier Battalion, survived only briefly into the new century. Having survived legions of outlaws, it was a legal technicality that destroyed the old force. In an important judicial decision, the Texas courts ruled that ranger privates had no general arrest powers. The entire Frontier Battalion was abolished in 1901 as an anachronism. Its duty was done; the frontier was no more; its mission had been accomplished. Although the Texas Rangers recovered, reconstituted, and continued as an institution, the glory days of the Frontier Battalion were over. Company

B continued to troubleshoot under Captain McDonald and his nephew, Sergeant McCauley, but only as a reorganized outfit of greater mobility. The company's fortunes in the new century were closely tied to the service as a whole. Nadirs, such as when the disreputable Ferguson governors appointed gun-toting loyalists to ranger sinecures, drove away many rangers of talent and abilities.

Like the Frontier Battalion, few of the original communities survived the new age either. Old Tascosa hung on pitifully for a few more decades, but by the 1920s her adobe buildings had melted away. The archeological remains of Old Clarendon slid under the waters of Greenbelt Lake a century later. Mobeetie survived as a small Wheeler County community with a rich history—but then she too relocated when a later railroad passed near her. Historic Margaret quickly lost her place in the new order. Her decline was assured when the official Hardeman County seat moved to Quanah in 1890. After the formation of Foard County out of Hardeman a year later, Margaret suffered a further humiliation when the voters chose the hamlet of Crowell as the new county seat. When the only railroad in the county bypassed Old Margaret, its fate was sealed.

The historic site of Old Margaret is not a secret, but few people outside of Foard County know that it exists.[8] County Road 98 runs northeast of Crowell for some six miles, parallel to the Atchison, Topeka & Santa Fe tracks, before turning east at the present tiny community of (New) Margaret. A mile and a half farther east on County Road 98 is a plain dirt road that runs north about three-quarters of a mile to a T-intersection. Once upon a time this particular dirt corner was downtown Margaret, Texas. Down its vanished streets walked and rode our beloved western heroes: John and Mary Wesley, "Soft Voice" McMurry, Bill McDonald, Charles and Mary Goodnight, Pat Wolforth, Temple Houston, Jim Allee, Abner Miller, and hundreds of other pioneers.

For a crucial decade Margaret's streets, stores, and courts opened far Northwest Texas. It was a hospitable place where people helped one another and thought little of it. Eventually though the last townspeople gave up on the site of Wesley's dream. In 1908 the Santa Fe's "Kansas City, Mexico & Orient RR" bypassed the town. After a few meetings everyone simply relocated to a railroad townsite some three miles away. John Wesley's son (and Margaret postmaster) Hervey Wesley captured this transition period in a scarce 1908 photograph.

Old Margaret is still a remarkable place for its romantic perspectives and sense of history. The landscape is silent, lonely, and almost empty

Figure 15. Margaret, Texas—May, 1908. Author's collection

COMMENTARY ON 1908 MARGARET PHOTOGRAPH

Old Margaret died when the railroad finally built into Foard County. In this real photo postcard, postmarked "Margaret, Texas, May 9, 1908," local citizens celebrate the construction of New Margaret at a stop on the line. A message on back notes: ". . . I guess you know the horse and buggy to right in this picture." Hervey [Wesley] to Mattie Wesley.

once more, more like it was when the Comanche-Kiowa bands left and the first scattered pioneers were arriving. It is still possible to feel the Northwest frontier spirit here, to dream of carving farm and ranch empires all the way from the North Fork of the Red River to the Wichita River. To the west and northwest a scrubby pasture opens to a magnificent vista of the Pease Valley, with its variegated bluffs of Permian red and juniper green. Only a mile to the north lies the Pease River, its impressively broad course marked by dunes and invasive salt cedar thickets. Debris on the banks and meanders show the serious effects of periodic inundations flowing from the Llano Estacado. To the east of Old Margaret, cotton and grain fields slope gently down to Mule Creek. Improbably the creek still flows and retains a quaint lushness. Old trees mark its further course toward a confluence with the Pease River. Cynthia Ann Parker was recaptured beyond these banks in 1860.

Today there is not a trace of the Old Margaret jail, courthouse, post office, Thacker's store, Boren's livery, the blacksmith shop, church, or any former residences. I talked one hot afternoon with Foard County farmer Tom Smith, a genial soul with a deep appreciation of history. Mr. Smith stopped his tractor and shared his memory cup about Margaret with me. Tom Smith now cultivates cotton on top of Old Margaret. That is, his field embraces a substantial part of the site of former dugouts, houses, and streets. Traces of lost dugouts appear as localized caliche-white depressions in the field. Smith remembers as a child when state officials and old settlers arrived one day to dedicate an imposing Texas Centennial marker. The marker was placed at the dirt corner in 1936, where it still stands in commemoration of the region's most historic ghost town.[9] A venerable John Wesley was there; indeed, he guided state officials to the correct location. Mr. Wesley reminisced and wrote poetry for only two more years before dying in July of 1938. He was buried in the family plot in the Old Margaret cemetery.

Various fates also overtook the old Quanah rangers. Captain Bill McDonald, of course, achieved lasting fame in the years ahead. In contrast the talented and experienced Tom Platt faded from the service. He is hardly remembered today, while his brother John was fired from the company by McDonald. Tom Platt's replacement as company sergeant, W. John L. Sullivan, had a better idea about courting posterity. He wrote a cantankerous and anecdotal account of 1890s rangering for Company B—*Twelve Years in the Saddle for Law and Order on the Frontiers of Texas.* Sullivan's narrative is disjointed and opinionated, but his scarce 1909 book is strongly recommended for an understanding of Company B in the 1890s.

Southwesterners love reminiscences. The frontier passed so quickly that pioneers recognized its historicity in its fleeting, compressed, and harsh nature. They thought it special and wrote of the time with feeling and abundance. Texas Ranger reminiscences fit well into the emerging regional genre. Yet for every documented, well-reminisced life of an officer like Bill McDonald or John Sullivan, there were scores of ranger privates who came and went, their experiences and passing little marked.

Some of the Quanah ranger privates left the region and little is known about the rest of their lives. As Miller noted in his July 20, 1888, entry: "Severel of the boys has gone out to Mexico [Mexico, Missouri?] since the last of last month and nothing heard of them since." Still there are clues and fragments, service records and notices, articles and books that enable one to reconstruct some destinies. And what of Abner Miller himself?

Figures 16. Tom Platt (ex Fletcher Photograph). Courtesy Texas Ranger Hall of Fame and Museum, Waco

Let us therefore ponder the individual lives and fates—good, bad, or unknown—that befell the boys of Company B. Let us scout the last adventures of the old Quanah Texas Rangers.

Tom and **John Platt,** two of eight brothers and one daughter born to Rip Ford's old Sergeant Platt in the Mexican-American War, loyally served Company B for three more years. Rangering was in their blood. They largely had grown up with a family member in the Frontier Battalion. When older brother Sam Platt, a distinguished veteran of the 1870s warfare in the Nueces Strip, finally retired from Company B as lieutenant in the mid-1880s, he could note with satisfaction that two more Platts, Tom and John, were on the force to carry on the family tradition. Two other brothers—Jake and Radd Platt—would also join a ranger company for stints. Through their father and older brother, Tom and John Platt were steeped in the lore and legends of the early Texas Rangers.

Tom Platt's service was unusually long for a Texas Ranger. He joined in September of 1881 and served until February of 1891, almost ten years of riding and almost all of it with Company B. He witnessed the glory days of the last Texas frontier, working the boomtown conversion of the state from subsistence to commercial capitalism. Tom Platt rangered at

Figure 17. John Platt (ex Fletcher Photograph). Courtesy Texas Ranger Hall of Fame and Museum, Waco

Colorado City, Coleman, Wichita Falls, Harrold, Quanah, and most of the Panhandle. From time to time he was too boisterous and agitated in his personal ways. He did drink, as the Miller diaries attested. But Tom was a consistent and productive lawman and he remained a true Texas Ranger at heart.

One of his proudest memories came from the terrifying experience of facing down angry mobs in Fort Worth. Labor strikes, some violence, and a riot in 1886 brought well-armed rangers to the city to restore order. Tom Platt and other rangers assembled, then stood their ground before many hundreds of howling, angry strikers. Although the rangers carried the day, it had been a close call. He was personally a courageous man. Abner Miller certainly respected his abilities in law enforcement. Captain McMurry preferred Tom Platt of all the rangers to watch his back.

John Platt was a younger version of his tough brother. He is clearly a youth in the Fletcher photo of the Quanah rangers, with a baby face contrasted to the mustachioed older men. He nevertheless thrust himself into a man's job, joining the manhunts and guard duty. He was inoffensive to others, and kept up with the work. McMurry preferred to send Tom out alone on a dangerous assignment, rather than John, because

John Platt was still being seasoned. He was around the camp frequently. A. T. enjoyed his congenial willingness to help out with camp chores.

Tom Platt's experience, exuberance, courage, and popularity led Captain McMurry to appoint him as Company B first sergeant in March of 1888.[10] As sergeant he was often dispatched with a small detachment to various trouble spots around the Panhandle and Greer County. He served in this capacity until early 1891. Unfortunately Tom Platt was not as highly favored by Bill McDonald as he had been by Sam McMurry. There was possibly a personality conflict or an insubordination incident. Or maybe Tom simply found McDonald's grandstanding to be insufferable. In any case, when McDonald assumed command of Company B in February of 1891, Tom Platt resigned from the service after a demotion.

His brother John did not last much longer. John Platt found it hard to accept McDonald's supervision and his brother's absence. Recognizing his personnel problems, Captain McDonald fired John Platt, his good friend John W. Bracken, and Bill Neely as well in September of 1891.[11] There were allegations of drinking, poor discipline, and misuse of firearms, but McDonald essentially cleaned house by purging some of McMurry's men. For almost nine years John and Tom Platt followed other pursuits around Austin, Texas, where the Platt family had congregated. Tom's rangering days were far from over however. In April of 1900 Thomas Platt reenlisted as a lieutenant in Company D. Lieutenant Platt handled a variety of ranger matters for Company D before retiring from the service altogether.[12]

After riding many long trails, Tom returned to Austin to stay put. His brother John also lived in the sleepy capital. The Platt brothers won new friends in Austin in the 1920s. They also spun magnificent yarns of their glory days in the Texas Rangers. John Platt died first, leaving Tom to carry on with the storytelling. But on October 10, 1929, Thomas Platt died. He was buried in Austin by family and old friends. Almost a week later the entire stock market collapsed and the nation entered the Great Depression.

His death did not go unremarked. In the December, 1929, issue of *Frontier Times,* an old Company B fellow ranger penned a final tribute to Tom's passing. John Bracken, fired by McDonald at the same time as John Platt, wrote of the Platt boys: "they were my friends and I loved them as brothers. Tom Platt deserves more than a passing notice. He was known in the eighties from the Rio Grande to Texline, from Midland to Houston, and every old time officer in those days knew the Platt boys,

Figure 18. Sterling Price (ex Fletcher). Courtesy Texas Ranger Hall of Fame and Museum, Waco

Tom especially. Tom, old boy, goodbye. Sam and John are waiting for you on the other side."[13]

Sterling Price was twenty-six years old when he enlisted in Company B on September 1, 1887. He was born around 1861 in Vallejo, California, the beautiful north coastal community in San Francisco Bay near the Sacramento delta. At six-foot-five inches tall, the dark-haired, gray-eyed peace officer towered over most men. Powerfully built, Sterling intimidated miscreants and served warrants by his physical presence. This strong Californian easily blended with the Texas boys, enjoying camp humor and shirking his share of the chores. As the diarist noted, Price sometimes had "troubles," including at least two potentially fatal gunfights. He certainly was at ease in the use of weapons.

Sterling Price served ten months in Company B until resigning on June 30, 1888. A. T. reported that he went to Weatherford, Texas, that summer, likely on leave to visit family and do personal business. In any event his discharge was of a friendly and entirely temporary nature. Sterling Price reenlisted in Company B on September 3, 1888. He settled back into ranger camp life at Quanah and resumed regular duties. McMurry assigned him as an escort on October 16, 1888, for the notorious "Wm.

Brooken" or Bill Brooken, who was being transferred to Seymour to stand trial for murder.[14] Almost a month later Price joined nine other privates for a train ride to the new company town of Thurber.

Pay vouchers for 1889 suggest that Captain McMurry recommended Sterling Price for extended security work during the labor unrest at Thurber, Texas.[15] The anti-labor coal mines of the Texas & Pacific Coal Company needed extensive security, and company officials were happy to hire experienced men. First dispatched to Thurber by Captain McMurry, he spent some months in this company town as a Texas Ranger. There were payrolls to guard, fences to patrol, strikebreakers to protect, and entrances to monitor. He was likely hired away from the Texas Rangers, specifically to work as a Texas & Pacific Coal Company security guard after the rangers went back to Quanah.

Sterling Price was certainly in this notoriously anti-union town in the fall of 1893. There had been another spell of labor trouble that year. In October of 1893 Price was appointed a "Special Texas Ranger" at Thurber, a document signed by the union-buster Robert D. Hunter and Captain Bill McDonald.[16] This document gave Price the special powers of a state ranger while enabling him to stay on the payroll of a private company.

McDonald certainly had no qualms about appointing Price as a special ranger at Thurber. He remembered him well from their days of riding for the Brookens together. Sterling Price was both a good man and a fine ranger.

Dennis A. Peale [also spelled **Peal**] lingered in the Panhandle for years after his rangering days. He had been a solid ranger—calm, social, methodical, a good friend. These qualities served him in more private ventures in the years ahead. Dennis stayed in touch with some of the former ranger boys. He even convinced a respected former sergeant of Company B to join him in the semi-dangerous enterprise of selling liquor to Amarilloans shortly after the turn of the century.

By the early 1900s it was clear that only Amarillo had any real hopes of becoming a Panhandle metropolis. Dennis Peale and Grude Britton accordingly threw in together, pooled their money, and opened a saloon in downtown Amarillo around 1903. While not as glamorous as riding for the Brooken gang, the money was better and the living easier. For several years they worked at their business and they enjoyed the cowboy money that arrived with herds trailing into the Amarillo stockyards from the large ranches. Dennis and Grude sold out their saloon and separated their business affairs around 1906, but they both stayed in the liquor business.

Figure 19. Dennis Peale (ex Fletcher). Courtesy Texas Ranger Hall of Fame and Museum, Waco

Dennis continued to serve liquid libations to all kinds of folks in Amarillo, rich and poor, for some eight years. He was bartender in James H. Patton's saloon at 413A Polk Street in 1907, where he regularly provided cool mugs of Fred Miller's famous "Milwaukee Beer" to the thirsty and afflicted denizens.[17] A year later he took a room at 206 Tyler and tended bar with a Mr. Moore. Dennis maintained regular order in the saloon. He kept a gun under the counter in case of trouble, and most locals were aware that he knew how to use it. Judge James D. Hamlin recalled Dennis and Grude's early Amarillo saloon and that its owners were both seasoned ex–Texas Rangers.[18] The reputation of being a former Texas Ranger was therefore something of a deterrence.

After the summer of 1908 Dennis's former partner and old friend Grude Britton decided to go back to Fort Worth for new business dreams. There was more action in a bigger city. The two old rangers and former business partners said goodbye once again. Grude caught a train east and Dennis stayed behind in Amarillo. He kept his room at 206 Tyler and his routine bartending ways. His ambition was more limited. He was still there in the winter of 1910 when the awful news of Grude's violent end reached him. After 1911 Peale disappeared from the Amarillo city di-

Figure 20. Ed Furman (ex Fletcher). Courtesy Texas Ranger Hall of Fame and Museum, Waco

rectory and the paper trail grows cold.[19] Nothing is known of any subsequent career for Dennis A. Peale.

Edward E. Furman was mustered into the company on November 1, 1886. He saw the railroad town of Quanah grow from nothing but prairie. Private Miller liked "Mr. Furman." He did a good job, managed his personal life so as to avoid censure, and he seemed to avoid trouble in his law career. Although the captain kept him busy and he performed well enough, his heart was not into long-term rangering. Ed resigned from the Company on June 30, 1888, after twenty months of service. Miller reported a camp rumor that Furman was hired away as a security man by the railroad construction boss, Dan Carey, for work in "M.O.," possibly Mexico, Missouri.

J. M. Bradbury was a tried and true veteran of Company B. Jim Bradbury enlisted into the company on September 1, 1881, in the heyday of the reorganized outfit at Colorado City, Texas. He got on well with the new captain, Sam McMurry, and proved a steady and reliable lawman. Bradbury's school of criminal justice included some of the tougher new towns of West Texas. He saw Big Springs roar to life as a railroad town in 1884. He then rode north with the company to escort the FW&DC Railroad

Figure 21. James M. Bradbury (ex Fletcher). Courtesy Texas Ranger Hall of Fame and Museum, Waco

across the Rolling Plains, serving successively in Wichita Falls (1885), Harrold (1885), and Quanah (1886–87).[20]

Private Miller liked "Brad" and his quiet professionalism. He was not flashy or noisy like some men. After six years of distinguished state service, more years than most rangers of the era could muster, Private Bradbury finally resigned from Company B at Quanah on December 15, 1887. His subsequent fate is unknown. He may have been one of the boys hired away by the railroad as a protection man. Many rangers also graduated into or returned to law enforcement careers with county and city governments. Jim Bradbury's six years with the company was not only an enviable record, it was also a sign of perseverance in whatever he chose for his future.

James F. "Jim" Green resigned from Company B in June of 1888 for greener pastures. These fields of opportunity lay in Donley County. He soon settled in "New Clarendon," the designated railroad townsite whither residents were busy dragging their houses from Old Clarendon. There Jim Green put his criminal justice experience to good use as a well-paid ($75 per month) deputy for Sheriff Albert L. "Al" Gentry.[21]

Figure 22. Jim Green (ex Fletcher). Courtesy Texas Ranger Hall of Fame and Museum, Waco

Clarendon had started life as Carhart's Methodist colonization scheme on the Salt Fork of the Red River. As a Prohibition townsite or "drug-free" community, it attracted a diverse group of extraordinarily interesting people. In soddies and dugouts these highly educated pioneers gave music lessons and discussed great books. Few had the slightest criminal background or inclination. The 1887 arrival of the FW&DC railroad and its culture changed all that.

As others were doing, Deputy Green moved into the New Clarendon railroad townsite on the old Phillips's homestead section. New Clarendon tried to continue its pious "Saint's Roost" ways, but the town was now obviously unsheltered from the cruel outside world of dubious commerce, drink, gambling, drugs, theft, larceny, prostitution, and so on. Green was hired to help Sheriff Al Gentry cope with the difficult transition.

Jim Green did the new job with courage and zeal, and he quickly earned a local reputation as a reliable lawman. Al Gentry came to value his judgment and bravery. Here was a man not easily intimidated, even in a land of the brave. For Jim Green the change was good. There was less rough riding than with the rangers, the money was much better, and he exchanged a Quanah bedroll for a Clarendon soft bed and pillow. Green performed his duties with his customary aplomb and dispatch, and from time to time he may have ruffled feelings or trampled on an offender's dignity. Some resented Green's position and authority in the community.

Three brothers took special exception to Jim Green in the spring and summer of 1892. The Bell brothers—William "Bill," Robert "Bob," and Eugene "Gene"—resented the deputy's regulation of their behavior and gambling outfit in Clarendon's Cain's Saloon. Once Green noticed the brothers taking undue advantage of an inebriated trail hand at the gambling; the deputy ordered the Bells to refund the inexperienced cowboy's money, and then sent the prodigal youth on his way. The Bells resented this interference in their business. Were they not grown men, perhaps stronger and more valiant than the deputy himself? A personal feud quickly developed, fueled by idle town gossip.

In May of that year Jim Green found himself in the midst of a desperate fracas with Bill Bell and a ruffian named Bill Babb.[22] A mortally threatened Green brought his six-shooter into play and professionally cut down both men. It was an unfortunate incident. He was—once again—lucky to have survived a shoot-out. The subsequent investigation cleared him legally and in the community's mind, but not in the fevered brains of Bob and Gene Bell. Bob and Gene buried their brother and fell to brooding.

Even though the frontier was dying, the old Southern Highland traditions that migrated west remained strong. Shooting one supposedly innocent member of the Bells was taken as a shot at the entire family. The more Bob and Gene thought about poor Bill's shooting, the more devious, base, and unjust the deputy's actions seemed. Coaching each other and building their anger with the summer heat, the two brothers worked themselves into a state of action by early July of 1893.

The Fourth of July celebration always attracted a large crowd in Clarendon. The Bells enjoyed the festivities and business, but a darker scheme drove them the next day. On July 5, 1892, they walked down Kearney Street in Clarendon, armed and apparently prepared to take their vengeance. Bob and Gene Bell—already nervous and high-strung—quickened when they saw Jim Green in the shade of Cain's, one of Clarendon's three saloons. The brothers unobtrusively maneuvered around the deputy. In his 1945 reminiscence, William H. Patrick of Clarendon recalled Jim Green's last shoot-out: "One morning just as the golden God or day tinted the rosy East Jim found himself in need of thirty or forty drops of stimulant to clarify the mental makeup and went into Cain's saloon, ordered the necessary and was about to absorb it when one of the Bell boys who was standing just around the end of the bar with a six shooter in his hand coughed to attract Green's attention who immediately drew his gun and the battle opened."[23]

Jim Green had only a moment to consider the situation and the why of it all. The Fourth of July had been a busy day, and only now could he relax a bit. Perhaps he had only enough time to recognize the young men before him as angry brothers of that "bad hombre" Bill Bell. In that rush of awareness he recognized extreme danger. Whether he wanted it or not, he was suddenly in a fight to the death. All three men went for their guns.

Green was a good shot, and the odds and experience were with him in a man-to-man duel. Yet he hardly had time to ponder that, as he now was up against two men. In a blaze of close-quarters gunfire, Green quickly shot to death Robert Bell, the apparent leader. But Eugene Bell was steady and on fire too. While Green's instinctive aim and deadly attention were turned on Bob, Gene found the perfect opportunity to shoot the distracted deputy. A fatal shot at close range pierced the deputy and he collapsed. The pointless shoot-out lasted less than a minute, leaving two men sprawled in bloody death on the saloon floor. A shaken Al Gentry arrived and took charge of the surviving Gene Bell. Dr. Jerome Stocking, the physician and coroner, took charge of the corpses and investigation. News of the deputy's murder spread quickly.

The citizens of Clarendon mourned the loss of James F. Green. For almost four years he kept law and maintained order in the new community. If he were sometimes too scrupulous in his administration of the law, he was now forgiven for his sins and praised for his courage and virtues. For Sella Phillips Gentry the fresh grave of Jim Green was further evidence that her beloved husband, Sheriff Al Gentry, should consider a change of career. Albert L. Gentry finished his term in 1892 and stepped down as sheriff of Donley County. He had had enough.

Thomas M. "Red" O'Hare, the red-haired Irish muleskinner, served a teamster apprenticeship with Company B in 1887. Tom O'Hare became a Texas Ranger in his own right when McMurry allowed him to enlist on January 1, 1888. "Red Tom" or "Red" proved his mettle both as a teamster and as a ranger. Indeed, Red stayed in the company for years, seeing plenty of action while serving at Quanah from 1887–91.

He joined the company relocation to Amarillo in late 1891, and rode with the other outstanding rangers from their new Potter County headquarters. Dispatched to Thurber during the bitter strike of 1890, O'Hare joined Sam M. Platt, Tom Platt, John L. Sullivan, and a new group of privates in facing down angry strikers—so-called "dynamiters and anarchists." A photographer captured Red Tom's style in a contemporaneous pose in Amarillo.

The new captain, Bill McDonald, thought highly of Red Tom's general skills as a lawman, but the private's drinking was destined to lead to trouble. This trouble was noted in the Miller diaries early on, but it erupted violently in the fall of 1893. With all Company B officers busy with other troubles, Private Tom O'Hare found himself in November looking into rustlers and thieves operating around Lipscomb County, Texas. These artful dodgers would often flee across the convenient state line into the adjacent and new Oklahoma Territory. Joining with two Oklahoma lawmen, and with the connivance of the local sheriff, Ranger O'Hare left the borderline town of Higgins and rode directly into the Oklahoma Territory. This was a practice discouraged by distant state officials but sometimes winked at by local law enforcement. The sheriff of Lipscomb County had used O'Hare once before to track men wanted in Texas into Oklahoma. O'Hare was apparently foolish enough to go.

Red Tom was investigating and drinking—or vice versa—at a saloon in Cheyenne, Oklahoma Territory, on November 20, 1893, when he exchanged animadversions with a Cheyenne native named Wolf Hair. Frightened by O'Hare's suspicious questions, guns, and threats, the Indian jumped in his wagon and raced away. Determined to bring Wolf Hair back for further questioning, Red Tom mounted his horse and gave chase. As narrated by Harold John Weiss, Jr., from the later account in El Reno's *Globe:* "When O'Hare caught up with Wolf Hair, the Indian climbed off his wagon, according to the ranger's story, grabbed O'Hare's rifle, which was laying in front of him across his saddle, and pulled the trigger. O'Hare returned the fire with his revolver and killed Wolf Hair. Afterwards, the ranger turned himself in and townspeople went out to take care of the body."[24]

Charged with murder, Private O'Hare was lodged initially in the Cheyenne jail. McDonald's first impulse was the safety of his man; he feared a lynching by outraged Cheyenne townsfolk. But his request to supervise O'Hare's jailing was quickly denied by the adjutant general. McDonald's second impulse was to deny his knowledge or responsibility for

O'Hare's actions. Although the captain stoutly defended his ranger's abilities in public, in reports to superiors he stated that O'Hare had acted of his own accord and contrary to orders.[25] However much McDonald hated to see one of the boys in trouble, he knew Private O'Hare had to be immediately discharged.

Red Tom was fired from Company B and given his last pay voucher that fall.[26] Curiously, there is no mention whatsoever of the Wolf Hair homicide in his official ranger service file, which is largely blank save for pay vouchers.[27] O'Hare languished for over a year in the El Reno County jail, on the wrong side of the bars (as he knew now from experience), before his convoluted case reached trial. There were plenty of lawyers but absolutely no eyewitnesses to counter his claim of self-defense and justifiable homicide. The jury returned a controversial verdict of "not guilty." Red Tom was set free in December of 1894 to wander the earth again.

James Magruder "Grude" Britton served Company B for almost six and a half more years, rising to sergeant of the company and simultaneously serving as sheriff of Hartley County for much of 1893. He was capable, dependable, and respected by both Sam McMurry and Bill McDonald. He was also popular and trusted by the other boys.

"Of stern appearance and strong features," wrote historian Robert Stephens, "he can be described as having been typical in many respects of the early peace officer."[28] A native of Parker County, Grude's father died when he was sixteen, leaving the youth to help care for his mother and younger brothers. Grude entered law enforcement on the Weatherford police force. He matured and moved on to the Colorado City town police in West Texas, where he met ex-ranger Dick Ware and came to the recruiting attention of Sam McMurry. A. T. Miller noted his arrival at the Quanah ranger camp in June of 1887. Grude's municipal experience in criminal justice was helpful, but he still had to learn the trail rigors of state police manhunting in Greer and Hardeman Counties. Rangering was much more vigorous than walking the streets of Weatherford as a policeman.

Two of Grude's younger Parker County brothers, Ed and Joe Britton, also joined Company B and served in the Panhandle. Edward S. Britton watched the XIT at one point, and he worked with Sterling Price as a Special Texas Ranger in the Thurber mines at another. Ed eventually rose to a management position with the coal mining company. Joe Britton signed on as Company B teamster in 1894, a routine apprenticeship of sorts, and he also worked as a guard at Thurber. Both brothers resigned from the company for other pursuits.

Figure 23. Grude Britton (at right). Courtesy Texas Ranger Hall of Fame and Museum, Waco

More than six years of service took Grude Britton to virtually every corner of the Panhandle—and beyond. John L. Sullivan recalled the time in 1891 the two arrested a desperate escaped convict and his unusual, cross-dressing accomplice, (Miss) Jennie Bates, in the cedar brakes of Greer County.[29] Grude's work was so exemplary that a retiring Captain McMurry openly recommended this "conservative and brave" company veteran for the captaincy in a letter to Adjutant General Mabry on January 18, 1891.[30] Grude Britton followed McMurry's letter of recommendation with his own petition two days later.[31] Perhaps he would have gotten the position, but a politically connected rival emerged when Governor Hogg's old friend Bill McDonald applied for the job. Hogg chose his old friend for the captaincy.

Captain Bill McDonald remembered Grude's hard work in Hardeman County and made him the new company sergeant.[32] In fact McDonald chose Sergeant Britton to accompany him on an especially sensitive matter in the summer of 1891. Captain McDonald had been given a Texas requisition order to arrest the last two surviving Marlow brothers. McDonald and Britton caught a train to Ridgeway, Colorado, where Ouray County Sheriff J. H. Bradley found himself in a delicate situation. Charles and George Marlow, now deputized federal witnesses in legal actions against the '89 lynch mob that killed their brothers, were adamant about not surrendering to Texas lawmen. In truth Britton and McDonald needed to follow a proper extradition process, but rumors said the rangers would try to collect the Marlows in any case.

When Britton and McDonald returned to Ridgeway and got off the train at the depot, they found a large crowd facing them, a mass entirely sympathetic to the two brothers present under the sheriff's care. "McDonald and Britton strode briskly to the Marlows, nodding and extending their left hands," writes historian Glenn Shirley. "George and Charles extended their left hands. It was a left-handed shake all around."[33] A compromise was reached to settle the jurisdictional dispute at the governor's office in Denver. They all got on board a train, Grude and Bill at the front of a car with the suspicious Marlows and Sheriff Bradley taking rear seats, and rode on to Denver. There the issue of jurisdiction was settled in favor of the Marlows. Britton and McDonald took no offense, personally wished the Marlows well, and returned to their Texas headquarters.

One of Grude Britton's last stints was on the Texas–New Mexico border. He combined two jobs in much of 1893, working as both a Texas Ranger and as a sheriff of deeply troubled Hartley County. This unusual arrangement came about when Sergeant Britton and his men had to arrest the existing Hartley County sheriff for absconding with considerable county funds. And only months before, in 1892, the foreman of a Hartley County jury had been gunned down in cold blood by a townsman he sought to indict, George Knighton.[34] Grude headed the detachment that chased this fugitive to New Mexico. Making matters worse, the adjacent state border was plagued by rustlers working back and forth, possibly in cahoots with local renegade police. Replacement Hartley County officials petitioned McDonald to appoint Sergeant J. M. Britton as sheriff. McDonald consented to this unorthodox action on January 4, 1893. Grude went to Texline for the assignment and served until August 20. Adjutant General Mabry eventually terminated the arrangement.[35] The Hartley County sheriff's job was certainly dangerous work.

In December of 1893 Sergeant Britton assumed effective command of Company B while the captain was hors de combat from a gunfight. Grude did a good job. He officially left the force at Amarillo on March 17, 1894. He was well known in the Panhandle at the time. He moved to Fort Worth for seven years, but continued to work with Bill McDonald as a special hired gun from time to time. Indeed, he was one of McDonald's hand-picked men at the confrontation between capital and labor at Port Arthur, Texas.[36]

Grude Britton returned to Amarillo in 1903 to open a downtown saloon with an old friend, ex-ranger Dennis Peale. His affable ways and colorful experiences in law enforcement proved popular with locals like Judge James D. Hamlin. After Peale and Britton sold their business, Grude joined Frank Anderson in 1906–1907 in the retail liquor trade, rooming at 208 Fillmore. Anderson and Britton ran saloons at 404 Polk Street—"Phone 92"—and 417 Polk Street, giving some idea why this corridor was the Main Street of Amarillo.[37] After five years of barkeeping in Amarillo, Grude sold out, moved back to Fort Worth in the fall of 1908, and ran the Senate Saloon there for about a year.

On January 21, 1910, an ailing and frustrated Grude lost his temper against a Fort Worth police captain. There was an on-going dispute, some little thing that deeply offended Britton's sense of fair play and justice. Supposedly threats were made, and he apparently had tried to get the officer fired. That evening an unmollified and determined Grude Britton hunted down the offending captain at city hall. Mistaking the former Texas Ranger's stride and purpose, the police captain panicked and gunned down Grude as he approached. Grude staggered, collapsed from two massive wounds, and died on the cold floor at Fort Worth City Hall. The shooting and death were both sensational and pointless, as Grude Britton was found to have no guns or weapons whatever on his person. He had probably intended nothing worse than a public tongue-lashing of the police captain.

Despite the fact that a nervous captain had gunned down a well-known—and unarmed—former Texas Ranger, the Fort Worth Police force closed ranks. Officers had their image to consider. There were claims that Britton had twice threatened the life of the officer that day. An investigation and jury subsequently no-billed the captain on the assumption that he had acted in immanent fear for his life. One of the best ranger historians, Robert W. Stephens, noted that Grude "had been given authority to go armed as a result of having made enemies while in the service but Britton had surrendered the authority of his own accord shortly before his death."[38]

James Magruder "Grude" Britton thus died—ironically and pointlessly—in a dispute with a trigger-happy lawman. His body was collected by another ex-ranger from Company B, his brother, Ed Britton. Like Sam McMurry, Grude had never married or had children. Ed accompanied his brother's coffin westward to Parker County, where the Britton family interred the remains in Weatherford's Oakland Cemetery.

George Adamson enlisted in Company B on March 3, 1888, and resigned from the company on August 31, 1891, three years after A. T. Miller left the service. George had been born in Canada and somehow made his way to Texas.[39] He proved to be a steady ranger, sober and industrious. George Adamson also had an entrepreneurial spirit. He saved his pay while rangering and invested it in local enterprises. At one point he bought and sold livestock from the herds driven to the new cattleman's town of Quanah.

George Adamson liked Texas. His resignation from the service probably had little to do with McDonald's purge of some privates in 1891. It is more likely that George simply resigned in favor of a more settled and prosperous life. In any event after his last pay from the service, Adamson moved from the ranger camp into Quanah proper to make a living and to marry. At the time of his resignation he owned a saloon interest, a rather common commercial venture targeting thirsty cowboys. Adamson also bought and sold town lots. His prudent speculations in real estate in the 1890s eventually yielded a comfortable bourgeois lifestyle. Like A. T. Miller, rangering had been a means, not an end for him.

George Adamson married Miss Lillian Bowman, an attractive resident of Quanah, soon after turning in his resignation from Company B. Texas Rangers had always been popular in the town, and ex-rangers enjoyed plenty of esteem as well. George quickly made a good name for himself. He was a church-going husband, an honest businessman, and he participated in the civic life of Quanah. Sadly there were no children from the marriage, but the couple proved themselves assets to the community in many ways.

While still in his thirties, George Adamson was stricken with a grave illness. He died suddenly on March 28, 1901.[40] His death was so unexpected that it was a great shock to Lillian Adamson. George was buried by his widow and friends at the town cemetery north of Quanah, not far from the old company camp.

Samuel A. McMurry served Company B as captain for almost two and one-half more years, completing a sterling period of service as company captain from September 1, 1881, to January 31, 1891. His Texas Ranger record was impressive to say the least, even in an age of remarkable captains. An original veteran of Captain Lee Hall's Special Force in the Nueces Strip, McMurry rose from the ranks of the tough border rangers to become lieutenant by 1880. Detailed to law enforcement in counties opened by railroad construction, he emerged as captain of Company B in the 1881 reorganization of the Frontier Battalion. From wild West Texas in 1881 to the booming Texas Panhandle of 1890, Captain McMurry hastened the passing of the lawless frontier.[41]

His sobriquets of "Soft Voice" and "Say Nothing" tell us that he was a cool and calculating professional. His innate caution, diligence, precision, and restraint made him seem much less colorful than others. But then his cool professionalism led to fewer dead men, and his force took almost no casualties. He was proud of his remarkable record in taking wanted men without having to kill them, in an age when others might have been tempted to shoot first and shoot nervously. He deserves much more historical interest and acclaim. Abner Miller obviously respected his company commander.

McMurry only served a further twenty-nine months after Private Miller resigned in August, 1888. But these months were full of activity. Added to his prior service they brought him close to a decade of service as a captain in the Frontier Battalion. McMurry's steady nerves and analytical approach served Company B particularly well when state officials turned to the company to quell labor violence. Indeed, near the end of 1888 Sam McMurry was plunged into the historic labor unrest at Thurber, Texas. Around December 19, 1888, Captain McMurry and nine or ten privates from Company B caught a train out of Quanah. On December 20 the well-armed rangers arrived at the new town of Thurber, Texas.

Thurber was a town bought and paid for by the Texas & Pacific Coal Company. The company built the new community in 1888 around its recent purchase of the Johnson bituminous coal mines in north Erath

Figure 24. Captain Sam Alexander McMurry, Company B. Courtesy Texas Ranger Hall of Fame and Museum, Waco

County. The new town quickly gained a reputation for labor trouble and an atmosphere of repression. Led by an inflexible general manager, Colonel Robert D. Hunter, company management was virulently anti-union. Meanwhile angry immigrant workers were agitating under the influence of the Knights of Labor. A strike broke out that same year; Colonel Hunter fired workers en masse. By December of 1888 Thurber was a case study in historic labor strife. When some labor hotheads peppered Colonel Hunter's office quarters with gunshots, the general manager successfully appealed to the state for protection. The state's answer was to send Sam McMurry and his company.[42]

McMurry may have been aware that there were two sides to the violence, unrest, and strike at Thurber, but he had no sympathy for agitators, and he operated to remove the troublesome element. Thurber historian Madilyn Rhinehart notes that McMurry's periodic reports, "often written on Texas & Pacific Company stationery, displayed an obvious bias against the strikers."[43] The captain's anti-labor bias made him popular with company officials, of course, but he wisely resisted Colonel Hunter's rasher admonitions to crush the unions. Instead, he plotted to get strikebreakers past the intercepting screen of ardent union agitators in the surrounding cities. He also refused Hunter's offer of $5,000 (for ostensibly saving the manager's life) by noting simply that the State of Texas paid him for all services. A large barbed-wire fence surrounded the nine-hundred-acre company compound. Armed Texas Rangers and private guards secured the few entrances and patrolled the facilities inside by horseback.

McMurry played for time, arrested and harassed the rougher elements of labor camped nearby, and he appealed to his superiors for the company to remain at Thurber. He even persuaded Adjutant General W. H. King to visit Thurber in January, 1889, to assess the situation for himself. King gamely tried to play peacemaker with the strikers that January. His efforts were unavailing, so he decided to follow McMurry's advice and keep rangers on site indefinitely.[44] Captain McMurry saw it as his job to resolve the situation firmly in favor of management's resumption of operations.

With the connivance of Company B rangers, a large number of black strikebreakers were eventually transported to Thurber. Ranger John Sullivan claimed that McMurry also hired him to go undercover for $100 a month—to expose "dynamiters and anarchists." Sullivan's claims to have foiled a dynamiter plot were probably inflated versions of actual harassment arrests. In any case the strike petered out that spring and mine operations resumed by fall, 1889. McMurry's intervention had proved critical. He avoided real trouble—mob violence, shootings, and brutal labor repression—while still getting the mines back in production. A photograph of the Company B Texas Rangers at Thurber shows his men—and a woman—determined to clean up the town and sweep out the disorderly elements.

By the end of 1890 Sam McMurry was prepared to step down as company commander. When he finally resigned on January 31, 1891, he could look back to a remarkable career in law enforcement. As McMurry, now ex–Texas Ranger, caught a train and left Quanah forever, he could reflect that he left the region at least half-tamed. In fact he had left most of West Texas half-tamed, considering his ranger days in Colorado City, along the Texas & Pacific Railroad, and elsewhere. His friend and poker companion Bill McDonald was an interesting choice to complete the job. Bill Jess was a vain and boastful contrast to "Soft Voice" Sam, but at least

Sam's beloved Company B, Frontier Battalion, would be in brave and shrewd hands. Sam McMurry celebrated his forty-fourth birthday on April 25, 1891, and perhaps he was relieved that another man should now carry the burden.

Sam McMurry traded the strenuous job of rangering for the comforts and travels of a better-off salesman based in Louisville, Kentucky. He filled out with age and the better food, but he preserved his coolness and detachment of gaze. McMurry traveled widely for his Louisville firm, seeing the vast progress and pride of the settled nation from California to the East Coast. While visiting his sister in St. Louis in late 1913, he unfortunately caught pneumonia. Determined to make a business meeting back in Louisville, he struggled eastward to Kentucky. Weak and exhausted, he took a turn for the worse after the meeting. Sam McMurry died on January 8, 1914, at the age of sixty-six.

His body rode the steel rails one last time to the west. At St. Louis, the gateway to the western plains, his sister and other family members met the coffin. Samuel A. "Soft Voice" McMurry, an old warrior, was laid to rest in the town's Valhalla Cemetery on a winter day. As the Texas Ranger historian Robert W. Stephens noted, "He was born in Tennessee, died in Kentucky and is buried in Missouri but Sam McMurry belongs to Texas."[45]

William Jesse McDonald enjoyed his 1880s work in Quanah as a "special," particularly the local notoriety that began to attach to his name. He liked fame, and he courted its influence. The pioneer editor Harry Koch wrote of this time, "While running a newspaper I discovered that notoriety was something many Rangers aspired to and I had no trouble to stand well by them by giving ample space to their exploits."[46] McDonald also nursed old political connections, social ties that he used to his advantage in the 1890s and century ahead. And in the end McDonald had a passion for manhunting, a natural-born talent for capturing fugitives of all kinds, a skill that can be traced back to his youth when he pursued runaway slaves in the swamps of Mississippi.

It greatly helped his case when an old friend from Mineola, James Stephen Hogg, became the new governor of Texas. With the retirement of Sam McMurry, Governor Hogg thought about it and then recommended Bill Jess McDonald for the captaincy of Company B in January, 1891. Company B was still headquartered at Quanah, a convenient locale for McDonald with his ranch home nearby. His first action as captain was managing a hoax, the infamous "Indian Scare" of 1891 when wild reports

Figure 25. Captain Bill McDonald. Courtesy Texas Ranger Hall of Fame and Museum, Waco

of a hundred marauding braves circulated through panicked towns around Quanah. Soon Company B was back to its regular business of suppressing crime in the Panhandle, Greer County, and Rolling Plains.

By the middle of his first year, the new captain purged some of McMurry's men for indiscipline and related peccadilloes. He hired others more to his liking, including eventually his talented nephew, W. J. "Billy" McCauley. Following the adjutant general's sensible advice, McDonald relocated Company B to the booming cowtown of Amarillo at the end of the year. Company B arrived on December 8, 1891, and the men quickly knocked together some stables and winter structures for the new base camp.[47]

With McDonald's arrival in the Sanborn community, Amarillo became the geographic center for the suppression of outlawry in the Gay Nineties Panhandle. McDonald, a sergeant, a teamster, and the twelve privates in Company B proved very effective at closing illicit corridors and curbing lawlessness. With each new exploit and devious outsmarting of outlaws, his reputation also grew. During the 1890s he astutely cultivated friendships with other western legends such as Quanah Parker and Bat Masterson.[48]

McDonald's obsessive-compulsive personality was noted by some in Amarillo, especially his inveterate small-time gambling at the local faro bank.[49] He was regrettably a bigot and old-fashioned racist to boot, prone to regular derogation of minorities. But McDonald performed well in the Panhandle as captain of the company. He also enhanced his fame with intelligent examination of physical evidence, disguises and incognitos, and clever deduction skills. He examined hides with particular skill at detecting brand alterations. He doggedly chased the wicked and wild men throughout the Panhandle. "The Pan-handle was full of bad men in the early [eighteen] nineties," he recalled. "Most of them had graduated from other schools of crime and found here a last resort."[50] Invigorated municipal police forces elsewhere combed out their cities and sent streams of problem cases heading his way.

In the process of sorting it out, Bill Jess McDonald became a Texas Sherlock Holmes—eccentric, deductive, fearless, psychological, eager to examine arcane physical evidence, and ready to disguise or dissimulate to get his man. Arthur Conan Doyle's portrait of the deductive personality, *A Study in Scarlet,* appeared in 1888 just a year after McDonald was cracking his first cases as a Special Texas Ranger in Quanah.

The captain's most famous gunfight took place on the streets of Quanah on December 9, 1893.[51] While half the town watched in fascination, a classic western encounter and gunfight began as two sworn enemies—both prominent law officers—opened fire at arms length while Sheriff Coffer stood between them.[52] The renegade lawman Joe Beckham first caused trouble between Childress County Sheriff John Pierce Matthews and Captain Bill McDonald. McDonald refused to kowtow to Matthews's gruff claims of county governance over the despicable Beckham, and jurisdiction troubles escalated into personal threats. At the annual sheriff's convention in 1893, in Governor Hogg's presence, further philosophical and personality differences erupted in hot words and dirty names hurled at each other.

Matthews and two associates arrived at the Quanah train station on the morning of December 9, 1893. John Pierce Matthews had a domineering personality with a troubled past. He had killed an African American in Louisiana, come to Texas, dropped Matthews from his name for awhile, and was responsible for the 1884 accidental death of cowboy James Mankins in Wheeler County.[53] Despite all that—or maybe because of it—he handily won election in 1892 as Childress County's second sheriff. Sheriff Matthews and two companions did some drinking that day, according to the later report of Sergeant Grude Britton.[54] Mutual friends were worried by public hearsay rumors that Matthews had come to kill McDonald, and they were actively intervening. Around six o'clock that evening the two foes and their friends walked up to each other near the crowded Quanah train depot, ostensibly to make peace.

Reports said the two men met and McDonald had just queried Matthews about the sheriff, supposedly calling him a "damned, c— s— —, s.o.b." As Matthews tried to reply, McDonald pointed an accusing finger at him, Sheriff Coffer stepped between the two, and both antagonists instinctively went for their guns. Coffer dropped to the ground and bullets flew at the same time. Accounts vary in who fired the first shot but both men—and some of their associates—fired off shots.[55] It is impossible now to tell exactly who shot whom or when, and a mystery bullet is blamed for the only mortal wound. Both Matthews and McDonald were desperately wounded and fell bleeding into the street. Screams and confusion reigned supreme.

Sheriff Matthews survived long enough to apologize for his part in the shoot-out. But after days of recovery he contracted blood poisoning and died on December 30 in great agony. McDonald lingered in a critical state for weeks. Bill Jess recovered from his multiple wounds in the spring, and he even resumed his active captaincy of Company B. The Matthews shoot-out greatly enhanced his public reputation, despite the historical fact that McDonald was quietly and better known as a lawman who got his man alive. Nervous and inexperienced lawmen were the ones who too often took no chances and shot a wanted man needlessly.[56]

By late 1902 Captain McDonald was involved in troubles virtually across the entire state, from Gregorio Cortez in South Texas to horse thieves in the Oklahoma Territory. In December, 1902, the governor of Texas transferred a reorganized Company B from Amarillo to Fort Hancock on the Rio Grande for a spell of border trouble, then on to Alice in Jim Wells County in 1903. From September 1, 1902, to August 31, 1904, McDonald's Company B logged an incredible 74,537 miles in discharge of duties, making some 205 scouts and arresting 31 murderers among scores of investigations.[57] He became a magnificent troubleshooter for the state, dispatched hither and yon from 1904 to 1907 to stop riots and lynchings, to intimidate strikers and whitecappers, to break up white trash feuds, and generally to wholesale malefactors to the justice system for newly confident juries to sort out. He regaled Theodore Roosevelt so well with his bravado that he got an invitation to the White House, which he honored in 1906.[58]

Even a partial list of McDonald's famous cases resembles the romanticized casebooks of Doyle's fictional Sherlock Holmes. In "The Fruit Tree-man" he disguised himself as a traveling salesman, collecting orders for orchard trees while doing highly effective undercover investigations. In "The Hutchinson County Cattle Mutilations" McDonald destroyed a vicious rustler operation. In "The Cherokee Strip Campaign" he extended his avenging reach into Oklahoma's Panhandle. In "The Fitzsimmons-Maher Fight" he enforced state law against the entire boxing and gambling interests. In "The Murder Society of San Saba" he captained his Company B "Baker Street Irregulars" into shutting down a homicidal vigilante faction. In the "Wichita Falls Bank Robbery" McDonald and his men tracked down murderous bank robbers, but they soon found the real terror came from a determined lynch mob. They stoutly protected the robbers until relieved, whereupon the enraged mob had its way. There were many more cases: "The Reece-Townsend Feud"; "The Wichita Falls Bank Robbery"; "The Humphrey Murders, or Mystery in the Trans-cedar Bottoms"; "The Orange Race Riot"; "The Brownsville Incident"; "One Riot, One Ranger"; and "The Rio Grande City Ambush."[59]

A last and bloody gunbattle near Rio Grande City in late 1906 brought home to state officials just how easily they could lose their statewide press hero. Accordingly, Governor Thomas Campbell promoted Captain W. J. McDonald to the sinecure of state revenue agent in early 1907. McDonald attacked the statewide and inequitable system of tax assessment for two years, and, incredibly enough, he managed to win a major reform in the system. By cultivating his connections with Colonel E. M. House, established while both were in South Texas, McDonald eventually got on as Woodrow Wilson's personal bodyguard during the historic 1911–12 presidential campaign.

McDonald's job as bodyguard for Governor Woodrow Wilson was a serious one. The Bull Moose candidate, Teddy Roosevelt, had already survived one assassination attempt during the 1912 campaign. On

House's orders McDonald arrived with his weapons in New York City and joined the entourage around Wilson.[60] He kept his mouth shut, even earning the ironic nickname "Silent Bill" from reporters. Wilson and McDonald were thrown together frequently during the tumultuous campaign, and they formed a friendship. After winning the election, President Wilson appointed McDonald as U.S. Marshal of the Northern District of Texas, a prestigious position that Marshal Bill filled with honor, dash, and fairness. Despite all these impressive gains, he suffered an immeasurable personal loss with the passing away of wife Rhoda Carter McDonald.

After decades of bullets, bad men, and foul weather, it was a lowly microbe that finally brought tough, shrewd, deductive, and vain Marshal McDonald to a deathbed. He caught pneumonia in the pandemic winter of 1918. After a fight he died of respiratory failure at Wichita Falls on January 15, 1918. McDonald's body was brought westward for burial by his second wife, back to his hometown of Quanah.

On a winter day, cold as whiz, there was one last roundup of old friends, lawmen, and Texas Ranger companions in Quanah, Texas. Telegrams and messages of condolence poured into the community from all over the state. With much grief and memory, the legendary lawman was laid to rest with a dignified Presbyterian service. McDonald's funeral was the last reunion of the old boys of Company B, Frontier Battalion.

I paid my respects to McDonald's grave one summer afternoon. A number of the Quanah rangers are buried in the cemeteries serving the 1887–88 railroad townsites, towns that boomed and struggled with new economies. Driving along today's Highway 287 brings the sojourner close to the resting places of the old rangers. McDonald's grave is in the public cemetery just north of Quanah, a mile or so from the old ranger camp where fame dawned and his name lingered on the lips of outlaws and lawmen alike. The tombstone is impressive and even dominating, as was the man. Carved on it is McDonald's epitaph, a stricture that became his motto and governed his life: "No Man in the Wrong Can Stand Up Against A Fellow That's in the Right and Keeps on A-Coming."

Abner Theophilus Miller resigned from Company B on August 31, 1888, and relocated from Quanah to the vicinity of Margaret. He never stated a reason for resigning. He undoubtedly hoped to better his finances and condition in life with other opportunities. Abner Miller boarded in a Margaret hotel for a spell, and he laid plans to launch a new life with the coming year. Influenced by John Wesley's agrarian experiments and

Figure 26. Abner T. Miller. Courtesy Texas Ranger Hall of Fame Museum, Waco

community vision, Miller determined to engage in farming the fertile prairies southeast of Wesley's old townsite.

While going about his initial farming, Miller made the happy acquaintance in 1891 of George Burke's dark-haired sister, Naomi Catherine Burke Nixon. Naomi Nixon was a new schoolteacher at Margaret, a widowed Michigander trying to put family tragedy behind her. Born in 1859, she married Harry Nixon as a young woman. Harry and Naomi were childless, but the death of her mother in 1886 led the couple to take in two of her young siblings for official raising. In the unfortunate course of Harry Nixon's medical studies in the late 1880s, he contracted tuberculosis and died painfully. Fearful of her own exposure and unable to run a proper household for her siblings anymore, Naomi surrendered custody of the children and came to Texas, "seeking a climate to dry out her own lungs."[61]

Her brother, George Burke, likely introduced A. T. to Mrs. Nixon. A warm and mutual attraction developed. The two courted in a serious and traditional manner on evenings in 1891. The former Texas Ranger finally captured the one person on his most wanted list. Abner Theophilus and Naomi Catherine wedded in an old-fashioned Margaret ceremony, followed by a big wedding supper and dance. The Burkes and Wesleys and other pioneers toasted the newlyweds and celebrated the union.

Mr. and Mrs. Miller moved into a two-room frame house south of the new Thalia hamlet. A. T. farmed to win and Naomi kept a good house. Both were frugal and even anxious about money from time to time. But after six years of scrimping and saving they pooled their money and bought a magnificent new home place. On November 26, 1897, the Millers purchased an entire section of good farm land, then southwest of the McDonald ranch, now located one mile northeast of the *Last Picture Show* town of Thalia, Texas, in Foard County.

The modern and pleasant State Highway 70 touches the Miller section between Crowell and Vernon. Carpenters constructed a typical Victorian country cottage-house near the northeast corner of the section. A. T. and Naomi settled in their new house, putting in roots and helping establish the Thalia farming community. They farmed for years and built a solid life together on the Rolling Plains. A. T. Miller managed his farms and affairs well, acquired adjacent land with his brother R. L. as co-investor, and eventually employed hired hands and tenants to work his farms.

Childless after years of marriage, the Millers made a crucial decision after moving into their new home. Abner contacted and made an appointment with the Reverend I. Z. T. Morris, a Methodist minister who gave up the lofty pulpit for the lowly cradle. The same year A. T. Miller had joined Company B, the Reverend Morris and his wife, Isabella Morris, opened the door in Fort Worth to an unusual institution—the 1887 "Texas Children's Home and Aid Society."[62] The Reverend Morris was a brilliant advocate of child-welfare. With meager funds but much goodwill he and his wife established an innovative nursery and adoption service for the abandoned children of the teeming city. Later they worked with the shameful "orphan trains," trying to create western goodness from the eastern urban surplus of neglected and abandoned children who were loaded onto trains and shunted into the hinterland.

The Reverend Morris and his wife reversed the traditional cold perusal and selection of a child by prospective parents, however fit or abusive. They sought to place the child's interest first. In an age of notorious abuse, neglect, and abandonment of children, Morris's society interviewed and screened adoptive parents most carefully. Only after careful deliberations did it then consider an appropriate child in the interests of all. The Texas Children's Home and Aid Society was committed to placing unfortunate children into homes where they could grow to their fullest potential. Abner and Naomi Miller successfully passed their interviews with the Reverend Morris. They were then entrusted with an abandoned baby, an engaging and intelligent year-and-a-half-old girl.

The fair-haired and pretty baby otherwise suffered from disgrace, as she was illegitimate—a severe social and legal handicap in that prudish age. After months of caring for the child, A. T. and Naomi Miller formally adopted Lena Mae Miller on July 2, 1898. Decades later confidential family letters surfaced that suggested Lena's biological mother was possibly a Fort Worth prostitute, a woman no longer able to care for her child at a brothel. This possibility was socially dreadful, so a plausible cover story arose, one that explained Lena's birth and adoption as the unfortunate result of a soldier's dalliance with a Texas maiden during the Spanish-American War. The Reverend Morris knew the real truth. He believed that a black woman, a domestic worker, had simply delivered the babe in a basket one day to his Texas Children's Home doorstep. There was an attached note begging for care of the infant.[63]

The Reverend I. Z. T. Morris's innovations in child-welfare made a profound impression on another visitor, child-advocate Edna Gladney of Gainesville. Inspired by Morris's work, Edna Gladney reformed the Grayson County poor farm. She also personally directed neglected children to the Texas Children's Home. In 1910 Mrs. Gladney joined the society's board. Over the following decades she transformed the Texas Children's Home and Aid Society into the nationally recognized Edna Gladney Home. A tireless advocate for the rights of illegitimate children, Edna Gladney's life and Morris's home for homeless children were immortalized in the 1941 movie classic, *Blossoms in the Dust,* starring Greer Garson as Edna Gladney.[64]

The adopted blond child, named Lena Mae Miller, grew up with Abner and Naomi on their large farm in Foard County. There were inevitably many chores that fell her way. The Millers were strict and sometimes too frugal with their young daughter. Lena Mae celebrated one birthday with the present of a comb given her by a kind hired hand. But if the Millers refused to spoil their daughter with material success, they sincerely valued and promoted her educational prospects. The child was an excellent student with a flair for composition. As the Miller farm prospered they even began to think of her attending college. Like other adoptive couples of the era, the Millers counted on Lena Mae taking care of them in their old age. In the spring of 1914, A. T. and Naomi Miller relocated from Thalia to Clarendon in order for Lena Mae to attend Clarendon College.

A. T. and Naomi Miller settled into town life in Clarendon in 1914. The Millers bought an entire city block southwest of Clarendon College, and there they built a splendid Victorian house on the corner. Their adopted daughter did so well with her coursework at Clarendon College, "The Athens of the Panhandle," that she dreamed of further studies. The Millers watched with pride and sorrow as Lena Mae, a vivacious young woman with writing talent, left Clarendon by train in September, 1916. Their daughter arrived in Dallas to attend the second fall session of Southern Methodist University. Alone in a strange new dormitory on the edge of Dallas, Lena Miller started her own diary that night. At the end of her first entry she noted the sound of sobs in the women's dormitory. She felt like crying too—so far from home.

A. T. Miller stayed busy. He had duties as a Master Mason, and he joined the Scottish Rite in 1922. He frequently traveled to the old Miller homestead near Thalia in Foard County. He had to check on farm crops and tenant conditions. He drove a car now, but the landscapes rolling past recalled those seen from horseback over three decades ago.

By the early 1920s the Millers had new distractions. Lena Mae had graduated from SMU, and she was soon engaged to a bright and ambitious Texan, Sergeant Carl Bernard Morris. Sergeant Morris was a former schoolteacher, a veteran of Pershing's American Expeditionary Force, and a distant relation of the Reverend I. Z. T. Morris. He had known Lena Miller from his school and football glory days at Clarendon College. The couple fell in love and corresponded for years, especially during Morris's enlistment, training at Fort Bowie, and subsequent military service in France. When Sergeant Morris returned—unmutilated from trench warfare—they agreed to pledge their troth. A. T. Miller's idea of a honeymoon was to whisk his new son-in-law away after the ceremony, and to have him labor like a field hand for days on the Miller farm at Thalia, Texas. After showing his mettle and enduring his new wife's absence—for longer than he could stand anyway—Morris revolted and ran away to Clarendon to be with his bride.

Abner and Naomi Miller eventually adjusted to losing their daughter Lena and gaining a son-in-law, Carl Bernard "Cap" Morris. The newlyweds Cap and Lena settled on the Thalia farm, while the Millers kept their residence in Clarendon. Soon enough there were bright grandchildren. Abner and Naomi Miller made frequent trips to the Thalia farm to visit and inspect the operations. "Sometimes when distracted by bird watching and grandchildren," a granddaughter recalled of the frequent Miller visits, "they would forget who was to go first at the domino table. Abner's pocket knife was used as a marker."[65]

Mr. and Mrs. Miller lived a quiet, prosperous, and dignified life in Clarendon during the Roaring Twenties. When land prices tumbled at the end of the decade, A. T. saw opportunity and bought in March, 1930, a large nearby farm, the "Sunnyview Place," on the High Plains northeast of Clarendon. By the close of the decade Abner Miller's health began to fail. Cap and Lena Morris moved from Thalia to Clarendon to help care for him. Stricken with prostate cancer, Abner Theophilus Miller, former Texas Ranger, struggled for months before dying on September 6, 1931. Naomi Burke Miller, his loving wife, followed him to the grave two years later.

Abner Theophilus Miller was not an extraordinary Texas Ranger. His service was limited. He made few arrests and he clubbed down few citizens with his weapons. Given the extraordinary lawmen all around him, his personal talents were overshadowed in all save one respect: he recorded the daily experience. Unlike the filtered, bowdlerized, and sentimental reminiscences that dominate the portrayal of Texas Ranger camp life, the Miller diaries tell it as it appeared on the spot—with no thought of profit, glory, or justification. The boys were sometimes too rowdy, too drunk, too gambling, too cold, and too depressed for their own good. But this truth is also within the fabric of life, and it must likewise be restored to history. Deeply, directly, and in detail he captured—not outlaws—but the time and place, the working man's experience of riding for the Brookens with McMurry, McDonald, and Sheriff Barker. His camp reportage and casual gossip slashes at the cloying mythologies that have overgrown the real men and their natural behavior.

A. T. Miller was also a decent man. There is almost no trace of the vicious racism sometimes commonly associated with the Texas Rangers of the time. He saved his money, dressed well, was temperate in his habits, went to the Methodist church often enough, and was meticulous with tools and equipment. He was kind to ladies and attentive to the misses, played with children, kept up correspondences, and transformed himself from a Reconstruction refugee into a very successful middle-class farmer.

In the end Miller's most important contribution to the Texas Rangers was simply to record and preserve the daily experiences of the boys of Company B on the passing frontier of the Rolling Plains and Texas Panhandle.

A. T. Miller was buried at Citizen's Cemetery, on a prairie just south of Clarendon. His descendants still care for the grave and honor his memory.

The End of the Trail

APPENDIX A

Red Diary Addenda

The last three pages of the red diary contain notes and miscellanea, including the following items relevant to the life of an 1880s Texas Ranger private:

My Horses brand I got of W. R. Wheat. [?] on left Shoulder. And just behind the flank. Blaze face runs from brow. Band down over the left noze to the mouth. Left hind foot white half way up to the Neck. White in his right eye. 14 [hands] and a little over in high. Black. And saddle marks.

Feb 24/87 My wash acct.

2 shirts, 1 pr drawers. Socks	35[cents]
Mar 1st 2 shirts & a drawers	30[cents]
2 shirts & collar & socks	20[cents]

July 5 Quanah Tx

Jim Allee tells me that Em Harrington is wanted and old man Ben Backus son. And for us to Take them when ever we se them.

Paid W. R. Wheat 16.40 on June 1st/87, the balance on the Horse I owed him for, which makes us square.

$18.11 ⅔ Johnie [Miller]
12.66 ⅔ Lucus
$31.78 ⅓

I have in safe	$69.00
Tom Platt owes me 15.00	
	84.00
	31.78 ⅓ [debts]
	52.22 ⅔ [Net]

Paid to Johnnie Nov 15/87
in Settlement $18.10

1887 Discripion of a man
About Six ft high. Dark brown eyes and dark hare. Dark complexion. Wearing a brown ducking suit and black hat. With a Winchester. Name William Williams. Shot a Soldier at Ft Sill.

T. L. Keens Brand. Margaret Tx
[Illegible] on right side. 2 on right jaw. R on left shoulder and hip 1 cow -6 2 head. Branded U mule shoe left side.

J. N. Coleman. Kirkland [Texas]
1 oxen. Branded H left side
a red steer and a blase in forehead like a hart
Stolen Horses
1 Bay 77 on left shoulder
W. C. Lawson. Elm Spring
Chickisa Nation
1 Black Horse. Branded
on left Hip $50
Smith Brown. And Dock Pimiton is the owner
Pimiton
About six ft High Dark complexion. Coarse talking. Black Hare. Little mustash. Large teeth and sticks out. About 24 or 25 years old.
Smith Brown
Low Heavy set about 5 ft 3 in high. About 22 years old. Lite complection & Blew eyes. Sandy mustash.
Descripion of men

[end of red diary]

Black Diary Addenda

The following selected notes and accounts are found on the last pages of the second or black diary. The initial items concern the Miller brothers' speculative purchase of lots in John Wesley's townsite of Margaret. Like others, Miller came West for economic opportunity. His regular savings habits and investments bespeak a frugality born of the miserly Reconstruction period. Miller saved all his life and learned to invest wisely in farming.

Of further interest are detailed accounts of the Company B camp supplies and their costs. A good idea of the ranger mess can be gleaned from these records and the diary jottings about trading coffee for butter and eggs with locals. The inventory and accounting may have been a job duty that the captain imposed on Miller.

Margaret Lots

No [Number] Block	No [Number] of lots		
3	19. 20. 21	J. W. Miller	$ 50.00
8	13. 14	A. T. Miller	$ 75.00
	front on west side square		
6	10	R. L.(50) & A. T. Miller(10)	$ 60.00
9	7. 8. 9. 10. 11. 12.	A. T. Miller	$120.00
	106 Seven Acres of which five is Johnnies & Two is Ja W & A. T. Miller		$300.00
			$605.00

[The following accounts record the typical and seasonal supplies for the ranger camp at Quanah. The diet was southern in fashion. Note that Miller uses the ubiquitous # sign to indicate lb. or poundage, and "bu" or "bus" for bushels. Sam Walton would have approved of their bulk buying.]

Dec 6th/27 Tom Platt got some supplies to day. molasses 1 qt. salt one little sack, candles nine Sugar 12# coffee 12# onions 15# potatoes 15# baking p[owder] 2# corne 10bu Bacon 31#

[Dec] 17th/27 Flour 50#. 25# Potatos Appls as[?] Beans 5# 1 gal P Alieas[?] vinger Lard 10# as Bacon 5 sacks corne 15 bushels

Dec 27	to day 4 bu corne 6 of oats 10# sugar 2# Baking P[owder] 4 boxes pepper (1# candles 8) Salt about 5 or 10# potatoes 10#
Dec 29	we got 5 bales Hay.
Jan 6/88	6 bales of hay.
"3	15 bus corne 5 bales hay 12# coffee 2# B Powder 1# [candles] 4# salt 2 gal molasses 30# potatoes 10# Lard
Jan 11th	1 sack flour
Jan 14	Six 6 bales of hay
"18	6 bales of hay
Jan 25th	12# coffee 10# sugar 2# Baking Powder 10# lard 15#Potatos 1 sack flour 1# candles 15 bu corne
Jan 2.4	6 bales of hayJan 26th 15# potatos
Feb 1st	1# candles. potatoes 20# oat meal 15# Lard 5# corne 10bu. 6 bales hay
Feb 9th	14bu & 31# of corne 6 bales of hay 10# sugar, ¼# Tea, 5# Lard, 1 sack flour (50#), 1 sack meal (50#), 23# potatoes
Feb15th	5bu 4# oats 3 bales hay 30# potatos 20# Lard 10# salt 1# candles small box of spice & the peper he gave me.
Feb 28th	Mike & Tom Platt got 4 sack corne 2 sack oats 3 ba[r]ley 12# coff[ee] 12# sugar 1# candles & 2 bottles of pickles 1 sack flour 20# potatoes 2 cans Tomatoes
March 2	2 55# corne 15# potatoes 1 axhandle 1# candles 1 sack flour

Bought of Robinson Bros & co.

Quarter from Sept 1st to Nov 30/87

1350	#	Flour	2.90 [=]	39.15
540	#	Bacon	11 ½ c	62.10
108	#	Rice	7 ½	8.10
162	#	Beans	6c	9.72
216	#	Coffee	24 ½	52.92

216	#	Sugar	8c	17.28
10 ¾	Galls	Pickles	50c	5.38
43	#	Salt	1 ½	.65
21	#	Soap	6c	1.26
18	#	Baking Powder	20c	3.60
2 ¾	#	Pepper	20c	.55
11	#	Candles	12c	1.32
324	#	Potatoes	2 ½	8.10
11520	#	Corne 205 20/28 bus	77c	158.40
	23			
				[Total=] 368.53

[Crossed out and marked "Paid"]
Oct 10 Monday /[18]87
I Loaned to Dennis Peal untill Payday Dec 1st/87 $5.00
[Signed] A. T. Miller
[Signature]
C Sparmann
Quanah Tx
Boot Maker

[end of the black diary]

NOTES

Prologue

1. Mike Cox notes, "Judging from the number of times he uses the word, 'boys' must have been in common usage among comrades in arms in frontier Texas." Mike Cox, *Texas Ranger Tales: Stories that Need Telling,* p. 308. Cf. A. J. Sowell, *Rangers and Pioneers of Texas* . . . .
2. See Alonzo Van Oden's *Texas Ranger's Diary & Scrapbook,* edited by Ann Jensen. This slender but interesting scrapbook is not a true journal, as Van Oden's entries are random (not daily), usually undated, and sometimes consist principally of collected writings then current. Ranger historian Mike Cox notes, "As remarkable as Oden's diary was, it is a shame he did not record more of his day-to-day activities as a Ranger." Mike Cox, "Ranger Oden's Diary," in *Texas Ranger Tales,* p. 97.
3. W. John L. Sullivan, *Twelve Years in the Saddle for Law and Order on the Frontiers of Texas.* Mike Cox comments on Sullivan's book in "Appendix," *Texas Ranger Tales,* pp. 308–10.
4. John H. Jenkins, *Basic Texas Books,* pp. 526–28. Jenkins selected Sullivan's work as Basic Texas Book (BTB) #200.

Chapter 1

1. Alex Mathews Arnett, *The Story of North Carolina,* pp. 159–62.
2. Compiled from research in the Carolina Room, Public Library of Charlotte and Mecklenburg County, Charlotte, North Carolina. See Julia Pollock Harriet, comp., *The History and Genealogy of Jones County, North Carolina;* William Harris Miller, *History and Genealogy of the Families of Robert Miller* . . . ; Roger E. Kammerer and David Carpenter, comps., *Onslow Register: Records of Onslow and Jones Co.;* and Surena B. Henderson, *Jones County: Fact and Folklore.*
3. Naomi M. Green, "Miller, Abner and Naomi," in [Donley County], *Donley County History 1879–1990,* pp. 318–19; A. T. Miller's maroon diary (1888), where genealogical notes are appended by Miller to page 71.
4. Green, "Miller, Abner and Naomi," *Donley County History,* pp. 318–19.
5. Miller's maroon diary, p. 71. In notes for "Miller Heirs Tax acct on land in Jones Co N.C." the first entry records that on May 18, 1884, A. T. Miller sent $2.93 to Thomas A. Miller "at Gainesville, Tex" to pay his share of 1883 taxes on the farm.
6. Walter Prescott Webb, editor-in-chief, *The Handbook of Texas,* vol. 1, p. 974, and Ron Tyler, Douglas E. Barnett, Roy Barkley, eds., *The New Handbook of Texas,* vol. 3, p. 1163.
7. Z. T. Fulmore, *The History and Geography of Texas as Told in County Names,* revised edition, pp. 79, 215; Webb, ed., *The Handbook of Texas,* vol. 1, pp. 766–67.

8. Bailey Phelps, *They Loved the Land: Foard County History,* p. 130 and *passim.* Phelps's work is an important compilation and guide to the pioneers of the area. George Burke is usually spelled "Geo. Burk," but Miller family records on his sister, Naomi Burke, suggest a best spelling with a final "e."
9. Green, "Miller, Abner and Naomi," *Donley County History,* pp. 318–19.
10. See W. G. Kerr, *Scottish Capital on the American Credit Frontier,* pp. 7–8, 22–25.
11. See the entries for M. M. Hankins and J. C. Ferguson in Bill Neal, *The Last Frontier: the Story of Hardeman County,* pp. 114–15, 128.
12. For "Yampareka, Texas" see Phelps, *They Loved the Land,* p. 110; for "Yamparika" Comanche, see Tyler, et al., *The New Handbook of Texas,* vol. 6, p. 1108.
13. Quoted from Dorothy Scarborough's 1926 letter to a Dallas bookseller, in Sylvia Ann Grider's foreword to the 1979 reprint edition. Grider's introduction explicitly ties the novel to the 1886–87 weather extremes. See Dorothy Scarborough, *The Wind,* pp. vii–x.
14. J. Evetts Haley, *Charles Goodnight: Cowman and Plainsman,* new edition, pp. 381–401.
15. Reminiscence of John Campbell, "Drought of 1886," *Foard County News* (Apr. 7, 1941), cited in Phelps, *They Loved the Land,* p. 31.
16. For the best account of the "Texas Drouth," see William Curry Holden, "West Texas Drouths," *Southwestern Historical Quarterly* 22:2 (Oct., 1928): 103–23.
17. Quoted in C. Richard King, *Wagons East,* p. 17.
18. Holden, "West Texas Drouths," pp. 117–18.
19. Clara Barton, *The Red Cross,* p. 141.
20. Phelps, *They Loved the Land,* pp. 121–22.
21. See J. W. Klepper entry in Charles P. Ross and T. L. Rouse, eds., *Early-Day History of Wilbarger County,* p. 108.
22. Haley, *Charles Goodnight,* pp. 54–55. At the end of a Foard County dirt road, about a mile east of the Old Margaret townsite, another state historical stone marker commemorates the Pease River battlefield.
23. Phelps, *They Loved The Land,* p. 261.
24. Ibid., pp. 112–14.
25. The 1880 U.S. census records John and Mary Wesley and four children, Hurley, Abner, Sarah, and Maggie, as part of the fifty residents of the county.
26. Phelps, *They Loved the Land,* pp. 32–33, 114. The old ULA is now part of the Halsell Ranch.
27. Fulmore, *The History and Geography of Texas,* p. 169; Joe Beverly, "Foard County History," in *Foard County News,* Crowell, Tex., 1930. Special issue.
28. Neal, *The Last Frontier,* p. 66.
29. Note "Monthly Return of Captain S. A. McMurry's Company B, Frontier Battalion State of Texas, for the Month Ending February 28th, 1887" (hereafter [date] *Monthly Return,* Co.B, FB), Adjutant General's Record Group (hereafter AGR) 401-1247/14, Archives Division—Texas State Library, Austin. In the "Remarks" column on his February, 1887, *Monthly Return,* Captain McMurry wrote: "Enlisted Feb. 12th A. T. Miller."
30. Robert W. Stephens, *Texas Ranger Sketches* ([Dallas]: privately printed, 1972),

pp. 26–32. Stephens presents the best biography of Sam McMurry [also spelled McMurray]. For other details on McMurry's enlistment and service see S. A. McMurry File, Texas Ranger Service Records, Adjutant General's Record Group (AG's RG) 401-162, Archives Division—Texas State Library, Austin (hereafter TSL-A).

31. S. A. McMurry File, AG's RG 401-162, TSL-A; Dora Neill Raymond, *Captain Lee Hall of Texas,* pp. 177 and 192.
32. Frederick Wilkins, *The Law Comes to Texas: The Texas Rangers 1870–1901,* pp. 225–28.
33. For the connection of McMurry to Porter, see Chuck Parsons and Gary P. Fitterer, *Captain C. B. McKinney: The Law in South Texas,* p. 36.
34. A useful recent history of the Texas Rangers during this period is Wilkins, *The Law Comes to Texas.*
35. J. Evetts Haley, *Jeff Milton: A Good Man With a Gun,* pp. 66–67.
36. Cf. 1883–1885 *Monthly Returns,* Co.B, FB, AG's RG 401-1247/10–13, TSL-A.
37. McMurry, letter to Capt. L. P. Sieker, Sept. 1, 1886, Frontier Battalion Correspondence, AG's RG 401-1160/5, TSL-A. McMurry notes, "I will get more [men] when I reach Hardeman Co."
38. See Raymond, *Captain Lee Hall of Texas,* pp. 50, 177, and 192; and John W. Bracken, Obituary, "Tom Platt, Texas Ranger," *Frontier Times* 7:3 (Dec., 1929): 144.
39. The Texas case for the North Fork as the boundary was argued well in John M. Swisher (with the opinions of Ex-Governor E. M. Pease and Major William M. Walton), *Title of Greer County Investigated.* See also C. A. Welborn, *The Red River Controversy, The Western Boundary of the Louisiana Purchase;* Webb L. Moore, *The Greer County Question;* and Tyler, et al., *The New Handbook of Texas,* vol. 3, pp. 326–27.
40. Feb., 1887, *Monthly Return,* Co.B, FB, AG's RG 401-1247/14, TSL-A.
41. Ibid.
42. Ibid.
43. Albert Bigelow Paine, *Captain Bill McDonald, Texas Ranger: A Story of Frontier Reform,* p. 55. John H. Jenkins has an excellent discussion of the book (BTB#158) in *Basic Texas Books,* pp. 424–26.
44. Paine, *Captain Bill McDonald,* p. 61. Paine's biographical account gives little credit to others, including Pat Wolforth, due to its excessive adulation for McDonald. Note also Captain McMurry's February, 1887, *Monthly Return,* Co.B, FB, AG's RG 401-1247/14, TSL-A, which sums up the entire incident in a sentence: "Sergt. McNelly arrested Pat Wolforth chg assault to murder del[ivered] to authorities of Hardeman Co."
45. Bracken, Obituary, "Tom Plat, Texas Ranger," p. 144.
46. The location for Teepee City is given as Cottle County in Webb, ed., *Handbook of Texas,* vol. 2, pp. 718–19, but note the corrected locale in Tyler, et al., *The New Handbook of Texas,* vol. 6, pp. 234–35.
47. Documentary evidence on McDonald's ranger activities in 1887 is rare. After his appointment as a Texas ranger captain in 1891, McDonald filed reports on his ac-

tivities, located in File Box 2–11, Records of the Adjutant General of the State of Texas, Texas State Library, Austin. Some additional 1890s McDonald transcripts are in the Ranger Correspondence, Webb Papers, Barker Texas History Center Archives, Austin.

48. Charles Seymour, *The Intimate Papers of Colonel House,* pp. 20–21.
49. J. Paul Jones, "History of Hardeman County," Master's Thesis, University of Texas at Austin, 1949.
50. Mar., 1887, *Monthly Return,* Co.B, FB, AG's RG 401-1247/14, TSL-A.
51. Haley, *Charles Goodnight,* p. 363.
52. Paine spells the name consistently as "Bull Turner," but the Miller diary provides strong evidence that it should be "Bill" not "Bull." (Sometimes one wonders how much "Bull" is actually in Paine's book.) See Paine, *Captain Bill McDonald,* p. 58.

Chapter 2

1. Madeline Mason-Manheim [using pseudonym of Tyler Mason], *Riding for Texas: The True Adventures of Captain Bill McDonald of the Texas Rangers . . . As told by Colonel Edward M. House to Tyler Mason.* Other important sketches are found in: Walter Prescott Webb, *The Texas Rangers, A Century of Frontier Defense,* new edition, pp. 444–69; Eugene Cunningham, *Triggernometry: A Gallery of Gunfighters,* chapter 14, "Rush One Ranger," pp. 315–31; William Warren Sterling, *Trails and Trials of a Texas Ranger,* pp. 334–61; and Lee McGiffen, *Ten Tall Texans,* pp. 182–205. Two essential modern discussions are Harold J. Weiss, "'Yours to Command': Captain William J. 'Bill' McDonald and the Panhandle Rangers of Texas," Dissertation, Department of History, Indiana University (1980), and Virgil L. Baugh, *A Pair of Texas Rangers: Bill McDonald and John Hughes.*
2. See Wilkins, *The Law Comes to Texas,* "The Vanishing Frontier, 1881–82," chapter 8, pp. 215–36.
3. Paine, *Captain Bill McDonald, p.* 141.
4. T. R. Fehrenbach, *Lone Star: A History of Texas and the Texans,* pp. 576–77, 588–90.
5. Frederick Wilkins comments on the 1880s, "There was little glory in any of their efforts to enforce law and order and make the laws work." Wilkins, *The Law Comes to Texas,* p. 240.
6. Ibid., p. 249.
7. Phelps, *They Loved the Land,* pp. 63–65.
8. Lee Gilmore, "The Mill Iron Ranch," *Panhandle-Plains Historical Review* 5 (1932): 57–66.
9. James R. Gober and B. Byron Price, eds., *Cowboy Justice: Tale of a Texas Lawman Jim Gober, p.* 88.
10. Incident reported in Dulcie Sullivan, *The LS Brand, The Story of a Texas Panhandle Ranch,* pp. 60–61.
11. See John Arnot, "My Recollections of Tascosa Before and After the Coming of

the Law," *Panhandle-Plains Historical Review* 6 (1933): 58–79; and Wayne Gard, *Frontier Justice*, pp. 230–34.

12. Austin, Texas: KVUE "Six O'Clock News," May 17, 1995. Governor George Bush's remarks to the press were reported after the passage of the concealed-handgun bill by the Texas Legislature.
13. Captain William Scott, letter to Quartermaster L. P. Sieker, July 3, 1886, Frontier Battalion Correspondence, AG's RG 401-1160/5, TSL-A.
14. Captain William Scott, letter to L. P. Sieker, July 31, 1886, ibid.
15. For further details on the Conner fight, see William Warren Sterling, *Trails and Trials of a Texas Ranger*, pp. 309–11, 372, and 381. For a modern cinematic treatment of a similar theme, note the National Guardsmen tangling with Cajun outlaws in the movie *Southern Comfort*.
16. A scrap of paper torn from a small notebook is in the Frontier Battalion Correspondence, AG's RG 401-1160/5, TSL-A., with the plaintive message: "Hemphill, Tex. Mch 31st 1887. [To] Dr. F. H. Tucker San Augustine. Capt. Scott and two of his men was shot this morning by the Conners, and asking that you come at once to this place as they need & wish your service and attention on them. Be sure and come right away as they are badly wounded. Your Friend, Jas. Polly."
17. Dora Neill Raymond, *Captain Lee Hall of Texas*, p. 177; Webb, *The Texas Rangers*, *pp*. 239–80.
18. See John McNelly File, Texas Ranger Service Records, AG's RG 401-162, TSL-A.
19. Cf. Apr., 1887, *Monthly Return*, Co.B, FB, AG's RG 401-1247/14, TSL-A.
20. Wayne Gard, *Frontier Justice*, p. 51.
21. Like Comanche raiders, the Texas Rangers are well aware of the advantages of a full moon. The calculation of moon phase is by Brad Armovsky, McDonald Observatory Public Information Office, using the "Voyager II" software program made by Corina Software Company.
22. "Record of Scouts," Apr., 1887, *Monthly Return*, Co.B, FB, AG's RG 401-1247/14, TSL-A.
23. Phelps, *They Loved the Land*, p. 64.
24. For nearby Wheeler County, "The expression 'disturbing the peace' was used occasionally at first then after 1888 used altogether," according to Millie Jones Porter, *Memory Cups of Panhandle Pioneers*, p. 161.
25. Neal, *The Last Frontier*, *p*. 275.
26. "Two ex-Texas Rangers, Peale and Britton, ran a saloon for awhile, and then sold it to Wally Bills." J. Evetts Haley and Wm. Curry Holden, eds., *The Flamboyant Judge: James T. Hamlin*, p. 15.
27. Tyler, et al., *The New Handbook of Texas*, vol. 1, p. 17.
28. Sterling, *Trails and Trials*, pp. 393–94. Sterling notes other colloquial names such as "Black Book" and "Bible Number Two."
29. In editing his county history of Foard County, *They Loved the Land*, Bailey Phelps deliberately chose the spelling "Wanders Creek." He found it the common orthography in old documents. A. T. Miller also spelled it "Wanders," but his spelling often reflects a phonetic rendering of Upper South dialect. The U.S.

Geological Survey, Texas Department of Transportation, and other current cartographic users prefer a spelling of "Wanderers Creek," but to be fair we should pronounce it "Wanders Creek."

30. For the active service of the rangers during the fence-cutting wars, see Webb, *The Texas Rangers,* pp. 426–37, and Raymond, *Captain Lee Hall of Texas*, pp. 193–96.
31. Sterling, *Trails and Trials*, p. 311.
32. Cf. "Public Property" column, Apr., 1887, *Monthly Return,* Co.B, FB, AG's RG 401-1247/14, TSL-A.
33. Gunnar Brune, *Springs of Texas,* p. 118.
34. Virginia Browder Rogers, *The Giles Chronicle: Vignette of Panhandle History, 1887–1956;* Brune, *Springs of Texas, p.* 169; and Tyler, et al., *The New Handbook of Texas,* vol. 3, p. 162.
35. An endearing work on the town and period is Willie Newbury Lewis, *Between Sun and Sod.*
36. Tyler, et al., *The New Handbook of Texas,* vol. 1; Lewis, *Between Sun and Sod,* pp. 97–99 and 221–23.
37. The old wagon roads of the Panhandle are discussed in C. Robert Haywood, *Trails South: The Wagon-Road Economy in the Dodge City–Panhandle Region.*
38. Brune, *The Springs of Texas*, p. 109.
39. See the illustration of a stagecoach and ad copy for the "Vanita and Las Vegas Mail Route at Fort Elliott," in Haywood, *Trails South*, p. 205.
40. The Canadian Valley explorers are discussed in John Miller Morris, *El Llano Estacado: Exploration and Imagination on the High Plains of Texas and New Mexico, 1536–1860.*
41. Margaret Sheers, "The LX Ranch of Texas," *Panhandle-Plains Historical Review* 6 (1933): 45.
42. J. I. Romero, as told to Ernest R. Archambeau, "Spanish Sheepmen on the Canadian," *Panhandle-Plains Historical Review* 19 (1946): 45–72.
43. Richard L. Nostrand, *The Hispano Homeland, pp.* 77–82. The Hispano eastward expansion down the Canadian Valley was blunted by W. M. D. Lee (who bought them out), Charles Goodnight (who discouraged them), and Bates and Beales (who blocked them). Nevertheless, Nostrand persuasively argues that eastward expansion from Mora and Las Vegas contributed to the formation of an Outland—a peripheral zone of Hispano acculturation and significant settlement.
44. The ruins still existed in the 1930s. See the Floyd Studer photo in Pauline D. Robertson and R. L. Robertson, *Panhandle Pilgrimage,* p. 135.
45. Walter Prescott Webb, "George W. Arrington: The Iron-Handed Man of the Panhandle," *Panhandle-Plains Historical Review* 8 (1935): 7–20.
46. A well-researched biography of G. W. Arrington [John C. Orrick, Jr.] is in Mike Cox, *Texas Ranger Tales II,* pp. 97–109. See also Jerry Sinise, *George Washington Arrington: Civil War Spy, Texas Ranger, Sheriff, and Rancher.*
47. Webb, *The Texas Rangers,* pp. 411–22.
48. Della Tyler Key, *In the Cattle Country: History of Potter County, 1887–1966,* second edition, pp. 18–19.

49. Helen Bugbee Officer, "A Sketch of the Life of Thomas Sherman Bugbee," *Panhandle-Plains Historical Review* 5 (1932): 8–22; Virginia Browder, *Donley County, Land O' Promise,* pp. 120–24.
50. Porter, *Memory Cups,* pp. 521–22.
51. Ibid., p. 525.
52. "Record of Scouts," May, 1887, *Monthly Return,* Co.B, FB, AG's RG 401-1247/14, TSL-A. See also the "Arrests" column of McMurry's report.
53. Jim Gober discusses working for the LX Ranch around this time in Gober and Price, eds., *Cowboy Justice,* 69–84. See also John Arnot, "The Famous LX Ranch had its Beginning on the Arkansas," *Amarillo Globe News,* Special Edition (Aug. 21, 1938), section E, p. 23.
54. Millie Jones Porter, *Memory Cups of Panhandle Pioneers,* 165 and 521.
55. John L. McCarty, *Maverick Town, The Story of Old Tascosa,* pp. 238–39.
56. Charles Rudolph, Dec. 8, 1886, article, "Shot Thirteen Times," reprinted in Ernest R. Archambeau, ed., "Old Tascosa, Selected News Items from *The Tascosa Pioneer* 1886–1888," *Panhandle-Plains Historical Review* 39 (1966): 44–46. Dr. Croft arrived on the scene to treat John Leverton, but it was too late. Croft's version of the tragic event reached Rudolph who wrote a scathing attack on Arrington's handling of the situation.
57. Porter, *Memory Cups,* p. 522; John McCarty, *Maverick Town,* p. 238.
58. See Vance Johnson, *Amarillo-Globe News,* Anniversary Special Edition, *op.cit.*, 2–4.
59. Charles Rudolph, "Shot Thirteen Times," in Archambeau, ed., *op.cit.*, pp. 45–46.
60. Porter, *Memory Cups,* p. 521.
61. Ibid., pp. 165–167. Some of the females charged with vagrancy are identified as a "common prostitute." Many names also appear in other courthouse records relating to assaults, threats, and fights, as when May McAfee accused Rube Sealer of "attempting her life" in 1887, ibid., 159.
62. Ibid., 166–67.
63. Ibid., 168–69.
64. Quote from Haley and Holden, eds., *The Flamboyant Judge,* Appendix, p. 302. For a broader context see Anne M. Butler, *Daughters of Joy, Sisters of Mercy: Prostitutes in the American West, 1865–1890* (Urbana: University of Illinois Press, 1987).
65. Rudolph in Archambeau, ed., *op. cit.*, p. 88, reprint article from *The Tascosa Pioneer,* Sat., May 21, 1887.
66. "Record of Scouts," May, 1887, *Monthly Return,* Co.B, FB, AG's RG 401-1247/14, TSL-A.
67. Raymond, *Captain Lee Hall of Texas,* p. 50. These exciting years are also covered in the sensational, first-hand journalistic account by N. A. Jennings, *A Texas Ranger.*
68. S. M. Platt File, Texas Ranger Service Records, AG's RG 401-168, TSL-A.
69. Ross and Rouse, eds., *Early-Day History of Wilbarger County,* p. 106.
70. Paine, *Captain Bill McDonald,* p. 143.
71. Edward Bellamy, *Looking Backward: 2000–1887,* later edition with S. Baxter introduction, pp. 20–21. Bellamy's novel was first published by Boston's Ticknor & Co. in 1888. The novel deserves a renewed interest.

72. See the state pay vouchers signed by McMurry in the A. T. Miller File, Texas Ranger Service Records, AG's RG 401-164, TSL-A.
73. Phelps, *They Loved the Land,* pp. 126 and 220. The arrival date given for both Ayers and Moore is 1888, but the diary suggests they actually arrived in 1887. Mrs. Moore gave birth on February 8, 1888, to a daughter in their new home, further implying that they had been in the area for awhile.
74. Names and spellings are taken from McMurry's "Arrests," June, 1887, *Monthly Return,* Co.B, FB, AG's RG 401-1247/14, TSL-A. McMurry's "Ben Tutt" seems preferable to Miller's "Ben Tuck." McMurry's report merely gives the barest details, making Private Miller's account a veritable gossip-sheet.
75. "Record of Scouts," June, 1887, *Monthly Return,* Co.B, FB, AG's RG 401-1247/14, TSL-A.
76. Ann Seagraves, *Soiled Doves: Prostitutes in the Early West.*
77. This was the typical charge in Wheeler County according to local historian Millie Jones Porter, *Memory Cups,* pp. 165–66.
78. Haley and Holden, eds., *The Flamboyant Judge,* p. 55.
79. Ibid., pp. 105–107. For Temple Houston's impassioned trial speech in defense of transient prostitute Milly Stacy, see the Appendix, "Plea For A Fallen Woman," pp. 301–302. Millie Stacy afterward moved to Canadian, Texas, took in washing, joined the Methodists, and married, ibid., 54f. Various spellings of her name exist.
80. "Record of Scouts," June, 1887, *Monthly Return,* Co.B, FB, AG's RG 401-1247/14, TSL-A.

Chapter 3

1. FW&DC Railroad Company, *Annual Report,* 1887.
2. Richard C. Overton, *Gulf to Rockies: The Heritage of the Fort Worth and Denver—Colorado and Southern Railways, 1861–1898,* pp. 127–29. Overton cites from the "Memo Outline" original in FW&DC Files.
3. Ibid., p. 129.
4. Amarillo historian Laura Hamner eloquently recalled the life of a child, Addie Brown, who lived in "Tent City" in 1887. See Laura V. Hamner, *Light 'n Hitch,* pp. 184–88. "Tent City" called itself Rag Town in Potter County after months of wind and weather had taken their toll on the tents.
5. Paine, *Captain Bill McDonald,* p. 64.
6. The July, 1887, "Record of Scouts" notes that on July 10 Privates Green and Furman were detailed to accompany the sheriff of Wilbarger County "to Baylor Co in pursuit of Bill Brooken & Pet[e] Rose. failing to catch them ret[urned] [July] 12th travelled 150 miles." Thus, both company records and Miller's diary mention a "Pet[e]" Rose for this time period. Neither company records nor Miller's diary mention McDonald's participation, but this absence should not impeach his general account of the events. McDonald's version is given in Paine, *Captain Bill McDonald,* 65–66.

7. See Glenn Shirley, *The Fighting Marlows: Men Who Wouldn't Be Lynched.* Sheriff Marion Wallace's death is on pages 41–44.
8. Overton, *Gulf to Rockies,* p. 122.
9. Charles N. Gould, *Oklahoma Place Names,* p. 112. "Navajoe" was a ghost town by the 1930s.
10. Shirley, *The Fighting Marlows,* pp. 14, 29–33.
11. The best source on the old Texas town of Navajoe is Cecil R. Chesser, *Across the Lonely Years, The Story of Jackson County,* pp. 104–105.
12. Quoted from "Corwin F. Doan Tells Experiences at the Gateway to Greer County," in *Mangum Daily Star,* vol. 45 (Nov. 16, 1932), p. 16. See also the entry for Corwin F. Doan in Tyler, et al., *New Handbook of Texas,* vol. 2, p. 660.
13. Phelps, *They Loved the Land,* p. 153.
14. Miller's "Ammerias" is a phonetic Anglo rendering of the correct Spanish pronunciation for "Amarillas," with the liquid LL-ending. Railroad conductors soon corrupted the "ree-yo" to a "rill-o" pronunciation.
15. Ernest R. Archambeau, ed., introduction to "Old Tascosa: Selected News Items from *The Tascosa Pioneer,* 1886–88," *Panhandle-Plains Historical Review* 39 (1966): v–vii.
16. Tyler, et al., *The New Handbook of Texas,* vol. 5, p. 825.
17. Amarillo's evolution may be traced in the successive comments and articles about the new village by Charles F. Rudolph, editor of *The Tascosa Pioneer.* Note Rudolph's pertinent article, "The Election in Potter," published on Sept. 3, 1887, and reprinted in Archambeau, ed., "Old Tascosa," p. 123.
18. Two worthwhile sources on the founding of Amarillo are Key, *In the Cattle Country,* pp. 36–65 and 77–89; and B. Byron Price and Frederick W.Rathjen, *The Golden Spread,* pp. 68–73.
19. Texas Adjutant General Service Records, Frontier Battalion, 401-162 (John McNelly).
20. Texas Adjutant General Service Records, Frontier Battalion, 401-168 (Thomas Platt).
21. "Record of Scouts," Sept., 1887, *Monthly Return,* Co.B, FB, AG's RG 401-1247/14, TSL-A.
22. "Record of Scouts," Sept., 1887, *Monthly Return,* Co.B, FB, AG's RG 401-1247/14, TSL-A.
23. "Record of Scouts," Sept., 1887, *Monthly Return,* Co.B, FB, AG's RG 401-1247/14, TSL-A.

Chapter 4

1. "Record of Scouts," Sept., 1887, *Monthly Return,* Co.B, FB, AG's RG 401-1247/14, TSL-A.
2. Ross and Rouse, eds., *Early-Day History of Wilbarger County,* p. 80.
3. Fred Rathjen, *The Texas Panhandle Frontier,* p. 245.
4. "Record of Scouts," Sept., 1887, *Monthly Return,* Co.B, FB, AG's RG 401-1247/14, TSL-A.

5. Alfred J. Watkins and David C. Perry discuss the class implications of western growth in "Regional Change and the Impact of Uneven Urban Development," in Watkins and Perry, *The Rise of the Sunbelt Cities,* pp. 19–54. I also drew upon my unpublished 1985 research paper, "Amarillo: The Perils of Prosperity," originally written for the graduate program in Community and Regional Planning at the University of Texas at Austin.
6. "Record of Scouts," Oct., 1887, *Monthly Return,* Co.B, FB, AG's RG 401-1247/14, TSL-A.
7. Lester Fields Sheffy, *The Franklyn Land & Cattle Company, A Panhandle Enterprise, 1882–1957,* pp. 156–57.
8. Ernest B. Zeisler, *The Haymarket Riot, pp.* 101–39.
9. "Record of Scouts," Nov., 1887, *Monthly Return,* Co.B, FB, AG's RG 401-1247/14, TSL-A.
10. I am endebted to T. Lindsay Baker for calling my attention to the above remedies, as well as the rich literature on their formulas and bottling. "Spirits of Nitra" are given in *Mackenzie's Five Thousand Recipes in all the Useful and Domestic Arts,* Kay's improved and enlarged edition, p. 156. References to "Hamlin's Wizard Oil" are in: Joseph K. Baldwin, *A Collector's Guide to Patent and Propietary Medicine Bottles of the Nineteenth Century,* p. 222; Kay Denver, *Patent Medicine Picture,* pp. 41–42; and Larry Freeman, *Grand Old American Bottles,* p. 428.
11. Overton, *Gulf to Rockies,* pp. 169–74; McCarty, *Maverick Town,* pp. 210–24.
12. Lewis Nordyke, *Cattle Empire,* pp. 169–71.
13. A contemporary account of Montgomery's arrival was penned by editor Charles F. Rudolph, *The Tascosa Pioneer,* Sept. 17, 1887. For an interesting modern conjecture on the meeting, see Donald F. Schofield, *Indians, Cattle, Ships, & Oil, The Story of W. M. D. Lee,* p. 89.
14. McCarty, *Maverick Town,* p. 227.
15. Charles F. Rudolph, "Old Tascosa, Selected News Items from The Tascosa Pioneer 1886–1888," Ernest R. Archambeau, ed., *Panhandle-Plains Historical Review* 39 (1966): 141.
16. "Record of Scouts," Dec., 1887, *Monthly Return,* Co.B, FB, AG's RG 401-1247/14, TSL-A.
17. "Arrests," Sept.–Dec., 1887, *Monthly Return,* AGR 401-1247/14, TSL-A.

Chapter 5

1. Neither Mr. Fletcher nor Mr. Adamson are listed as Texas photographers in David Haynes's directory, *Catching Shadows, A Directory of 19th-Century Photographers.*
2. "Greer County Subject of Historic Lawsuit," feature article in special edition of *The Mangum Daily Star* 45:108 (Nov. 16, 1932): 8–9.
3. Quoted from "The Greer County Bachelor" in Francis Edward Abernethy, "Texas Folk and Modern Country Music," pp. 148–49 in Glen Lich and Dona Reeves-Marquardt, eds., *Texas Country, The Changing Rural Scene.*

4. An advertisement for W. E. Johnson's grocery store appeared in the November 22, 1888, issue of *The Star,* the Greer County newspaper that Major A. M. Dawson published at Mangum. Quanah merchants advertised heavily for the trade of Old Greer. These advertisements are summarized in the article, "Early Newspapers Told Story of Development," *Mangum Daily Star* 45:105 (Nov. 16, 1932): 12.
5. Robertson and Robertson, *Panhandle Pilgrimage,* pp. 278–79.
6. "Early Newspapers Told Story of Development," *Mangum Daily Star,* p. 12.
7. Jan., 1888, *Monthly Return,* Co.B, FB, AGR 401-1247/15. McMurry's report says the two were dispatched on the 16th.
8. Jan., 1888, "Record of Scouts," *Monthly Return,* Co.B, FB, AGR 401-1247/15.
9. Feb., 1888, "Record of Scouts," *Monthly Return,* Co.B, FB, AGR 401-1247/15.
10. Feb., 1888, "Record of Scouts" and "Arrests," *Monthly Return,* Co.B, FB, AGR 401-1247/15.
11. Feb., 1888, "Record of Scouts," *Monthly Return,* Co.B, FB, AGR 401-1247/15.
12. Neal, *The Last Frontier,* p. 112.
13. Feb., 1888, "Record of Scouts,"*Monthly Return,* Co.B, FB, AGR 401-1247/15.
14. The best account is in A. C. Greene, *The Santa Claus Bank Robbery.*
15. Otta, Texas, is not listed in *The New Handbook of Texas* but it can be found in Arthur Hecht, comp., *Postal History in the Texas Panhandle, p.* 12. The Otta post office functioned 1879–92 with episodic closings.
16. Feb., 1888, "Record of Scouts,"*Monthly Return,* Co.B, FB, AGR 401-1247/15.
17. Feb., 1888, "Record of Scouts," *Monthly Return,* Co.B, FB, AGR 401-1247/15.
18. Tyler, et al., *New Handbook of Texas,* vol. 5, p. 39; Feb., 1888, "Record of Scouts," *Monthly Return,* Co.B, FB, AGR 401-1247/15.
19. Shirley, *The Fighting Marlows,* pp. 29–34, passim.
20. Paine, *Bill McDonald,* p. 68.
21. Ibid.
22. Mar., 1888, "Record of Scouts," *Monthly Return,* Co.B, FB, AGR 401-1247/15.
23. Cf. Robert W. Stephens, *Texas Ranger Sketches,* p. 12.
24. Mar., 1888, "Record of Scouts," *Monthly Return,* Co.B, FB, AGR 401-1247/15.
25. Ibid. Founded in 1877 as the "Stock-Raisers' Association of North-West Texas," the cattlemen's association is also known under a variety of names. The "Record of Scouts" notes that McMurry attended the "N.W. Cattle Association" at the invitation of the secretary.
26. Ibid.
27. John Edwards, "Baseball in Texas: The Early Years." Paper presented to the Texas State Historical Association, Austin, Feb. 29–Mar. 2, 1996. Copy provided by Dr. Ty Cashion.

Chapter 6

1. The author is endebted to the staff of the Denver Public Library for access to their March, 1888, issues of the *Rocky Mountain News* and *Daily News.* See the daily stories in volume 29 (Mar. 27–31, 1888). Limited extracts and quotes from

this reportage also appear in Overton, *Gulf to Rockies, pp.* 182–83. Overton's book is an excellent source of scarce railroad company documents and accounts.

2. "Enthusiam in Texas," in *Rocky Mountain News,* vol. 29 (Mar. 26, 1888), p. 1.
3. There is no mention of this grand excursion (akin to today's "junket" for state employees) in the March, 1888, "Monthly Return." However Captain McMurry carefully notes his leaving for Denver "by permission of Genl King," and the rangers paid for their own tickets, of course.
4. "List of the Excursionists," in *Rocky Mountian News,* vol. 29 (Mar. 28, 1888), p. 4.
5. "Street Decorations," in *Rocky Mountain News,* vol. 29 (Mar. 29, 1888), p. 1.
6. "Gulf to Peak," in *Rocky Mountain News,* vol. 29 (Mar. 28, 1888), p. 1. As this lead article on the railroad noted, the strategic region between the two commercial empires was the "Panhandle of Texas."
7. Governor John Evans's address was reprinted in "Denver's Crisis Passed," *Rocky Mountain News,* vol. 29 (Mar. 28, 1888), p. 17. For the news story on the address, see "Ovation to Gov. Evans," *Rocky Mountain News,* vol. 29 (Mar. 27, 1888), p. 10.
8. "Through the Panhandle," *Rocky Mountain News,* vol. 29 (Mar. 29, 1888), pp. 9–10. Illustrations for the guide included a new wood-framed Panhandle homestead, Indian scouts at Fort Elliott, and a large panorama of the Fort Worth Union Stock Yards.
9. See "The Railroads," in Jan Blodgett, *Land of Bright Promise, Advertising the Texas Panhandle and South Plains, 1870–1917,* chapter 3, pp. 26–42; Ida Marie Williams Lowe, "The Role of the Railroads in the Settlement of the Texas Panhandle" (master's thesis, West Texas State College, 1962); and F. Stanley [pseudonym of Father Stanley Francis Louis Crocchiola] *Railroads of the Texas Panhandle.*
10. "Special," *Rocky Mountain News* (Mar. 27, 1888), p. 1; Overton, *Gulf to Rockies,* pp. 183–84.
11. "Ovation to Gov. Evans," *Rocky Mountain News,* vol. 29 (Mar. 27, 1888), p. 10.
12. "Denver's Grand Jubilee," *Rocky Mountain News,* vol. 29 (Mar. 27, 1888), p. 1.
13. Quoted in Overton, *Gulf to Rockies,* p. 188. See also "The Grand Jubilee Ball, One of the Greatest Social Receptions in the West," *The Daily News* (Mar. 30, 1888), p. 2.
14. "They Will March," *The Daily News* (Mar. 30, 1888); Overton, *Gulf to Rockies,* p. 188.
15. Robert Julyan, *The Place Names of New Mexico,* pp. 132–33.
16. Pauline and R. L. Robertson provide an illustrated overview of the OM, H Bar Y, and similar Greer County ranches in *Cowman's Country: Fifty Frontier Ranches in the Texas Panhandle, 1876–1887, pp.* 75–77, 131, and *passim.*
17. For McMurry's trip to Mobeetie, see Apr., 1888, "Record of Scouts," *Monthly Return,* Co.B, FB, AGR 401-1247/15; for Goodnight and the Panhandle Stock Association, see Tyler, et al., *The New Handbook of Texas,* vol. 5, pp. 43–44, and J. Evetts Haley, *Charles Goodnight,* "The Panhandle Stock Association," chapter 21, pp. 356–80.
18. Robertson and Robertson, *Cowman's Country,* pp. 100–101.

19. Historian Frederick Rathjen notes the through service began April 1, but Miller's entry suggests that such service started almost a week later. Rathjen, *The Texas Panhandle Frontier,* p. 246.
20. Overton, *Gulf to Rockies,* p. 193.
21. Apr., 1888, "Record of Scouts," *Monthly Return,* Co.B, FB, AGR 401-1247/15.
22. Ibid.
23. The best history is Estelle D. Tinkler, "Nobility's Ranche: A History of the Rocking Chair Ranche," *Panhandle-Plains Historical Review* 15 (1942): 1–96. An abbreviated version appears as Estelle Tinker, *Archibald John Writes the Rocking Chair Ranche Letters.*
24. Laura Hamner, *Short Grass and Longhorns,* p. 79.
25. Sullivan, *Twelve Years in the Saddle,* pp. 89–97. All of chapter 27 is devoted to Corporal Sullivan's investigation on the Rocking Chair Ranche.
26. Sullivan, *Twelve Years in the Saddle,* p. 93.
27. Estelle D. Tinkler, "Nobility's Ranche," pp. 76–80; see also Tyler, et al., *New Handbook of Texas,* vol. 5, p. 36.
28. This pasture was "in the extreme south-eastern corner of the Rocking Chair pasture, on the 100° meridian line, [which] divided Collingsworth and Greer counties." Estelle D. Tinkler, "Nobility's Ranche: A History of the Rocking Chair Ranche," *Panhandle-Plains Historical Review* 15 (1942): 30.
29. May, 1888, "Record of Scouts," *Monthly Return,* Co.B, FB, AGR 401-1247/15.
30. Wilkins, *The Law Comes to Texas,* p. 358.
31. Mary Starr Barkley, *History of Travis County and Austin, 1839–1899,* pp. 202–209.
32. May, 1888, "Record of Scouts," *Monthly Return,* Co.B, FB, AGR 401-1247/15.
33. Ibid.
34. May, 1888, "Record of Scouts," *Monthly Return,* Co.B, FB, AGR 401-1247/15.
35. "Ferguson resisting arrest was killed." Ibid.
36. Tom Smith, local farmer and long-time resident, interview by John Miller Morris, near Thalia, Texas, Foard County, June 22, 1995. I am indebted to Mr. Smith for sharing his local expertise.
37. Tyler, et al., *New Handbook of Texas,* vol. 3, pp. 720–21.
38. Details of Gentry's career are in two books by Willie Newbury Lewis: *Between Sun and Sod,* pp. 156–57 and *passim,* and *Tapadero, The Making of a Cowboy,* pp. 141–45. See also Robertson and Robertson, *Panhandle Pilgrimage,* p. 248.
39. June and July, 1888, "Remarks," *Monthly Return,* Co.B, FB, AGR 401-1247/15.
40. June, 1888, "Record of Scouts," *Monthly Return,* Co.B, FB, AGR 401-1247/15.
41. Wilkins, *The Law Comes to Texas,* p. 210.
42. Ross and Rouse, eds., *Early-Day History of Wilbarger County,* p. 174.
43. Paine, *Bill McDonald,* p. 68.
44. Glenn Shirley, *West of Hell's Fringe,* p. 28.
45. Webb, *The Texas Rangers,* pp. 386–87; R. W. Stephens, *Texas Ranger Sketches,* pp. 95, 151–52. Webb credited Harrell with the kill of Sam Bass, while Stephens championed Dick Ware.
46. June, 1888, "Record of Scouts," *Monthly Return,* Co.B, FB, AGR 401-1247/15.
47. June, 1888, "Record of Scouts," *Monthly Return,* Co.B, FB, AGR 401-1247/15.

48. This contention is supported by a comparison of the handwriting styles for Company B *Monthly Reports* in 1888.
49. Archambeau, ed. "Old Tascosa, Selected News Items from *The Tascosa Pioneer*," pp. 170–72.
50. Robertson and Robertson call this competitive event "The First Rodeo in Texas" in *Panhandle Pilgrimage*, p. 276. For the historical background, see "Rodeos," in Tyler, et al., *The New Handbook of Texas*, vol. 5, pp. 646–47.

Epilogue

1. Sept.–Dec., 1888, "Remarks," *Monthly Returns*, Co.B, FB, AGR 401-1247/15.
2. Sullivan's twelve years ran from 1889 to 1900. For the date of enlistment, see Apr., 1889 "Remarks," *Monthly Return*, Co. B, FB, AGR 401-1247/16.
3. Gober, *Cowboy Justice*, p. 149.
4. See John W. Reese and Lillian E. Reese, *Flaming Feuds of Colorado County*.
5. Stephens, *Texas Ranger Sketches*, pp. 22–23. A fuller version of this incident is in Sterling, *Trails and Trials of a Texas Ranger*, pp. 336–38. Sterling claimed, "All the bullet holes could be covered with a silver dollar."
6. For Billy McCauley at Alice in 1906, see Jack Martin, *Border Boss, Captain John R. Hughes—Texas Ranger*, pp. 176–77.
7. Sullivan, "Battle in the Dugout," *Twelve Years in the Saddle*, pp. 144–54. See also Shirley, *West of Hell's Fringe*, pp. 348–49.
8. Note "General Highway Map Foard County Texas" by Texas State Department of Highways (Austin: n.p., 1971), which marks "Original Site of Margaret."
9. Tom Smith, interview by John Miller Morris, June 22, 1995, Old Margaret townsite. I am grateful to Mr. Smith for sharing his knowledge of Old Margaret.
10. Mar., 1888, "Record of Scouts," *Monthly Return*, Co.B, FB, AGR 401-1247/15.
11. W. J. McDonald to Adjutant General W. H. Mabry, Sept. 30, 1891, AGR 2–11/43, TSL-A.
12. See the AGR Service Records files for "Thomas Platt" (FB 401-168), and "John R. Platt" (FB 401-168) in the TSL-A.
13. John W. Bracken, "Tom Platt, Texas Ranger," *Frontier Times* 7:3 (Dec., 1929): 144.
14. Oct., 1888, "Record of Scouts," *Monthly Return*, Co.B, FB, AGR 401-1247/15.
15. "Sterling Price" Service Records, AGR, FB 401-168, TSL-A. In the teeth of labor strife, company guards might be appointed as Special Rangers, or rangers might emerge as guards.
16. Ibid.
17. *City Directory of Amarillo, Texas, 1907* (Dallas: Worley Directory Co., 1906) with entries for "Peale, Dennis A." and "Patton, James H."
18. "Two ex-Texas rangers, Peale and Britton, ran a saloon for awhile, and then sold it to Wally Bills." Haley and Holden, eds., *The Flamboyant Judge*, p. 15.
19. The last entry for Dennis Peale, "bartender," is in *Worley's Directory of Amarillo, Texas, 1911* (Dallas: Worley Printing Co., 1911).

20. J. M. Bradbury Ranger Service Records, AGR 401-144, TSL-A.
21. Albert Bigelow Paine erred in his noted biography when he placed Jim Green with Captain McDonald in Amarillo in 1891. Paine, *Captain Bill McDonald,* p. 143.
22. Browley, *Donley County, Land O' Promise,* p. 264.
23. W. H. P. [William H. Patrick], "Jim Green," May 25, 1945, Interview Files, Research Center, Panhandle-Plains Historical Museum, Canyon, Texas. West Texas A&M University Registrar Mary Moore identified the interview initials with the inimitable Mr. Patrick of Clarendon, Texas. The original typescript reads "fourty drops of stimulent," but the misspellings were corrected for this volume.
24. Harold John Weiss, Jr., "'Yours to Command': Captain William J. 'Bill' McDonald and the Panhandle Rangers of Texas." Dissertation, Indiana University, 1980, 87n. Available from University Microfilms International.
25. Ibid., pp. 86–88. Weiss performed an admirable job of tracing the Wolf Hair episode through the collateral ranger documents.
26. Ibid.
27. Thomas M. O'Hare Ranger Service Records, AGR 401-166, TSL-A.
28. Robert W. Stephens, *Texas Ranger Sketches,* p. 29.
29. Sullivan, *Twelve Years in the Saddle,* pp. 51–52.
30. Capt. S. A. McMurry to Adjutant General W. H. Mabry, Jan. 18, 1891, AGR File 2–11/40, TSL-A.
31. J. M. Britton to Adjutant General W. H. Mabry, Jan. 20, 1891, AGR File 2–11/40, TSL-A. See also, Wilkins, *The Law Comes to Texas,* pp. 296–97.
32. Paine spelled Grude's name as "J. M. Brittain" in *Captain Bill McDonald,* p. 143.
33. Shirley, *The Fighting Marlows,* p. 138. Shirley gives the name as A. J. Britton.
34. Laura Hamner, *Light 'n Hitch,* pp. 118–21.
35. Weiss, Jr., "'Yours to Command,'" pp. 85–86; Stephens, *Texas Ranger Sketches,* p. 30.
36. Paine, *Captain Bill McDonald,* pp. 262–63.
37. [Amarillo], *Worley's Directory of Amarillo, Texas, 1908.*
38. Robert W. Stephens's *Texas Ranger Sketches, op. cit.,* is an indispensable and accurate source for many of the Boys of Company B who served under Captain McMurry and Captain McDonald.
39. Robert W. Stephens, *Texas Ranger Sketches,* 12.
40. Ibid.
41. Samuel A. McMurry Ranger Service Records, AGR 401-162, TSL-A.
42. Marilyn D. Rhinehart, *A Way of Work and a Way of Life: Coal Mining in Thurber, Texas, 1888–1926,* pp. 74–75.
43. Rhinehart, *A Way of Work, p.* 76.
44. Wilkins, *The Law Comes to Texas,* pp. 284–85.
45. Stephens, *Texas Ranger Sketches,* p. 102. Stephens's book has important biographical research on Captain McMurry. See also, Wilkins, *The Law Comes to Texas, passim,* and S. A. McMurry Ranger Service Records, AGR 401-162, TSL-A.
46. Harry Koch, *Quanah Tribune-Chief,* Aug. 26, 1938.

47. Weiss, Jr., "'Yours to Command,'" p. 76.
48. Details of Company B's multitudinous actions under Captain McDonald are admirably surveyed in Harold Weiss, Jr., "'Yours to Command,'" pp. 61–105.
49. Haley and Holden, eds., *The Flamboyant Judge,* p. 78. McDonald later repented his gambling habits.
50. Paine, *Captain Bill McDonald,* 158.
51. Most accounts date the Matthews-McDonald showdown in December, *1895,* but Texas Ranger documents in the Texas State Library confirm that the year was 1893.
52. Paine, *Captain Bill McDonald,* pp. 165–75.
53. Millie Jones Porter cites Wheeler County records and the recollection by Mr. Henry of "John Pierce" and his past, in *Memory Cups of Panhandle Pioneers,* pp. 337–38.
54. Sergeant J. M. Britton to Adjutant General W. H. Mabry, Dec. 16, 1893, AGR File 2–11/50, TSL-A.
55. A summary and factual account of the romanticized fight is in Weiss, Jr., "'Yours to Command,'" pp. 88–96. For other testimony, see Michael Ehrle, comp., *The Childress County Story* (Childress, Tex.: Ox Bow Printing, 1971), pp. 59–62.
56. Weiss, Jr., "'Yours to Command,'" *passim.*
57. Paine, *Captain Bill McDonald,* "Appendix C," p. 417.
58. Ibid., pp. 273–89.
59. The romanticized case titles are primarily taken from Paine, *Captain Bill McDonald, Texas Ranger.* See also Virgil Baugh, *A Pair of Texas Rangers: Bill McDonald and John Hughes;* Lee McGiffen, *Ten Tall Texans, pp.* 182–205; and Tyler Mason [Madeline Mason-Manheim], and E. M. House, *Riding for Texas: The True Adventures of Captain Bill McDonald of the Texas Rangers.*
60. Weiss, Jr., "'Yours to Command,'" pp. 234–38; Arthur D. Howden Smith, *Mr. House of Texas, pp.* 57–58; Charles Seymour, *The Intimate Papers of Colonel House,* vol. 1, pp. 79–81.
61. Naomi M. Green, "Miller, Abner and Naomi" entry in [Donley County] *Donley County History 1879–1990,* p. 319.
62. Tyler, et al., *New Handbook of Texas,* vol. 3, pp. 177–78.
63. Naomi M. Green, interviews by John Miller Morris, Clarendon, Donley County, Texas. Mrs. Green has been extremely helpful with information on the Millers. A. T. Miller was her maternal grandfather.
64. Ibid.
65. Green, "Miller, Abner and Naomi," in *Donley County History,* p. 319.

BIBLIOGRAPHY

Manuscripts and Documents

Eugene C. Barker Archives, Center for American History, Austin, Texas: Texas Ranger Papers and Walter Prescott Webb Papers

Panhandle-Plains Historical Library and Archives, Canyon, Texas: William H. Patrick Interview, "Jim Green" and Photographic Collections

Texas and Oklahoma County Records: Donley County Records (Clarendon, Texas): Deeds, A. T. Miller Will and Probate. Foard County Records (Crowell, Texas): Deeds, Marriage Licenses. Greer County Records (Mangum, Oklahoma): [Few documents survived a disastrous arson fire.] Hardeman County Court Docket Records (Quanah, Texas). Oldham County Records (Vega, Texas).

Texas Adjutant General Records (AGR) and Files, Archives Division, Texas State Library, Austin: (Official documentation for the Frontier Battalion, including Company B, can be found in the old Adjutant General Records [AGR]. These records were later transferred to the Texas State Library for preservation and conservation.) "Correspondence Files," Frontier Battalion, AGR File Box 401-1160/6 (1887) and 401-1160/7 (1888). "List of Fugitives from Justice," Austin, State Printer [1887–1888]. (Known as the "Fugitive List," "Black Book," or "Bible II.") "Monthly Reports" [January, 1887, to December, 1888], Samuel A. McMurry, Captain, Company B, Frontier Battalion, Attorney General's Record Group 401-1247/14 and 401-1247/15. (Capt. McMurry filed these monthly reports with the adjutant general's office, summarizing Company B activities, equipment, and arrests.) "Muster and Pay Roll Records," 1886–88. "Quarter Master Records," 1886–90

Individual Texas Ranger Service Files: A. T. Miller (FB 401-164); Samuel A. McMurry (FB 401-162); William Jesse McDonald (FB 401-162); Samuel M. Platt (FB 401-168); Thomas Platt (FB 401-168); John R. Platt (FB 401-168); James M. "Grude" Britton (FB 401-144); Sterling Price (FB 401-168); Ed E. Furman (FB 401-152); Dennis A. Peale [also spelled "Peal"] (FB 401-167); J. F. Green (FB 401-153); J. M. Bradbury [also spelled "Bradberry"] (FB 401-144); J. R. Bishop (FB 401-143); John McNelly (FB 401-162); and Thomas M. O'Hare (FB 401-166).

Reports of the Adjutant General of the State of Texas. Austin: State Printer, 1889–1902.

United States Bureau of the Census (Microfilm versions): Foard County, Texas—1900 Census and 1910 Census. Hardeman County, Texas—1880 Census and 1900 Census. Jones County and Iredell County, North Carolina—1860 Census. Potter County, Texas—1900 Census and 1910 Census.

Theses, Dissertations, and Papers

Boaz, Sallie R. "A History of Amarillo, Texas." Master's Thesis, University of Texas at Austin, 1950.

Edwards, John. "Baseball in Texas: The Early Years." Paper presented to the Texas State Historical Association, Austin, February 29–March 2, 1996.

Holden, William C. "Frontier Problems and Movements in West Texas, 1846–1900." Doctoral Dissertation, University of Texas at Austin, 1928.

Jones, J. Paul. "History of Hardeman County." Master's Thesis, University of Texas at Austin, 1949.

Lowe, Ida Marie Williams. "The Role of the Railroads in the Settlement of the Texas Panhandle." Master's Thesis, West Texas State College (West Texas A&M University), 1962.

Morris, John Miller. "Amarillo: The Perils of Prosperity." Paper written for the Community and Regional Planning graduate program at the University of Texas at Austin, 1985.

Pope, Billy N. "The Freighter and Railroader in the Economic Pattern of Panhandle History." Master's Thesis, West Texas State College (West Texas A&M University), 1956.

Weiss, Harold John, Jr. "'Yours to Command': Captain William J. 'Bill' McDonald and the Panhandle Rangers of Texas." Doctoral Dissertation, Indiana University, 1980. (Available from University Microfilms International.)

Williamson, Robert L. "A History of Company E of the Texas Frontier Battalion, 1874–1879." Master's Thesis, University of Texas at Austin, 1952.

Wilson, Torrence. "A History of Wilbarger County, Texas." Master's Thesis, University of Texas at Austin, 1938.

Interviews and Correspondence

Peggy Crabb Bielich, Old Greer County Museum, Mangum, Oklahoma
Lewis Buttery, Lampasas, Texas
Naomi M. and Horace A. Green, Clarendon, Texas
R. Frank Heflin, Amarillo, Texas
Betty Hoover, Quanah, Texas
Geraldine Meason, Quanah, Texas
Joan and Carl Bernard Morris, Jr., Horseshoe Bay, Texas
Mae Morris Naylor, Vernon, Texas
Tom Smith, Margaret, Texas

Books and Articles

Adams, Ramon F. *Six-Guns and Saddle Leather: A Bibliography of Books and Pamphlets on Western Outlaws and Gunmen.* Revised edition, Norman: University of Oklahoma Press, 1969.

Adler, Larry. *The Texas Rangers.* New York: McKay, 1979.

Allen, Allyn [Eberle, Irmengarde]. *The Real Book About the Texas Rangers.* Garden City, N.Y.: Doubleday & Company, 1952.

[Amarillo]. *Worley's Directory of Amarillo, Texas.* Dallas: Worley Printing Co., [1907–13].

Archambeau, Ernest R. "The First Federal Census in the Panhandle—1880." *Panhandle-Plains Historical Review* 23 (1950): 22–132.

Arnett, Alex Mathews. *The Story of North Carolina.* Chapel Hill: University of North Carolina Press, 1942.

Baldwin, Joseph K. *A Collector's Guide to Patent and Propietary Medicine Bottles of the Nineteenth Century.* Nashville: Thomas Nelson, 1973.

Banister, John. *Banister: A Greer County Farm Family.* Roswell, N.Mex.: Old-Time Publications, n.d.

Barkley, Mary Starr. *History of Travis County and Austin, 1839–1899.* Second edition. Austin: Steck Company, 1967.

Barton, Clara. *The Red Cross.* Washington, D.C.: American Historical Press, 1899.

Baugh, Virgil. *A Pair of Texas Rangers: Bill McDonald and John Hughes.* Washington, D.C.: Potomac Corral, The Westerners, 1970.

Bellamy, Edward. *Looking Backward: 2000–1887.* Boston: Ticknor & Co., 1888. Revised edition with Introduction by S. Baxter, New York: Grossett and Dunlap, 1898.

Billington, Ray Allen. *America's Frontier Heritage.* New York: Holt, Rinehart & Winston, 1966.

Beverly, Joe. "History of Foard County." *Foard County News,* Crowell, Texas, 1921. Special commemorative edition.

Blodgett, Jan. *Land of Bright Promise, Advertising the Texas Panhandle and South Plains, 1870–1917.* Austin: University of Texas Press, 1988.

[Bracken, John W.] "The Obituary of Tom Platt." *Frontier Times* 7:3 (December, 1929): 144.

Browder, Virginia. *Donley County: Land O' Promise.* Burnet, Tex.: Nortex Press, 1975.

Brown, Richard M. *Strain of Violence: Historical Studies of American Violence and Vigilantism.* New York: Oxford University Press, 1975.

Brune, Gunnar. *Springs of Texas.* Fort Worth: Branch-Smith, 1981.

Burton, Harley True. *A History of the J A Ranch.* 1927. Reprint, Ann Arbor, Mich.: Argonaut Press, 1966.

Carlson, Paul H. *Empire Builder in the Texas Panhandle, William Henry Bush.* College Station: Texas A&M University Press, 1996.

Cashion, Ty. "(Gun)smoke Gets in Your Eyes: A Revisionist Look at 'Violent' Fort Griffin." *Southwestern Historical Quarterly* 99:1 (July, 1995): 80–94.

———. *A Texas Frontier: The Clear Fork Country and Fort Griffin, 1849–1887.* Norman: University of Oklahoma Press, 1996.

Castleman, Harvey N. *The Texas Rangers: The Story of an Organization that is Unique, Like Nothing Else in America.* Girard, Kan.: Haldeman-Julius Publications, 1944.

Chesser, Cecil R. *Across the Lonely Years: The Story of Jackson County.* Second edition. Altus, Okla.: Altus Printing Co., 1976.

Conner, Seymour V. "Reminiscences of the Southwest." *Texas Quarterly* 7:2 (summer, 1964): 41–53.

Cook, David J. *Hands Up! or Twenty Years of Detective Life in the Mountains and on the Plains.* Reprint, Norman: University of Oklahoma Press, 1958.

Coolidge, Dane. *Fighting Men of the West.* New York: Dutton & Co., 1932.

Cox, Mike. *Silver Stars and Sixguns: The Texas Rangers.* Austin: Texas Department of Public Safety, 1987.

———. *Texas Ranger Tales: Stories That Need Telling.* Plano, Texas: Republic of Texas Press, 1997.

———. *Texas Ranger Tales II.* Plano, Texas: Republic of Texas Press, 1999.

Cronon, William. *Nature's Metropolis, Chicago and the Great West.* New York: W. W. Norton, 1991.

Cunningham, Eugene. *Triggernometry: A Gallery of Gunfighters.* Caldwell, Idaho: Caxton Printers, 1941. Reprint, Garden City, N.Y.: Country Life Press, 1952.

Davis, John L. *The Texas Rangers, Images and Incidents.* San Antonio: Institute of Texan Cultures, 1991.

Davis, Richard Harding. *The West From a Car Window.* New York: Harper & Bros., 1892.

DeArment, Robert K. *George Scarborough: The Life of a Lawman on the Closing Frontier.* Norman: University of Oklahoma Press, 1992.

Denver, Kay. *Patent Medicine Picture.* Tucson: privately printed, 1968.

Dobie, J. Frank. *A Vaquero of the Brush Country: Partly from the Reminiscences of John Young.* Dallas: Southwest Press, 1929.

[Donley County] *Donley County History, 1879–1990.* Dallas: Curtis Media Corporation, 1990.

Doughty, Robin W. *Wildlife and Man in Texas: Environmental Change and Conservation.* College Station: Texas A&M University Press, 1983.

Douglas, C. L. *The Gentlemen in the White Hats: Dramatic Episodes in the History of the Texas Rangers.* Dallas: Southwest Press, 1934.

Draper, Robert. "The Myth of the Texas Rangers." *Texas Monthly* 22:2 (February, 1994): 76–82, and *passim.*

Duke, Cordia Sloan, and Joe B. Frantz. *6,000 Miles of Fence, Life on the XIT Ranch of Texas.* Austin: University of Texas Press, 1961.

Duke, J. K. "Bad Men and Peace Officers of the Southwest." *West Texas Historical Association Year Book* 13 (1932): 51–61.

Ehrle, Michael G., ed., *The Childress County Story.* Childress, Tex.: Ox Bow Printing, 1971.

Emmons, David M. *Garden in the Grasslands, Boomer Literature of the Central Great Plains.* Lincoln: University of Nebraska, 1971.

Fehrenbach, T. R. *Lone Star: A History of Texas and the Texans.* New York: Macmillan Company, 1968.

———. *Seven Keys to Texas.* El Paso: Texas Western Press, 1983.

Fite, Gilbert C. *Farmer's Frontier, 1865–1900.* Albuquerque: University of New Mexico Press, 1977.

Frantz, Joe B. "The Frontier Tradition: An Invitation to Violence," in H. D. Graham and T. R. Gurr, eds., *Violence in America: Historical and Comparative Perspectives.* New York: New American Library, 1969.

Freeman, Larry. *Grand Old American Bottles.* Watkins Glen, N.Y.: Century House, 1964.

Fulmore, Zachry T. *The History and Geography of Texas as Told in County Names.* Revised edition. Austin: S. R. Fulmore, 1926.

Gard, Wayne. *Frontier Justice.* Norman: University of Oklahoma Press, 1949.

———. *Sam Bass.* New York: Houghton Mifflin, 1936.

Gillett, James B. *Six Years with the Texas Rangers, 1875 to 1881.* Austin: Von Boeckmann–Jones, 1921. Reprint, edited with introduction by M. M. Quaife, New Haven, Conn.: Yale University Press, 1925. Second printing, with new foreword by Oliver Knight, New Haven, Conn.: Yale University Press, 1963.

———. and Howard Driggs. *The Texas Ranger: A Story of the Southwestern Frontier.* Yonkers-on-Hudson, N.Y.: World Book Co., 1926.

———. *Fugitives from Justice: The Notebook of Texas Ranger Sergeant James B. Gillett.* Austin: State House Press, 1997.

Gilliland, Maude T., comp. *Wilson County Texas Rangers 1837–1977.* N.p.: n.p., 1977.

Gober, James R., and B. Byron Price, eds. *Cowboy Justice: Tale of a Texas Lawman Jim Gober.* Lubbock: Texas Tech University Press, 1997.

Gould, Charles N. *Oklahoma Place Names.* Norman: University of Oklahoma Press, 1933.

Gournay, Luke. *Texas Boundaries, Evolution of the State's Counties.* College Station: Texas A&M University Press, 1995.

Graves, Richard S. *Oklahoma Outlaws: A Graphic History of the Early Days of Oklahoma. . . .* Oklahoma City: State Printing & Publishing Co., 1915.

Greene, A. C. *The Santa Claus Bank Robbery.* New York: Knopf, 1972.

Greer, James K., ed. *A Texas Ranger and Frontiersman: The Days of Buck Barry in Texas, 1845–1906.* Dallas: Southwest Press, 1932.

Grinstead, J. F. *Texas Ranger Justice.* New York: Dodge, 1941.

Haley, J. Evetts. *Charles Goodnight: Cowman and Plainsman.* Norman: University of Oklahoma Press, 1949.

———. *Jeff Milton: A Good Man with a Gun.* Norman: University of Oklahoma Press, 1948.

———. *The XIT Ranch of Texas and the Early Days of the Llano Estacado.* Norman: University of Oklahoma Press, 1953.

———. and William Curry Holden, eds. *The Flamboyant Judge: James D. Hamlin, A Biography.* Canyon, Tex.: Palo Duro Press, 1972.

Hamner, Laura. *Light 'n Hitch.* Dallas: American Guild Press, 1958.

———. *Short Grass and Longhorns.* Norman: University of Oklahoma Press, 1943.

Harriet, Julia Pollock, comp. *The History and Genealogy of Jones County, North Carolina.* New Bern, N.C.: J. P. Harriet with Owen G. Dunn Co., 1987.

Harrison, Lowell H. "British Interest in the Panhandle Plains Area, 1878–1885." *Panhandle-Plains Historical Review* 38 (1965): 1–44.

Haynes, David. *Catching Shadows: A Directory of 19th-Century Texas Photographers.* Austin: Texas State Historical Association, 1993.

Haywood, C. Robert. *Trails South: The Wagon-Road Economy in the Dodge City–Panhandle Region.* Norman: University of Oklahoma Press, 1986.

Hecht, Arthur, compiler. "Postal History in the Texas Panhandle." Canyon, Tex.: Panhandle-Plains Historical Society, 1960.

Henderson, Surena B. *Jones County: Fact and Folklore.* Henderson, N.C.: n.p., 1979.

Henry, Will. *The Texas Rangers.* New York: Random House, 1957.

Hobart, T. D. "Some of the Characters and Customs of Old Mobeetie." *Panhandle-Plains Historical Review* 2 (1929): 123–28.

Hobart, Mrs. T. D. "Pioneer Days in the Panhandle Plains." *Panhandle-Plains Historical Review* 8 (1935): 65–78.

Holden, William Curry. "Frontier Defense, 1865–1889." *Panhandle-Plains Historical Review* 2 (1929): 43–64.

———. "Law and Lawlessness on the Texas Frontier, 1875–1890." *Southwestern Historical Quarterly* 44:2 (October, 1940): 188–203.

———. "A Spur Ranch Diary, 1887." *West Texas Historical Association Yearbook* 7 (June, 1931).

———. "West Texas Drouths." *Southwestern Historical Quarterly* 32:2 (October, 1928): 103–23.

Hollon, W. Eugene. *Frontier Violence: Another Look.* New York: Oxford University Press, 1974.

Hough, Emerson. *The Story of the Outlaw: A Study of the Western Desperado.* New York: Grosset & Dunlap, 1905.

House, [Colonel] Edward Mandell. *Riding for Texas.* New York: John Day, 1936.

Hughes, W. J. *Rebellious Ranger: Rip Ford and the Old Southwest.* Norman: University of Oklahoma Press, 1964.

Ingmire, Frances Terry. *Texas Ranger Service Records, 1847–1900.* St. Louis: Ingmire [privately printed], 1982.

James, Bill C. *Jim Miller: The Untold Story of a Texas Badman.* Ed. by Robert W. Stephens. Wolfe City, Tex.: Hennington Pub. Co., 1989. Revised edition.

Jenkins, John H. *Basic Texas Books: An Annotated Bibliography of Selected Works for a Research Library.* Revised edition. Austin: Texas State Historical Association, 1988.

Jennings, Napoleon Augustus. *A Texas Ranger.* New York: Scribner's, 1899. Reprint, Dallas: Southwest Press, 1930.

Jordan, Philip D. *Frontier Law and Order: Ten Essays.* Lincoln: University of Nebraska Press, 1970.

Jordan, Terry. "The Anglo-Texan Homeland." *Journal of Cultural Geography* 13:2 (1993), 75–86.

———. "Early Northwest Texas and the Evolution of Western Ranching." *Annals of the Association of American Geographers* 67 (March, 1977).

———. *North American Cattle-Raising Frontiers, Origins, Diffusion, and Differentiation.* Albuquerque: University of New Mexico Press, 1993.

———. *Trails to Texas: Southern Roots of Western Cattle Ranching.* Lincoln: University of Nebraska Press, 1981.

Julyan, Robert. *The Place Names of New Mexico.* Albuquerque: University of New Mexico Press, 1996.

Kammerer, Roger E., and David Carpenter, comps. *Onslow Register: Records of Onslow and Jones Co.* [North Carolina]: Privately printed, 1984.

Keating, Bern. *An Illustrated History of the Texas Rangers.* New York: Rand McNally, 1975.

Kerr, W. G. *Scottish Capital on the American Credit Frontier.* Austin: Texas State Historical Association, 1976.

Key, Della Tyler. *In the Cattle Country: A History of Potter County, 1887–1966.* Amarillo: Tyler-Berkley Co., 1961. Second edition, Quanah–Wichita Falls, Tex.: Nortex, 1972.

Kilgore, Daniel Edmond. *A Ranger Legacy: 150 Years of Service to Texas.* Austin: Madrona Press, 1973.

King, C. Richard. *Wagons East.* Austin: University of Texas School of Journalism, June, 1965.

King, W. H. "The Texas Ranger Service," in Dudley Wooten, *A Comprehensive History of Texas,* vol. 2. Dallas: William Scarff, 1898.

Lewis, Willie Newbury. *Between Sun and Sod.* Clarendon, Tex.: Clarendon Press, 1938.

———. *Tapadero: The Making of a Cowboy.* Austin: University of Texas Press, 1972.

Lich, Glen E., and Dona B. Reeves-Marquardt. *Texas Country: The Changing Rural Scene.* College Station: Texas A&M University Press, 1986.

Maltby, [Captain] Jeff. *Captain Jeff, or Frontier Life in Texas with the Texas Rangers.* Colorado City, Tex.: Whipkey Printing Co., 1906. Facsimile reprint, Waco, Tex.: Texian Press, 1967.

Marlow, Charles, and Marlow, George. *Life of the Marlows: A True Story of Frontier Life in the Early Days.* Revised by William Rathmell, Ouray, Colo.: Ouray Herald Print, W. S. Olexa, publisher, 1928.

Marshall, James. *Santa Fe: The Railroad that Built an Empire.* New York: Random House, 1945.

Martin, Jack. *Border Boss: Captain John R. Hughes—Texas Ranger.* Austin: State House Press, 1990.

Mason, Tyler [pseudonym for Madeline Mason-Manheim]. *Riding for Texas: The True Adventures of Captain Bill McDonald of the Texas Rangers . . . As told by Colonel Edward M. House to Tyler Mason.* New York: Reynal & Hitchcock, 1936.

McCarty, John L. *Maverick Town: The Story of Old Tascosa.* Norman: University of Oklahoma Press, 1946.

McConnell, Joseph C. *The West Texas Frontier.* Jacksboro, Tex.: privately printed, 1933, 1939.

McGiffen, Lee. *Ten Tall Texans.* New York: Lothrop, Lee & Shepard, 1956.

Meeks, Beth Thomas, with Bonnie Speer. *Heck Thomas, My Papa.* Norman: University of Oklahoma Press, 1988.

Meinig, Donald W. *Imperial Texas: An Interpretive Essay in Cultural Geography.* Austin: University of Texas Press, 1975.

Miller, Floyd. *Bill Tilghman, Marshal of the Last Frontier.* Garden City, N.Y.: Doubleday & Company, 1968.

Miller, William Harris. *History and Genealogy of the Families of Robert Miller . . .* Richmond, Ky.: Press of Transylvania Co., 1907.

Moore, Webb L. *The Greer County Question.* San Marcos, Tex.: Press of the San Marcos *Record,* 1939.

Morgan, E. Buford. *The Wichita Mountains: Ancient Oasis of the Prairie.* Waco, Tex.: Texian Press, 1973.

Morgan, Jonnie R. *The History of Wichita Falls.* Wichita Falls, Tex.: Nortex, 1971.

Morris, John Miller. *El Llano Estacado: Exploration and Imagination on the High Plains of Texas and New Mexico, 1536–1860.* Austin: Texas State Historical Association, 1997.

Neal, Bill. *The Last Frontier: The Story of Hardeman County.* Quanah, Tex.: Quanah *Tribune-Chief* and Hardeman County Historical Society, 1966.

Nix, Evett Dumas. *Oklahombres, Particularly the Wilder Ones.* St. Louis: Eden Publishing House, 1929.

Nordyke, Lewis. *Cattle Empire.* New York: William Morrow & Co., 1949.

Nostrand, Richard L. *The Hispano Homeland.* Norman: University of Oklahoma Press, 1992.

Olive, Thelma, ed. *A History of Old Greer County and its Pioneers.* Mangum, Okla.: Old Greer County Museum and Hall of Fame, Inc., circa 1980.

O'Neal, Bill. *Encyclopedia of Western Gunfighters.* Norman: University of Oklahoma Press, 1979.

Ord, Paul, *et al.*, eds. *They Followed the Rails: In Retrospect, A History of Childress County.* Childress, Tex.: Childress *Reporter*, 1970.

Overton, Richard C. *Gulf to Rockies: The Heritage of the Fort Worth and Denver—Colorado and Southern Railways, 1861–1898.* Austin: University of Texas Press, 1953.

Paine, Albert Bigelow. *Captain Bill McDonald, Texas Ranger: A Story of Frontier Reform.* New York: J. J. Little & Ives, 1909. Reprint, Austin: State House Press, 1985.

Parsons, Chuck, and Gary P. Fitterer. *Captain C. B. McKinney: The Law in South Texas.* Wolfe City, Tex.: Henington Publishing, 1993.

Peare, Catherine Owens. *The Lost Lakes: A Story of the Texas Rangers.* Phildelphia: Winston, 1953.

Petulla, Joseph M. *American Environmental History.* Second edition, Columbus, Ohio: Merrill Publishing Company, 1988.

Phelps, Bailey. *They Loved the Land: Foard County History.* Burnet, Tex.: Nortex Press, 1969.

Pomeroy, Earl S. *The Territories and the United States, 1861–1890: Studies in Colonial Administration.* Seattle: University of Washington Press, 1975.

Porter, Millie Jones. *Memory Cups of Panhandle Pioneers.* Clarendon, Tex.: Clarendon Press, 1945.

Prassel, Frank Richard. *The Western Peace Officer: A Legacy of Law and Order.* Norman: University of Oklahoma Press, 1972.

Preece, Harold. *Lone Star Man: Ira Aten, Last of the Old Texas Rangers.* New York: Hastings House, 1960.

Price, B. Byron, and Frederick W. Rathjen. *The Golden Spread.* Northridge, Calif.: Windsor Publications, 1986.

Raine, William MacLeod. *45-Caliber Law: The Way of Life of the Frontier Peace Officer.* Evanston, Ill.: Row, Peterson & Co., 1941.

———. and Will C. Barnes. *Cattle, Cowboys, and Rangers.* New York: Grosset & Dunlap, n.d. (originally published as *Cattle* in 1930).

Rathjen, Frederick. *The Texas Panhandle Frontier.* Austin: University of Texas Press, 1973.

Raymond, Dora Neill. *Captain Lee Hall of Texas.* Norman: University of Oklahoma Press, 1940.

Reese, John W., and Lillian E. Reese. *Flaming Feuds of Colorado County.* Salado, Tex.: Anson Jones Press, 1962.

Reps, John W. *Cities on Stone, Nineteenth Century Lithograph Images of the Urban West.* Fort Worth: Amon Carter Museum, 1976.

Rhinehart, Marilyn D. *A Way of Work and a Way of Life: Coal Mining in Thurber, Texas, 1888–1926.* College Station: Texas A&M University Press, 1992.

Rigler, Lewis C., and Judyth Wagner Rigler. *In the Line of Duty: Reflections of a Texas Ranger Private.* Houston: Larksdale, 1984.

Rister, Carl Coke. "Outlaws and Vigilantes of the Southern Plains, 1865–1885." *Mississippi Valley Historical Review* 19 (March, 1933): 537–54.

———. *Southern Plainsmen.* Norman: University of Oklahoma Press, 1938.

———. *The Southwestern Frontier.* New York: Russell and Russell, 1928.

Roberts, [Captain] Daniel Webster. *Rangers and Sovereignty.* San Antonio: Wood Printing & Engraving Co., 1914.

———. *Rangers and Sovereignty*, and Mrs. D. W. Roberts. *A Woman's Reminiscences of Six Years in Camp with the Texas Rangers.* Austin: State House Press, 1987. Reprints.

Robertson, Pauline Durrett, and R. L. Robertson. *Cowman's Country: Fifty Frontier Ranches in the Texas Panhandle, 1876–1887.* Amarillo: Paramount Publishing, 1981.

———. *Panhandle Pilgrimage.* Amarillo: Paramount Publishing, 1978.

Robinson, Charles M., III. *The Men Who Wear the Star: The Story of the Texas Rangers.* New York: Random House, 2000.

Rogers, Virginia Browder. *The Giles Chronicle: A Vignette of Panhandle History.* Clarendon, Tex.: Clarendon Press, 1956.

Rosa, Joseph G. *The Gunfighter: Man or Myth?* Norman: University of Oklahoma Press, 1969.

Ross, Charles P., and T. L. Rouse, eds. *Early-Day History of Wilbarger County.* Vernon, Tex.: *The Vernon Times,* 1933.

Rudolph, Charles Francis. "Old Tascosa, Selected News Items from *The Tascosa Pioneer* 1886–1888." Selected and edited by Ernest R. Archambeau. *Panhandle-Plains Historical Review* 39 (1966): 1–208.

Samora, Julian; Joe Bernal, and Albert Peña. *Gunpowder Justice: A Reassessment of the Texas Rangers.* Notre Dame, Ind.: University of Notre Dame Press, 1979.

Scarborough, Dorothy. *The Wind.* Foreword by Sylvia Ann Grider. 1925. Reprint, Austin: University of Texas Press, 1979.

Schivelbusch, Wolfgang. *The Railway Journey: Trains and Travel in the 19th Century.* New York: Urizen Books, 1980.

Schofield, Donald F. *Indians, Cattle, Ships, & Oil: The Story of W. M. D. Lee.* Austin: University of Texas Press, 1985.

Seagraves, Anne. *Soiled Doves: Prostitutes in the Early West.* Hayden, Idaho: Wesanne Publications, 1994).

Seymour, Charles. *The Intimate Papers of Colonel House.* New York: Houghton Mifflin, 1926.

Sheers, Margaret. "The LX Ranch of Texas." *Panhandle-Plains Historical Review* 6 (1933): 45–57.

Sheffy, Lester Fields. "The Arrington Papers." *Panhandle-Plains Historical Review* 1:1 (1928): 30–66.

———. *The Franklyn Land & Cattle Company: A Panhandle Enterprise, 1882–1957.* Austin: University of Texas Press, 1963.

Shirley, Glenn. *Law West of Fort Smith: A History of Frontier Justice in the Indian Territory, 1843–1896.* New York: Collier, 1961.

———. *The Fighting Marlows: Men Who Wouldn't Be Lynched.* Fort Worth: Texas Christian University Press, 1994.

———. *Heck Thomas: Frontier Marshall.* Philadelphia: Chilton Co., 1962.

———. *Six-Gun and Silver Star.* Albuquerque: University of New Mexico Press, 1955.

———. *Temple Houston: Lawyer with a Gun.* Norman: University of Oklahoma Press, 1980.

———. *West of Hell's Fringe: Crime, Criminals, and the Federal Peace Officer in Oklahoma Territory, 1889–1907.* Norman: University of Oklahoma Press, 1978. Reprint, 1990.

Sinise, Jerry. *George Washington Arrington: Civil War Spy, Texas Ranger, Sheriff, and Rancher—A Biography.* Burnet, Tex.: Eakin Press, 1979.

———. *Pink Higgins: The Reluctant Gunfighter and Other Tales of the Panhandle.* Quanah, Tex.: Nortex Press, 1973.

Siringo, Charles A. *A Lone Star Cowboy.* Santa Fe, N.Mex.: Chas. A. Siringo, 1919.

———. *Two Evil Isms: Pinkertonism and Anarchism* . . . Chicago: Chas. A. Siringo, 1915.

Sowell, A. J. *Rangers and Pioneers of Texas.* Reprint, Austin: State House Press, 1991.

Spratt, John S., Sr., Edited by Harwood P. Hinton. *Thurber, Texas: The Life and Death of a Company Town.* Austin: University of Texas Press, 1986.

Stanley, F. [pseudonym of Father Stanley Francis Louis Crocchiola] *Railroads of the Texas Panhandle.* Borger, Tex.: Hess Publishing Co., 1976.

Stephens, Robert W. *Texas Ranger Sketches.* Dallas: privately printed, 1972.

———. *Tribute to a Ranger: Captain Alfred Y. Allee, Company D Texas Rangers.* N.p.: privately printed, 1969.

———. *Walter Durbin: Texas Ranger and Sheriff.* Clarendon, Tex.: Clarendon Press, 1970.

Sterling, William Warren. *Trails and Trials of a Texas Ranger.* Norman: University of Oklahoma Press, 1968.

Strong, Captain Henry W. *My Frontier Days & Indian Fights on the Plains of Texas.* N.p.: privately published, circa 1925.

Sullivan, Dulcie. *The LS Brand, The Story of a Texas Panhandle Ranch.* Austin: University of Texas Press, 1968.

Sullivan, W. John L. *Twelve Years in the Saddle for Law and Order on the Frontiers of Texas.* Austin: Von Boeckmann–Jones, 1909. Reprint by Michael Ginsberg. New York: Buffalo-Head Press, 1966. Reprint, Lincoln, Neb.: Bison Books, 2001.

Swisher, John M., with opinions of E. M. Pease and William M. Walton. *Title of Greer County Investigated.* Austin: American Sketch Book Publishing House, 1883.

Texas Live Stock Journal. Special Edition—Descriptive of the Panhandle Country. 8:2 (October, 1887): 1–32. Fort Worth.

[Texas Rangers.] *Former Texas Ranger Straight Talk.* 1:1 (1995). Former Texas Rangers Association. San Antonio.

Tilghman, Zoe A. *A Marshal of the Last Frontier: Life and Services of William Matthew (Bill) Tilghman.* Glendale, Calif.: Arthur H. Clark Co., 1949.

Timmons, William. *Twilight on the Range, Recollections of a Latterday Cowboy.* Austin: University of Texas Press, 1962.

Tinker, Estelle. *Archibald John Writes the Rocking Chair Ranche Letters.* Burnet, Tex.: Eakin Press, 1979.

———. "Nobility's Ranche: A History of the Rocking Chair Ranche." *Panhandle-Plains Historical Review* 15 (1942): 1–96.

Tise, Sammy. *Texas County Sheriffs.* Albuquerque: Oakwood Printing, 1989.

Tole, Eva Kay, ed. *Quanah Centennial: 1884–1984.* Quanah, Texas: privately printed, 1984.

Turner, Thomas F. "Prairie Dog Lawyers." *Panhandle-Plains Historical Review* 2 (1929): 104–22.

Tyler, Ron, Douglas Barnett, and Roy Barkley, eds. *The New Handbook of Texas.* 6 Vols. Austin: Texas State Historical Association, 1996.

Van Oden, Alonzo. Edited by Ann Jensen. *Texas Ranger's Diary & Scrapbook.* Dallas: The Kaleidograph Press, 1936.

Walsh, C. C. *Early Days on the Western Range.* Boston: Sherman, French & Co., 1917.

Watkins, Alfred J., and David C. Perry. *The Rise of the Sunbelt Cities.* Beverly Hills, Calif.: Sage Press, 1977.

Webb, Walter Prescott. "George W. Arrington: The Iron-handed Man of the Panhandle." *Panhandle-Plains Historical Review* 8 (1935): 7–20.

———, editor-in-chief. *The Handbook of Texas.* 2 Vols. Austin: Texas State Historical Association, 1952.

———. *The Texas Rangers: A Century of Frontier Defense.* Boston: Houghton Mifflin, 1935. New edition, Austin: University of Texas Press, 1965.

Welborn, C. A. *History of the Red River Controversy: The Western Boundary of the Louisiana Purchase.* Burnet, Tex.: Nortex Press, 1973.

Wellman, Paul. *A Dynasty of Western Outlaws.* Garden City, N.Y.: Doubleday & Co., 1961.

Wheeler, David L. "The Blizzard of 1886 and Its Effect on the Range Cattle Industry on the Southern Plains." *Southwestern Historical Quarterly* 94:1 (January, 1991): 415–32.

White, Lonnie J., comp. and ed. "Old Mobeetie 1877–1885: Texas Panhandle News Items from the Dodge City Times." *Panhandle-Plains Historical Review* 40 (1967): 1–162.

Wilkins, Frederick. *The Law Comes to Texas: The Texas Rangers 1870–1901.* Austin: State House Press, 1999.

———. *The Legend Begins: The Texas Rangers, 1823–1845.* Austin: State House Press, 1996.

Williams, J. W. *The Big Ranch Country.* Burnet, Tex.: Nortex Press, 1971. Second edition.

Wilson, George W. *High Plains Justice? A True Tale of Murder and Mystery in the Texas Panhandle of the Old West.* Manvel, Tex.: n.p., 1993.

Woodard, Don. *Black Diamonds, Black Gold: The Saga of Pacific Coal and Oil Company.* Lubbock: Texas Tech University Press, 1998.

Zeisler, Ernest B. *The Haymarket Riot.* Chicago: A. J. Isaacs, 1956.

INDEX

Pages containing illustrations appear in *italics*. Page containing maps appear in **bold.**

ISBN 0-89096-964-7
90000
9 780890 969649